Emerging Trends in LIS Research

Emerging Trends in LIS Research

V.V. Suryanarayana

AKANSHA PUBLISHING HOUSE
NEW DELHI • GUWAHATI • VISAKHAPATNAM

AKANSHA PUBLISHING HOUSE
4649-B/21, Ansari Road
Darya Ganj, New Delhi - 110 002
Ph.: 23263193 / 9811582579 / 09435116718
Fax: 011-23263193
Email: ektabooks@yahoo.com
www.akanshapublishinghouse.com

Emerging Trends in LIS Research

First Published 2011
ISBN 978-81-8370-259-1

PRINTED IN INDIA

Published by Akansha Publishing House, New Delhi and Printed at Harmain Offset Press, Delhi.

Contents

Preface

The main aim of bringing out this book is to provide a comprehensive information book on Bibliometrics and its applications. The book covers all the aspects of Bibliometrics that covers most of the syllabi of different Universities.

This book mainly discuss about Bibliometrics and its relation to Librametry, Scientometrics, Informetrics, Cybermetrics; the laws of bibliometrics like Bradford Law of Scattering, Lotka's Law, Zipf Law; and various techniques of Bibliometrics like Citation Analysis, Citation counting, Bibliographic coupling, Obsolescence and Half-life.

The book includes the practical application of various bibliometric techniques in order to find out Bibliographic Form wise distribution of citations in Library and Information Science and its sub-disciplines; Subject-wise distribution of citations in Library and Information Science and its sub-disciplines; Language-wise distribution of citation; Authorship Pattern; Self-citations; Ranking of Journals; Application of Bradford Law of Scattering; Obsolescence and half-life of literature; and Age-wise distribution of citations.

Author

Acknowledgements

It is my privilege to express my utmost gratitude to Dr. M.V.V.S. Murthi, the President of GITAM University for his inspiration and encouragement in bringing out this book.

I convey my sincere thanks to Sri V. Seetaramaiah, Vice-President, Sri B.V. Mohan Rao, Secretary, Sri V.V.S.N. Murthy, Treasurer, and Memebers of Board of Management, GITAM University for their continuous encouragement and cooperation.

I also thak Prof. G. Subrahmanyam Vice-Chancellor, Prof. M. Potha Raju, Registrar and Prof. D. Harinarayana, Pro-Vice-Chancellor for their valuable support in my academic pursuit.

I would like to specifically thank Prof. C. Sasikala, Department of Library and Information Science, Andhra University for being a philosopher and guide to me in writing this book.

I am grateful to Dr. K. Satyanarayana, University Librarian, GITAM University for his cooperation and support.

It is my duty to express my deep sense of gratitude to my parents and my family who always stood behind me in the completion of this book.

Last but not the least, I am indebted to Sri M.P. Misra, tne publisher and his staff who are instrumental in publishing this book in the shortest time possible.

V.V. Suryanarayana

List of Tables

1

Introduction

These days information has been increasing exponentially in large quantities and in complexity of various subjects with inter-disciplinary and multi-disciplinary nature which has been called "Information Explosion". The availability of large number of books; rise of middle class; development of public libraries, more people becoming literate, passing of renaissance, the advent of reformation, continued interest in humanism, the beginning of scientific progress and industrial revolution, political revolutions like French revolution, American Revolution, etc.—all these led to "Information Explosion". At the same time "Information" is now considered by all countries as an important national resource for their socio-economic development. Consequent upon 'Information explosion' the literature in various disciplines scattered over a large number of different forms of documents including doctoral dissertations, in different languages and originating from different countries. The multiplicity of journals and their specializations, the increasing needs of user communities, substantial increases in subscription costs of journals, and the constraints of limited financial resources- which all make it necessary for Librarians to design and develop need-based information systems and services to meet information requirements of users. A thorough understanding of the characteristics of the subject literature required by users is very essential in planning and designing of such information systems and services. In order to overcome these problems and to acquire a thorough knowledge of the characteristics of the literature, the early twentieth-century documentalists applied mathematical and statistical techniques to bibliographic units. This has led to emergence of new concept of "Bibliometrics" in the discipline of Library and Information Science.

Origin of the Concept of Bibliometrics

"Bibliometrics" is a quantitative study of various aspects of literature of a subject (Sharada, B.A.).[1] Though Alan Pritchard[2] coined this term for the first time in 1969, the use of this concept can be traced back to 1896 when Campbell[3] used statistical methods for studying subject scattering in publications. This was probably the earliest bibliometric study. In 1917, Cole and Eales[4] analysed the publications in comparative anatomy from 1543 to 1860 by simply counting the number of titles and grouping them by country. In 1922 Hulme[5] introduced the term "Statistical Bibliography". He used statistical measuring techniques to quantify the growth of scientific knowledge, and thereby to assess the overall development and growth of modern civilization. At this stage it is useful to explain for a better understanding of the terms "Bibliography" and "Statistics".

Bibliography

The word 'Bibliography' was originated from the two German roots 'Biblion' and 'Graphos' which give the meanings as: 'the book' and 'to write' respectively.[6] Over the centuries the meaning of bibliography underwent a number of changes. In the post-Classical Greek period for instance Monks while copying manuscripts, also made lists of books being copied. These lists, catalogues or inventories are considered as early bibliographies.

George Schneider[7] stated that in the narrow sense, 'Bibliography is a study of lists of books'. From individual listings the bibliography progressed to attempt to produce a "world bibliography".

In 1545 Konrad (Conrad) Gesner produced in one list all the scholarly publications in the world in bibliographic form.

During 17th and 18th centuries some bibliographies on particular subjects were published. All these are of the nature of 'descriptive accounts of the literature, of the subjects...' (1917)[8]. By the end of 18th century bibliography was taken to mean 'writing about books'. Later it was called 'the science that deals with literary production', and finally, 'the science of books'.

According to Thomas Hartwell Horne:

> 'General Bibliography' comprises works or catalogues, whose design is to give us knowledge of every kind of book whatsoever...[9].

In 1935 Theodore Besterman[10] divided Bibliography in two parts as: 'enumeration and classification of books', and the 'comparative and historical study of their make-up'. His research indicated that "bibliographies started as biographies in which the writings of the subjects were referred to as facts in their lives". Consequently this slant changed, with the emphasis on the writings becoming the more important.

Current Bibliography may be said to be the result of demands of research, development of numerous journals, and formation of many societies, literary and scientific (1956).[11] It can be concluded that the most important change in the meaning of bibliography was caused by change in its purpose. Today the primary purpose of bibliography is to aid in dispensing knowledge. This supports the definition of bibliography given by E. Wyndham Hulme[12] as "the science of the organization of recorded knowledge".

The term "Statistics" was derived from the German word "Statistik", which came from the Latin word "Status" meaning 'state, position, standing'.

Statistics "as a plural noun means collections or sets of facts that are recorded.... In particular its meaning is restricted to facts which are numerical or related to numbers. As a singular collective noun, statistics means the science of collecting or selecting statistical facts, sorting and classifying them and deriving conclusions from them.[13]

In other words, "statistics" means facts or data of a numerical kind, assembled, classified and tabulated so as to present information about a subject. Originally it referred to physical, social, economic, intellectual, political and industrial state of a country or its people as indicated in tables or numerical statements.

The term 'Statistik' was used for the first time by Gottfried Achenwall in 1748 in his statistical work.

The meaning of statistics gradually changed from a listing of Landownership and progressing to a description of states.

Sebastian Muenster[14] described the world, giving maps of known countries, history, organization, laws, customs "and in detail the chief cities with their wealth and trade" in his *Cosmographia* sometime between 1536-1544.This is called as "descriptive statistics".

It was during the 17th century the games of hazard such as lotteries, probabilities in games of chance, annuity life insurance became prominent and this is considered as the beginning of 'inductive statistics.'

Walpole[15] explained that "any treatment of data leading to predictions or inferences is known as inductive statistics".

Based on the theory of probability, which had beginning in gambling or games of chance, inductive statistics projects or determines probable outcome.

During 18th century the subject of probability developed rapidly and in the 19th century it found application in the mathematical study of statistics.

In 1853 Adolph Quetelet a Belgian statistician "developed the conception of statistics as a general method of research applicable to any science of observation". He applied statistical methods to education and sociology.

In 1872 M.Hashofer stated statistics as a method and science. This was supported by August Meitzen[16], who in 1886 evaluated statistics as a 'method of scientific investigation by means of enumeration of objects and the numerical comparison of the results of such enumeration".

Thus, Statistics may be divided into two areas as 'descriptive' and 'inductive'. Descriptive statistics is description or compilation of data in a usable form, while in inductive statistics data pertaining to a sample of a population are used to arrive at a probable conclusion or prediction concerning the whole.

It seems logical that librarians or the Bibliographers would also have Applied science of probability and statistics to the field of bibliography. So statistics, employing the theory of probability (counting, analysing, interpreting) combined with bibliography (knowledge dispensers) became statistical bibliography, as Pritchard defined it.

Statistical Bibliography

Application of quantitative techniques to libraries is known as "Statistical Bibliography". As stated earlier Wyndham Hulme was the first person to express the concept of "Statistical Bibliography" in 1922. Next the expression was used by Gosnell in 1943 in his dissertation on "The Rate of Obsolescence in College Library Book Collections". Later in 1962 Raisig[17] defined "Statistical Bibliography" as "the assembling and interpretation of statistics relating to books and periodicals; it may be used in a variety of situations for an almost unlimited number of measurements".

There were several other scholars who also used the expression "Statistical Bibliography". For instance H.H. Henkle[18] in 1938 used the expression in his article "Periodical Literature of Bio-Chemistry"; in 1948 Herman H. Fussler[19] in his dissertation "Characteristics of the Research Literature used by Chemists and Physicists in the Soviet Union"; and in 1966 Dale Lockard Barker, in his dissertation "Characteristics of Scientific Literature cited by Chemists of Soviet Union"..

Later in 1968 Alan Pritchard[20] used the phrase "Statistical Bibliography" in his unpublished paper "Computers, Statistical Bibliography and Abstracting Services", and in 1969 in his article "Statistical Bibliography: An Interim Bibliography". He defined "Statistical Bibliography" as "the statistical analysis of the means of communication in order to illuminate the processes of communication, the factors which influence them and the inter-relationships between the history and sociology of science and the literature of science.

Pritchard also used the term "Bibliometrics" in 1969 in his article "Statistical Bibliography or Bibliometrics?" But in 1970 he preferred the term "Bibliometrics" than the phrase "Statistical Bibliography" as is evident when he stated that 'the phrase "Statistical Bibliography" was clumsy, not very descriptive and could be confused with statistics itself or bibliographies on statistics'. Therefore the term "Bibliometrics" in now accepted in print.

Meaning and Definitions of Bibliometrics

The word "Bibliometrics" has two roots i) "biblio" and ii)

"Metrics". The term "biblio" is derived from the combination of a Latin and Greek word "biblion" equivalent to Bybl(os) meaning book. The word "metrics" indicates the science of meter, i.e. measurement and is derived from Greek word "metricus". As already stated the word bibliometrics was first used by Alan Pritchard. Following statements explain the meaning and purpose of bibliometrics.

Bibliometrics is a quantitative study of all aspects of the literature of a subject and the bibliographic variables of documents, both the sources and their references (1992).[21]

Bibliometrics is unique type of research method developed by Library and Information Science. Bibliometrics utilizes quantitative analysis, statistics and data visualization (i.e. dimensional mapping) to investigate.[22]

Bibliometrics is an established knowledge domain unique to Library and Information Science and incorporates its own set of laws and theories, its own methodologies, its own technologies, and its own specialized journals, conferences and associations.

Bibliometrics is also a primary tool for analysis of scientist/ researcher behaviours (citation decision processes, user needs, etc). It is used for design and evaluation of Information Retrieval (IR) systems (i.e. search engines, online databases).

Bibliometrics is a decision support methodology used by LIS professionals in and across virtually every discipline, including computer science, telecommunication, political science, agriculture, biology, neuroscience, education, mathematics, business, industry, religion and art.

Bibliometrics is build on advanced knowledge of online searching of databases and databanks; familiarity with the various traditional and emerging classification and cataloguing practices and theories, and an understanding of the fundamental concepts of Information science, including precision, recall, relevance, pertinence, and entropy.

Pritchard (1969) defined it as 'the application of mathematical and statistical methods to books and other media of communication'. In his later article, 'Bibliometrics and Information transfer', he explained "Bibliometrics" as 'the methodology of information transfer process... (1972)[23].

After Pritchard many scholars have defined the concept of Bibliometrics, each in his own way, but to give the same meaning.

Robert A. Fairthrone (1969)[24] defined Bibliometrics as 'quantitative treatment of the properties of recorded discourse and behaviour appertaining to it'.

The British Standard Glossary of Documentation[25] of Terms explained Bibliometrics as 'the study of the use of documents and patterns of publication in which mathematical and statistical methods have been applied' (1976).

Hawkins (1977)[26] defined Bibliometrics as 'quantitative analysis of the Bibliographic features of a body of literature'.

Lancaster (1977)[27] defined it as "the study of patterns of authorship, Publication and literature use by applying various statistical analysis".

Schrader (1981)[28] defined Bibliometrics as "the scientific study of recorded discourse".

According to William Gary Potter (1981)[29] "bibliometrics is the study and measurement of the publication pattern of all forms of written communication and their authors".

According to Hertzel (1987)[30] "bibliometrics, the source of recorded discourse- which uses specific methodologies, mathematical and scientific, in its research- is a controlled study of communication. It is the body of a literature, a bibliography quantitatively or numerically or statistically analysed- a statistical bibliography, a bibliography in which measurements are used to document and explain the regularity of communication phenomena".

According to Egghe (1988)[31] Bibliometrics "is the development and application of mathematical models and techniques to all aspects of communication.

White and McCain (1989)[32] defined bibliometrics as the "quantitative study of literature as they are reflected in bibliographies".

According to Gupta (1991)[33] Bibliometrics is the study and measurement of the pattern of all forms of recorded information and their producers.

Humayoon Kabir (1993)[34] defined "Bibliometrics" as that branch of information theory that attempts to analyse quantitatively the properties and behaviour of recorded knowledge.

Diodato (1994)[35] defined it as "the study of publications and communication patterns in the distribution of information by using mathematical and statistical techniques, from counting to calculus".

Essentially all these definitions of "bibliometrics" connote the same meaning.

Scope of Bibliometrics

The scope of subject "Bibliometrics" is until recently limited only to the application of quantitative methods to library management. Its scope is so far restricted to study and understand the quantitative behaviour of certain characteristics of documents.

To Simon (1973)[36], the scope of "Bibliometrics", includes studying the relationship within a literature (e.g. citation studies) or describing a literature. Daniel O'Connor and Henry Voos [37]expressed the same view and further said that "Bibliometrics" aim at consistent patterns, involving authors, monographs, journals etc.

According to Nicholas and Ritchie (1978)[38] the scope of Bibliometrics was to provide information about the structure of knowledge and how it is communicated, and classified bibliometrics into two groups: Descriptive bibliometrics and Behaviourial bibliometrics. Descriptive Bibliometrics describes the characteristics or features of a literature whereas behaviourial bibliometrics examines the relationships formed between components of literature. Rolland E. Stevens (1953)[39] also considered bibliometrics as quantitative science and more or less divided bibliometrics just as Nicholas and Ritchie did into two broad areas and added several sub-areas as follows:

1. Descriptive Bibliometrics or Productivity Count

1.1 Geographic (countries)

1.2 Time Periods (Eras)

1.3 Disciplines (subjects)

2. Evaluative Bibliometrics or Literature Usage Count

2.1 Reference count

2.2 Citation count.

According to Diodato (1994)[40] there are three major areas in bibliometric research. They are

1. Bibliometric Laws or distributions, such as Lotka's Law, Zipf's Law, Bradford's Law of Scattering.
2. Citation Analysis; and
3. Indicators of research performance.

Thus Bibliometrics includes (but is not limited to) analysis of publication and transfer patterns within a given field, for instance, a body of literature, an organization, an environment or enterprise, and within and between disciplines. Bibliometrics is standard method of information analysis applied in Library and Information Science.

Bibliometrics and its Relation with Librametry Scientometrics, Informetrics and Cybermetrics

"Bibliometrics" as a quantitative study of various concepts of literature of a subject is closely related to similar other concepts such as librametry, scientometrics, informetrics and cybermetrics which can be described briefly as below:

Bibliometrics vs. Librametry

In 1948 Dr. S.R.Ranganathan propounded the concept Librametry on the lines of Bibliometry, as many matters connected with library work and services involved large numbers. He therefore thought that they can be subjected to the techniques of mathematical and statistical analysis and for providing efficient library services.

He illustrated how he had applied librametric techniques in organizing library activities and services in Madras University Library. In the library he maintained systematically the statistics relating to various library operations. On the basis of these statistics he calculated man hours needed in a year for each item of work in the library. This helped him to deduce a staff formula. The formula can be used for the determination of the strength of staff in an objective and impersonal way. Similarly this concept helps in determining the optimum size of a service library, design of library building, size of reading rooms and so on.

Thus measurement of library activities and results of its services is the core of librametry. Bibliometrics and Librametry may, therefore, be defined as areas in which one studies information processing and information handling in libraries and information centres by quantitatively analysing the characteristics and behaviour of documents, library staff and library users.

Bibliometrics vs. Informetrics

The term "Informetrics" connotes the use and development

of a variety of measures to study and analyse several properties of information in general and documents in particular. The term was first introduced by Otto Nacke in 1979 and was later adopted by VINITI and International Federation of Documentation (FID). Its scope covers bibliometrics, scientometrics and other quantitative studies related to information science.

Informetrics seeks to develop statistical and mathematical techniques to evaluate and improve the efficiency of information services and their use. Its important applications fall in the areas of collection management and library and information services. Most of the Informetric studies are connected with different types of users and the degrees to which the user needs are fulfilled.

From simple data analysis of library statistics, informetrics has now grown to a well defined concept involving applied statistics, modeling, simulation, cluster analysis etc. The trend in "Informetrics" is mostly towards discovery of theory and/or a generalized mathematical model which can help in achieving both services to library and information users and efficiency in the management of information systems and services as envisaged in Ranganathan's five laws of library science.

Bibliometrics vs. Scientometrics

The terms "Bibliometrics" and "Scientometrics" were introduced almost simultaneously by Alan Pritchard and Nalimov and Mulchenko in 1969. While Pritchard[41] explained the term bibliometrics as "the application of mathematical and statistical methods to books and other media of communication. Nalimov and Mulchenko defined scientometrics as "the application of those quantitative methods which deal with the analysis of science viewed as an information process. According to these interpretations, scientometrics is restricted to the measurement of science communication, where as bibliometrics is designed to deal with more general information processes.

Bibliometrics vs. Cybermetrics

The term Webometrics or Cybermetrics has been named by Almind and Ingwersen (1997).[42] Webometrics can be defined as using of bibliometric techniques in order to study the relationship of different sites on the World Wide Web. Such techniques also be used to map out (called "scientific mapping" in traditional bibliometric research) areas of the web what appears to be most useful of influential, based on the number of times they are hyperlinked to other websites".

Webometrics displays several similarities to informetrics and scientometrics studies and the application of common bibliometric methods. For instance, simplistic counts and content analysis of web pages are like traditional publication analysis; counts and analyses outgoing links from web pages, here named out links, and of links pointing to web pages, can be seen as reference and citation analysis, respectively. Out links and in links are then similar to references and citations, respectively, in scientific articles. However due to its dynamic and distributed nature, the web often demonstrates web pages simultaneously linking to each other—a case not possible in the traditional paper-based citation world.

In this way Bibliometrics has close relation with the concept cybermetrics which employ measuring techniques in the evaluation of development of science and its impact and relevance to human society. Thus it may be finally concluded that Bibliometrics, librametrics, scientometrics, informetrics and cybermetrics have certain basic similarities to each other and all these branches have great potentiality and application in the field of Library and Information Science.

Application of Bibliometrics

Alan Pritchard[43] the originator of the term "Bibliometrics" stated the following purposes or functions or applications of it as:

1. To shed light on the processes of written communication and of the nature and course of development of a discipline, by means of counting and analysing the various facets of written communication.

2. "The assembling and interpretation of statistics relating to books and periodicals... to demonstrate historical movements, to determine the national or universal research of books and journals, and to ascertain in many local situations the general use of books and journals.

According to Lawani (1981)[44], bibliometric studies are applicable in many fields such as selection of books and periodicals; features of subject literature; evaluation of collection and bibliographies; and historical and sociological studies.

According to Ravichandra Rao (1983)[45], bibliometric techniques are used in identification of trends in a subject and also in the study of scientific communication. He states that "bibliometrics" has been accepted as a research area that gives us additional understanding of the form and structure of scientific communication".

Lancaster (1991)[46] states that bibliometric studies are applicable to any form of "... quantitative analysis relating to the production, distribution and use of the published or semi-published literature. Bibliometric studies include studies of: the growth of the literature in some subject; how much literature is contributed by various languages; how the literature on some subjects is scattered (e.g. over documentary types, languages, journals); and how quickly the literature on some subjects becomes out-of-date (studies of obsolescence)".

Bibliometric studies are used to identify the pattern of publication, authorship, citations and / or secondary journal coverage in the hope that such regularities can give an insight into the dynamics of the area under consideration. This consequently leads to better organization of information resources which can be effectively used.

Bibliometrics is applied for developing and measuring information and knowledge transfer in traditional, that is, print based, as well as proprietary electronic information environments that is, databases and databanks.

The huge amount of documents available through networks gives great possibilities to apply bibliometrics within the framework of librarian's work. Different bibliographic databases register daily thousands of references to literature in almost in every subject field.

Management of catalogue can be assisted by the knowledge that most entries appear only a few times. A small number or authors appear many times, and these cause the most problems, as they are most likely to be inconsistent. Bibliometrics helps to choose where to spend more time maintaining catalogue. Search commands can be analyzed. The development of a catalogue can use bibliometrics to show which terms are used most often, in order to be sure the terms used match those chosen by the users.

Thus Bibliometrics may be employed in the illumination of the development of subjects as displayed in their literature; provision of reliable data on which to make adequate provision of information facilities; definition of the limits of subject areas; indication of the relative importance of various types of documents in different subject areas; determination of the use of information materials and sources; investigation of reading habits and pattern of information transfer; and so on.

Bibliometrics can be used to study productivity count (number of publications) of literature in a given field for the purpose of comparing the amount of research in different countries, or the amount of research produced in different subdivisions of a field, or types of publications, or amount of publications by an individual or an organization.

It can be used to study pattern of scatter of literature on a subject in different periodicals, relationship of quantity of publications of individuals and their recognition, identification or peers, impact of social change on the production of literature. Bibliometrics can also be used to study in terms of references cited by researchers and citations.

As enumerated by Sengupta (1992)[47] the bibliometric techniques can be applied in the following areas:

1. To identify research trends and growth of knowledge of different scientific disciplines;
2. To estimate comprehensiveness of secondary periodicals;
3. To predict productivity of publishers;
4. To identify users of different subject;
5. To identify authorship and its trends in documents on various subjects;
6. To measure usefulness of ad hoc and retrospective SDI services;
7. To forecast past, present and future publishing trends;
8. To develop experimental models correlating or bypassing the existing ones;
9. To identify core journals in different disciplines;
10. To formulate an accurate need-based acquisition policy within limited budgetary provision;
11. To adapt an accurate weeding and stacking policy;
12. To initiate effective multilevel network systems;

13. To regulate inflow of information and communication;
14. To study obsolescence and dispersion of scientific literature (clustering and coupling of scientific papers etc);
15. To predict productivity of publishers, individual authors, organizations, countries or that of an entire discipline;
16. To design automatic language processing for auto-indexing, and auto classification; and
17. To develop norms for standardization.

In short, Bibliometric studies can help to achieve:

(a) identification of core journals;

(b) ranking of journals;

(c) selection of journals;

(d) weeding of journals;

(e) growth of publications / structure of literature;

(f) trends in a subject / study of scientific communication;

(g) impact of one journal on another;

(h) clues for predicting future use;

(i) contribution of scientists (scientific productivity)/ contribution of organizations / contribution of countries; and

(j) areas of deficiency within an existing information system whose major concern being documents.

Analysis of the statistical records of a library can be used for collection development. Not only knowing a user group's needs, but knowing that most of their needs can be filled by only a small number of books or journals can help with the difficult process of selection or weeding. If your library has limited amount of space, you can use your statistics to determine what books need to be on the open stacks and what books can be placed in storage because they are rarely used.

Empirical Laws of Bibliometrics

Certain regularities are derived in the study of the concept of "Bibliometrics" and these regularities are taken as empirical laws. Of these the most significant laws are of these formulated by Bradford, Lotka and Zipf.

Though it is claimed that the three laws are basically the same, still some differences lie in the type of data. Bradford's law is concerned with the scattering of articles on specific subjects in various journals; Lotka's law deals with authors publishing and the number of papers published; and Zipf law relates to ranking of frequencies of words.

Bradford's Law

In the study of 'Bibliometrics' the observations of Samuel Clement Bradford regarding distribution of articles on a subject in different periodicals has come to be referred as the law of scattering.

Bradford[48] published his observation first in his article in the Engineering in 1934. This paper was reproduced in his book *Documentation* in 1948. Analysing the periodical literature in two different subjects, geophysics and lubrication, he found that if the source periodicals were arranged in decreasing order of productivity, a number of zones of these periodicals could be created according to their yields. Each zone contributed the same number of articles but from increasing number of periodicals. The number of periodicals in each successive zone increased at geometric progression. In the first zone or the 'nucleus' will come the periodicals which are more particularly devoted to the subject. The relation between the number of periodicals coming in the nucleus and the successive zones could be represented as

1: a: a2. Apart from the verbal formulation, Bradford also gave a graphical representation of the scattering of articles in periodicals. The value of 'a' in Bradford's analysis of data was found to be about 5.0. So, according to the formulation, if the total literature on a subject is contributed by 248 journals they might be divided into a nucleus zone of 8 highly productive journals, a second zone of 5x8 or 40 journals of moderate productivity and a third zone of 5^2x8 or 200 journals of low productivity.

However, Bradford did not express his discovery in a more precise mathematical form. He even left some aspects uncertain. This was even expressed by Fairthrone when he expressed that during his discourses with Bradford through correspondence, he would understand that the later had not enough evidence or explanation to sustain the law in public debate.

Applications of Bradford's Law

Hyperbolic distribution can be used to study "the completeness of the bibliography in a given subject; the fraction of the total coverage available at a specified cost limit; the optimum distribution of journal or document collections between stores admitting frequent, occasional or rare access; and questions relating to the information loss produced by document retirement (Salton,1975).[49] Other areas include study of citation frequency data, collection build up, journal acquisition Vs photocopying or borrowing desired articles, study of circulation statistics to decide minimal collection, and distribution of documents from IR searches.

Lotka's Law

Author productivity is one of the many factors to identify or to distinguish eminent scholars in the field [Price: 1963]. Alfred J. Lokta[50] who was a mathematician was the first person to study the frequency distribution of productivity of authors of scientific papers. He formulated his law known after his name as Lotka's law in 1926. He proposed that the number of authors making n contributions is about $1/n^2$ of those making one contribution, and the proportion of all contributors who make a single contribution is about 60 percent and proportion of authors making two contributions is $1/2^2 x 60 = 15\%$ or $a(n) = k/n^2$

Where a is the number of authors producing n papers and k a constant (Lotka, 1926).

Lokta's law on productivity of authors

Authors	Papers
100	1
25	2
11	3
6	4
4	5

Zipf's Law

One of the most puzzling phenomena in bibliometrics – and more broadly in quantitative linguistics – is Zipf's law. George Kingsley Zipf[51] was a philologist from Harvard University. He was the next scholar after Bradford to make extensive study on Bibliometrics. While studying linguistics at the University of Berlin, he had an idea that "speech as natural phenomena" is "a series of communicative gestures'. After extensive research he found that "the length of a word is closely related to the frequency of its usage – the greater the frequency, the shorter the word" (1935)[52]. He also discovered that "the distribution of words in English approximates with remarkable precision a harmonic series... an unmistakable progression according to the inverse square, valid for well over 95% of all the different words used in the sample" (1935)[53]. He worked on the theory and application of his principle of 'relative frequency' in the structure and development of language (1936).[54]

His law states that if words are ranked on the basis of the frequency of their occurrence in a long text in decreasing order, the frequency of occurrence f(r) of a word is the reciprocal of its rank n (Zipf, 1949)[55]. The law is represented by f (r) = c/n, where c is a constant, or log f(r) + log n = log c

Zipf Distribution

Word	*Rank*	*Frequency*	*Rank frequency*
The	1	245	245
Of	2	135	270
Terms	3	98	294
To	4	81	324
A	5	65	325
And	6	61	366
In	7	55	385
Were	8	52	416

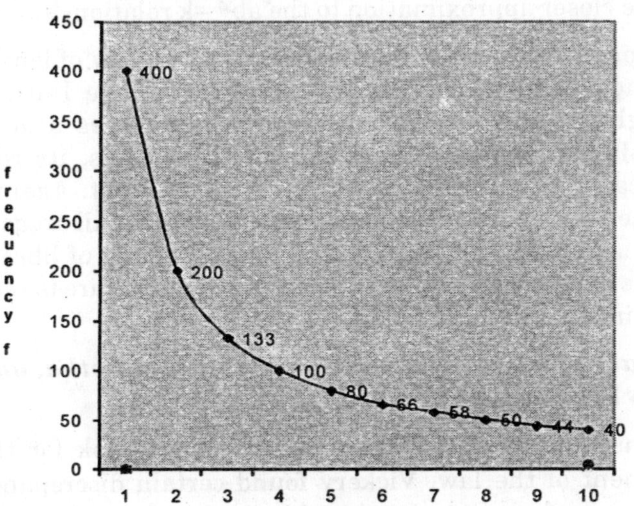

Fig. 1 : Zips distribution with an exact fit, giving a hyperbolic curve

The law represents only an approximation of the relationship between rank and frequency, which is hyperbolic.

Zipf stated that the philosophy behind the rank-frequency phenomenon as 'principle of least effort'. In any language the words which have high frequency of occurrence are those that cost less in usage or require less effort in communication. A feature of Zipf's law is that it highlights the phenomenon that once, by chance, a group has achieved a dominant position it retains that position for a long time and indeed, is more likely to be promoted than less fortunate groups (Scarrot, 1974)[56]. This feature is also known as "success breeds success phenomenon that is success increases the chances of further success.

Zipf developed a formula $ab^2 = k$, where a is the number of words occurring b times. He also concluded the $ab^2 = k$ relationship is valid only for the less frequently occurring words which represent the greater part of the vocabulary in use, though not always a great majority of occurrences, but it is in the frequency distribution of the rarer words that we find the closer approximation to the $ab^2 = k$ relationship.

Though the law has been applied to the study of length of monographs in Harvard University College Library through the measure of the number of pages and in vocabulary control in the design of IR systems, its real significance to a library is yet to be brought out. Against this, the least effort principle has significance for all areas of library activities. Those planning and designing of library systems must consider the tendency of human nature to seek things involving least effort.

Critical appraisal of the laws of Bradford, Lotka, and Zipf by different eminent scholars

Consequently B.C.Vickery (1948)[57] undertook for the refinement of the law. Vickery found certain discrepancy between verbal and the graphical representations in

Bradford's statement. The mathematical expression was restated by him as follows:

$$T_2: (T_{2x} - T_x): (T_{3x} - T_{2x}):: 1: n: n^2$$

Where Tx T2x are related in this way, we are told, the plot of R against T is not a straight line. Thus, the above expression comes closer to the graphical expression of Bradford. Vickery also simplified the technique of deriving the ratio of α.

Kendal (1960)[58] the next paper on Bradford's law was that of M.G. Kendal. He supported the idea that the Bradford type of distribution is really a Zipf distribution and he also provided "a more refined statistical explanation of the straight line observed by Bradford".

Cole (1962)[59] took "A New Look at Reference Scattering" whereby he plotted the cumulative fraction of references against the logarithm of the cumulative fraction of the titles and the resultant slope he named "reference scattering coefficient". He came to the conclusion that the reference-scattering coefficient "may be characteristic of the subject field and found that a comparison of reference-scattering coefficients derived from data obtained in three published petroleum literature-usage surveys shows that the reference-count method gives untrustworthy results.

Leimkuhler (1967)[60] took a lead to study the practical application of Bradford's Law in information work. He has derived a mathematical expression by inverting the relationship of number of papers and number of journals in Bradford law and calls it Bradford Distribution. This expression is meant to show the distribution of productivity in a collection of source documents.

This expression is $F(x) = 1n\ (1+\beta x)/1n\ (1+\beta)$, $(0 < X<1)$ where F(x) is cumulative fraction of the references, x is the corresponding fraction of the most productive journals and â a constant related to the document collection.

Leimkuhler's formula (Bradford Distribution) can be utilized in a number of ways. When an estimate is available of the total number of relevant references on a given topic during a period, a distribution pattern of the number of journals and their productivity can be predicted.

B.C.Brookes (1969)[61] further refined the theory by ranking journals according to their productivity and derived the formula (Brookes, 1968)[62]

$$R(n) = K \log(n/s)$$

Where n is the rank of each journal, R (n), the total number of articles yielded by first 'n' journals and k and s are constants with values depending on the collection studied. The values of k and s can be determined by plotting R(n) and log(n) on a semi logarithmic graph paper, when the slope and the intercept of the resulting straight line represent n and s, respectively. The graphic formulation of Bradford's law called a bibliography is shown in the figure.

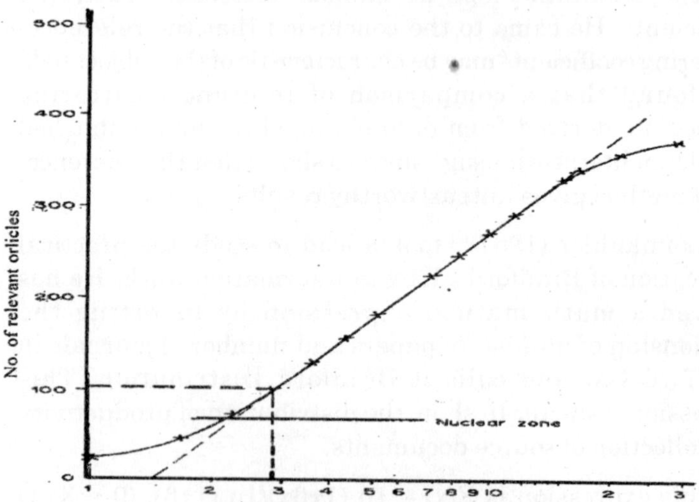

Fig. 2 : A Bibliograph

Naranan (1970)[63], in his "Bradford's Law of Bibliography of Science: An Interpretation" called attention to the Brookes papers: "An interesting discussion of the law and its application in library systems is given by Brookes".

For the conclusion of his own paper, he wrote: in summary, it is shown, that the essential features of Bradford's law of bibliography of scientific literature can be explained in terms of an underlying power law distribution of the number of articles in scientific journals. It is suggested that the law emerges as a natural consequence of exponential growth of scientific literature and journals at comparable rates. Such a model predicts a strong correlation between age of a journal and number of articles it carries. The proposed mechanism is likely to find wider application in many other fields of science.

Goffman and Morris (1970)[64] applied Bradford's Law to library acquisitions. They stated that Bradfrod's law should apply to the use of periodicals in a library as well as to the dispersion of articles among journals. These are both acquisition processes; namely, processes of obtaining relevant items by means of selection.

Wilkinson (1972)[65] pointed out, that despite the limitations of our understanding of such laws; Bradford promises useful application in the design of more rational and economic information systems.

Library Trends published an issue, "Analyses of Bibliographies", to which Brookes (1973)[66] listed the five main objectives of numerical analyses based on the belief that quantification is a necessary component of the design of economic information systems and that measurement of the key processes of an information system is a necessary component of management control.

Sengupta (1973)[67] stated that during phases of rapid and vigorous growth of knowledge in a scientific discipline, article of interest to that discipline appear in increasing numbers in periodicals distant from that field.

Pope (1975)[68] claimed that the area where the Bradford distribution has the greatest potential is in collections development, both in individual libraries and in library systems.

Worthan's (1975)[69] findings supported the statement that Bradford's law of distribution can be applied to the monograph publisher relationship for a subject literature.

Aiyepeku (1977)[70], in an extensive analysis of the periodical literature in geography for the whole world and for the USA, British Isles, France and Germany found evidence that data conforming with the verbal formulation of Bradford's distribution theory may not necessarily conform with its graphical representation and vice versa, which is in agreement with investigations by other researchers.

Brookes (1977)[71] describes how Bradford's law can be regarded as a particular example of empirical law of social behaviour which pervades all social activities. Bradford without knowing what he was doing in this respect, may have initiated a new branch of statistics – the statistics of individuality – which may lead to an extension of fundamental mathematical ideas which would make mathematics more useful in the social sciences.

Rapaport (1957)[72] in writing about the "Principle of Least Effort" stated Zipf's arguments are vague appeals to the recognition of the principle in a great variety of situations simply on the basis of its plausibility.

Simon and Mandelbrot (1960)[73] attempt to put Zipf's investigations on a more scientific basis. Mandelbrot has published several studies of generalizations of Zipf's law dealing both with the question of whether the slope is –1 and with the deeper problem of explaining why the rf products should be relatively constant.

Hill (1970)[74] was responsible for a group of papers regarding Zipf's Law. Hill's first paper was "Zipf's Law and Prior Distributions for the Composition of Population" (1970) in which he cited Wills for first noting the law and discussed the fact that "theoretical models yielding such a law have been proposed by Yule and Simon". In the paper "Rank-Frequency Form of Zipf's Law" (1974), Hill presents a theoretical derivation of the rank frequency form of Zipf's Law based on a Bose-Einstein form of the classical occupancy model.

Sichel (1975)[75] developed a new model to which twenty observed distributions quoted in the literature were fitted and good results obtained.

Wylls (1975)[76] mentioned that Zipf not only leaped to the conclusion that the "true" slope of rank-frequency curves was –1, but also claimed that this regular slope resulted from more fundamental force of nature. In the broad sense, this claim had to be correct : but Zipf variously described the force as that of struggle between the "life tendency" and "death tendency" or the "Force of Diversification" and the "Force of Unification", and finally the "Principle of Least Effort", for none of which did he furnish an operable definition. Wyllys claimed that his report and study established that significant detectable variations in rank-frequency curve slope do exist, that they appear to have potential for subject-field discrimination, and that they may perhaps also be usable for the identification of subfields of especially rapid development.

Murphy (1973)[77] did a study of "Lotka's Law in the Humanities". He chose for his work the first decade of the publication "Technology and Culture", and found the actual number of single authors. He rounded off his numbers and plotted the results, leading him to conclude, without any statistical test for goodness of fit, that the tabulation essentially verifies that Lotka's Law applied to this field within the humanities.

Voos (1974)[78] measured the productivity of authors in the field of information science and compared his results with Lotka's observation. Using all the articles indexed in Information Science Abstracts form 1966 to 1970 for his data, he made a rank-frequency listing all the authors and their articles by year. Voos "found that the relationship for information science seems to be $1/n^{3.5}$ instead of Lokta's $1/n^2$ and instead of Lotka's 60% producing one paper, "in information science the figure tends to be 88% writing only one paper" the results of using the chi-square test show that one can be more than 95% certain that the actual population fits the theoretical distribution. Voos published his first application study in the year 1974, in conjunction with library science, and used data Library Quarterly and College and Research Libraries from 1963 to 1972. His analysis indicated that Lotka's Law does not apply to the field of library science, where four-fifths of all papers represent the only contribution of individual.

Schorr (175)[79] found that authors with multiple contributions fall below the numbers expected by Lotka's Law (e.g., authors with two publications account for 18.1% of single author entries instead of 25% ; authors with five publications comprise 1.8% instead of 4%)... The results do not support the inverse square law and thus Lotka's Law does not hold true for the history of legal medicine.

Hubert (1977)[80] in a letter to the editor of the Journal of the American Society for Information Science evaluated Murphy's work with the x^2 goodness of fit test. His conclusion was, "By using an exact interpretation of the law and by applying a valid statistical test, it can be shown that this data does not follow Lotka's Law.

Russell Coile (1977)[81] also did an evaluation of the Murphy results, and he too found that Lotka's Law did not apply to the particular sample of authors.

Radhakrishnan and Kernizan(1979)[82] found that (i) Lotka's Law , in its generalized form, seems applicable when we consider the publications of authors in one periodical and (ii) when we consider the publications of authors in various journals, the observed values deviate considerably from the predictions of the law. This may be due to differences between pure and applied science.

Subramanyam (1981)[83] found that the pattern did not conform to Lotka's results and suggested more work to be done.

Richardson (1981)[84] stated that Frankston data do fit Lotka's law in the general form, but since the slope of the Frankston line is greater than 2, the data do not correspond to the inverse square law.

Pao (1982)[85] analysed the above problems neatly and opines that several studies have assumed the inverse square relation as the basis for testing. Others derived the value of the constant c from the percentage of single paper contributors. None of these assumptions can be traced back to Lotka. Her deduction is well taken. "Therefore, she suggests that a uniform method should be agreed upon by these attempting such a test. Comparison and generalization on author productivity may be possible only if compatible data are available and results are significant".

Formulation of General Theory

The common features of Bradford, Lotka and Zipf laws are those that represent hyperbolic distributions in which the product of the fixed powers of the variables is constant. These laws are based on rank-order frequencies or rank-size relationships. The inter-relationships that exist among these three laws have been recognized and efforts are being made to develop a general theory covering all the three.

Citation Analysis

Citation analysis is another important area of bibliometrics. It represents a relationship between the cited and citing documents. The study of this relationship in all aspects is the function of citation analysis.

Reference or Cited: An item designating the source unit; thus it is always in Pre-dated in relation to the reference.

Citation or Citing: An item designating the receiving unit; this it is always post-dated in relation to the reference

The following reasons are given for using citations:

1. Paying homage to pioneers.
2. Giving credit for related work.
3. Identifying methodology, equipment etc.
4. Providing background reading.
5. Correcting one's own work.
6. Correcting the work of others.
7. Criticizing previous work
8. Substantiating claims.
9. Alerting researchers to forthcoming work.
10. Providing direction to poorly disseminated work, poorly indexed or uncited work.
11. Authenticating data and classes of fact-physical constants etc.
12. Identifying original publications in which idea or constant was discussed.
13. Identifying the original publication describing eponym concept or term as e.g. Hodgkin's disease Pareto's law.

14. Describing work or idea of others.
15. Disputing priority claims of others.
16. Self citation for its own sake.
17. Sometimes citations are made in the bibliography to provide up-date ness.

The coverage of citation analysis has now been extended from citations of articles to other items such as books, journals, authors, industrial organizations, academic departments, universities, countries and many others. The prominent techniques of citation study are citation counting, bibliographic coupling, and co-citation analysis.

Citation Counting

This technique involves counting the number of citations received by a given document or set of documents over a period of time from a particular set of citing documents. Citation counting has been utilized for measuring the impact of individual scientific journals. The term impact factor was coined by Garfield to indicate the number of citations received by a paper during a specified period of time.

Bibliographic Coupling

Two documents are bibliographically coupled if both of them have at least one reference in common. The number of such common references represents the coupling strength. The common sharing of a document need not necessarily mean sharing the same information. The coupling links two or more documents later in time in relation to one or more earlier documents.

Co-citation

Two documents are co-cited if both of them are commonly cited in papers published subsequently. Co-Citation links two or more documents published earlier in relation to a later document.

Applications

Citation analysis has been applied extensively to study various aspects of documents in their subject context and use environment. The techniques can be used in:

Collection development, user studies; Information Retrieval; development and growth of subjects and their literature; historical and research standing studies; and pattern of research communication.

Obsolescence

Growth in collections of documents as well as files representing them affects all aspects of library management. Every addition of a document beyond a size calls for extra space, adds to maintenance problems and hampers easy and effective access to all documents. To overcome these problems or at least to minimize their adverse effects, there is need to exercise control over the size of collections. Discarding documents or relegating them to less frequented areas constitutes one such control. A discarding and/or relegating policy has to be based on sound principles. Statistical methods aid in developing such principles. The relative importance or utility of a document is a key element of all such policies. This leads to the concept of obsolescence.

Obsolescence is defined as the "decline over time in validity or utility of information" (Line and Sandison, 1974)[86]. The same applies to documents. Assessing decline is subjective and not easy.

Four reasons are given to explain obsolescence:

1. The information is still valid, but is now incorporated into later work.
2. The information is valid, but is now superceded by later work.

3. The information is valid, but is now in a field of declining interest.
4. The information is no longer valid.

The criteria generally employed to measure the decline are:

- Age factor of the document
- Citations to the document in subsequent literature
- Utilization of the document.

Half life of literature is another method which helps in identifying obsolescence.

Half-life of Literature

Papers have high utility during a short period of time after publication and their utility diminishes rapidly as time progresses. The rate of obsolescence varies from subject to subject. The measure to compare the speed of decay among different subjects is called 'half life'. A half life refers to the time taken for half the currently published information to obsolescence.

Subject	*Half life in years*
Metallurgical Engineering	3.9
Physics	4.6
Chemical Engineering	4.8
Mechanical Engineering	5.2
Physiology	7.2
Chemistry	8.1
Botany	10.0
Maths	10.5
Geology	11.8

The validity of theory of obsolescence itself has been questioned. The best policy for coping with obsolescence is to combine criteria of age, citation and use. Besides these methods many mathematical models for measuring obsolescence have been developed.

These three laws accelerated the growth of research activities and as a result there has been exponential growth of literature in bibliometrics during the past two decades. Many standard statistical tests have been made either to substantiate, modify, extend link or criticize these laws by subsequent researchers which give rise to new empirical laws and models providing a solid theoretical foundation for bibliometric studies.

The bibliometric laws are useful in understanding some of the information phenomena and may help in planning many of the library activities as they indicate certain basic patterns and relationships governing information items and activities. The study mostly relates to quantification of items and their pattern of distribution.

These studies throw light on the pattern of growth of literature, productivity and influence of authors, interrelationships among different branches of knowledge, distribution of items in information storage and retrieval (IR), pattern of collection build up, their use and the like.

Nevertheless the application and utility of these laws to practical problems have some limitations. Bibliometric laws are empirical laws and hence remain valid so long as the sociology, structure and pattern of information generation, communication and dissemination remain the same and may not hold good once the pattern of basic organization changes due to social and scientific phenomena.

Probably, with greater insight into the library/information phenomena coupled with the refinement of these laws, they may contribute to library planning and management decision-making more effectively than is possible at present. As theories, they have enriched the field of library and information science.

Bibliometrics is the analysis of the structure of literature using various tools, counting, rank-frequency distributions, and citation analysis; and although the structure of literature is basic to all disciplines, it is particularly important in the area of information retrieval.

Thus it is evident that bibliometrics which was first used in evaluating journals for collection development in libraries, has been recognized and expanded to the study of the structure of literature in the field of information science. At present it is composed of methods and techniques without a coordinating theory; but it seems possible that as more theoretical information is converted to fact, and behaviourial patterns are established for the assessment and evaluation of the structural components of literature (i.e. authors, publications, words, laws) and their relationships, the more probable casual explanations will be evident and bibliometrics will be closer to being recognized universally as a science.

Present Status

Bibliometrics has contributed greatly to the development of Library and information science, particularly on the theoretical side. The subject is still at a developmental stage. Except for citation analysis, the practical utilization of bibliometrics is presently very limited. To make it a theory and more useful, researchers must concentrate on the casual factors underlying Bibliometric phenomena" (Hubert, 1981)[87].

Research in Library and Information Science

The term research refers to diligent search for knowledge characterized by systematic and disciplined enquiry. It is the pursuit of truth through study, observation, comparison and experimentation.

Ranganathan views research as a critical and exhaustive investigation to discover new facts, interpret them in the light of knew ideas – laws and theories, revise the current laws and theories when warranted by new facts and apply the conclusions to some practical purposes.

Role of Research in Development of a Subject

Research plays a key role in the educational process as a source of new knowledge both for the field of librarianship in general and for library education in particular. To quote Shera "Research is an intellectual process whereby a problem is perceived, divided into its constituent elements and analysed in the light of certain basic assumptions, valid and relevant data are collected and hypothesis (if any) are through objective testimony, rejected, amended or proved.

Research is thus the only sure way to constantly expand the fund of human knowledge. Research is useful as it

- Extends the boundaries of knowledge, thereby creating new knowledge.
- Makes it possible for new application of existing knowledge.
- Helps in finding solution to the problem.
- Leads to continuing advancement of scholarship.
- Brings prestige to the individual undertaking research and also to the institution where research is being conducted.
- Promotes faculty development in a teaching department intellectually and professionally.
- Enables the teachers engaged in or guiding research to become better teachers because they can integrate knowledge gained through research into their teaching programme.

- Enables the parent body to procure financial assistance through funded research and consultancy services.

Need for Research in Library and Information Science

Research in Library and Information Science unlike in Science and Technology is not well established, though it is imperative for librarians and scholars to find the best methods of acquiring, organizing, storing, accessing, retrieving and disseminating information. Waples states "The purpose of Library Science Research is clearly to support the functioning and development of library as a social and educational institution".

Moreover information is now regarded as a national resource which is vital for the development of any nation. To utilize the information effectively specialized manpower and research into information systems is necessary. For the advancement of Library and Information Science, strong research programmes are required.

Development of Research

Research in Librarianship existed since earlier times. History of Library reveals that librarians in earlier times have undertaken a great deal of experiments to solve the problems encountered by them. Research then was empirical which solved the immediate and practical problems. The importance and need of research into librarianship was realized for the first time in USA during the 30s. The opening article of the first issue of *Library Quarterly* in January 1931 entitled "The place of research in library science" written by C.C. Williamson revealed important points. Said C.C. Williamson "If the library is to rise to its opportunity as a social institution and educational force it must begin very soon to attack its problems by a thorough going application of the spirit and methods of research that are being found so effective in every other field". With the proliferation of library schools and acceptance of doctorate as legitimate course of study within the library field, research became firmly rooted within library educational process.

The recent decades witnessed a tremendous change in the research activities which may be attributed to increasing social pressures, financial support from library associations and governments and realisation of librarians to raise the status of library science on par with other disciplines.

LIS Education in India

LIS education in India started as non-university or non-college phenomena. The history of LIS education in India dates back to 1911 when for the first time LIS School was started at Baroda by W.A. Borden. In 1915 a part time course of 3 months duration was organized by Asa Don Dickinson at the Punjab University. Later Dr. S.R. Ranganathan gave a positive direction to Library Science education and started a certificate course under auspices of Madras Library Association in 1929. It was taken over by Madras University in 1931. This was basically an undergraduate educational programme. The University Education Programme was started by Ranganathan from Madras university in 1937 when he instituted the post graduate diploma course in Library Science. Later several other Universities followed the example and introduced diploma course in Library Science. Now M.L.I.Sc in India is a two year Post Graduate programme.

A number of studies have been carried out on the implications of Information Technology on Library and Information Science and the need for restructuring the curriculum of LIS education to meet the global information environment. (Singh, Jagtar[88]; Santosh Kumar[89]; Harinarayana, J, Giri Naidu, P., and Gopal Reddy, G.[90]; Muralidhar, G. and Yadigiri Reddy, J[91])

Research Activities in India

The concept of library research in its present day meaning is in fact a phenomenon of the post-independence period. The credit for initiating and stimulating scientific investigation in librarianship goes to the doyen of library and information science education Dr. S.R. Ranganathan. Under his dynamic leadership the 'era' of research in library science in India started. He was a genius and an innovator par excellence. He derived theories by challenging the concepts intellectually and expanded the horizons of library science discipline. His experiments and innovations gave solutions to various library operations and set a tradition which is significant and influential even today. The research activities in India can be broadly classified into two categories.

- Research conducted in library schools leading to the award of M.Phil. and Ph.D. degrees or fellowships by professional associations or research institutions.
- Research carried out by individual researchers or research teams in library schools, libraries and documentation centres etc. on certain problems without leading the award of any formal degree.

Research Levels

Ph.D.

Research courses leading to the award of M.Phil. and Ph.D. are offered by the University Library and Information Science Departments in India. Research at the Ph.D. level was initiated by Dr. S.R. Ranganathan in 1948 at the University of Delhi, with the active support and encouragement of Sir Maurice Gwyer, the then Vice-Chancellor. The first candidate who obtained his Ph.D. degree in 1957 was Dr. D.B. Krishna Rao for his work on "Facet Analysis and Depth Classification of Agriculture". It was only after 20 years (1977) that the second Ph.D. in India in Library

Science was awarded by Panjab University, Chandigarh to Pandey S.K. Sharma. Other universities soon launched research programmes. As per latest trends 63 universities are offering Ph.D. programme. The objectives of Ph.D. are to make a significant contribution to existing knowledge, to give evidence of carrying out independent research and ability to advance knowledge in the field of Library and Information Science, to promote cross fertilisation of ideas through interdisciplinary studies and to produce a selected number of candidates for testing positions in Library and Information Science.

M.Phil.

On the basis of recommendations made by Sen Committee (UGC) M.Phil. programmes in various disciplines were started in different universities. University of Delhi was the first to introduce M.Phil. programme in Library and Information Science in 1980. Today nearly 20 universities are offering this programme. The objectives of M.Phil. programme are to make students proficient in the methods and techniques of research and their applications to problems in Library Science and service, to give the student specialized knowledge in selected areas of Library Science, to train students for doing research work leading to Ph.D., and to expose the candidate to teaching methods relevant to Library and Information Science.

In addition to M.Phil. and Ph.D. programmes most university LIS departments prescribe a dissertation for M.L.I.Sc. as a partial fulfillment of the degree.

Besides universities, research work is also carried out by centers like The Documentation Research and Training Centre (DRTC) and Indian National Scientific Documentation Center (INSDOC). The Documentation Research and Training Centre (DRTC) set up in 1962 has done outstanding research work under the supervision of Dr. S.R.

Ranganathan. The results of DRTC research are communicated in the journal "Library Science with Slant to Documentation and Information Studies" and annual DRTC Seminars. It is the only institute which is engaged in individual and team research so far as the aspects of Library and Information Science are concerned. Recently INSDOC has been merged with National Institute of Science Communication and Information Resources (NISCAIR) and various activities performed by INSDOC were now taken up by NISCAIR.

Research works on special projects are also being done by individuals like teachers, students and librarians and team research funded by UGC, ICSSR, Dept of Science and Technology, Govt. of India etc. The Government of India also realized the importance of research for national development and established several research institutes and laboratories which function under Council for Scientific and Industrial Research (CSIR).

LIS research is also carried out at international level by professional organizations such as IFLA and FID. Besides, UNESCO, International Atomic Energy Agency is also actively involved in conducting and supporting research through publications conferences seminars, and the development of information systems. UNESCO has been particularly prominent internationally in conducting statistical and other research and in supporting the projects of other international organisations and national associations.

Several authors have written articles pertaining to different dimensions of research in Library and Information Science and suggested the application of latest information technology gadgets at each stage to complement the manual and conventional procedures to improve the quality of the research work. (Mathew Raju[92]; Mangla, P.B.[93]; Satija, M.P.[94] Sasikala, C.[95]; Padmini, K.[96])

Areas of Library and Information Science(LIS) Research

Research in the past focused its attention mostly on the historical aspects of the profession since the scope of library and information science at that time was limited and it was in its emergent state. It was only from the later years of 19th century that librarians paid increasing attention into the problems and functions of librarianship when the craft of the profession began to crystallize. As Melvin Voight[97] and Carl White point out "... it is apparent that systematic advancement of library science through research is still in the beginning stage". The dominant areas of research in olden days were academic and research libraries, bibliography, cataloguing and classification.

The development of Information Technology, and inter-disciplinary nature of the subjects, compelled research in the discipline of LIS to undergo seesaw changes. Increasing research activities within library and information science began to interface with other subject areas such as audio-visual technology, microform technology, computer science, communications and instructional technology. These developments enhanced the research potentialities of library and information science and gave scope to develop new theories, principles and practices.

In view of this changing scenario, a number of articles have been published by authors on different areas of research done in the discipline of Library and Information Science. The results indicated that most of the research has been done on traditional areas and suggested the researchers to exploit new areas which is the result of information technology revolution and inter-disciplinary nature of the subjects.(Rosemary, McGrill[98]; Subba Rao, C.V.[99]; Kumbhar, M.R. and Karisiddappa, C.R.[100]; Karande, A.G.[101]; Mahapatra, M.[102]; Shailendra Kumar and Ravindra Kumar[103]; Sivan Sen

Gupta[104]; Karande, A.G.[105]; Anandamurugan, M., Sasirekha, G., and Pandian, Murugaesha[106]).

Profiles of Universities, Libraries and LIS Departments

ANDHRA UNIVERSITY

Andhra University was constituted in response to a widely voiced demand in Telugu districts to the erstwhile Madras Province by the Madras Act No. II of 1926. The University was formally inaugurated at Bezawada (now Vijayawada) on August 30, 1926 by Lord Goschen, the first chancellor with C.R. Reddy as the founder Vice-Chancellor. The University was shifted to Vizagpatnam (Visakhapatnam) and started functioning in the Uplands of Waltair from September 5, 1930. Dr. Radhakrishnan, who had already renown as an exponent of Indian Philosophy, took charge as Vice-Chancellor on July 1, 1931. He inaugurated the University College of Arts on July 1, 1931 with two departments Telugu and History. A year later, the College of Science and Technology came into being with honours courses in Physics and Chemistry. Steps were initiated to construct permanent buildings for the two university colleges and hostels for students.

Shri Vikram Deo Varma Rajah Saheb of Jeypore, came forward with a donation of Rs. 75,000 for 1934-35 and a lakh of rupees each year thereafter, till such time as he or his heirs paid up a sum of fifteen lakhs for the maintenance of University College of Science and Technology. It was in recognition of this gesture that the syndicate renamed the College as Jeypore Vikram Deo College of Science and Technology and also conferred D. Litt. on the Raj Saheb.

In 1934, the University introduced the first ever honours course in Commerce in the country. Dr. C.R. Reddy came back to the University as Vice-Chancellor on May 20, 1936 and this time his term of office was marked by intense activity

– coming up of new buildings, flourishing laboratories and opening of new colleges and departments. Emphasis was laid on research and the University found itself in the forefront of Indian Universities and compelled international recognition. Dr. Reddy formulated an ambitious five year plan for the development of the University. The outbreak of second World War II in 1942, the University was shifted to Guntur and again it was shifted back to Waltair in 1946.

Dr. C.R. Reddy was succeeded by Dr. V.S. Krishna (1949). With a steady flow of funds from the Government of India and the University Grants Commission and matching funds from the state government the University witnessed an accelerated growth. Several new courses were introduced and departments established and the University celebrated its Silver Jubilee in January, 1953 and the College of Engineering was started in 1955. In 1961, Dr. A.L. Narayana who was a syndicate member since its inception became the Vice-Chancellor. During his tenure the engineering college and chemical engineering units developed at a steady pace. The chemical engineering building was declared open by Dr. S. Radhakrishnan in January 1963 and in the same year he laid foundation for convocation hall. B. Gopala Reddy laid foundation for Venkateswara Prayer Hall which was funded by Tirumala Tirupati Devasthanams. The UGC helped in the construction of Gandhi Bhavan and University press.

In 1966, Dr. K.R. Srinivas Iyengar became the Vice-Chancellor of Andhra University. During his tenure a Postgraduate centre was started in Guntur in July 1967 which subsequently blossomed into the present Nagarjuna University.

In 1968, Dr. L. Bullayya, who was the Director of Public Instruction in the Government of Andhra Pradesh became the Vice-Chancellor. Many affiliated colleges were permitted to introduce postgraduate courses and research work received full attention.

In the year 1974, Sri M.R. Appa Row became the Vice-Chancellor. He was a former Minister for Cultural Affairs and his tenure brought upsurge in sports and cultural activities in the campus. In 1975, three Postgraduate Extension Centres in Srikakulam, Kakinada and Nuzvid were started besides the establishment of 21 new affiliated colleges. Golden Jubilee of the University was celebrated in 1978.

In 1980, Dr. Avula Sambasiva Rao an eminent person from judicial family became the Vice-Chancellor. He was soft-spoken and had an open approach to administration. New courses including B.E. Metallurgy in the Department of Mechanical Engineering and Bachelor's course in Journalism and Mass Communication were started in 1981-1982. The Institute for Coastal Offshore Research and a Centre for Remote Sensing and Information Systems were also established in the College of Engineering.

In 1984, Prof. K. Ramakrishna Rao, an internationally renowned Professor of Psychology took over as Vice-Chancellor. An Institute for Yoga and Consciousness and a Centre for South Asian Research were established in the University.

In 1988, Dr. K.V. Ramana was appointed as Vice-Chancellor. There were fresh appointments in the University which provided young generation an opportunity to serve the esteemed institute.

Dr. M. Gopalakrishna Reddy, who served as Registrar of the University for over 25 years assumed the office of In-charge Vice-Chancellor on March 23, 1991. However he took over as full time Vice-Chancellor on September 18, 1991. There was another round of teachers recruitment during his tenure. In recognition to his rich contributions to the allround development of the University, the Governor of Andhra Pradesh has reappointed Dr. Gopalakrishna Reddy as Vice-Chancellor for second term on September 18, 1994.

In the year 1998, Prof. Rokkam Radhakrishna, an eminent economist assumed the post of Vice-Chancellor. He gave much importance to research and worked hard to regularize the academic calendar and examinations.

In 2002, Prof. Y.C. Simhadri, an alumni and former teacher of Andhra University became the Vice-Chancellor. By that time he has already served as Vice-Chancellor of Banaras Hindu University and Nagarjuna University. His appointment was crucial, as the University was on the threshold of downfall. He introduced reforms in admission procedure, allocation of hostels, attendance, examinations, enforced discipline to students and staff and beautified the campus. During his tenure the National Assessment and Accreditation Council has awarded A++ status to Andhra University which gave boost to achieve great heights.

In 2006, Prof. Y. Venugopala Reddy, was appointed as Vice-Chancellor of Andhra University. He insisted that massive and quality research should be undertaken in Universities and followed the pursuit by giving the research admission notification. He reinstated some of the Professors and Non-teaching staff with the view of creating a congenial atmosphere in the campus.

Dr. V.S. Krishna Library

> "... the University should provide great libraries and great laboratories of research with great scholars to direct them".

Genesis

The Andhra University Library is one of the best libraries of its kind in this country. It came into existence with the birth of University at Bezawada in August, 1926 with a humble collection of a few thousand books donated by Rao Bahadur D. Lakshminarayana, an Andhra industrialist and philanthropist of Nagpur.

In the middle of 1930 with the settlement of the problem of permanent venue of the University Head-quarters in favour of Waltair-uplands, the University was once for all shifted to Waltair along with the Library. Soon the library grew in size considerably and in 1935 it was housed in its own building, specially designed on the model of European Library Buildings, at Waltair.

A steady progress marked the period from 1937 to 1942 when along with the University, the Library had to be shifted to Guntur as a safety measure on account of the World War II. In 1946 the library reoccupied its own building at Waltair. With its rapid growth the collection of the Library was confronted with special problem which became acute by the beginning of 1959. Meanwhile the University Grants Commission came to the rescue in the cause of higher education in the country and with its gracious grant the present spacious building was built. By the end of 1962 the Library was completely shifted into the present building. The foundation stone for new building was laid by Sri Neelam Sanjiva Reddy, the then Chief Minister of Andhra Pradesh and it was declared open by Dr. K.L. Shrimali, the then Union Education Minister in 1962.

Library System

Over these years the Library is now developed not a system consisting of the Main Library, the Law College Library and the Engineering College Library besides the individual libraries of each Department in the campus.

The Main Library is named as Dr. V.S. Krishna Memorial Library in honour of late Dr. V.S. Krishna, the former Vice-Chancellor of the University and the Chairman of the UGC.

Membership

The services of the Library systems are extended only to its members. The students, the scholars, the faculty members, the officials of the University and the deposit borrowers as permitted by the Vice-Chancellor are the Library members.

Holding of the Library

The library witnessed a commendable growth in its comprehensive collection covering all branches of knowledge which at present stands at 4,31,799 apart from important journals. The collection includes books, bound volumes of periodicals, films, tapes, Xerox copies etc. In addition to this there are about 3000 palm-leaf manuscripts which were mostly donated by Paravasthu family and others. The library has also sizeable collection of audio and video cassettes.

Gifts and Special Collections

Very useful books were received were received as gifts from the Britain Council, the French Government, the Asia foundation, the U.S.I.S. and from the individuals. The special collections are those of many benefactors like Rao Bahadur D. Lakshminarayana, Dr. V.S. Krishna, Sri. A.V. Bhanoji Rao, Sri Gidugu Rama Murthy Pantulu, Sir S. Radhakrishan, Sir Kurma Venkata Reddy Naidu and Sri. K.V. Gopalaswamy.

Staff

The staff of the library includes 45 qualified professionals and 80 supporting staff for the smooth functioning of the library.

Services Offered

- Reference Services
- Inter-Library Loan Service
- Reprographic Service
- Audio-Visual Service
- E-Mail Service
- Content Page Service

- OPAC (On-line Public Access Catalogue)

UGC and its Role in the development of University Libraries – X Plan Development Programmes

For the development Andhra University Library, the UGC has sanctioned an amount of Rs. 571.50 lakhs which is to be divided among the following heads. Building (Rs. 70.00 Lakhs), Equipment (Rs. 256.00 Lakhs), Books and Journals (Rs. 60.00 Lakhs) and for central facilities (Rs. 185.50 Lakhs). The UGC has already released 367.90 lakhs as per the agreement.

Information explosion on one hand and ever changing demands of the user community have compelled the present day libraries whether it may be University library, College library, School library or Special library to go for automation. The Andhra University Library in order to mechanize the in-house operations acquired a library software viz., SOUL (Software for University Libraries) developed by INFLIBNET, Ahmedabad. The data entry of all the records have been completed and the users can access the OPAC. The total computerization of the library is still in progress.

UGC and ERNET India on collaborative basis operate UGC-INFONET. UGC is the owner of this network and it will provide funds to the Universities for this purpose. The University network managers will be trained by ERNET at New Delhi and also at various university sites. INFLIBNET will act as a focal point between the ERNET and the Universities. The library professionals will be given training in the use of this network by INFLIBNET to render efficient and effective services i.e. providing access to E-Journals to academic community.

The University library acts as a central hub of the campus and renders services to 900 teachers, 1000 scholars and 9000 students covering all the disciplines. However the local users from industries and other institutions also utilize the library for their information requirements. The present collection of books is about 450000. The total number of national and international journals subscribed by the library are more than 260.

List of Online sources accessible through UGC-Infonet in Dr. V.S. Krishna Library, Andhra University

A.C.S (American Chemical Society) URL : http://pubs.acs.org

A.I.P (American Institute of Physics) URL : http://www.aip.org/

A.P.S (American Physical Society) URL : http://www.aps.org

A.R: (Annual Reviews) URL : http://www.annualreviews.org/

B.A : (Biological Abstracts)

URL : http://web5s.silverplatter.com/webspirs start.ws?customer=c1804700

CUP : Cambridge University Press URL : http://www.cup.org

I.P. Institute of Physics URL : http://www.iop.org/EJ/

JSTOR : Journal Store URL : http://www.jstor.org/

Nature : URL : http://www.nature.com

P.M. Project Muse URL : http://muse.jhu.edu/journals/

R.S.C. Royal Society of Chemistry URL : http://www.rsc.org/

S.C. Science Online URL : http://www.scienceonline.org/

S.D. Science Direct URL : http://www.sciencedirect.com/

Number of Electronic Journals and Databases accessible through UGC Infonet are 86 which include both foreign and Indian.

Department of Library and Information Science, Andhra University

The Department of Library and Information Science,

Andhra University had its origin in 1935 when the senate sanctioned a summer school as well as a regular school of librarianship. Dr. M.O. Thomas, M.A, B.D., Ph.D., Dip. L.S. (London), F.L.A. organized these courses. According to him the courses were designed to suit the requirements to both the higher and the lower orders of librarianship and they led either to a graduate University diploma or a certificate of proficiency course was the first of its kind conducted in our country. However it appears the course had checkered progress after 1938 when both Dr. M.O. Thomas and Sri. C.G. Viswanathan left the University. During Second World War the University was shifted to Guntur. The courses were revived in 1948, and C.L.Sc. and D.L.Sc. courses were conducted till 1958.

In 1961 Prof. Koneru Ramakrishna Rao took charge as Chief Librarian and Head, Department of Library Science. He bought with him a rich and varied experience of Library Science education and Library services from Western countries. The organization of the department on a regular basis and modernization of the curriculum were initiated by Prof. K. Ramakrishna Rao. He took steps to constitute the Board of Studies in Library Science and thus facilitated the constant revision and updating of the curriculum. As part of the programme to strengthen the Department, a full-time lecturer post was created and Sri K. Siva Reddy was appointed. Sri K. Venkataratnam, Sri. P. Vasudeva Rao, Sri M. Satyanarayana were associated with the teaching programme as part-time lecturers for D.L.Sc. In compliance with the U.G.C. recommendations, the C.L.Sc. course was discontinued in 1962. In the year 1968 the Department attained the status of a full-fledged teaching department. Under the leadership of Prof. K. Siva Reddy it grew from strength to strength. Consequently the practice of employing Library staff as part-time teachers was given up. The Diploma course was redesigned as Bachelor of Library and Information

Science (1979). These changes indicate the change and modernization of the curriculum. In 1979-80, the Master of Library and Information Science programme was started in response to the felt need of the students of this department.

The Department has been providing facilities for the pursuit of research studies leading to the award of Doctor of Philosophy since 1966 for part-time while full time research admissions took place from 1980-81. M.Phil. course, both full time and part time have been in offer since 1980.

Curriculum Design and Review

The present curriculum has been framed based on the recommendations of the UGC panel on LIS Education and it is subject to revisions every three years.

Teaching Learning and Evaluation

Classroom instruction relies mainly on the lecture method, supported by audio-visual teaching aids such as OHP, computers, seminars etc. Students knowledge is assessed through assignments and unit tests.

Research/Consultancy/Evaluation

The department has produced 39 Ph.Ds and more than 17 M.Phils. 12 books and over 200 articles have been published. Most of the teachers are on Expert Committees and Board of Studies of other Universities. The department is active in organizing national seminars, workshops and training programmes.

Infrastructure and Learning Resources

The department has a computer laboratory which helps to augment the academic activities of the students as well as the staff.

SRI VENKATESWARA UNIVERSITY

Sri Venkateswara University, Tirupati was established

in 1954, in the famous temple town of Tirupati, South India, the SRI VENKATESWARA UNIVERSITY is a standing testimony to the wisdom and foresight of Late Tanguturi Prakasam Pantulu, the then Chief Minister of Andhra Pradesh, and to the munificence of Tirumala Tiripati Devasthanams. Intended to fulfill the long felt educational needs and aspirations of the people of Rayalaseema, this University has been carefully nurtured and developed by eminent Vice-Chancellors such as Prof. S. Govindarajulu, Dr. V.C. Vamana Rao, Dr. D.J. Reddy and Prof. K. Satchidananda Murthy during its formative years.

Located in a sprawling thousand acre campus at the foot of the picturesque Seven Hills (Seshachala Hills of Eastern Ghats), the University has been emphasizing teaching and research programmes in different faculties right from its inception. The range of subject departments, courses and research programmes undertaken and promoted during the last 40 years reflect the Sri Venkateswara University's commitment to promoting socially relevant programmes on one hand and to catch up with frontier areas of research and training on the other. Starting with basic science and social science departments of Chemistry, Physics, Mathematics, Botany, Zoology, Economics and Philosophy in 1954-1955, the University today has over 40 subject departments including Biochemistry, Virology, Management, Home Science, Computer Applications, Computer Science, Electronic Space and Communication Engineering. The University offers more than 40 graduate and Post graduate programmes in all branches of humanities, social sciences, basic sciences, engineering management and in some of the frontier areas such as Environmental Studies, Atmospheric Science, Computer Applications, Computer Science and Engineering, Virology, Biotechnology, Sericulture, Fishery Science, Fashion Technology and Engineering Physics. Besides, the University has been offering M.Phil. and Ph.D. research programmes in almost every subject discipline.

Equipped with the most modern laboratory facilities and very strong library resource system, the University has been conducting sponsored and funded research in several key areas such as Water Resource Management, Rural Sanitation, Low Cost Housing, Alternative Systems of Energy, MST Radar Applications, and Environmental Studies. A good deal of research activity of Sri Venkateswara University is a response to the problems of drought prone semi-arid Rayalaseema region.

The University has been a centre for intellectual activities, growth of ideas and experimentation. A large number of outstanding scholars have been visitors of this University. Eminent persons like Dr. Sarvepalli Radhakrishnan, Pandit Jawaharlal Nehru, His holiness Sankaracharya, Sri P.V. Narasimha Rao, Dr. Shankardayal Sharma, Dr. Karan Singh, Prof. Nilhar Ranjan Ray, Justice Ranganath Mishra, Dr. S. Gopal, Dr. H.N. Detna, Dr. Homi Baba and Prof. G.K. Menon visited this University and stimulated the academic activity at various points of time during the last 40 years.

In the life of a University, 40 years is but a brief period, yet it is vitally important. It is during this stage that sound academic foundations are laid on which a lasting superstructure can be built. The S.V. University has been successful not only in laying solid foundations but in completing the superstructure. The UGC, the Government of Andhra Pradesh, several funding agencies, University bodies, faculty and students have contributed to the successful development of the University which is well poised to take a big leap forward.

Vision

- Promotion of Academic Excellence
- Resource Generation/Mobilization
- Networking

- University - State/Industry and Community Interaction
- Student Counseling, Placement and Training.

Mission

The "Mission" is to develop qualified and competent citizens through teaching and training, expand the horizons of knowledge through research, to lend knowledge and support to various organizations for their effective functioning, to contribute to the creation of a happy and healthy society through fruitful interaction with it, and to participate in the development of the society.

Goals

- Designing and implementing educational and training programs of high standard
- Promoting research in an environment conducive for exploration, experimentation and expansion
- Creating awareness and disseminating knowledge through various media, forums and programs
- Undertaking extension activites, providing consultancy to various organizations for solving their problems and improving their functioning
- Organizing extracurricular activities to develop sporting skills, promote literary and cultural events, social services, national integration and discipline

Academic Excellence

- The University envisages comprehensive academic excellence by adopting an integrated approach involving students, staff and community
- Curriculum development will be based on periodical review complying with Industry/Social requirements

- International conferences, Educational and Industrial tours
- Effective measures will be taken to modernize the curriculum at U.G. and P.G. level through integrated approach
- The University plans to play effective role in supporting and facilitating the organizing process and providing scientific and technical guidance and advice for comprehensive societal development
- One of the challenges posed by gloabalization is the entry of Foreign Universities into India with highly attractive course modules in the Distance learning mode. Distance Education has therefore become very convenient, economic and cost-effective for the common man. The University proposes to strengthen the Directorate of Distance Education as a model institution to attract large number of student into its fold.

Sri Venkateswara University Library

Overview

The University Library was started in the year 1955 with a small collection of 6,700 books taken from Sri Venkateswara College, Tirupati, administered by Tirumala Tirupati Devasthanams. Initially the library was housed in one portion of the college main building. Later, it was shifted to the present building which was declared open in July 1964, by Late Dr. S. Radhakrishnan, the then President of India. He described it as "Taj Mahal of the South". University Library is the common facility for SVU College of Arts & Sciences and SVU College of Engineering and serves the information needs of the students, research scholars, teaching faculty, non-teaching staff of the University and deposit borrowers numbering around 7000.

Document Collection

The total collection of the library is 3,27,500 documents, which includes books, reference books, reports, back volumes of journals, theses and dissertations. The Library subscribes to about 360 journals of National and international importance.

Organization

In order to achieve functional efficiency, the library is organized into 12 different sections. They are Circulation Section, Book Acquisition Section, Technical Section, Periodical Section, Binding Section, Stack Area, Reference-Cum-Dcoumentation Section, Text Book and Competitive Examinations Cell, Electronic Data Processing Section, University Publications Section and Administrative Section.

Membership

The membership of library comprises of Students, Research Scholars, Faculty Members, Non-Teaching Staff, Deposit Borrowers.

Library Services

Book Lending Service, Reader's Advisory Service, Reference Service, Reprography Service and Inter-Library Loan Facility.

Special Features

The novel feature of S.V. University Library is the establishment of Competitive Examinations Cell in the year 2000 with main objective of providing reading material for student community preparing for various competitive examinations like TOEFL, GATE, GRE, GMAT, CAT, UPSC, APPSC etc.

Automation

The S.V. University Library is a participating member in

the INFLIBNET programme of the UGC. It has procured SOUL, integrated library automation software from INFLIBNET, UGC, for automation of various in-house operations of the library.

UGC-INFONET Programme

UGC in its Golden jubilee year 2003 launched a consortium of Universities known as UGC-INFONET E-Journals Consortium to provide electronic access over the internet to scholarly literature in all areas of learning to the university sector in India. Our University is also member of this programme and as on today, INFLIBNET has provided access to about 4,000 full-text E-Journals.

Digital Library

SVU Library is establishing a Digital Library by spending an amount of Rs. 23 lakhs to ensure students, research scholars and faculty members access to all E-Journals provided under INFONET programme and other E-Resources available in the library.

The Vision and Future Plans

- Establishment of separate cell for books and journals on 'Information Technology'
- Automation of all the in-house operations of the library
- Integration of SVU library OPAC (Online Public Access Catalogue) with SVU campus LAN.
- Compilation of INTERNET information sources for all disciplines
- Training of Library Professional in Automation, Networking and INTERNET searching
- Training of library users in using OPAC facility, E-Journals and INTERNET resources.

Department of Library and Information Science, Sri Venkateswara University

The B.L.I.Sc. and M.L.I.Sc. courses were started in the Department in the year 1974 and 1985 respectively. The present system of Library and Information Science curriculum has been designed keeping in view the fast development of Information Technology and its applications in Libraries. In order to produce efficient manpower to manage digital environment of the libraries the Department instituted two year MLISc course with effect from 1996-1997 along with research leading to M.Phil. and Ph.D degrees. The Department has so far produced 18 Ph.D. and 13 M.Phil degrees and presently 18 students are doing research. The Department has completed one project and has 125 publications including books and research papers. Five conferences/seminars have been organized by the Department

OSMANIA UNIVERSITY

History

Founded in 1917 by the VII Nizam of Hyderabad, Nawwab Mir Osman Ali Khan, Osmania University is the seventh oldest institution of higher learning in India, the third oldest in southern India and the first to be established in the erstwhile princely state of Hyderabad. Throughout its existence of almost nine decades, it has shown remarkable progress and sustained an integrated development of all faculties. It has made significant contributions to the academic, social, and economic development of not only the region but to the nation as a whole. Its alumni have distinguished themselves nationally and internationally in various spheres of life and are spread far and wide around the world.

Reputation and Offerings

With a sprawling campus of nearly 1600 acres and

buildings of majestic beauty and architectural splendour, Osmania University is perhaps the symbol of the largest higher education system in the country. With its strong reputation, the University has always attracted students from all across the nation as well as from various other countries. It is the home to nearly 3,00,000 students pursuing higher studies in its campus, constituent affiliated colleges and district centres. Its faculty and staff number nearly 5,000.

It is a multi-faculty and multidisciplinary University, offering rich and varied courses in the fields of Humanities, Arts, Sciences, Social Sciences, Law, Engineering, Medicine, Technology, Commerce and Business Management, Information Technology and Oriental Languages. The University's strategic planning, teaching-and-learning policies and research direction have always emphasized respect for the concerns of the society and need to address the issues that challenge it.

In the year 2001, Osmania University had the distinction of being awarded the five-star status by the National Accreditation and Assessment Council (NAAC) of the University Grants Commission, part of the Government of India.

Business

The department of Business Management, Osmania University has been offering an MBA Program since 1964. This program has been constantly ranked as one of the best MBA Programs in India.

Geography

The Department of Geography is the oldest and largest geography department in South India. Established in 1942, it has a substantial infrastructure with high-tech labs for geography and geoinformatics. The Department of Geography has some of India's best known geographers on its faculty.

Engineering

The College of Engineering (OUCE), established in 1929, offers B.E. (Bachelor of Engineering), M.E. (Master of Engineering), and Ph.D. Programs in various engineering fields. It is autonomous college and arguably the best engineering college in Andhra Pradesh. An affiliation with the IIT is suggested due to its achievements and excellent academic pursuits.

Notable Alumni

- Late Muhammad Raziuddin Siddiqui, Mathematician, Physicist, and Nobel Prize Nominee
- Late P.V. Narasimha Rao, Scholar, Statesman and former Prime Minister of India
- Barrister Asaduddin Owaisi, Politician and Current Member of Parliament of India
- Late Syed Ali Mohammed Khusro, Economist, Director, Reserve Bank of India, and former Indian ambassador to the Federal Republic of Germany
- Muhammad Khutub Uddin, M.D., Ph.D., Physician and Professor of Religious Studies and Theology
- Haroon Siddiqui, Indo-Canadian journalist
- Ramulu Komireddi, journalist, lawyer and politician
- Late Prof. Afzal Mohammad, former Vice-Chancellor, BRAOU, Hyderabad
- Ali Ejaz, M.D., Ph.D., Physicist and educator.

Osmania University Library

In the picturesque Osmania campus, a stately building up the hillock attracts your attention as you approach the Arts College. As you climb up the driveway, the Saraswati temple to your right is some indication that you are nearing a book-centered world. Up a flight of spacious steps is the Osmania University Library, which in addition has departmental libraries, like the one located in the Arts College building.

The library, which is one of the oldest in twin cities, began functioning as early as in 1918. It has kept itself contemporary, though. Right next to the librarian's office, for example, is the staircase to the "Competitive Examinations Reference Library", a section not to be found in any of the university libraries though many students still fancy the power-driven civil services for a career. Similarly, to the right of the librarian's office, you will find the vision of Osmania. It contains important documents of the Nizam period. You need official permission to get to see these *famans*, manuscripts and photographs.

The holdings of library include 5 lakhs books, 58000 bound volumes of journals, 3858 government documents, 272 films, 6428 manuscripts, 143 microfilms and 9 CD ROMs.

The library prides itself on its collection of government and UN documents. The government documents include budget papers and census and statistical reports acquired by the library, which are processed and are made available. The library is also a depository for materials brought out by the UN and its agencies. It receives books, journals and mimeographed documents (verbatim debates of the General Assembly and the Security Council) published by the United Nations and its agencies. It also has a UNESCO Information Centre.

The other specialty of this typical University library is its gift collection of the personal libraries of such stalwarts as Nawab Ali Yawar Jung. Its manuscripts collections include palm-leaf manuscripts, illustrations, calligraphy and scripts of the rare variety.

The entire collection of the library is automated using LIBGEN software. Users of the library can access the database of the University library through OPAC (On-line Public Access Catalogue).

Department of Library and Information Science, Osmania University

The Department was established in 1959 as a result of concreted efforts made by Sri. B.P. Shenoy and Sri K. Raghava Reddy. Initially, it offered a post- graduate diploma and a post-matric certificate course. The certificate course was given up in 1962 following the recommendations of Sinha Committee appointed by the Government of India.

The Diploma was replaced by a post-graduate degree in Library Science (BLSc) in 1965. The Department was renamed as 'Department of Library and Information Science' in the mid-80s as per the UGC directive. The master's degree programme (MLISc) was started in 1979-80 and the M.Phil. programme was introduced in 1993-94.

A self-financing MLISc (summer programme) spanning two summer vacations was started in 1993 for in-service librarians and it was discontinued in 2000.Eminent academicians and librarians like Masood Yazdani, K. Raghava Reddy, Smt. Malathi Reddy, R.K. Gupta, Abdul Mahamood, Prof M.V. Venugopal, Prof. A.A.N. Raju have served as Heads of the Department. Prof. A.A.N. Raju also served as Dean, Faculty of Social Sciences and was UGC Emeritus Fellow. The Department has awarded 17 Ph.Ds. and seven M.Phil. degrees. The Department also offers outreach and extension services and organizes campus placements.

SRI KRISHNA DEVARAYA UNIVERSITY

Sri Krishna Devaraya University, Anantapur, came into existence on July 25, 1981 fulfilling a silent demand and a long cherished dream of the people of Rayalaseema. The University is named after a great patron of learning and the arts, Sri Krishna Devaraya, of the glorious Vijayanagara empire of the sixteenth century. The University is an offshoot of the erstwhile Postgraduate Centre of Sri Venkateswara University started in 1968. Subsequently in 1976, the S.V.U. Postgraduate centre attained autonomous status. In 1987, with a capital outlay of Rs. 1.2 crores, Sri Krishna Devaraya Institute of Management was started with funding from the University Grants Commission. In 1988, the University which was originally a unitary, residential institution, became full-fledged affiliating University. Yet another landmark in the history of the University is that the Postgraduate centre at Kurnool under the jurisdiction of Sri Venkateswara University was made over to Sri Krishna Devaraya University in 1993. Thus the University has an academic history of 33 years. Situated in rural environs in an extensive campus of over 500 acres of land, the University has ample scope for development as also an infrastructure which includes a Library, University Science Instrumentation Centre, a Computer Centre, a Health Centre, a Gymnasium, an Outdoor Stadium, an Auditorium and adequately built up space to accommodate departments of studies, laboratories, hostels and housing for the staff, teaching and non-teaching.

Sri Krishna Devaraya University Library

The University has a Central Library. It has a rich collection of over 97,000 books, periodicals, charts and other reading materials. It has a collection of 14,000 back volumes of periodicals. It subscribes to 141 periodicals of which 28 are foreign periodicals. In addition, as many as 65 reading room journals are subscribed by the Library. It makes special provision in its budget for resource materials for competitive examinations preparation. IX plan allocations amounting to Rs. 35 lakhs have been utilized in a phased manner for a further updating of the library. The Library has entered the networking era by acquiring the INFLIBNET facility to offer more wide ranging services to its users and to focus on the expansion of the knowledge base. Yet another important feature of the library is that it maintains a textbook collection for SC/ST students.

Department of Library and Information Science, Sri Krishna Devaraya University

The Department was established in 1982. In order to meet the human resource needs of libraries during Nineteen Eighties, the University authorities took steps to start certificate course in Library and Information Science with the available resources in the library due to the efforts of Prof. P. Kamaiah. B.L.I.Sc., was started with the permission from the UGC during 1984-85. The M.L.I.Sc. and research courses leading to M.Phil., and Ph.D., were started during Nineties. The department has the credit of running summer course for college librarians leading to M.L.I.Sc. Degree for the first time in the country. The Department of Library and Information Science, Sri Krishna Devaraya University has been offering M.L.I.Sc., M.Phil. and Ph.D. for its students. The department has accomplished faculty to train the students in order to meet the challenges posed to them in their future. The department has the credit of handling a project titled "Education and Information for empowering rural women through community library and information services in Rayalaseema of Andhra Pradesh", which was funded by University Grants Commission. The amount sanctioned for this project is Rs. 1,97,040.00. The areas of specialization offered by the Department of LIS are Academic Library System at P.G. Level, Personnel Management in Libraries at the Ph.D. and individual teacher level.

This chapter covers various areas of Bibliometrics like citation analysis, bibliometric laws, bibliographic coupling, citation counting, co-citation, obsolescence and half-life of literature. This chapter also covers the history of Library and Information Science Education , Library and Information Science Research and profiles of four universities in Andhra Pradesh namely Andhra University, Sri Venkateswara University, Osmania University and Sri Krishna Devaraya University.

REFERENCES

1. Sharada, B.A. Bibliometric Statistics in Linguistics and Bibliometric Laws. *Library Science*, 30(2), 1993, pp. 71-75.
2. Pritchard, Alan. Statistical Bibliography or Bibliometrics. *Journal of Documentation*, 25, 1969, pp. 348-349.
3. Campbell, F. *Theory of the National and International Bibliography*. London. 1896.
4. Cole, F.J. and Eales, N.B. The History of Comparative Anatomy. Part I: A Statistical Analysis of Literature. *Science Progress*. 11, 1917, pp. 578-596.
5. Hulme, E.W. *Statistical Bibliography in Relation to the Growth of Modern Civilization*. London: Grafton, 1922.
6. Webster, N. *Webster's New Twentieth Century Dictionary of the English Language*. New York: Standard Reference Works Publishing Company, 1956, p. 172.
7. Schneider, George. *Theory and History of Bibliography*. New York. 1926.
8. Murray, David. *Bibliography. Its Scope and Method*. Glasgow. 1917.
9. Horne, T.H. *An Introduction to the Study of Bibliography*. London: G. Wood fall, 1814.
10. Besterman, T. *The Beginning of Systematic Bibliography*. London: Oxford University press, 1935.
11. Malcles, L.N. *Bibliography*, Translation by Theodre Christian Hines. New York: Scarecrow Press, 1956, p. 93.
12. Hulme, E.W. *Statistical Bibliography in Relation to the Growth of Modern Civilization*. London: Grafton, 1923.

13. Levinson, H.C. *The Science of Chance from Probability to Statistics*. New York: Rinehart and Company, 1950.

14. Meitzen, A. History, Theory and Techniques of Statistics. translated by Ronald P. Falkner. Philadelphia: American Academy of Political and Social Science, 1891. Part First: History of Statistics, p. 15.

15. Walpole, R.E. *Introduction to Statistics*. New York: Macmillan, 1968.

16. Meitzen, A. History, theory and technique of statistics. translated by Ronald P. Falkner. Philadelphia: American Academy of Political Social Science, 1891. Part First: *History of Statistics*, p. 20.

17. Raisig, L.M. Statistical bibliography in the Health Sciences. *Bulletin of medical library association*, 50, 1962, pp. 450-461.

18. Henkle, H.H. The periodical literature of Biochemistry. *Bulletin of medical libraries association*. 27, 1938, pp. 139-147.

19. Fussler, H.H. Characteristics of the Research Literature used by Chemists and Physicists in the United States. Ph.D. dissertation, University of Chicago. 1948.

20. Pritchard, Alan. *Computers, Statistical Bibliography and Abstracting Services*. Unpublished paper. 1968.

21. Sengupta, I.N. Bibliometrics, Informetrics, Scientometrics and Librametrics: An Overview. *Libri*. 42, 1992, pp. 75-98.

22. http:// WWW. Du.edu/~ jtwining/ LIS 4236.

23. Pritchard, Alan. Bibliometrics and Information Transfer. *Res. Librarianship*. 4, 1972, pp. 37-46.

24. Fairthorne, R.A. Empirical Hyperbolic Distributions (Bradford-Ziff-Mandelbrot) for Bibliometric Description and Prediction. *Journal of documentation*. 25, 1969, p. 319-343.

25. *British Standard Glossary of Documentation Terms*. London: British Standards Institution, 1976.

26. Hawkins, D.T. Unconventional use of on-line information retrieval system: On-line bibliometric studies. *Journal of*

American Society for Information Science. 28, 1977, p. 13-18.

27. Lancaster, F.W. *The Measurement and Evaluation of Library Services*. Washington D.C: Information Resources Press, 1977.
28. Schrader, A.M. Teaching bibliometrics. *Library Trends*. 30, 1981, p.151-172.
29. Potter, W.G. Introduction to Bibliometrics. *Library Trends*. 30, 1981, p. 5-7.
30. Hertzel, D.H. History of the Development of Ideas in Bibliometrics. In Kent, A, ed. *Encyclopedia of Library and Information Science*. V 42. New York: Marcel Dekker, 1987, p. 144-219.
31. Egghe, I. And Rousseau, R. *Introduction to Informetrics, Quantitative Methods in Library, Documentation and Information Science*, Amsterdam. Elsevier Science Publishers. 1988.
32. White, H.T. and Mc Cain, K.W. Bibliometrics. In: *Annual Review of Information Science and Technology*.M.E, ed. Williams, V 24. New York: Elsevier Science, 1989, pp. 119-186.
33. Gupta, D.K. Application of Bradford's Law to Citation Data of Ethopian Medical Journal. *Annals of library science and documentation*. 38, 1991, pp. 85-88.
34. Humayoon Kabir, S. World Literature on Bibliometrics: Authorship and Growth Patterns. *ILA Bulletin*, 28(3/4), 1993, pp. 87-94.
35. Diodato, V. *Dictionary of Bibliometrics*. New York: Haworth Press, 1994.
36. Simon, H.R. Why Analyse Bibliographies. *Library trends*. 22, 1973, pp. 3-8.
37. Connor and Voos. Emperical laws. Theory construction and bibliometrics. *Library trends*. 30; 1981.
38. Nicholas, D. and Ritchie, M. *Literature and Bibliometrics*. London: Clive Bingley, 1978.
39. Stevens, R.E. *Characteristics of Subject Literatures*. Association of College and Research Libraries, USA: American Library Association, 1953.

40. Diodato, V. *Dictionary of Bibliometrics*. New York: Haworth Press, 1994.

41. Pritchard, Alan. Statistical Bibliography or Bibliometrics. *Journal of documentation*, 25, 1969, pp. 348-349.

42. Almind, T.A. and Ingwersen, P.I. Informetric Analyses on the World Wide Web: Methodological Approaches to "Webometrics". *Journal of Documentation*, 53, 1997, pp. 404-426.

43. Pritchard, Alan. *Computers, Statistical Bibliography and Abstracting Services*. Unpublished, 1968.

44. Lawani, S.M. Bibliometrics: Its Theoretical Foundations, Methods and Applications. *Libri*. 31; 1981, pp. 294-315.

45. Ravichandra Rao, I.K. *Quantitative Methods for Library and Information Science*. New Delhi: Wiley Eastern, 1983.

46. Lancaster, F.W. Bibliometric methods in assessing productivity and impact of research. Bangalore: Sarada Ranganathan Endowment for Library Science, 1991.

47. Sengupta, I.N. Bibliometrics, Informetrics, Scientometrics and Librametrics: An Overview. *Libri*, 42, 1992, p. 75-98

48. Bradford, S.C. Documentation. Washington: Public Affairs Press, 1950, chapter IX.

49. Salton, Gerard. *Dynamic Information and library Processing*. Englewood Cliffs (New Jersey): Prentice Hall, 1975, pp. 25-33, 181,195-214.

50. Lotka, A.J. The Frequency Distribution of Scientific Productivity. *Journal of the Washington Academy of Science*, 16, 1926, p. 317-323.

51. Zipf, G.K. *The Psycho-Biology of Language: An Introduction to Dynamic Philosophy*. Houghton Mifflin, Boston: Riverside Press, 1935.

52. Zipf, G.K. *op.cit.*

53. *Ibid.*

54. Martin Joos. *Book Reviews, George K. Zipf's The Psycho-Biology of Language*. Boston: Houghton Mifflin Company, 1936.

55. Zipf, G.K. *Human Behavior and the Principle of Least Effort*. Reading (Mass): Addison-Wesley, 1949.

56. Scarrott, G. Will Zipf join Gauss. *New Scientist*, 62, 1974, pp. 402-404.

57. Vickery, B.C. Bradford's Law of Scattering. *Journal of Documentation*, 4(3), 1948, pp. 198-203.

58. Kendall, M.G. Bibliography of Operations Research. *Operational research quarterly*, 11, 1960, pp. 31-36.

59. Cole, P.F. A New Look at Reference Scattering. *Journal of Documentation*, 17, 1962, pp. 58-64.

60. Leimkuhler, F.F. The Bradford distribution. *Journal of Documentation*, 23, 1967, pp. 197-207.

61. Brookes, B.C. Complete Bradford-Zipf "Bibliograph". *Journal of Documentation*, 25(1), 1969, pp. 58-60.

62. Brookes, B.C. The Derivation and Application of the Bradford-Zipf Distribution. *Journal of Documentation*, 24(4), 1969, pp. 247-265.

63. Naranan, S. Bradford Law of Science Bibliography: An Interpretation. *Nature*, 227, 1970, pp. 631-632.

64. Goffman, W and Morris, T.G. Bradford's Law and Library Acquisitions. *Nature*, 226, 1970, pp. 922-923.

65. Wilkinson, E.A. The Ambiguity of Bradford's Law. *Journal of Documentation*, 28, 1972, pp. 122-130.

66. Brookes, B.C. Numerical methods of analysis. *Library Trends*, 22, 1973, pp. 18-43.

67. Sengupta, I.N. Recent growth of the literature of biochemistry and changes in ranking of periodicals. *Journal of Documentation*, 29(2), 1973, pp. 210-211.

68. Pope, A. Bradford's Law and the Periodical Literature of Information Science. *Journal of the American Society for Information Science*, 26(4), 1975, p. 212.

69. Worthan, D.B. The Application of Bradford's Law to Monographs. *Journal of Documentation*, 31(1), 1975, pp. 19-25.

70. Aiyepeku, W.O. The Bradford Distribution Theory: The Compounding of Bradford Periodical Literature in Geography. *Journal of Documentation*, 33(3), 1977, p. 218.

71. Brookes, B.C. Theory of Bradford Law. *Journal of Documentation*, 33, 1977, p. 180-209.

72. Rapaport, A. The Stochastic and the Teleological Rationals of Certain Distributions and the So-called Principle of Least Effort. *Behav-Science*, 2(2), 1957, p. 150.

73. Simon, H.A. Some further notes on a class of Skew Distribution Functions. *Information Control*, 3(1), 1960, pp. 80-88.

74. Hill, B.M. Zipf's Law and prior Distributions for the Composition of a Population. *Journal of the American Society for Information Science*, 65(331), 1970, pp. 1220-1232.

75. Sichel, H.S. On a Distribution Law for Word Frequencies. *Journal of the American State Association*, 70, 1975, pp. 542-547.

76. Wyllys, R.E. Measuring Scientific Prose with Rank Frequency (Zipf) Curves: A New Use Ford Old Phenomenon Proc. ASIS 38th Annual Meeting. Information Revolution, 12, 1975, p. 30.

77. Murphy, L.J. Lotka's Law in the Humanities. *Journal of the American Society for Information Science*, 24(4), 1973, pp. 461-462.

78. Voos, H. Lotka and Information Science. *Journal of the American Society for Information Science*, 25(4), 1974, p. 270.

79. Schorr, A.E. Lotka's Law and the History of legal Medicine. *Research Librarianship*, 30(3), 1975, pp. 205-209.

80. Hubert, J.J. Letters to the Editor. *Journal of the American Society for Information Science*, 28(1), 1977, p. 66.

81. Russel, C.C. Lotka's Frequency Distribution of Scientific Productivity. *Journal of the American Society for Information Science*, 28(6), 1977, p. 366.

82. Radhakrishnan, T and Kerinzan, R. Lotka's Law and Computer Science Literature. *Journal of the American Society for Information Science*, 28(6), 1979, p. 366.

83. Subramanyam, K. Lotka's Law and Library Literature. *Library Research*, 3, 1981, p. 167.

84. Richardson, V.L. Lotka's Law and the Catalogue? *A.A.R.L*, 12(3), 1981, p. 185.

85. Pao, K.L. Test-*Collection Management*, 4(3), 1982, p. 112.

86. Line, M.B. and Sandison, Alexander. "Obsolescence" and Changes in the use of Literature with Time. *Journal of Documentation*, 30, 1974, pp. 283-350.

87. Hubert, J.J. General Bibliometric Models. *Library Trends*, 30, 1981, pp. 65-81.

88. Singh, Jagtar. Looking Beyond Globalization of LIS Education. In. *Globalization of Library and Information Science Education* edited by N. Laxman Rao, S. Sudarshan Rao and J. Yadagiri Reddy, Hyderabad, IATLIS, 2004.

89. Santosh Kumar, K.T. Redefining LIS Education in the changing Environment. In. *Globalization of Library and Information Science Education* edited by N. Laxman Rao, S. Sudarshan Rao, and J. Yadagiri Reddy, Hyderabad, IATLIS, 2004.

90. Harinarayana, J. Giri Naidu, P., and Gopal Reddy, G. Reforms in LIS Education to meet the Global Information Environment. In. *Globalization of Library and Information Science Education* edited by N. Laxman Rao, S. Sudarshan Rao, and J. Yadagiri Reddy, Hyderabad, IATLIS, 2004.

91. Muralidhar, G. and Yadagiri Reddy, J. Curriculum for Global Education in LIS. In. *Globalization of Library and Information Science Education* edited by N. Laxman Rao, S. Sudarshan Rao, and J. Yadagiri Reddy, Hyderabad, IATLIS, 2004.

92. Mathew Raju, M. The Indian Council of Library and Information Research and Training: A proposal. *ILA Bulletin*, 24(3), 1980, pp. 179-183.

93. Mangla, P.B. Research in Library and Information Science and the Contribution of S.R. Ranganathan. *Journal of Education for Librarianship*, 9(1), 1970, pp. 6-14.

94. Satija, M.P. Sources of Library and Information Science Dissertation Literature with Special Reference to India. *Herald of Library Science*, 26(2), 1987, pp. 61-64.

95. Sasikala, C. Impact of Information Technology (IT) on Research in LIS. In. *Infrastructure facilities for Library and Information Science Education*, Mysore, IATLIS, 1999.

96. Padmini, K. LIS Research in the Globalization Era. In. *Globalization of Library and Information Science Education* edited by N. Laxman Rao, S. Sudarshan Rao and J. Yadagiri Reddy, Hyderabad, IATLIS, 2004.

97. Melvin Voight, *Advances in Librarianship*, 10, 1977.

98. McGrill, Rosemary. Conducting Library Research. *College and Research Libraries*, 41(3), 1980, pp. 200-206.

99. Subba Rao, C.V. Research in Libraries: Some Steps for Action. *Herald of Library Science*, 11(3), 1980, p. 163-170.

100. Kumbhar, M.R. and Karisiddappa, C.R. Perspective of Research in Library and Information Science in Karnataka University. *Journal of Library and Information Science*, 8(2), 1983, pp. 137-145.

101. Karande, A.G. A Review of Research in Library and Information Science. *Lucknow Librarian*, 18(3), 1986, pp. 83-89.

102. Mahapatra, M. Research in Library and Information Science in India: Status and Prospects. *Hundred Years of Library Education and its Future: National Seminar*, November 1987.

103. Shailendra Kumar and Ravindra Kumar. Research Work at Post Graduate Level in Library and Information Science: Dissertation Study of PU & DU. *Annals of Library Science and Documentation*, 34(3), 1987, pp. 119-129.

104. Sengupta, Sivani. Areas of Research in Library and Information Science. *XVI IASLIC Conference*, Tirupathi, 1987.

105. Karande, A.G. Areas and Methods of Research in Library and Information Science. *IASLIC Bulletin*, 34(3), 1989, pp. 105-113.

106. Anandamurugan, M, Sasireka, G., and Pandian, Murugaesha. Trends in LIS Research in India. In. *Globalization of Library and Inforamtion Science Education* edited by N. Laxman Rao, S. Sudarshan Rao and J. Yadagiri Reddy, Hyderabad, IATLIS, 2004.

2

Review of Literature

Bibliometrics is a type of research method used in library and information science. It utilizes quantitative analysis and statistics to describe patterns of publication within a given field or body of literature. Another major area of bibliometric research uses various methods of citation analysis in order to establish relationships between authors or their work. When one author cites another author, a relationship is established. Citation analysis uses citations in scholarly works to establish links. Many different links can be ascertained, such as links between authors, between scholarly works, between journals, between fields, or even between countries. Citations both from and to a certain document may be studied. One very common use of citation analysis is to determine the impact of a single author on a given field by counting the number of times the author has been cited by others. As doctoral dissertations are scholarly works, they are important source for conducting citation analysis. All the libraries and library administrators are susceptible to the problems arising due to declining library budgets. In this juncture citation analysis serves as a tool for the librarians in making judicious judgement regarding collection development, individual item selection, binding and retention decisions. The literature in bibliometrics is growing rapidly and it has been the subject of great interest to the researchers. An attempt has been made in this chapter to summarize the important works and literature related to the various aspects of the present study.

Alan Pritchard[1] used the word "bibliometrics" in 1969 in his article "Statistical Bibliography or Bibliometrics" in the December issue of the *Journal of Documentation*. Apparently he was not satisfied with "Statistical Bibliography" as it is very clumsy, not very descriptive, and can be confused with statistics itself or bibliographies on statistics. As a result of the prompting of his friend, M.G. Kendall, Pritchard suggested that the word "Bibliometrics", i.e. the application of mathematics and statistical methods to books and other media of communication" be substituted for "statistical bibliography".

The present study reveals that out of the 71 theses awarded in so far in Library and Information Science in the four universities of Andhra Pradesh, six are on Bibliometrics (Vagiswari[2], Valasayya[3], Vimala[4], Aruna Prasad Reddy[5], Dheerendra[6], Andhramatha[7]). Based on the analysis of research activity at the doctoral level in various Indian Universities it is found that a good number of theses were being awarded in the field of Bibliometrics by various Indian Universities. (Sengupta[8], Singh[9], Mahapatra[10], Sengupta[11], Sangam[12]. Vyas[13], Roy[14], Taher[15], Savanur[16], Kannappanavar[17], Parvathamma[18], Rajendra Prasad[19], Berhamuddin[20], Maheswarappa[21], Ratnakar[22], Shailendra Kumar[23], Tripathy[24], Mahapatra[25], Arora[26], Binwarilal[27], Munshi[28], Srivastava[29], Vearma[30], Humayoon Kabir[31], Jalaja[32], Aravind[33], Misra[34], Ravi[35], Sahu[36], Thoidingian[37], Meera[38], Sacham Anitha[39], Khokale[39A]).

Bibliometric Studies in Library and Information Science

Different authors have considered different sources of

information for the purpose of bibliometric studies. This section covers exclusively the literature published in Library and Information Science. The findings of review of literature are grouped based on the sources of information consulted in the studies.

Theses and Dissertations

Kubota (1976)[40] studied the citations in 113 graduation theses in the field of library and information science presented to the Keio University during the period 1973 to 1974. The results showed that journals contributed 62.2 percent of the total citations; more than 50 percent of the literature cited was under four years old; citations to foreign literature comprised 23.1 percent; and nine journals accounted for more than 50 percent of citations to domestic journals. The holdings of Keio University Libraries and Information Centres were the main important sources of information for the students accounting for 80.8 percent of the total cited literature.

LaBorie and Halperin (1976)[41] analysed the citations in library and information science dissertations to find out the adequacy of Drexel University Library in supporting research programmes in library science.

Meera, Deshpande and Rajyalakshmi (1997)[42] made a study of 65 dissertations on Library and Information Science submitted to Nagpur University (India) during the period 1990-1994. Citation analysis have been carried out to find the types of cited source materials, authorship pattern, and chronological distribution of cited references. The results indicate that – Highest citations are in the field of journals. Majority of works are in the field of literature and survey. Year-wise submission of dissertations indicates that 15 dissertations were submitted during 1991, 1992, and 1993. Chronological distribution of citations reveals that maximum citations were in period of 1984-88. The ranked list of journals indicates that the *Annals of Library Science and Documentation* is the most cited journal.

VijayaKumar, Padmamma and Sampat Kumar (2000)[43] paper identifies forms, average number of citations per dissertation, year-wise distribution of literature, area-wise distribution of dissertations, availability of cited journals in Kuvempu University, frequency distribution of periodicals, and the core journals by analysing references appended to eighty postgraduate Library and Information Science dissertations, submitted to the Department of Library and Information Science, Kuvempu University during 1995-1999. The results of this study indicated that average number of references per dissertation is found to be 38.66. The form-wise distribution pattern of citations shows that books topped the list with 57.81% citations followed by periodicals with 32.7% citations. The number of dissertations on college libraries is found to be maximum (42.5%) while dissertations on University libraries is 12.5%.

Journal Articles, Reviews and Bibliographies

Kundu (1981)[44] studied the self citation pattern of Indian library scientists by analysing the citations appended to the journal *Annals of Library Science and Documentation* during 1974-1975 and found that 14.5 percent of citations were self-citations.

Hart (1990)[45] studied the authorship characteristics of articles in library and information science journals which were published in the year 1986. He compared the characteristics of authors of articles that resulted from funded research with those of articles that were not supported by funding. The findings revealed that the authors of funded research collaborated with other authors, possessed doctoral degrees and were employed in college or university.

Raptis (1992)[46] studied the authorship characteristics in five international library and information science journals and found a self-citation rate of 27.6 percent.

Afolabi (1992)[47] studied the productivity of journals, the language, subject and title dispersion of journals which published articles on librarianship in Nigeria during the period 1910 to 1985. The observation was that there were four core journals with respect to Nigerian library literature; ten percent of the journals were published in Nigeria; title dispersion of journals was low; and articles were predominantly in English (99.7%) while the remaining articles were published in Russian, French and Scandinavian languages.

Subramanian and Navaneethan (1992)[48] in their paper discusses various features of the issues of the quarterly Library Science with Slant to Documentation and Information studies published during 1981-1990. The results of study show that number of papers per volume is not uniform. Major part of papers fall within the subject field of computer application of library and information work. Maximum articles published by Research organizations. LSD publishes majority of its papers by Indian authors. The average length of article is 11-15 pages.

Gupta (1994)[49] in his paper made an attempt to study librarianship literature on Ethiopia comprising of 240 items produced between 1944 and 1991. The findings of study indicate that vast amount of literature was produced between 1967 and 1978. Journal articles and reports being almost equal in number dominated the literature. Most of the journal items are descriptive in nature. Majority of items are single authored items. 78 authors are responsible to produce 167 items which on average is about 2.2 items per author.

Mahapatra (1994)[50] carried out a citation analysis of authors and journals in Indian Library and Information science literature. The results of study show that Indian authors and journals occupied the highest rank, whereas books published from USA ranked as the top core books. The comparative analysis of core authors, core journals and core books indicate that out of 10 highly cited authors, journals and books, 50 percent of the authors and books are of Indian origin. Amongst journals only 30 percent are published in India. The *Annals of Library Science and Documentation* continues to top the list of core journals both according to present and earlier ranking. It is concluded that Bradford's bibliograph is more suited to the developing subjects like Library and Information Science than his mathematical derivation of scattering of journals.

Dimitroff and Arlitsch (1995)[51] found that the rate of self-citation was 50 percent and the percentage of self-citation was 6.6 percent in library and information science literature through an analysis of 1,058 articles collected from 28 core library and information science journals.

Bose and Goria (1995)[52] made a systematic study of the articles published in different volumes of INICAE (International Information Communication and Education) journal and found that the subject-wise breakup of articles revealed that a bulk number of articles produced in computer application area, information system, communications etc are latest in origin and thought. The study indicates that single author contribution is maximum (82.25%), double authors (10.83%) and corporate authors (6.37%). In the beginning the number of foreign contributors were high but the number of Indian contributors were increasing by the time and at present they are sharing almost equal number of papers. The institution-wise distribution shows that educational institutions are the chief contributors. 42.67 percent of articles are without references because most of papers published here, convey original ideas and novel concepts. Articles with an average length of 7-9 pages is setting the highest percentage (27.39%). In country-wise distribution India is getting the highest percentage (29.30%) followed by USA (18.47%).

Mahendra and Deshmukh (1996)[53] in their study analysed 1824 citations from 202 articles published in *Annals of Library Science and Documentation*, Vol.31 to 40 (1984-

1993). The findings of study show that journals are most cited form of communication amongst the library and information scientists and the source journal is the most cited publication. Bradford's law of scattering is testified with the journal citations and it was found that 23.13% of total journals could meet 67% of the requirements. The most devoted core periodicals in Library and Information Science have been found out and listed according to productivity. The half life of LIS literature is found to be 8 to 12 years for journals and books respectively. The study reveals that library professionals most frequently refer to the journals in which they write.

Ramesh and Hussain (1997)[54] in their article studied various features of the issues of the quarterly *Herald of Library Science* published during 1985-1994. The area-wise distribution of articles indicates that Andhra Pradesh has the maximum contributions at an average of 11.72 percent and USA among the foreign countries with (8.36%). Out of the total papers published during 10 years span, 66.11 percent were contributed by Indian library professionals, 28.45 percent by foreign contributors and 5.44 percent are anonymous works. The data on authors show that *Herald of Library and Science* bags credit of introducing 158 authors in 10 years span and P.N. Kaula tops the list with 20 papers. On an average, *Herald of Library Science* had brought out 24 papers per year, which means approximately 6 papers per issue. The subject-wise analysis of articles shows that Library Management and Librarianship and different types of libraries top the list with an average of 21.75 percent followed by miscellaneous subjects (14.64%). Articles with 1-5 pages constitute the maximum (52.72%) and articles of 21-25 pages contribute the least (0.41%). Contribution without citations constitute the maximum (38.07%).

Blaise Cronin and Debora Shaw (1999)[55] developed a bibliometric profile of four information science journals. Data on acknowledgements to funding sources, authors nationalities and the citedness of published articles are analysed. The relationships among these variables are explored. Citedness appears to be associated with journal of publication and an author's nationality, but not with funding.

Ramesh and Nagaraju (2000)[56] analysed the citations provided in articles of Indian Journal of Information, Library and Society (IJILS). The findings of study indicate that on an average 7 citations were cited per article. The frequency distribution of citations per article showed that nearly 27 percent of the articles had no citations. 67.5 percent of articles were having citations between 1-20 while nearly 3 percent of articles have 20-30 citations and only 1.5 percent of articles have cited above 40 citations. Nearly 89 percent of citations belonged to Books and Journals, while nearly 11 percent of citations belonged to reports, conference proceedings, seminars, papers, theses, letters from library professionals. Dr. S.R. Ranganathan was first in the rank of authors whose valuable books have been utilized by several authors more frequently. English language was dominating amongst the cited articles, and it is cent percent. Only 14 percent citing authors had tendency of self-citation. Co-citation cases are 110, and only a couple of cases being repeated. More than 90 percent citations were from Library and Information Science Journals.

Dhiman (2002)[57] in his paper 'Self Citation Behaviour of Library Scientists : A case study of ILA Bulletin' discusses the trend of Self-Citation in this field based on the study of ILA Bulletin. Citing one's own earlier papers is known as self-citation. Like other fields the practice of self-citation has started in the field of Library and Information Science as well. The results of the study indicate that out of 71 articles published during the period only 11 had self-citations or 2 on average per volume. Maximum number of citations was from seminar proceedings. Most of citations were from single authors.

Kaur (2002)[58] in article analysed 544 citations appended to 59 research articles covered in the issues of 'ILA Bulletin' during 1996-2000. The conclusions of the study reveal that majority of library scientists prefer to contribute their papers individually. Most of the contributions in this journal are form Delhi. Most of the contributions in this journal are from teaching faculty and research scholars of various library schools. Most of the contributions are on Librarianship ; I.T applications in libraries. A majority of library scientists has cited books, followed by journals. Journal of Education for Library and Information Science occupies the first rank and Long range planning occupies second rank in the ranked list of journals.

Pratap Chandra Roy (2004)[59] in his article 'Authorship Pattern of Indian Library Science Journals for the Period of 1991-2000' made a study based on 1637 research papers in Library and Information Science published in 10 LIS journals. The article shows that single authorship is most popular among library scientists. Collaborative work is not much popular. So we can say that single authorship is most dominating in the field of LIS Research.

Pratap Chandra Roy (2004)[60] in his paper made a study based on 1637 papers in LIS published in 10 Indian LIS journals during the period 1991-2000. It is found that institutional collaboration in Indian LIS field is not high. 72% of articles are contributed by single institutes. Only 11% articles are published jointly by two institutions, 0.6% by three and 0.06% contributed by four institutes. In Indian LIS journals; foreign collaboration with Indian institutes is very neglible. Institutional collaboration among the authors has been notified only in the case of two journal articles. These journals are *Information Studies* and *SRELS Journal of Information Management.*

Databases/Indexing and Abstracting Sources

Humayoon Kabir (1993)[61] in his paper analysed 1372

citations form LISA (1964 to 1990) in order to determine the most frequently cited journals in bibliometrics. The most important journals identified were Scientometrics, Journal of American Society of Information Science, Nauch. Tech.Inf. Seriya, Journal of Documentation, Annals of Library Science and Documentation, Information Proc. Management, Journal of Information Science, Revista. Exp. De Doc. Cient, International Library Review and College and Research Libraries.

Humayoon Kabir (1994)[62] in his paper studied the authorship pattern and extent of research collaboration in the field of bibliometrics literature, based on the data collected from LISA (1964-1990). The study revealed that solo research is more favourable than collaborative research. The degree of collaboration ranged between 0.20 to 0.35 during the period of study, with an overall average of 0.31.

Parameswaran and Smitha (2001)[63] carried out Bibliometric analysis of LISA, covering 60 issues of LISA published during the period 1994 to 1998. Authorship Pattern shows that more people write individually and less number of people produce work of more than two authors. About 77.50 percent contributions were made by single authors, 15.83 percent works were by double authors and only 6.47 percent of contributions were made by more than two authors. This indicates that solo research predominates in the field of Library and Information Sciences.

Rajeev Vij (2001)[64] in his bibliometric study analysed LISA database form 1969 to 2000 covering 550 journals with over 2,06,091 abstracts. The important findings of the study indicate that 93.99% of records in the present LISA CD-ROM database are from journals, most of which are published in USA and UK. It is observed that Internet and World Wide Web are evolving subjects, where as CD-ROM's, Information storage, medical informatics and telecommunications are showing trends of decay. The maximum number of articles are published in English language followed by German, Russian and French. A majority of contributions included in LISA database are made by single author, while a considerable number of items resulted from contribution of two authors. Country wise analysis indicates that UK stands first followed by USA. Coverage of journals from developing countries is relatively poor. The ranking of journals show that majority of foreign journals have a better coverage than those brought out from India. *Herald of Library Science* and *Library Journal* are the top Indian and foreign journals respectively.

Others

Narayana and Reddy (2000)[65]. Bradford's law in bibliometrics consists of two aspects. First one is the distribution aspect which is purely a mathematical pattern. The other aspect is the relevance of such a distribution to bibliometrics. Narayana (2000) described the methodology for estimating Bradford groups within a given set of bibliometric data. The paper also proposes a simple and easily adaptable statistical research method (SSM) and illustrates the application of the method.

Satarkar, Dharmapurikar and Jadhava (2002)[66] in their article analysed citations appended to articles published in 37th conference proceedings of Indian Library Association. The main conclusions drawn from the study show that majority of articles have citations between 1 to 10. It means authors of Library and information science are having tendency to use minimum citations in their articles. Books are favourable information sources and they are preferred more for reading and citing. As far as authorship pattern is concerned, the study indicates that maximum citations are of single author. It is found that information sources from India are cited more.

Review of literature on bibliometric studies in Library and Information Science revealed interesting findings. The Bibliometric research has been done in the field using different types of sources. They include theses and dissertations, primary journals, indexing and abstracting journals, databases, reviews, bibliographies and conference proceedings.

It is observed from the methodology applied to these studies that majority of these studies used the techniques of citation analysis to study the literature use pattern by researchers in the field of Library and Information Science. In the case of studies based on journal literature, mostly the content of Indian journals has been analysed. Some of the studies covered single journals for a specific period and very few studies covered the foreign journals. However, studies made on Library and Information Science abstracts have covered the popular and peer reviewed journals in the Library and Information field analysing the research trends in the field.

Among the Indian journals, *Annals of Library Science and Documentation*, *Herald of Library Science* and *ILA Bulletin* are the popular journals attracted the researchers. Number of studies have also covered a group of Indian Library Science journals and made comparative studies on the characteristics of Library and Information Science literature published in these journals. These studies provided ranked list of Indian journals in Library and Information Science based on the citation count.

Bibliometric Studies in Other Subjects

Theses and Dissertations

Omoruyi (1978)[67] analysed the citations to journal articles in 18 social science theses and dissertations submitted to the University of Ibadan during 1965 to 1970. It was found that a large percentage (98.71%) of articles was in English, mainly from journals published in USA(38.50%) and the median age of the citations was nine years.

Maheswarappa and Prakash (1982)[68] studied the literature use pattern by researchers in the field of botany by analysing 2,726 citations appended to 15 doctoral theses accepted by the University of Mysore during 1973 to 1980.

The bibliographic form-wise distribution of citations showed that journals occupied the first place accounting for 75.61 percent of total citations, followed by books (12.42%) and conference proceedings (4.55%). The country-wise distribution of citations revealed that USA occupied the first place accounting for 29.25 percent of the total citations, followed by India (14.65%) and UK (13.29%). The half- life of botanical literature was found to be 12 years.

De Oliveira (1984)[69] studied citation patterns in veterinary sciences by analysing 495 citations in 14 master degree theses submitted to the Universidade Federal de Vicosa, Brazil. The bibliographic form-wise distribution of citations showed that journals accounted for 70 percent of the total citations followed by books (19%) and theses (3%). The country-wise distribution of cited journals showed that USA occupied the first position with 36.1 percent of total cited journals accounting for 51.1 percent of total citations, followed by UK (13.8%) and Brazil (12.5%). The half-life of veterinary medicine literature was about 12 years and the literature did not conform to Bradford's Law of Scattering.

Sangam (1985)[70] studied the citations in 131 doctoral dissertations in social sciences accepted by the Karnataka University during the period 1964 to 1982. The findings show that books are highly cited (56.17%) followed by journal literature (32.57%). The country-wise scatter of citations showed that India occupied the first position with 86.73 percent of total citations, followed by USA (7.35%) and UK

(4.76%). The researchers preferred documents published in the English language (95.75%), and 34.5 percent of the cited literature was available in the Karnataka University Library.

Nweke (1988)[71] studied 964 citations in eight theses in zoology submitted to the Ibadan University, Nigeria, during the period 1970 to 1975. Out of the total citations, 77.8 percent of citations were to journal articles, followed by books (10.6%), reports (3.5%), and others (8.1%). The language-wise distribution of citations revealed that English was by far the most used language (91.8%), followed by French (4.9%), German (1.6%), and others (1.7%).

Sangam and Biradar (1990)[72] studied the information use pattern by researchers in the field of surgery, by analysing 7,576 citations appended to 145 M.S. dissertations accepted by Gulbarga University, Gulbarga, during 1982 to 1989. The bibliographic form-wise distribution of citations revealed that journal articles are the major source of information accounting to 54.23 percent of the total citations, followed by books (35.39%), conference proceedings (5%), and others (5.38%). The language-wise scattering of cited documents showed that English was the predominant language with 99.78 percent of the total citations. The country-wise distribution of cited documents revealed that 41.71 percent of the cited documents were from USA, followed by UK (28.45%), India (26.38%), and other countries (3.46%). The half-life of cited journal literature was observed to be 12 years.

Madkey and Rajyalakshmi (1994)[73] carried out a citation analysis of doctoral dissertations in the field of environmental science and engineering, which were consulted by scientists working at National Environmental Engineering Research Institute, Nagpur, during 1977 to 1991. The results revealed that the single authored papers were maximum in number, USA occupied the prime place accounting for 52.05 percent of the total citations, and the half-life period for books and journals was found out to be 17 to 18 years.

Sylvia and Lesher (1995)[74] studied the citations appended to theses and dissertations of graduate students in the psychology and counseling departments of St. Mary's University, Texas, and prepared a rank list of journals in counseling and psychology. The top 75 titles contributed 62 percent of the total citations.

Deo and Mohlal and Survey (1995)[75] carried out bibliometric analysis of 4066 citations collected from the doctoral dissertations on the English language and literature accepted by Dr. Babasaheb Ambedkar Marthwada University to determine the use pattern of literature by researchers in English. Provides the main bibliographic forms of literature cited. Non-serial publications i.e. books, published from U.K and periodicals from U.S.A are mostly cited. Ranked list of periodicals, books and authors show that modern fiction studies and times literary supplement are most preferred journals, where as American fiction and Main currents in American thoughts are most frequently cited books. Amongst the first ten most cited authors, six are from U.S.A and two each are from U.K and India. English citations account for 99% and only one percent of the citations are shared by two other languages, namely Marathi and Sanskrit. Country-wise distribution of periodicals and chronological distribution of citations indicate substantial use of older literature with a half life value of 27.5 years. Authorship study indicates increasing trend towards multiple authorship. The data under study do not exactly fit into the Bradford's law of scattering.

Mubeen (1996)[76] in his paper studied the information use pattern by researchers by analysing citations of 22 doctoral dissertations in chemistry submitted to Mangalore University. The study has identified 60 core journals, out of total 418 journals referred to by the researchers. The bibliographic form-wise distribution of citations showed that majority of citations pertained to journals followed by books and patents. Regarding country wise citations, U.S.A occupies the first place followed by India. The application of Bradford's law of scattering to the literature of chemistry reveals an exponential trend when plotted on the graph. The Bradford's multiplier is seen to observe a geometric series pattern over the literature.

Arjun Lal and Panda (1996)[77] study is based on 3685 references collected from 20 Ph.D. Dissertations (1980-1993). The study attempts to identify the different forms of literature used, and provides a ranked list of first 100 most frequently cited core journals. The findings reveal that plant pathology literature are scattered in 631 periodicals, of which more than 50 percent references are covered by first 20 periodicals. Among them, Indian Phytopathology tops the list followed by Phytopathology and plant disease respectively. The study also portrays a comparison of first 42 periodicals with that of the three previously published list. The first 10 periodicals are most productive and contribute quite considerable amount of total literature.

Vimala (1997)[78] studied the citations appended to 200 doctoral dissertations in the field of biological sciences submitted to the Sri Venkateswara University, Tirupati. The Bibliographic form-wise distribution of citations revealed that journal literature was the most preferred source of information (85.34%), followed by books (9.89%), and conference proceedings (2.05%). Researchers preferred documents published in the English language (91.63%), followed by French (0.40%) and Russian (0.19%). The country-wise scattering of citations revealed that USA alone covered 56.55 percent of citations, and UK and India covered 13.66 percent and 11.02 percent respectively. The study of the authorship pattern showed that papers with two authors were maximum in number (40.41%) and single authored papers constituted 26.67 percent of the total cited papers. The half-life period for journal citations was found to be 11.43 years and 12.79 years for book citations.

Biradar and Vijayalaxmi (1997)[79] in their study discusses the pattern of information use by researchers in the field of Neurology as indicated by citations in the D.M. (Neurology) dissertations submitted to the National Institute of Mental Health and Neuro Sciences (NIMHANS) deemed university Bangalore during 1979-1996. Identifies the average number of references per dissertation, the use of different sources of information, states the obsolescence of literature and lists the most frequently cited journals by Neurological scientists. The findings of the study have implications for the development of need based collection in library and information centres in the field of Neurology.

Biradar and Premalatha (1998)[80] studied forms, authorship pattern, language wise periodical and periodical articles, obsolescence of literature and the core journals based on the references appended to M.D Psychiatric (Alcoholism) dissertations accepted by the Department of Psychiatry Nimbans, a deemed university Bangalore during 1974-1995. Results indicated that major forms of reading materials is periodicals articles, predominant journals language and language of the journal articles are in English. Regarding Authorship pattern, maximum articles were written by two authors followed by single authors and three authors. It is evident that there are more number of citations distributed in the age ranking from 5 to 27 years. The maximum number of citations are of 5 years old. It is observed that number of citations decrease with increase in the age. It is also observed document as old as 67 years have been cited. 115 core journals are identified in the field of psychiatry. The first and second journals are from U.S.A viz American Journal of Psychiatry and Archives of General Psychiatry. Third rank of journal is "British Journal of Psychiatry". It is observed that "Indian Journal of Psychiatry" is placed at sixth rank.

Arjunlal and Panda (1999)[81] in their paper analysed the results of a citographical study comprising 3023 out of 3685 references yielded by 681 periodicals and arranged in order of frequency. These references were collected from 20 doctoral theses in plant pathology submitted to Rajendra Agricultural University, Bihar during 1980-1993. The applicability of two vital formulations (verbal and graphical) of Bradford's Law of Scattering was tested. The verbal formulation was tested in three separate parameters to avoid the arbitrary scattering of references to three zones and graphical formulation of the same data was determined with the help of computer. The study has shown that the verbal formulation of the present study was closer to the graphical formulation. The graphical formulation which confirmed to Bradford's Law of Scattering demonstrated a very meager strength of only nine most productive core periodicals in nuclear zone which constitutes considerable percent of the total periodical citations.

Tapaswi and Maheswarappa (1999)[82] carried out a bibliometric analysis of 2475 Indian oceanographic research contributions and 38886 references cited by them. The data was compiled using CDS/ISIS software. Subject wise distribution, forms of contributions and references cited, authorship pattern, non-textual characteristics were the parameters used for analysis. A shift in the number of contributions among the disciplines of Oceanography, the forms of documents as the communication channel and even the items cited is noticed over a period of three decades. The increase in the number of scientists did not proportionately yield the number of contributions. Single authored contributions tend to decrease as in other disciplines. The number of tables and figures in contributions are yet to stabilize. The results could be applied in the development of information systems.

Amit Kumar Bandopadhyay (2001)[83] studied the extent of multiple authorship, degree of authorship collaboration and their change with time by analysing references appended to 92 doctoral theses submitted to Departments of mathematics, physics, mechanical engineering, philosophy and political science, University of Burdwan, India from 1981 to 1990. The study identified that within broad subjects multiple authored articles are found to be maximum in physics (62.24%) while 36.6% of the articles in mechanical engineering, 36.3% of articles in mathematics, 12.3% of the articles in philosophy and only 3.85% of the articles in political science are multiple authored. Within specific subjects, multiple authorship is highest in Nuclear physics (72.52%). The multiple authorship trend has increased steadily through decades (1950 to 1990) in physics, mathematics and psychology. In mechanical engineering, philosophy excluding psychology and political science the multiple authorship trend has increased in the first few decades but then the trend had decreased for certain period. In mechanical engineering the multiple authorship was highest during 1951-1960. In philosophy excluding psychology, it was highest during 1971-1980 and in political science the multiple authorship was highest during 1961-1970.

Amit Kumar Bandyopadhyay and Amitava Nandi (2001)[84] in their article carried out citation analysis of nine doctoral dissertations in political science submitted at the Burdwan University (West Bengal) form 1991 to 1995. Discusses the bibliographic forms of literature used, ranked list of journals and normalized ranking of journals with corrected citation numbers according to Sengupta's formula are find out with help of a computer using the programme developed by Bandyopadhyay based on dBase III+. The results of the study reveal that book is most favoured form followed by periodical publications. Twenty Nine journals are used to satisfy 80% of the journal requirements. Seven journals can satisfy 50% of requirements. Economic and Political Weekly tops the ranked list of journals.

Hirwade and Dankhade (2002)[85] in their study analysed 1646 citations from 23 theses in Economics submitted to

Nagpur University during the period 1996-1999. The findings reveal that nearly 43 percent citations were from books and 33 percent from journals. The authorship pattern study reveals that highest number of citations is from single author, nearly 68 percent in journals, 75 percent in books and 70 percent in conference papers. The subject distribution of theses indicate that Industrial Economics and Agricultural Economics forms 57 percent i.e. more than half of the total theses submitted during the period.

Biradar and Thippeswamy (2004)[86] in their article analysed 3401 references appended to 61 M.D. Pediatric dissertations submitted to J.M.M. Medical college, Davanagere. The results of the study shows that average number of citations per dissertation is 55.75. Authorship pattern show that three authors stood in first place followed by two authors and single author. The chronological dispersion of the cited articles (age wise) in the field of pediatrics that more number of citations are distributed in the age group of 0-15 years. It is noted that 25% of refrerred journals and 76.70% of cited journal articles are avalibale in the institution library. Indian Pediatrics is most heavily cited journal and Journal of Pediatrics from U.S.A is second most frequently used periodical. Among the first 11 journals 8 journals are directly related to the pediatrics and gynecology subjects.

Krishna and Kumar (2004)[87] in their paper made a study of 68 doctoral theses on Agriculture and Veterinary Sciences submitted to Rajasthan Agriculture University, Bikaner during 1996-2000. The study reveals that joint authors contribute 61%, single 37% and corporate authors contribute 2% of the total citations. Among joint authors ; two contribute 33%, three 17%, >3 11% and corporate authors contribute 2% only. In all 9 subjects, single and two authors contribute more research work in comparison to three and corporate authors. Authorship trend graph for books and journals show a decreasing trend form single to two, triple, >3 and corporate authors.

Journal Articles, Reviews, Bibliographies

A significant study prior to the publication of *Science Citation Index* was by Fussler[88] in 1949. He studied the characteristics of literature used by chemists and physicists of American origin and ranked the journals according to their use. Another significant study supported by Brown (1956)[89], was an attempt to ascertain what conclusions and inferences can be drawn from a study of lists of most frequently cited journals in different fields of science.

Burton and Kebler (1960)[90] compared the rate of obsolescence with that of radioactive substances. They applied the term 'Half life' to the decrease in use of scientific literature in the same way in which the decay of radioactive material is preferred to.

Raisig (1960)[91] in his article discussed the uses of citation data in evaluating scientific journals and was of the view that the amount of material published in a particular journal must be considered in calculating the weightage of citations of that journal. He suggested a measure called 'index of research potential realized'. It is calculated by dividing the number of articles cited by the number of articles published.

The concept of Bibliographic coupling was introduced by Kessler[92] of the Massachusetts Institute of Technology in 1963. He postulated that a number of scientific paper bear a meaningful relation to each other (they are coupled) when they have one or more references in common.

Brookes (1970)[93] developed an equation to show that the growth in the number of contributors to the literature on the same subject field will cancel the effect of the rate of growth of the literature if both the growth rates are equal, and disputed the need to correct for literature growth in obsolescence studies.

Chen (1972)[94] studied the use of 138 journals in physics at Massachusetts Institute of Technology, Science Library and observed a rapid decrease in use as the journal aged.

Seymour (1972)[95, 96] published two comprehensive review articles about weeding, one devoted to monographs and other to serials.

Rangra and others (1972)[97] studied the coverage of Indian literature on chemistry and chemical technology excluding metallurgy in *Referativinyi Zhurnal – Khimiya,* based on the literature reported in *Indian Science Abstracts,* and found that only 31 percent of the literature had been covered in the journal.

Small (1973)[98] studied the application of co-citation analysis as a useful tool in mapping the structure of science and described co-citation as the frequency with which twc documents are cited together.

The most comprehensive review was published by Line and Sandison (1974)[99] covering the concept of obsolescence, patterns of document use, synchronous and diachronous studies; the relationship between citations and actual use; and practical value of obsolescence studies.

Ravichandra Rao (1974)[100] studied the obsolescence of literature in sociology by analysing the citations in the *American Journal of Sociology*. The results showed half-life values of 9.2 years, 5.85 years, 5.8 years and 5.8 years for the years 1950, 1969, 1970 and 1972-73 respectively

Grefrath (1974)[101] analysed the citations appended to 308 journal articles in the field of chemistry published in 1963. The results showed that theoretical articles had a longer lifetime than articles on practical aspects.

Sengupta (1974)[102] studied the growth of literature of pharmacology and microbiology by analysing the citations in *Annual Review of Pharmacology* and the *Annual Review of Microbiology* for the period 1968 to 1970, and prepared a ranked list of journals in pharmacology and microbiology.

Longyear (1977)[103] analysed 1,374 citations in six major journals in musicology for the period 1973 to 1975, and found that journal articles in musicology do not show any obsolescence pattern as does scientific literature

According to Tagliacozzo (1977)[104], "self-citing is a common and fundamental attribute of scientific articles and has a function which essentially is not different from other forms of citing". The extent of self-citing varies considerably in different research papers within a discipline and also amongst disciplines. Generally two methods are employed to assess self-citation behaviour. The first method involves tallying all citations as well as all self-citations and calculating the ratio of self-citations to all citations. The second method involves analysing the citations and tallying articles that contain one or more self-citations and comparing this figure with the total number of articles in the sample. This is called the self-citation rate. The results showed that 16.6 percent of citations in plant physiology and 17.5 percent of citations in neurobiology were self-citations. The extent of self-citing did not appear to be related to the number of co-authors or to the size of the bibliography of the citing article or to their author's productivity.

Gupta and others (1978)[105] carried out a study to ascertain the active life of periodicals in structural engineering after taking into consideration the ageing factor, obsolescence factor, half-life, mean life and utility factor on the basis of citations in the *Journal of Structural Division of the American Society of Civil Engineering*. It was observed that the periodicals in structural engineering lost their utility value after eight years of their publication.

Griffith and others (1979)[106] studied the ageing of scientific literature and observed that ageing depends not merely on the material itself, but also on its users; a single journal may be aged very differently by different user communities; and ageing rates vary among journals.

Brown (1980)[107] studied the half-life of chemical literature using the Poisson frequency distribution and found it to be 9.3 years.

Balog (1980)[108] studied the increase in the frequency of multiple author papers and the number of authors per paper in an agricultural journal for the period 1958 to 1978. The findings showed that the frequency of single authored papers decreased from 65.5 percent in 1958 to 34.3 percent in 1978, and the frequency of papers with two authors increased from 28.1 percent to 41.4 percent for the corresponding years. Over the same period, the average number of authors per paper had increased from 1.43 to 1.99.

Gordon (1980)[109] showed a significant relationship between levels of multiple authorship of papers submitted to a leading astronomy journal for a period of six years and their frequency of acceptance for publication. It was found that 26 percent of single authored papers were rejected, compared with 12 percent with two authors, and nine percent for papers with three or more authors.

Dewitt and others (1980)[110] studied the use of citations as a tool for studying the sociology of chemical research and the feasibility and accuracy of using automatically generated data.

White and Griffith (1981)[111] developed author co-citation based on co-citation analysis as a new tool for providing a method for tracing the intellectual structure of science.

Anand (1981)[112] studied the citing pattern of Indian chemists by analysing the citations in the *Journal of the Indian Chemical Society* for the year 1979. The authorship pattern revealed that papers with two authors were maximum in number accounting for 50.87 percent, followed by papers with three authors (31.22%), and single authored papers accounted for 8.52 percent. The bibliographic form-wise distribution of citations showed that journals accounted for 88.56 percent of total citations and self-citations accounted for 11.26 percent.

Ayers (1981)[113] studied the journal articles and conference proceedings relating to chemical history, education, and documentation based on the data collected from *Chemcial Abstracts* for the years 1969 and 1979. The results showed that the percentage of articles published in the English language has decreased from 62.5 percent in 1969 to 55.8 percent in 1979, and in the Russian language from 18.1 percent in 1969 to 14.5 percent in 1979, whereas the percentage of articles published in German and Japanese language has increased from six percent to 12.3 percent and 0.8 percent to 3.6 percent respectively for corresponding years.

Nagappa and Maheswarappa (1981)[114] analysed 2,663 citations appended to the articles in the journal *Indian Phytopathology* for the years 1971 and 1972. The bibliographic form-wise distribution showed that journal articles accounted for 83.3 percent of total citations followed by books (10.40%) and conference proceedings (2.30%). The first 20 journals in the ranked list contributed 55.77 percent of total citations.

Maheswarappa (1983)[115] analysed 5,533 citations in the journal *Phytomorphology* for the period 1975 to 1979. The bibliographic distribution of citations showed that citations to journals occupied the first place accounting for 78.85 percent of the total citations, followed by books (17.53%), theses (1.69%) and conference proceedings (1.44%). The productivity of cited journals showed that 50 percent of the journal literature used by the phytomorphologists was contributed by the first 24 journals in the ranked list and remaining 50 percent of the literature was scattered in the remaining 640 journals. The geographical distribution of citations showed that USA occupied the first place accounting for 28.44 percent of the total journal citations, followed by India (14.85%), UK (13.45%) and Germany (11.29%).

Gupta (1984)[116] in his study found the average half-life of the literature of exploration geophysics to be 9.4 years, on analysing the citations in journal *Geophysics* for the year 1980.

Kapoor (1984)[117] studied the citations in the journal *Annual Review of Earth and Planetary Sciences* for the period 1973 to 1981 and prepared a ranked list of 82 journals contributing 76 percent of the total citations out of the 833 titles cited. The country-wise distribution of citations showed that USA occupied the prime position by contributing 56.02 percent of the total citations, followed by UK(23.25%), The Netherlands (8.54%) and Germany (4.12%).

Bottle and Gong (1987)[118] studied the ageing phenomenon of biochemical periodical literature by analysing the citations in the journal *Cell* for the year 1983. They found that the citation frequency distribution followed a negative exponential distribution for the period 1972 to 1982, with a median citation age of three years.

Stinson and Lancaster (1987)[119] compared the results of a synchronous citation study of obsolescence over a 19 year period, with the results of a diachronous citation study using the literature of human and medical genetics. They found that if the first two years of synchronous data was excluded, the rate of obsolescence measured synchronously was statistically equivalent to the rate of obsolescence measured dichronosuly.

A bibliography comprising 316 items on AIDS for the period 1981 to 1984 was analysed by Gupta (1988)[120] to study the characteristics of AIDS literature. The rate of growth has found to be exponential after the first publication; journal literature constituted the major portion accounting for 86 percent of the total literature, followed by books, conference proceedings, audio-visual materials and reports.

Ijari and Kannappanavar (1989)[121] studied the characteristics of literature of geology by analysing the data of *Journal of Geological Society of India* 1980 volume to determine the half-life and other factors related to obsolescence applying citation techniques. The distribution of citation frequencies was statistically tested and found to be of negative exponential distribution type. The average half-life of literature was determined and was found to be 10.2 years. Brookes technique of calculating Annual Aging Factor (AAF = a) was applied to demonstrate its applicability for the literature. The average value of 'a' is .886. The utility factor was calculated and found to be 8.772.

Musib (1989)[122] analysed the citations appended to the articles published in the *Journal of International Economics* covering the period 1971-1985 to determine the nature of the literature of the International economics. Results show that 75 percent of citations belonged to the subject groups of international trade, production economics, financial economics, and international finance. In the field of international economics 9 subject groups are sufficient to cover 90 percent of total literature. X^2 test has been applied to determine the possible association among the prominent subfields and to assess the mutual relationship of one cited subject with another in international economics. Study of mutual relationship among the branches of discipline reflected in the co occurrences of the citations is helpful for assessing dependence of one branch over the other, and for subject mapping. As the bond of association among its branches grows stronger, the more unitary becomes its structures.

Sengupta (1989)[123] studied the growth of knowledge and literature in the neurosciences by analysing 5,785 citations collected from the bibliographic database published in the source journal *Annual Review of Neuroscience.* The first nine journals in the ranked list contributed 50 percent of the total citations; the country-wise distribution of citations showed that USA occupied the first position with 50.15 percent of total citations, followed by UK (19.58%) and Germany (10.68%); and language wise distribution of journals showed that 75.37 percent journals were exclusively in English, and together contributed 68.77 percent of total citations.

Moed and Vriens (1989)[124] presented a detailed analysis of discrepancies between target articles and cited references with respect to author names, publication year, volume number and starting page number. The data consisted of some 4,500 target articles published in five journals containing 25,000 citations. It was found that the percentage of citations not showing any discrepancy accounted for 91 percent of the total citations, while the citations with discrepancies in one data field only (author name, volume or page number) accounted for almost five percent of the total citations.

Gupta (1990)[125] carried out a synchronous citation study of 15 leading journals in physics to determine the obsolescence of articles in *Physical Review*, with age. He found that the density of citations to *Physical Review* decreased exponentially with a half-life of approximately 4.9 years.

Usha and others (1991)[126] studied the citing behaviour of scientists of India, USA, UK and Canada by analysing the the citations in some selected journals of chemistry and chemical technology. It was found that Indian authors generally cited older literature whereas American authors cited more recent literature irrespective of their place of work. The citation practice of British and Canadian scientists had fallen between USA and Indian Scientists.

Deo (1991)[127] made a citation analysis of 1906 citations collected from Marathwada University Journal covering the period 1975-1984. The main findings of the analysis shows that scholars conducting research in the field of zoology heavily depend on the periodical literature (71%). Only 19 percent of the cited journals are from India. Citations to English literature account for 98.7 percent. '*Marathwada University Journal*', the source journal scores the highest citation percentage. Among monographs "Systems Helminthum" and "Zoology of Tape Worms" are most frequently cited. The half life of the zoological literature is 23.5 years. The literature of zoology under consideration confirms Branford's Law of distribution.

Hurd (1992)[128] studied the information use pattern by chemists of the Department of Chemsitry, Illinois University, Chicago. The results revealed that 49 percent of citations belonged to disciplines other than chemistry indicating the interdisciplinary nature of chemical research.

Mahapatra and Kaul (1992)[129] studied the self-citation practice of Indian botanists by analysing the citations in the Bulletin of the Botanical Survey of India during the period 1981 to 1987, and found that the citation rate of Indian botanists was 37.36 percent.

Diodato and Smith (1993)[130] studied the median citation ages (a measure of synchronous obsolescence) of 9,850 references found in 37 journals in music education, music theory, and musicology. For six of the journals, the half lives (a measure of diachronous obsolescence) of citations to the journals were calculated. Results included average median citation ages of 14.0 years for references to journal articles and 16.0 years for references to all types of documents. Musicology obsolesced most slowly (median citation age equal to 22.0 years), followed by music education (14.3 years), and music theory (9.6 years). The average half life (7.0 years) for six journals was less than their corresponding average median citation age (27.0 years). However there was gross, though not statistically significant, similarity between diachronous and synochronous data when they were analysed using a procedure suggested by Stinson and Lancaster.

Parvathamma, Gunjal and Nijagunappa (1993)[131] in their paper made an attempt to determine the rate of growth of Indian earth science literature by calculating relative growth rates and doubling time for total number of all types of publications and pages separately for the period 1978-1988. The results show that the mean relative growth rate has shown a declining trend while the mean doubling time has increased. The mean doubling time for Indian earth science literature is slightly less than growth rate of earth science literature as a whole. The growth curves and chi-square values obtained show that the growth of Indian earth science literature follows logistic pattern of growth. The results of study related to scientific productivity of authors show that percentage of authors contributing one publication is fairly close to Lotka's predicted value. The scientific productivity of authors is found to conform to Lotka's law and distribution of scientific productivity follows negative bionomial distribution.

Norris (1993)[132] studied authorship patterns in the *Canadian Journal of Nursing Research* for the period 1970 to 1991. The results revealed a decrease in single authored papers from 77.50 percent during 1970-1976 to 33.67 percent during 1987-1991, whereas the papers with two authors and papers with three or more authors had increased from 16.25 percent to 42.86 percent and 6.25 percent to 23.47 percent respectively for the corresponding years. The author/article ratio had increased from 1.12 in 1970 to 2.55 in 1991.

Kalyane (1993)[133] in her paper discussed about the importance of Research on use of Neem plant products for control of insect pests, nematodes, fungus and virus. Year wise and domain wise publications and their scattering is analysed. The results indicate that highest research was done on Insect pests. Insect pests research communication channels had highest publication density followed bu nematodes. Publication concentration indicated that except insect pests other domains had very high level of scattering of publications, probably due to low coordination among research teams. Average Bradford multiplier for insect pests publications was 3.37.

Milman and Gavrilova (1993)[134] presented the results of the citation study in 24 leading journals on chemical engineering for 1987. The selective methodology or the analysis of co-citation limited only to this discipline is based on relatively low thresholds of citation and co-citation. The established research fronts refer mostly to basic research. The flow of information and knowledge to chemical engineering is determined to the extent of 70-90% by the works in this very field, as is indicated by the analysis of citations. The geography of research fronts was determined. The USSR has a very low fraction of frontal papers. This can be explained by the publication of papers in Russian and by a large number of secondary and applied research. This type of research is revealed by frequent citation of books and a small fraction of highly cited papers.

Rana and Sunita Agarwal (1994)[135] studied the authorship and collaborative research patterns in Indian Wildlife and fisheries based on the data collected from "*Wildlife Review and Fish Review*" published between 1980 to 1989. The proportion of single authored papers has decreased from 63.68% in 1980 to 52.74% in 1989. During the same period there was an increase in the average number of authors per paper from 1.57 in 1980 to 1.70 in 1989. The degree of collaborative research also increased form 0.36 to 0.47. The trend towards collaborative research is a good sign for a new discipline like wildlife and fisheries.

Mahapatra and Kaul (1994)[136] in their paper carried out a bibliometric analysis of 187 citation classics published in current contents (Agriculture, Biology, Environmental Sciences) during 1986 and 1991. The findings of study conclude that Environmental sciences are the most popular field of research and most of the classics have expressive titles.

Braun and others (1994)[137] presented a comprehensive and detailed study on the publication output and impact for individual countries in all science fields.

Arora and Kaur (1994)[138] carried out a bibliometric study on core journals in immunology derived from citations collected from the Annual Review of Immunology for four consecutive year's i.e. 1983 to 1986. The results of study reveal very high concentration of literature in a few scientific journals. The first four core journals constitute 47.96% of total citations while the first two top-ranked journals account for close to 30% of total citations. In addition to determining the country, subject, physical format, chronological and language distribution of core journals in immunology, the half life and citation peak of journals in immunology have been worked out. The scattering of literature in immunology is determined by applying Branford's Law. The core journals in immunology and other disciplines of biomedical sciences are also compared.

Mubeen (1995)[139] in his paper empirically tested concept of bibliographic coupling developed by Fano and Kessler in two important sub-disciplines of Economics namely, Monetary Economics and Welfare Economics. All the pertinent research papers in these two sub-disciplines from two journals viz., '*American Economic Review*' and '*The Economic journal*' over a period of ten years have been culled and 45 pairs have been established to ascertain the coupling strength. The study shows that there has been very little to choose between the two journals from the point of view of number of citations, though the average citations are greater in '*The Economic*

Journal' due to the presence of survey articles. In fact, both the journals cite more or less in a similar fashion. The variability is less for '*American Economic Review*' than '*The Economic Journal*'. This is amply evidenced by the presence of high coupling rate in the journal ('*American Economic Review*'). There have been a marginally higher number of citations in the discipline of monetary economics than welfare economics. A higher rate of coupling has been observed in the discipline of welfare economics than monetary economics in both the journals. Comparatively, a higher rate of variation can be observed in the discipline of welfare economics of '*The Economic Journal*' and that of monetary economics in '*American Economic Review*'. The range of citations is larger in the case of '*The Economic Journal*' than '*American Economic Review*'. Bibliographic coupling provides a great extent the relationship between a set of research papers pertaining to the field. This will certainly help the information seekers in searching the document and to a certain extent in classifying the information. It would be possible for a researcher to cover the area of his interest more comprehensively and systematically by referring to research papers having high coupling strength. Coupling index may also come in handy to compile special bibliographic materials.

Damodaram, Rajasekhar and Devarai (1995)[140] in their paper discusses the results of an informetrics study of the issues of the Journal of Oilseeds Research published during 1984-1993. The average collaboration coefficient during the period 1984-1993 in different oil seed crops and in various disciplines worked out to 0.86 indicating healthy trend of collaborative research in oil seeds. It emphasizes on the key role played by the Indian society of oil seeds research and its journal in the dissemination of oil sees information in India.

Dalai and Ramesh (1995)[141] presented a bibliometric analysis of papers published in the *Journal of Scientific and Industrial Research (J.S.I.R)* during the years 1988 to 1993.

The main findings of the analysis reveal that 82.282% of articles were published from India and only 17.718% were from other countries. Number of articles published per year varied between 45 to 68. Majority of the contributions belongs to educational and research institutions. Majority of contributions are by single author (50.75%) followed by more than two authors (19.82%). Subject-wise break up shows contributions in all areas of scientific and industrial research. Maximum length of article varies between 7 – 9 pages and minimum length of articles varies between 1 – 3 pages.

Suchitra Das and Seth (1995)[142] in their study analysed citations of the periodical *Hydrometallurgy*. The main findings of the study show that regarding country-wise analysis, maximum contribution is made by Canada followed by USA, India and South Africa. Almost all the countries bring out publications in collaboration with others. The variety of contributors from different organizations and countries indicate that the journal is well recognized throughout the world. The institution-wise distribution show that most of the contributions are either from Universities or research institutes. The authorship pattern reveals that team research is most pronounced, followed by solo research. The bibliographic form-wise distribution indicates that 76.9 percent of total citations are from journals, 13.2 percent from books and 5.3 percent from proceedings. Hydrometallurgy is the most referred journal. It is also well brought out that there is no time lag in publication of research papers.

Sarala (1995)[143] in her paper analyses the papers published in the Journal of Tropical Agriculture from 1989-1994. The findings of the study are – the journal of Tropical Agriculture publishes 2 types of contributions viz., full length articles as well as research notes. Contribution from scientists of Kerala Agricultural University is maximum. An average of 5.64 citations are appended to the articles published in source journal. Periodical articles are cited in large numbers by scientists. *Journal of Tropical Agriculture* occupies the first place in ranked list. Indian journals occupy the first three positions in the rank list.

Senapati (1995)[144] in his paper analyses numerically the year and language-wise distribution and break up of papers published on 'studies in conservation' for five years from 1988 to 1992 . The results of the study indicate that distribution of articles from 1988 to 1992 in studies in conservation is consistent as the difference between maximum and minimum number of articles is five. Maximum number of articles is in English. U.S.A contributed the maximum number of articles. On an average 13.88 references appeared in papers in Studies in conservation. The average length of papers is 8.47 pages. Average number of illustrations is 6.23.

Kalyane and Sen (1995)[145] in their paper 'A Bibliometric study of the *Journal of Oil Seeds Research*' carried out an analysis of 498 research articles comprising 241 full length research papers and 257 short communications published during 1984 to 1992 in *Journal of Oil Seeds Research* (Vol 1-Vol 9). Some important findings are – the number of pages allotted per issue for full length papers as well as short communications varies widely. Two authored papers are found to be maximum. Hissar, Rajendranagar (Hyderabad), Bangalore, New Delhi, Kanpur, Dhanbad, Ludhiana and Pantnagar are found to be important areas of research in India. On an average a full length research paper has 3 to 4 tables, and short communications 1 to 2 tables. No set pattern is observed in other types of graphic presentations. Important countries and highly cited journals have also been listed. Citations appended to articles do not follow Bradford's Law.

Haiqi (1996)[146] studied authorship patterns by analysing the citations in the *Japaneese Journal of Pharmacology and Acta Pharmacologica Sinica,* published from Japan and China respectively for the period 1991 to 1995. The results revealed that there were considerable variations in the number of authors per article from the two countries. National and International collaboration had increased annually.

Kulkarni (1996)[147] studied authorship pattern in his paper 'Scientific Research on Yoga: A Bibliometric study' and found that most of the papers were contributed by single author.

Kajberg (1996)[148] carried out a citation analysis of library and information science literature published in Denmark during the period 1957 to 1986 to study the characteristics of the periodical literature and communication patterns. The country-wise distribution of citations showed that Denmark accounted for 64.1 percent of total citations, followed by USA (9.5%) and UK (7.4%). The bibliographic form-wise distribution of citations showed that journals accounted for 40.5 percent followed by Monographs (18.8%) and Technical reports (15.8%). Findings on the age dispersion of citations revealed that 69.1 percent of citations were to works which were five years old, or less, at the time the article was written.

Joshi and Maheswarappa (1997)[149] studied the authorship trends and collaborative research among Indian Phytopathologists by analysing a total of 4,943 articles published during 1950-1989 in the journal of *Indian Phytopathology*. Out of the total articles, papers with two authors accounted for 54.38 percent, papers with three authors accounted for 19.33 percent and single authored papers constituted 19.16 percent. The average number of authors per paper had increased from 1.92 in the 1950's to 2.26 in the 1980's with an average of 2.16 for the period as a whole.

Jose and Korah (1997)[150] attempted a bibliometric study of natural rubber bibliographies published in India during the period 1983 to 1994. The main findings of study reveal that Journal articles predominated among the bibliographic forms. Maximum number of publications was in the field of chemistry, physics and technology. The core author was M.R.Sethuraj and the core journal was Rubber Board Bulletin.

O'Neill (1998)[151] studied the authorship patterns in two theory based journals namely *Educational Theory* and *Journal of Educational Thought* for the period 1955 to 1994 respectively. The results revealed that the majority of papers were single authored in both the journals irrespective of the date of publication.

Sornam and Gopi (1998)[152] made a citation study of AIDS literature and observed that majority of contributions were made by joint authors. The authorship pattern reveals that joint authorship is a much acclaimed one. This is not surprising especially like a medical area AIDS, which has drawn the world's attention, that most of the research is being carried out as team work in laboratories, research institutions and hospitals. A maximum number of articles are contributed by two authors (20%). Even among the joint more than ten authors have contributed a total number of 4 articles. The growth of literature is exponential. USA produced the greater number of research articles followed by UK. The journal AIDS is ranked number one for publishing more number of articles on AIDS-DIAGNOSIS.

Wai Sin Tiew (1998)[153] analyses the authorship pattern, the range and frequency of references cited and extent of acknowledgement, appendix or appendices being included in research articles of natural rubber, the types of collaborative research in natural rubber and the international collaboration scenario. Results indicated that number of multi-authored research papers is high at 72.1%. This indicates that in the years to come, the trend is towards multi-authorship. The range of references cited in the research articles of Journal of Natural rubber research is 16.49. It is found that acknowledgement is common practice among natural rubber researchers. On other hand only minor percent of research articles contained appendix indicating lack of habit on the part of the researchers to furnish additional information. The percentage of collaborative paper among natural rubber researchers is quite high, at 72.09%. This means that team research is going to be a common practice in scientific activity, especially natural rubber research.

Meera (1998)[154] carried out a bibliometric study of journal citations in the field of plant ecology for the years 1994 and 1995. The results revealed that the first 15 journals in the ranked list accounted for 35 percent of the total citations. The country-wise distribution of citations showed that USA occupied the first position with 19.7 percent of the total citations, followed by UK (18.00%), and The Netherlands (12.31%). English was the most preferred language of communication of research findings accounting for 85.58 percent of the total citations, followed by Chinese (3.12%), Italian (1.89%), and Russian (1.81%).

Patil and Kumar (1998)[155] study deals with citation analysis of pedological literature from the Journal of Indian Society of Soil Sciences 1988-1992. The study reveals that journal citations meet the major information requirements of users. Productivity of cited journals reveals that quite considerable numbers of citations are from the first 5 journals of ranked list thus signifying their high degree of productivity. Pedology literature and distribution of literature in journal confirm closely to Braford's law of scattering signifying developed nature of subject.

Halkar, Senapati and Salekchand (1998)[156] in their paper deals with a bibliometric study on *Journal of Family Welfare* during the period 1990-1997. The following specific conclusions can be drawn from the present study:

Distribution of articles from 1990 to 1997 in the *Journal of Family Welfare* is consistent. Maximum number of articles published in 1993 is same as 1997. Maximum articles are contributed from Academic institutions. India contributed more number of articles since journal is published in India. On average of 17.76 references appeared in papers. The average length of papers is between 4-9 pages which show ideal length of research articles.

Kumbar and Akhtary (1998)[157] in their paper carried out bibliometric analysis for 7451 references/citations appended to 322 articles published in the *American Journal of Ophthalmology*, Vol 117 to Vol 120 during the year 1994-1995. Results indicate that major type of document is periodical; in this field research goes back to 25 years and *Ophthalmology Journal* scores the highest number of citations.

Fernandez (1998)[158] analyzed the trend towards collectivization in Astronomy during this century (1901-1996), as measured by the increase in the number of authors per paper. For this purpose, two leading astronomical journals: The Astrophysical Journal and Monthly Notices of the Royal Astronomical Society are surveyed. It is found that the average number of authors per paper has jumped from a little more than one in the first half of this century to about three at present. Most of this dramatic increase has taken place during the last 20-25 years. At the same time, the ratio of collective papers (three or more authors) to single-authored ones has passed from nearly zero to 3-4 at present. The latter means that collective papers were almost nonexistent until the fifties or sixties to become nowadays 3-4 times more frequent than single-authored ones. The reasons underlying the collectivization of Astronomy (and perhaps of all natural sciences) are analyzed. The growing professionalization of science accompanied by a massive influx of graduate students into University research institutes, the revolution in communication, the pressure to publish in order to progress in a scientific career, and the growing complexity of knowledge are invoked as causes for the abandonment of the traditional individualism in science to a collective regime.

Rana and Sunita Agarwal (1999)[159] conducted a bibliometric study of the bibliography on application of telemetry technique in wild life science for the period 1956-1994 to understand various characteristics of literature on the subject. The study revealed that most of the studies are communicated through journals, with the most productive journal in the field of telemetry in wildlife science being *Journal of Wildlife Management*. There has been a gradual increase in overall growth pattern of literature, which is a good sign for any new discipline such as wildlife conservation. Most of the studies conducted are on mammals, followed by birds and reptiles/amphibians. Most of the studies are collaborative in nature and the trend is towards multi-disciplinary research.

Ming - Yueh Tsay (1999)[160] in his study library journal use and citation age in Medical science explores the in-house use age distribution of journals in the Library of Veterans General hospital, Taipei, Taiwan, their citation age distribution and the difference between them. The use study employed the sweep method and the study period lasted for six months. The citation age for each journal in this study was based on the data listed in the Science Citation Index, Journal Citation Reports, 1993. The results of this study illustrate that the use age distribution for the mean of all the journals is an exponentially decaying curve. On the other hand, the citation age distributions show a sharp initial rise from age one to three or four years and then fall off in a sort of exponential decay; and the age of maximum citation is typically three years. About 80% of uses are attributed to journals less than ten years old, while these journals contribute about 70% of total citations. The Kolmogorov - Smirnov two-sample test indicates that the use age distribution does not fit the citation age distribution.

Mahapatra and Das (2000)[161] conducted a study to derive the nature of growth of literature in Geology during 1987-1996. From the study of five very old journals of Geology it was noticed that out of 4481 articles published 70.64 percent were written by more than one author. So the percentage of Collaborative publications was increased in recent years. However, the number of single and even two author publications are also declining. But the number of three and multiple authors has been increased. The increase in collaboration and simultaneously decrease in the amount of publications verifies that Geology is a quite a fully developed field, although the number of collaborative publications are more, the rate of growth of publications is low. It can conclude that team research is now quite popular in Geology.

Bahr and Zemon (2000)[162] studied the collaborative authorship in Journal literature. The findings of the study reveal that there is direct relationship between collaboration and publication acceptance. In fact, one pair of researchers noted that multi-authored papers in '*The Physical Review*' had a 95 percent acceptance rate. The quality of multiauthored papers is better than single authored papers. The relationship between collaboration and productivity appears to rest on the number of collaborators. The greater the number of collaborators, the greater for increased productivity. University librarians are greatest contributors to the field's premier research journals, but they are also are its most significant collaborators. 84 percent of collaborative articles were by University librarians. College librarians collaborate much less frequently than their University library counterparts do. Despite the increase in coauthored articles, little in the literature advises prospective co authors on ways to work together successfully. The main aspect in collaborative process is determining credit fairly, a particularly difficult problem when number of collaborators are large.

Dutta and Sen (2000)[163] study covers 743 citations appended to 41 research articles published in the January to

April 2000 issues of Indian Journal of Pure and Applied Physics, the articles being contributed by 124 authors (117 Indian; 7 foreign). Results show that solo research is still quite substantial (25%) in India. Team research is of course the most prevalent form of research where the team size is rather small ranging usually from two to four researchers.

Arundhaty Das (2000)[164] analysed 145 articles published by Institute for Plasma Research in the field of Plasma Sciences, and 2324 citations appended to them. The main findings reveal that majority of the articles were published in scientific journals. Most of the citations were drawn from journals. A sizable number of citations were from books and proceedings. Most articles were published in core subjects of research, which include Plasma-waves, Oscillations, Turbulence, Instabilities, Equilibrium, Confinement, Transport, Impurities, Fluctuations and flow. Multiple authorship is common; 2 or 3 author teams wore most articles. However significant number of articles was written by single authors. The frequency of citation ages is highest for citations with an age range of 2 to 9 years. From the frequency distribution curve of citations versus their age, it is deduced that the literature is nearly doubled in about 7 years of time.

Dhiman (2000)[165] in his paper deals with the bibliometric study of Ethnobotany Journal published during 1989-1998. The results indicate that distribution of articles form 1989-1998 in Ethnobotany Journals is not consistent as the difference between maximum and minimum is 21. Maximum articles contributed from research institutions followed by colleges. India contributed the maximum number of articles. On an average, around 16 references appeared per paper in these journals. The average length of paper comes to 6 pages, which shows ideal length of research article.

Kannappanavar and Vijayakumar (2001)[166] studied the authorship pattern of International Monetary Fund (IMF) literature. The study revealed that team research is more favourable than the solo research. The degree of collaboration in IMF research ranged from 0.45 to 0.62 during the period of study, with an overall average of 0.56.

Kannappanavar and Vijayakumar (2001)[167] applied citation analysis to the data of the *Journal of Plant and Cell Physiology* for the year 1998. The distribution of citation frequencies was statistically tested and found the negative exponential distribution type. The obsolescence factors were determined. The average half-life of literature was found to be 6.2 years. Brooks technique of calculating AAF (Annual Aging Factor) = a was applied to determine its applicability for the literature. The values of 'a' was found to be 0.85 and the utility factors were calculated and found to be 6.67.

Dutta and Sen (2001)[168] study covers 427 citations appended to 30 articles appeared in January to March 2000 issues (no.s 1 to 3) of the Indian Journal of Pure and Applied Mathematics. The authorship pattern shows that single-authored citations amount to 51.40 percent of total citations. The high percentage of single authored citations clearly indicates the dominance of individual research in mathematics unlike physics, chemistry, biosciences and medicine where single authored contributions cover around 20 percent of total citations. Team research in the subject is found to be less than 50 percent and team size is also small usually restricted to two or more members.

Das (2001)[169] studied the collaboration pattern in computer science research in India by analysing 1408 research papers published in international journals on computer science contributed by the Indian scientists from 1991 to 2000. The domestic and international collaboration patterns have been studied. The results show increasing trend of international collaborations and plateau in domestic collaboration. In domestic collaborations, the number of institutions involved varied from two to four, wherein two-institution collaboration was found to be maximum. Most of the domestic collaborations took place between two R&D institutions. Academic institutions regularly collaborated with R&D institutions. Corporate organizations also collaborated with R&D institutions and academic institutions. International collaborations with India mostly take place with the developed countries. Top three collaborating countries are USA, Canada and Germany. USA topped the list with 48.8% of the total international collaboration with India. Continentally, India collaborated mostly with North America (viz. USA and Canada). Among the Asian countries, India collaborated most with Japan followed by Singapore. India's collaboration with Europe involves maximum number of countries, i.e. eighteen. The study shows that India has the potential of carrying out computer science research of international standard.

Dhiman and Sinha (2001)[170] made an attempt to study the impact of research collaboration on growth of literature in Ethnobotany during 1998-1999. The main findings of the study reveal that the total number of articles published during this period is 175. Out of these articles 39.42 percent were contributed by single authors; 34.85 percent by two authors; 18.28 percent by three authors while only 7.42 percent were contributed by multi-authored papers. Out of total articles published 107 (61.14%) were written in collaboration by more than one author. So the percentage of collaborative publications have increased in recent years which means the subject is getting much concentration of researchers from different fields. This further supports the fact that Ethnobotany is growing day by day because collaboration of authors is helping in the increase in the number of publications in the subject.

Das and Sen (2001)[171] study *Indian Journal of Medical Research* – An analysis pattern is based on 781 citations appended to 43 research articles pertaining to January to June 2000 issues of volume 109 of Indian Journal of Medical Research. The authorship pattern of the citations shows that more than 15% contributions are single authored and about 85% are the result of team work. The team size of this field is bigger than those in the fields of chemistry and physics. Single authored articles amount to 15.52 percent of the total citations and about 28 percent resulted through the collaboration of five or more authors.

Das and Sen (2001)[172] study is based on 1049 citations appended to 34 research articles pertaining to issue no.2 to 4 of volume 20 of Journal of Biosciences for the year 2000. The authorship pattern of the citations shows that 18.68 percent papers are single authored, 52.71 percent are double and triple-authored, and the remaining 28.61 percent are joint contributions of four or more authors. As in the case of medicine, the team size of this field is also bigger than those in the fields of chemistry and physics. As many as 25 articles of mega authorship (i.e. contributions by ten or more authors) have been encountered in this study, and one of them was by 22 authors.

Sinha and Dhiman (2001)[173] studied the research articles published in Indian and foreign journals by Dr. R. C. Sinha, a plant virologist. This bibliometric study is an attempt to analyze his articles using science citation index and study their impact on the world literature.

Biradar, Anita and Ushalatha (2001)[174] attempted to know the use pattern of periodicals by Medical Practioners. The study reveals that majority of medical practioners need current information on new procedures and medicine respectively. Most of medical practioners get periodicals through medical associations. Major percent of them get current information through seminars, conferences and workshops. Besides these Doctors use E-mail and Internet as a major communication media.

Sahoo (2001)[175] undertook bibliometric study of the journal "*Conservation of Cultural Property in India*" for the period 1993-1997 to understand various characteristics of literature on the subject. The findings of the study reveal that distribution of articles from 1993-1997 in CCPI is not consistent as the difference between maximum and minimum is 16. Out of 129 articles 46 papers have no citations and on an average, around 5-6 citations appears per paper in this journal during the period of study. The average length of paper comes to 7 pages which show ideal length of article. From the subject analysis it is observed that more articles are published on the subject conservation of archaeological monuments and sites.

Barooh and Sharma (2001)[176] in their article evaluated the journal collection of Library of Regional Research Laboratory, Jorhat (RRLJ) through a study of use of journal titles for publication of research by the scientific community of the laboratory. Journals ranked on the basis of their use for individual groups and percentage of used journals is shown.

Gupta and Suresh Kumar (2001)[177] in their paper described the broad characteristics of Theoretical Population Genetics (TPG) literature. The main findings of study indicate that majority of citations are in the form of serial articles. A subject-wise analysis of citations based on journal classification indicates that largest number of citations appeared in genetics journals. An age wise distribution of citations indicate that around 60% of all citations belong to first 10 years, and around 75% belong to first 20 years. A rank list of journals compiled on the basis of number of citations appearing in selected source articles from core journals shows that the most heavily cited journal, and thereby securing the first rank is Genetics followed by Heredity. The application of Bradford law was found positive in distribution of citations in 1959 and 1969, but not during

1979. By putting the distribution of citation in Bradford's Zones, one gets an idea about the core journals and their stability over a period of time and also an indication of the maturity of the field.

Dutta and Sen (2001)[178] in their paper analysed 1011 citations appended to 27 research articles of January-March 2000 issue of '*Indian Journal of Chemistry*' contributed by 61 authors. The main findings of study shows that group research or team-work is mostly dominating the field. Journals are most cited documents followed by monographs. The percentage of author self citations is 15.43. Journal self citation is 0.50% indicating thereby the abnormally low popularity of the journal among the chemical scientists of world. The percentage of clubbed citations is 3.36 and the ratio of clubbed citation to the unclubbed citations is 1:30.

Udofia (2002)[179] compared author collaboration in the periodical literature of African Trypanosomiasis. The study was based on the literature abstracted in the 1990 – 2000 articles of *Tropical Diseases Bulletin* and *Tsetse and Trypanosomiasis Quarterly (TTQ)* using the counting method. Concludes that multiple authorship was the most productive publication with a total of 2,587 (70.99%) papers while single authorship had 1,057 (29.01%) papers. The extent of collaboration was up to 11 authors per article and this call for more collaboration to extend the authorship beyond 11 authors per paper, as it is noted in other scientific disciplines. The study like other does not support Price's hypothesis (1963) of a likelihood that single authored papers would disappear as time went on. The author collaboration increases as the number of publication decreases and vice versa. The findings have provided factual information in support of information service in the field of African Trypanosomiasis research.

Bidyarthi Dutta, Anup Kumar Das and Sen (2002)[180] study considered Impact factor as very good indicator about the quality of journal. Journal Citation Reports (JCR) published by Institute of Scientific Information, USA provides impact factor of less than 6,000 journals every year. There is practically no way to decide the quality of those journals objectively which are not covered by JCR. The paper has attempted to show that Internal Impact Factor determined on the basis of journal self citation can quite reliably indicate the quality of a journal as is done by the impact factor. The internal impact factor of all research journals can be calculated manually with little effort and cost.

Glanzel (2002)[181] in his paper aims at describing both the common and the distinguishing features of co-authorship trends and patterns in selected science fields. The relation between co-authorship schemes and other bibliometric features, such as publication activity and citation impact are analysed. While co publication activity has grown considerably, the extent of co-authorship and its relation with productivity and citation impact largely varies among fields.

Tilak Hazarika, Kusuma Goswami and Pritimoni Das (2003)[182] analysed *'Indian Forester'* for the period 1991-2000. The conclusions of the study reveals that number of papers published in the *'Indian Forester'* from 1991-2000 is not consistent. The maximum number of papers published in the year 1996 and minimum in the year 1992. ICFRE and its institute contributed maximum papers to Indian Forester. Uttar Pradesh contributed maximum number of papers followed by Madhya Pradesh. Multiple authorship papers are dominant in *Indian Forester* followed by single and double author. Maximum number of papers are found in the area of Siviculture, followed by Ecology, Environment and biodiversity. On average 4-6 citations are appended followed by 1-3 references. Average length of papers is 4-6 pages.

Nabi Hasan and Mukhtiar Singh (2003)[183] in their study analysed *'The Himachal Journal of Agricultural Research'* and derived the following results: the average number of articles published is 28.1 per year. Authorship pattern shows that emphasis is on joint authorship. Maximum number of articles have 3-4 page length. Intra-departmental collaboration tops the list followed by inter-departmental collaboration. On an average every article has 0.10 acknowledgements. Regarding the type of literature cited in the articles, periodicals received the maximum number of citations followed by books. Among the 20 top cited journals in *Himachal Journal of Agricultural Research*, Indian Journal of Agricultural Sciences received maximum number of citations.

Nutan Johry (2003)[184] made a bibliometric study of '*International Social Science Journal*' and conclude that each issue of *International Social Science Journal* is devoted to specific theme and focus is usually on current and policy issues. The contributions to the journal are predominantly specialists from a broad spectrum of disciplines. The highest number of contributions are from universities/colleges. Single authors have contributed most of papers. It is interesting to note that in case of joint authors, all have same affiliation. There are only five contribution made by Indian diaspora. Social scientists from countries like U.K, U.S.A, France and India have contributed to *International Social Science Journal*.

Ashu Shokeen and Kaushik (2003)[185] in their paper made a critical analysis of '*Indian Journal of Economics*' to find out authorship pattern and citation patterns of articles published in *Indian Journal of Economics* between January-December 2002. The findings of the study show that majority of articles published in these issues are single-authored. Journal articles are predominant. The ratio of author self citation to total citations is 1:46.73. The ratio of journal self citation to total citations is 1:350.5. It is also clear that majority of documents cited in these issues were published not more than twenty years ago.

Kaushik (2003)[186] in his paper 'Citation Pattern of Sociologist' analysed *American Journal of Sociology* published from July 2002 to May 2003. The main findings of the study reveal that majority of citations are single-authored. Journal articles and books both are almost equally cited sources. The ratio of author self citation to total citations is 1:29.53. The ratio of journal self citation to total citations is 1:22.26. It is clear that a majority of documents cited in these issues were published not more than twenty years ago.

Ganapathi and Ashok (2003)[187] in their article conducted a bibliometric study of '*Journal of Entrepreneurship*' till Volume 11. The results indicate that international exposure of *Journal of Entrepreneurship* is more. The distribution of articles from 1993 to 1999 is consistent but form 1998 onwards, the trends towards that number of articles is diminishing. Journal of Entrepreneurship does not contain any articles without references. It is observed that average length of papers is between 11 and 20. Acknowledgement is not a common practice among contributions of *Journal of Entrepreneurship*. Concentration of article publication is less.

Senthilkumaran and Vadivel (2003)[188] made a bibliometric study of the '*Spice India*' journal for the period 1997-2001. The study indicated that single authored papers were maximum which shows that more people write articles individually. This clearly indicated that solo research dominated in the field of Spice crops. Subject-wise break up of articles of Spice India Journal during the period of study shows that maximum number of publications fall under broad fields, major spice crops and its produces.

Nalini (2003)[189] in her article examined 31 articles on Occupational Health related problems published in journals (both Indian and foreign) during the year 2000. The number of publications on health consequences of chemical and textile workers topped the list with respiratory problems being predominant area of study. Most of the articles appeared in Indian journals and *Indian Journal of Occupational and Environmental Medicine* was found to be the most preferred journal. Majority of publications came from a team work of 2-3 authors. On an average, a publication contained 5 pages. Analysis of references showed that the citations ranged from 2 to 73, with the oldest being for the year 1916.

Kannappanavar, Chidananda Swamy and Vijay Kumar (2004)[190] in their paper studied authorship trend and collaborative research in Chemistry in India during 1996-2000. The study found that team research is preferred in the field of chemistry rather than solo research. The degree of collaboration is calculated and found to be 0.76. The degree of collaboration varies from year to year and is found to be 0.72 to 0.83. Average number of authors per paper increased from 7.52 to 8.39.

Praseeda and Vasudevan (2004)[191] in their article analysed the articles of Journal '*The University News*' and derived that more people tend to write individually and only less people like to produce collaborative work. The subject-wise break up shows that maximum number of articles fall under 'Education' followed by 'Library and Information Science' and 'Management Education'. Analysis of references used reveals that majority of authors have referred to books. Majority of articles are without references and most of the articles have 5-6 references. The author who contributed maximum articles to the journal has also been found.

Asha Narang (2004)[192] in her paper critically examined 8396 citations appended to 737 articles published in the '*Indian Journal of Pure and Applied Mathematics*' during the years 1998-2002. The results of the study indicate that highest number of papers have been written by joint authors. The most cited documents are articles from research journals. The contributions in this journal from India and other countries are almost equal. Among the Indian states, Uttar Pradesh is the top contributor whereas among the Indian universities, University of Delhi is at the top. At the international level, India is top contributor followed by China. The growth and popularity of this journal is found to be showing an upward trend.

Ashu Shokeen and Kaushik (2004)[193] in their article analysed 1149 citations that appeared in '*Indian Journal of Plant Physiology*'. The finding of the study reveals that two-authored citations are more common which is followed by single-authored papers. The results reveal that journal articles are predominant with 81% of total citations. The ratio of author self citation to total citations is 1:16.65. The ratio of journal self citation to total citations is 1:31.91. It is clear that a majority of documents cited in these issues were published not more than twenty years ago.

Mahapatra and Panda (2004)[194] in their article studied Health Science Literature on Orissa published from 1993-2002. The results indicate that majority of authors are jointly publishing their papers. Research work on malaria is most popular branch of health science research compared to other subjects. Papers are more published in clinical journals than in non-clinical journals. Health science authors prefer to publish their papers more in Indian journals than in foreign journals. The length of papers is more in the range of 5-6 pages. Two journals such as '*Journal of Communication Diseases*' and '*Indian Journal of Malaria*' rank the highest position in publishing papers on Health literature in Orissa.

Mahapatra and Rudranarayan (2004)[195] in their paper critically examined 115 research papers on 'Tribal Studies' from 46 Indian journals. The findings of the study show that single authorship is most dominant in tribal research. Regarding subject-wise breakup 'Tribal Communities' appears to be highest category. It is evident from the study that tribal researchers are prone to contributing more papers in anthropology journals. Majority of authors prefer to contribute their papers in national journals. Majority of papers have the length of 8 and above pages range. As far as ranking of journals in tribal research is concerned 'Adivasi' has published largest number of papers followed by 'Man and Life'.

Senthilkumar and Vadivel (2004)[196] in their paper made a bibliometric study of the '*Journal of Spices and Aromatic Crops*' for the period 1992-2000 and concluded that the total number of articles appearing in this journal varied from volume to volume. Maximum number of articles were published during 1999 and minimum during 1993. Joint authors wrote maximum number of articles. This trend indicated that nowadays the research works/projects are carried out on collaborative basis. On an average, the authors in their articles appended 4-6 citations. The scientists of Indian Institute of Spice Research, Calicut published the highest number of research articles. Indian scientists contributed maximum number of articles.

Databases

Price (1963)[197] described the phenomenon of multiple authorship from a historical perspective. Based on data from Chemical Abstracts, he showed that that at the beginning of this century more than 80 percent of papers were by single authors and almost all the remaining were multiple author papers. Since then, the trend towards multi-authored papers has increased steadily. He predicted "if it continues at the present rate, by 1980 the single author paper will be extinct".

Hawkins (1977)[198] carried out a bibliometric study of journals publishing papers in electrochemistry. The data was collected by searching the *Chemical Abstracts Condensates* for 1972 through 1976, using the on-line literature searching system namely DIALOG. He identified the most productive journals in electrochemistry by preparing a list containing 149 journals.

Maheswarappa and others (1984)[199] studied collaborative research in science and technology in India based on the authorship data collected from *Indian Science Abstracts* covering the calendar years 1965, 1975, 1980 and 1983. The results showed that papers with two authors were maximum in number in science and technology in India; the proportion of papers with three and four authors had doubled as a function of time and correspondingly papers with single authors declined approximately by half; the average number authors per paper had increased from 1.84 in 1965 to 2.33 in 1983; and the relative figures for the degree of collaboration ranged between 0.61 to 0.80.

Guay (1986)[200] conducted a quantitative survey of the emergence of organic chemistry in India based on the data collected from *Chemical Abstracts* for the period 1907 to 1926. Chemists who were conducting research in India were grouped under three distinct groups on the basis of their cultural identity and educational background. The important disparities between these three groups both in terms of research fields and in terms of publication outlets were identified.

Maheswarappa and Mathias (1987)[201] studied the authorship pattern and collaborative research in different disciplines of physical sciences based on the data collected from *Indian Science Abstracts* for the years 1965, 1970, 1975, 1980 and 1983. An increasing trend towards collaboration was found in all disciplines of physical sciences, but the actual increase varied from discipline to discipline. Among the different subjects in the field of physical sciences, the highest number of multi-authored papers was found in chemistry. The average number of authors per paper in chemistry had increased from 2.15 in 1965 to 2.61 in 1983 and the degree of collaboration had increased from 0.81 to 0.92 for the corresponding years.

Klaic (1990)[202] studied the research activity of chemists belonging to the Rugier Boskovic Institute, Yugoslavia for the period 1976 to 1985, covering 1,149 *Science Citation Index* registered papers. The results showed that the average number of authors per publication was 3.05 (range: 2.76 to 3.42), and papers published by two or three authors accounted for 60 percent, while papers published by seven or more authors represented only three percent of the total number of publications. The papers were published in 235 different journals, most frequently in the national *Croatica Chemica Acta.*

Mishra and Mishra (1991)[203] studied the authorship pattern and research collaborations in the field of Medicinal and Aromatic Plants based on the data collected from the *Medicinal and Aromatic Plants Abstracts* (1979-89). The major findings of the study reveals that papers with two and three authors constitute a major part (55.42%) of literature. States the multiple authorship is predominant in the field of study. The average number of authors per paper has remained almost consistent, ranging between 2.83 to 3.20 and the degree of collaboration ranges between 0.85 to 0.89 during 1979-89 in the field of Medicinal and Aromatic Plants. It is apparent from this study that research collaboration in the field is common.

Sharada (1991)[204] in her paper studied the authorship pattern in the field of linguistics by analysing the articles abstracted in *Linguistics and Language Behaviour Abstracts (LLBA).* The results reveal that 79.87 percent of articles are single authored while multiple authorship in linguistics account for 20.13 percent. From this study we may infer that in Linguistics, research is mostly individualistic rather than team-oriented. Multiple authorship is on the developing line, especially in interdisciplinary topics, experiment-oriented studies and multi-language oriented researchers.

Gupta (1992)[205] studied author productivity trends by analysing a cumulative index of geophysics for the two important journals "Geophysics" and "Geophysical Prospecting" for the period 1936-1985. Author productivity trends were tested by applying *K-S* statistical test. Two files were generated out of this database; one for the period 1936-1985 and the other for the period 1936-1976 to test the time sensitivity of Lotka's law. Lotka's law did not apply as inverse square law but could apply satisfactorily with exponent value of 2.1 on author productivity distribution patterns of both the files.

Vaishnav and Deo (1993)[206] in their paper analysed a database consisting of 25,669 items to study the growth of literature and subjectwise growth, while a database of 15287 items was analysed to study the authorship trend, author's publishing outlets, journal literature, its distribution and application of Bradford's Law. The main findings of the study reveal that the growth of literature was slow in the beginning while from 1980 onwards a stage of exponential growth started. Computerised information storage and Retrieval are the most popular subjects. Computerised financial management, computerized classification are evolving subjects. Computer output on Microforms, computerized citation indexes are decaying subjects. The tendency of team work is evident at the stage of maturity of the subject. There is very high proportion of authors contributing only one paper each. The K-S test confirmed the applicability of Lotka's law with slight variations. The popular carriers of information are journals, reports and conference proceedings. U.K and U.S.A are the most productive countries with English as the predominant language. The ranking of journals showed that first 16 journals covered 1/3 articles published on the subject. The data under study does not fist the Bradford's distribution.

Ramakrishna and Panganayya (1999)[207] analysed the science and business databases with most entries containing the term biotechnology in their title from the DIALOG databases to see how the number of references with biotechnology in the title has changed over a period of time within the group of a particular type of publications. The Relative Growth Rate (RGR) and doubling time for the publications during 1985 to 1997 were determined. The size of the literature was calculated by applying logistic growth formula.

Suresh Kumar (2003)[208] in his article analysed computer science data set comprising of 1661 authors contributing 4128 articles. The authors have made contributions ranging from 1 to 77 papers. The distribution is characterized by dispersion of papers over a large number of low productive authors and the concentration of contributions made by a very few highly productive authors. It is observed that 96.45% low productive authors have made 10 or less contributions representing about 72% of the total contributions produced. Where as only 1.62% highly productive authors have contributed more than 15 contributions each representing 18% of total contributions received.

Gupta and Jha (2004)[209] in their paper conducted a study on the outputs of India's S&T collaboration with Far East Asia countries on the basis of joint co-authored papers published from 1996 to 2000 and covered in Science Citation Index database. The findings show that India's collaboration with Japan was strongly bilateral and with other countries it was multilateral. The most preferred areas of research under bilateral collaboration has been found to be physics, chemistry and engineering & technology. In terms of overall impact, India's bilateral collaborative papers with Japan received the highest impact followed by Taiwan.

Others

Clarke (1964)[210] refuted Price's contention and showed

that the average number of authors per paper had remained almost constant at about 2.3 based on the authorship data collected from biomedical papers presented at the annual meetings of the Federation of American Societies for Experimental Biology for the period 1934 to 1963.

Zuckerman (1967)[211] studied 41 Nobel laureates in science and observed a high degree of collaboration between collaboration and productivity. In general, laureates in science published more and were more apt to collaborate.

Beaver and Rosen (1978, 1979, 1979)[212 213 214] studied the history of research collaboration from the 17th century onwards. They showed that research collaboration is related to professionalization of the scientific community; and collaboration generally leads to greater productivity and mobility.

Heffner (1981)[215] studied the relationship between collaboration and financial support for research in the fields of political science, psychology, biological sciences and chemistry. It was observed that in all these disciplines, financial support for research was associated with an increase in the total number of authors involved in the production of knowledge per research paper, and the association was particularly strong in biological sciences and chemistry.

Lawani (1982)[216] in his study discussed the heterogeneity of author self-citations by grouping them under synchronous self-citations and diachronous self-citations and presented a systematic scheme for their classification by identifying four categories within each group.

Subramanyam and Stephens (1982)[217] showed that collaborative research papers were supported by research grants to a large extent compared to single author papers in biochemistry and chemical engineering.

Subramanyam (1983)[218] reviewed the research in collaboration studies and developed a formula for computing the degree of collaboration of a discipline.

Sridhar (1985)[219] studied the citing pattern of Indian space engineers and found the overall self-citation rate to be 3.5 percent, and the average number of self-citations per article was 3.44.

Snyder and Bonzi (1989)[220] examined the motivation of authors in citing themselves and others. They observed that there were relatively few significant differences between the reasons for which authors cite themselves and the reasons for which they cite others.

Bonzi and Snyder (1990)[221] compared the self-citation pattern in physical sciences of chemistry and geology to those in the social sciences of economics and sociology.

Kalyane and Vidyasagar Rao (1992)[222] investigated collaboration trends in sugar cane research by studying the publications of Sugarcane Breeding Institute, Coimbatore, for the period 1948 to 1987. They calculated discipline-wise collaboration coefficient (CC) and average authorship per paper (AAP). It was noticed that both CC and AAP increased steadily over a period of time.

Sharada (1993)[223] in her paper examined the feasibility of the three laws of bibliometrics formulated by Bradford, Lotka, and Zipf in various studies conducted in Humanities and Sciences. In the light of these results, this paper examines the results obtained from bibliometric studies conducted on the corpus of Linguistics. Individual research dominates in field of linguistics. Such studies provide analytical insight to the scholars in linguistics. It is helpful to find density and intensity of topics in linguistics, in particular, the concentration of studies on languages.

Joshi and Maheswarappa (1994)[224] reviewed the literature of multiple authorship trends in different disciplines of science and technology. The subjects covered were mathematics, astronomy and allied sciences, physics, chemistry, geology, paleontology, genetics, biochemistry, botany, zoology, entomology, biomedical sciences, engineering, agricultural sciences, chemical technology and space technology.

Sudhier (1997)[225] carried out a quantitative treatment of characterstics and behaviour of scientific research output in Kerala during 1979-1994. The major findings of study indicate that research is more active in the field of agriculture followed by medical sciences. Academic institutions dominate in research front compared to research institutions. Analysis of institutional affiliation of authors revealed that majority of papers were contributed by research scholars and teachers working in Universities and colleges. The University wise distribution of papers revealed that University of Kerala stood first upto 1989. But in 1994 Kerala Agricultural University surged forward with more contributions. As far as contribution from different districts is concerned, Thiruvanthapuram was the largest contributor.

Gupta (1997)[226] studied the characteristics of theoretical population genetics in terms of obsolescence measures such as half-life, Price index, and found that the age of references cited in source papers of theoretical population genetics, irrespective of the period studied, was found to be best modeled according to a simple lognormal probability density function.

Manoj Kulkarni (1997)[227] in his study attempted to analyse quantitatively the contribution of Dr. Bhole towards the field of yoga research. 147 research papers are analysed and authorship pattern, collaboration trends, year wise distribution, media utilized, types of research design etc are highlighted. The results indicate that Bhole wrote most of the papers as second author and tendency for collaboration in work is increased with peak between 1981-1985. Yoga Mimamsa was most useful journal for expressing himself and

Bhole has aptly used the media of seminars and conferences for communicating the message of yoga research to the world. Yogic therapy seems to be the favoured topic.

Kalyan, Prakasan and Vijaikumar (2001)[228] in their study analysed 91 publications by Ranjit Kumar Mitra, during 1965-2001 in domains: Biochemical Genetics (30), Molecular Biology (16), Bioenergetics (12), Plant Biochemistry (11), Biotechnology (10), Methodology (5), Popular science (4), Gene Accessions (2), and Cytogenesis (1) revealed his research team (53 collaborators), prominent ones with their authorship credits being : C.R. Bhatia (43), T. Gopalakrishna(19), K.N.Suseelan(10), and S. E. Pawar(9). Other indicators are productivity coefficient 0.59, overall collaboration coefficient 0.95, publication concentration 36, publication density 1.28. Major achievements, authorship pattern, channels used, central tendencies on bibliographic characteristics, synchronous self-citation rate, and keyword frequencies in titles of the publications are documented.

Shukla, Saksena and Riswadkar (2001)[229] in this paper attempts to apply Bradford's Law of Scattering and Lotka's Law of productivity to bio-energy literature and to verify if the law holds good for ten abstracting services (eight international and two Indian).

It has been verified that literature related to bio-energy conforms to Bradford's Law of scattering and that grouping of services also yields a Bradford Distribution. The new model developed in this study fits the data very satisfactorily r value ranged from 0.952 to 0.998 (for papers from journal titles) and 0.989 to 0.998 (for papers from conference proceedings). The value of P (multiplication factor) for bio-energy literature ranged from 2.19 to 4.09 (except for IEA and ISA) for articles from journals and from 2.02 to 4.59 for papers from conference titles.

Results of linear regression showed that Lotka's distribution holds good for bio-energy literature and the value of n ranged between 2.5 and 4.5. The Kolmonogorov-Smirnoff test of goodness of fit confirmed these findings.

Review of literature on the application of bibliometric techniques in the various disciplines reveals some interesting findings. Majority of the earlier papers published during late 60's and 70's have discussed about the basic concept of bibliometrics, bibliometric laws and their applications in libraries theoretically. However, a shift from the theoretical discussion to exploring the possibility of application of bibliometric techniques to the published literature is noticed from 1980s onwards. This trend is still continuing even after 2000.

Authors traced the development of the application of quantitative methods in Library and Information Science starting from librametry to informetrics. Number of articles published in journals of library and information science reported the findings of wide range of research done in the area of bibliometrics. Majority of the bibliometric studies have considered journals as the source of information in various subjects. Secondary sources like abstracting and indexing periodicals have also been used as the base for such studies. Citations appended to dissertations and theses have also became the source of information for some of the bibliometric studies. A study made by Kabir, indicates that literature in the field of bibliometrics is doubling every ten years. Few studies have applied bibliometric techniques to analyze the literature in the form of books. Many of the research studies published in the late 1990s were based on the content of electronic databases.

Another aspect of bibliometrics that has been focused upon is measuring the research productivity of scientists, research projects and institutions. However, the number of such studies is relatively small compared to number of studies published on literature use pattern in different subject fields.

Among three principal laws of bibliometrics, Bradford's law was found to be the most popular as it attracted many researchers. Starting with the first article published by Vickery in 1948, it may be observed that even after 2000 study on the implications of this law on periodical literature seems to be the favourite topic for researchers in the field of bibliometrics. Besides the basic application and impact on distribution of periodical literature, many researchers have suggested and formulated new theories and formulae based on the original Law of Scattering (Vickery, Brookes, Leimkuhler).Few studies have been reported on the application of Lotka's law on author productivity and Zipf's law on word count compared to those on Bradford's Law.

The review of literature also points out the works of some of the dedicated scholars like Hulme, Gross, Lotka, Bradford, Zipf, Cole, Garfield, Leimkuhler, Vickery, Brookes etc who have enriched the field of Bibliometrics.

The research reported in the literature shows that various techniques of bibliometrics have been applied by the researchers in Library and Information Science to study different aspects of literature use, productivity of journals, authors and institutions at micro and macro levels. The objectives and purpose of these studies are varied. Some of the studies assessed the quality and relevance of the periodical collections to justify the expenditure on them. Few studies have tried to provide guidelines on selection, retention and archiving of highly useful periodical back volumes in libraries and information centers. Some of the studies used the findings to make decisions related to funding the research projects.

Majority of the studies are individual studies done by library professionals and academicians. Few studies were done by institutions and associations. Collaborative studies between the institutions were also found to be very limited in number. International collaboration to study variations in the research productivity and literature use pattern at the national level has been reported only in one case.

It is observed from the review of literature that active research has been done and also is continuing applying bibliometrics techniques in various subjects with different objectives. But , a few studies have focused on the implications of the findings of Bibliometric research on the management, the services and users of library and information centers on one hand and the research activity in the concerned field on the other hand. Studies have also not made any effort to assess the economic implications of the findings of such studies on individual research projects, libraries and information centers and institutions both at local, regional and national levels. There is a need to conduct elaborate in-depth research in these areas in the future.

REFERENCES

1. Pritchard, Alan. "Statistical Bibliography or Bibliometrics?" *Journal of Documentation*, 25(4), 1969, pp. 348-349.

2. Vagiswari, A. Publishing Patterns of Scientists in India with Special Reference to Astronomers and Astrophysicists, Andhra University, 1997.

3. Valasayya, G. "Literature Use Patterns of Scholars in Telugu Language and Literature: A Bibliometric Study of the Ph.D. Theses Submitted to Andhra University during 1945-1992", Andhra University, 1997.

4. Vimala, V. "Bibliometric Study of Citations in Ph.D. Theses in Biological Sciences", Sri Venkateswara University, 1999.

5. Aruna Prasad Reddy, C. "Bibliometric Study of Citations in Ph.D. Theses in Chemistry Accepted by Sri Venkateswara University, Tirupathi: 1964-1997", Andhra University, 1999.

6. Dheerendra, P.T. "Bibliometric Analysis of Citation Patterns in Indian Periodical Literature on Economics", Osmania University, 1999.

7. Andhramatha, K. "Bibliometric Study of Citations in Ph.D. Theses in Physics Awarded by Andhra University, Visakhapatnam: 1943-2002.

8. Sengupta, I. Recent Direction of Growth in Biomedical Knowledge: An Analytical Study based on Observed Changes in Scientific Impact on Serial Publications, Calcutta, 1983.

9. Singh, S.M. The Use of Social Science Literature in India: A Bibliometric Study, Benares, 1983.

10. Mahapatra, M. Growth of Literature and Citation Pattern among the Indian Journals in the Field of Botany – 1950-1980, Burdwan, 1984.

11. Sengupta, I.N. Bibliometric Analysis of the Impact of the Growth of Biomedical Knowledge on the other Biological and Medical Science, Karnataka, 1984.

12. Sangam, S.L. Citation Analysis of Doctoral Dissertations in Social Sciences Accepted by Karnataka University during 1964-1982, Gulbarga, 1986.

13. Vyas, S.D. Bibliographic Controls of Social Science Literature in Post Independent India, Rajasthan, 1986.

14. Roy, Paul M. Bibliometric Analysis and Evaluation of Indian Research Writing in Physics, Madurai, 1988.

15. Taher, Mohd. Bibliometric Analysis of the Literature in the Field of Islamic Studies, Calcutta, 1989.

16. Savanur, S.K. Reviewing of Library Science Books: A Content Analysis Approach, Karnataka, 1990.

17. Kannappanavar, B.U. Citation Analysis of Doctoral Dissertations in Library and Information Science Accepted by the Universities in Karnataka, Karnataka, 1991.

18. Parvathamma, N. Trends in Growth in Indian Earth Science Literature 1918-1988: A Bibliometric Study, Gulbarga, 1991.

19. Rajendra Prasad. Validity of Bibliometric Laws in the Field of Social Sciences, Benaras, 1991.

20. Berhamuddin, M. Indian Contribution to American Studies: An Investigation in to Growth of Literature Using the Bibliometric Analysis, Jiwaji, 1992.

21. Maheswarappa, B.S. A Bibliometric Analysis of Phytopathology Literature, Gulbarga, 1992.

22. Ratnakar, A. Trends in Scientific Communication in India Historic Sociometric and Bibliographic Analysis of the Scientific Journals in Physical Science especially Physics and Astronomy, Karnataka, 1992.

23. Shailendra Kumar. Information Sources in History of Science in India: A Scientometric Study of Periodical Literature, Rajasthan, 1992.

24. Tripathy, Tridib. Growth and Development of Indian Library and Information Science Periodical Literature from 1920-1985, Burdwan, 1992.

25. Mahapatra, G. Citation Pattern among the Indian Library and Information Science in English from 1975-1985, Utkal, 1993.

26. Arora, J. Bibliometric Analysis and Bibliographic Control of Literature in Immunology, Rajasthan, 1994.

27. Binwarilal. Bibliometric Study of Contribution made to Documentation as Reflected in Select Periodicals of Library and Information Science Published in India: A Quantitative Analysis 1969-1988.

28. Munshi, U.M. Assessment of Agriculture Research Output: A Bibliometric Analysis of Research Output of Indian Agriculture Universities, Jiwaji, 1994.

29. Srivastava, R. An Investigation in to the Literature Use Pattern of Researchers in Chemistry: A Bibliometric Study, BHU, 1994.

30. Vearma, Maya. Use Pattern of Literature in Economics Researchers: A Bibliometric Study, Ravishankar, 1994.

31. Humayoon Kabir, S. Growth of Indian Horticultural Literature during 1980-1989 and the Contribution of Indian Horticultural Scientist in Foreign Horticultural Periodicals: A Quantitative Study, Bangalore, 1996.

32. Jalaja, V. Bibliometric Analysis of Science Journals Published from India, Calicut, 1996.

33. Aravind, N. *The Literature of Physical Anthropology*: A Citation Analysis, Padmavati, 1997.

34. Misra, R. Citation Analysis of Doctoral Dissertations in Library and Information Science Accepted by the Universities of Orissa and Manipur till 1993: A Comparative Study, 1997.

35. Ravi, S. *Nuclear Science Research Productivity of Indian Annamalai Scientist: A Bibliographic Analysis*, 1997.

36. Sahu, K.C. Literature Use Pattern in Biosciences, Ecology, Biochemistry, Biophysics, Physiology of the University of Sagar and Sambalpur: A Bibliometric Study Based on Ph.D. Theses, HS Gour, Sagar, 1997.

37. Thoidingian, P.D. Citation Analysis of the Ph.D. Theses in Social Sciences Accepted by Guwahati University during 1970-80, Manipur, 1997.

38. Meera, B.M. *Statistical Quality Control Studies in Library and Information Science*, Bangalore, 1998.

39. Sacham Anitha. Scientometric Study of Chemical Literature Cited in Doctoral Theses of Chemistry Submitted to University of Jammu, Jammu, 1999.

39A. Khokale, Revati R. Bibliometric Analysis of Ph.D. Theses Awarded by Amravati University, Amaravati: A Study of Information Flow in Some Selective Disciplines, 2005

40. Kubota, Akiko. A Citation Analysis of Graduation Theses of the School of Library and Information Science, Keio University. *Library and Information Science*, 14, 1976, p. 193-209.

41. LaBorie, Tim. and Halperin, M. Citation Patterns in Library and Information Science Dissertations. *Journal of Education for Librarianship*, 16, 1976, p. 271-283.

42. Meera, Deshpande and Rajyalakshmi, D. Citation Study of Doctoral Dissertations in Library and Information Science. *Annals of Library Science and Documentation*, 44(2), 1997, p. 41-53.

43. Vijaykumar, M, Padmamma, S. and Sampat Kumar, B.T. Information Use by Library Professionals : A Scientometric Analysis. *ILA Bulletin*, 36(1), 2000, p. 19-23.

44. Kundu, A.K. Self-citations by Indian Library Scientists. *Annals of Library Science and Documentation*, 28, 1981, p. 39-41.

45. Hart, R. and others. Funded and Non-funded Research: Characteristics of Authorship and Pattern of Collaboration in the 1986 Library and Information Science Literature. *Library and Information Science Research*, 12, 1990, pp. 72-86.

46. Raptis, P. Authorship Characteristics in Five International Library Science Journals. *Libri*, 42, 1992, pp. 35-42.

47. Afolabi, M. Productivity of Journals which Published Nigerian Library Literature. *Annals of Library Science and Documentation*, 39, 1992, pp. 139-144.

48. Subramanian, R. and Navaneethan, R. Library Science with a Slant to Documentation and Information Studies, 1981-1991 : A Bibliometric Study. *Library Science with a Slant to Documentation*, 29(3), 1992, pp. 157-161.

49. Gupta, Davendra K. Bibliometric Study of Literature on Ethiopian Librarianship1944-1992. *Library Science with a Slant to Documentation and Information studies*, 31(4), 1994, pp. 208-216.

50. Mahapatra, Gayatri. Highly Cited Authors, Journals and Books in Indian Library and Information Science Literature. *Annals of Library Science and Documentation*, 41(4), 1994, pp. 127-134.

51. Dimitroff, A. and Arlitsch, K. Self-citations in the Library and Information Science Literature. *Journal of Documentation*, 51, 1995, pp. 44-56.

52. Bose, Kausik and Goria, Sunil. Bibliometric Study of INICAE. *International Information Communication and Education*, 14(1), 1995, pp. 39-50.

53. Mahendra and Deshmukh, P.P. Citation Analysis of Annals of Library Science and Documentation. *Annals of Library Science and Documentation*, 43(1), 1996, pp. 11-25.

54. Ramesh, L.S.R.C.V. and Hussain. Herald of Library Science: A Bibliometric Study. *Herald of Library Science*, 36(3-4), 1997, pp. 176-190.

55. Cronin, Blaise and Shaw, Debora. Citation Funding Acknowledgement and Author Nationality Relationship in Four Information Science Journals. *Journal of Documentation*, 55(4), 1999,p p. 402-408

56. Ramesh, L.S.R.C.V. and Nagaraju, A.V.S.S. Citation Analysis of the Indian Journal of Information, Library and Society. *Indian Journal of Information, Library and Society*, 13(3-4), 2000, pp. 171-179.

57. Dhiman, A.K. Self-citation Behaviour of Library Scientists: A Case Study of ILA Bulletin. *CLIS Observer*, 19(1-2), 2002, pp. 31-35.

58. Kaur, Amritpal. ILA Bulletin 1996-2000: A Bibliometric Study. *ILA Bulletin*, 38(3), 2002, pp. 126-134.

59. Roy, Pratap Chandra. Authorship Pattern of Indian Library Science Journals for the Period 1991-2000. *SRELS Journal of Information Management*, 41(4), 2004, pp. 393-404.

60. Roy, Pratap Chandra. Institution Collaboration in Indian Library and Information Science Journals 1991-2000. *ILA Bulletin*, 40(2), 2004, pp. 16-26.

61. Humayoon Kabir, S. Citations in World Bibliometrics Research : An Analysis. *Library Science with a Slant to Documentation and Information Studies*, 30(4), 1993, pp. 155-157.

62. Humayoon Kabir, S. Authorship Trend and Solo Research in Bibliometrics. *Library Science with a Slant to Documentation and Information Studies*, 31(2), 1994, pp. 87-90.

63. Parameswaran, M. and Smitha, K.G. Bibliometric Analysis of LISA. *Annals of Library and Inforamtion Studies*, 48(4), pp. 149-156.

64. Rajeev Vij. Library and Information Science Abstracts on CD-ROM : A Bibliometric Study. *ILA Bulletin*, 37(4), 2001, pp. 135-142.

65. Narayana, N.S.S. and Aruna Prasad Reddy, C. A Statistical Search Method for Estimation of Bradford Groups. *SRELS Journal of Information Management*, 37(1), 2000, pp. 5-16.

66. Satarkar, S.P., Dharmapurikar, R.G. and Jadhava, M.B. Citation Analysis of Indian Library Association Proceedings Vol. XXXVII. *ILA Bulletin*, 38(4), 2002, pp. 123-125.

67. Omoruyi, J. Social Science Dissertations: Characteristics of Bibliographic Citations. *UNESCO Bulletin for Libraries*, 32, 1978, pp. 172-177.

68. Maheswarappa, B.S. and Prakash, B.P. Literature Use Pattern by the Researchers in the field of Botany: A Citation Study of Doctoral Theses. *Journal of Library and Information Science*, 7, 1982, pp. 15-32.

69. De Oliveira, Silas Marques. Citation Pattern in Veterinary Medicine Dissertations. *Annals of Library Science and Documentation*, 31, 1984, pp. 147-155.

70. Sangam, S.L. A Citation Analysis of Doctoral Dissertations in Social Science Accepted by the Karnataka University, Dharwad, during 1964 to 1982. Gulbarga University, Ph.D. (Unpublished).

71. Nweke, Ken MC, The Language and Format of the Literature used by Research Scholars in Zoology at the Ibadan University, Nigeria. *Annals of Library Science and Documentation*, 35, 1988, pp. 128-133.

72. Sangam, S.L. and Biradar, B.S. Patterns of Information use by Indian Surgical Scientists. *Annals of Library Science and Documentation*, 37, 1990, pp. 133-142.

73. Madkey, V.D. and Rajyalakshmi, D. Citation Analysis of Ph.D. Theses in Environmental Science and Engineering used by NEERI Scientists during 1977-1991. *Annals of Library Science and Documentation*, 41, 1994, pp. 63-78.

74. Sylvia, Margaret and Lesher, Marcella. What Journals do Psychology Graudate Students need? : A Citation Analysis of Thesis References. *College and Research Libraries*, 56, 1995, pp. 313-318.

75. Deo, V.N., Mohlal, S.M. and Suvey, S.S. Bibliometric Study of Doctoral Dissertations in English Language and Literature. *Annals of Library Science and Documentation*, 42(3), 1995, pp. 81-95

76. Mubeen, M.A. Citation Analysis of Doctoral Dissertations in Chemistry. *Annals of Library Science and Documentation*, 43, 1996, pp. 48-58.

77. Arjun Lal and Panda, K.C. Research in Plant Pathology : A Bibliometric Analysis. *Library Science*, 33(3), 1996, pp. 135-147.

78. Vimala, V. Bibliometric Study of Citations in Ph.D. Theses in Biological Sciences, Sri Venkateswara University, Ph.D. (Unpublished) 1997.

79. Biradar, B.S. and Vijayalakshmi, T. Pattern of Information Use by Indian Neurological Scientists – A Bibliometric Study. *Annals of Library Science and Documentation*, 44(4), 1997, pp. 143-151.

80. Biradar, B.S. and Premalatha, R. Bibliometric Study of Psychiatric (Alcholism) Literature. *IASLIC Bulletin*, 43(4), 1998, pp. 163-170.

81. Arjunlal and Panda, K.C. Bradford's Law and its Application to Bibliographic Data of Plant Pathology Dissertations : An Analytical Approach. *Library Science with Slant to Documentation and Information Studies*, 36(3), 1999, pp. 193-206.

82. Tapaswi, M.P. and Maheswarappa, B.S. Some Trends in Indian Oceanographic Research Publications (1963-1992). *Library Science with a Slant to Documentation and Information Studies*, 36(3), 1999, pp. 173-192.

83. Amit Kumar Bandyopadhyay. Authorship Pattern in Different Disciplines. *Annals of Library and Information Studies*, 48(4), 2001, pp. 139-147.

84. Amit Kumar Bandopadhyay and Amitava Nandi. Citation Analysis of References Used in Doctoral Dissertations in Political Science. *Herald of Library Science*, 40(3-4), 2001, pp. 192-201.

85. Hirwade, Mangala Anil and Dankhade, Seema Sanjay Kumar. Citation Analysis of Doctoral Research in Economics. *ILA Bulletin*, 38(2), 2002, pp. 36-45.

86. Biradar, B.S. and Thippeswamy, K. Information Use Pattern by Pediatricians : A Bibliometric Study. *SRELS Journal of Information Management*, 41(1), 2004, pp. 107-120.

87. Krishna, K.M. and Kumar, S. Authorship Trends in Agriculture Research: A Bibliometric Analysis. *SRELS Journal of Information Management*, 41(2), 2004, pp. 229-234.

88. Fussler, H.H. Characteristics of Research Literature used by Chemists and Physicists in the United States. *Library Quarterly*, 1949, 19, pp. 19-35.

89. Brown, C.H. Scientific Serials. Assocation of College and Research Libraries Monograph No. 16. Chicago Libraries, USA.

90. Burton, R.E. and Kebler, R.W. Half-life of some Scientific and Technical Literature. *American Documentation*, 11, 1960, pp. 18-22.

91. Raisig, L.M. Mathematical Evaluation of the Scientific Serials. *Science*, 131, 1960, pp. 1417-1419.

92. Kessler, M.M. Bibliographic Coupling between Scientific Papers. *American Documentation*, 14, 1963, pp. 10-11.

93. Brookes, B.C. The Growth, Utility and Obsolescence of Scientific Periodical Literature. *Journal of Documentation*, 26, 1970, pp. 283-294.

94. Chen, Ching-Chin. The Use Pattern of Physics Journals in Large Academic Research Library. *Journal of the American Society for Information Science*, 23, 1972, pp. 254-270.

95. Seymour, C.A. Weeding the Collection: A Review of Research on Identifying Obsolete Stock Part I: Monographs. *Libri*, 22, 1972, pp. 137-148.

96. Seymour, C.A. Weeding the Collection: A Review of Research on Identifying Obsolete Stock Part II: Serials. *Libri*, 1972, 1972, pp. 183-189.

97. Rangra, V.K. and others. Reporting of Indian Chemical Literature in Referativinyi Zhurnal – Khimiya. *Annals of Library Science and Documentation*, 19, 1972, p. 81-86.

98. Small, H.G. Co-Citation in the Scientific Literature : A New Measure of the Relationship between two Documents. *Journal of the American Society for Information Science*, 24, 1973, 265-269.

99. Line, M.B. and Sandison, A. *op. cit.*

100. Ravichandra Rao, I.K. Growth of Periodicals and Obsolescence of Articles in Periodicals: A Case Study in Sociology. *Library Science with a Slant to Documentation*, 11, 1974, pp. 92-96.

101. Grefrath, Richard W. A Study of Citations to 308 Journal Articles in Chemistry Published in 1963. *Journal of Chemical Documentation*, 14, 1974, pp. 95-98.

102. Sengupta, I.N. Choosing Pharamacology Periodicals: Study of the Growth of Literature in the Field. *Annals of Library Science and Documentation*, 21, 1974, pp. 1-21.

103. Longyear, R.M. Article Citations and Obsolescence in Musicological Journals. *Notes*, 33, 1977, pp. 563-571.

104. Tagliacozzo, R. Self-citations in Scientific Literature. *Journal of Documentation*, 33, 1977, pp. 251-265.

105. Gupta, R.C. and others. Maintenance of Periodicals Collection: A Statistical Case Study. *Annals of Library Science and Documentation*, 25, 1978, pp. 101-105.

106. Griffith, B.C. and others. The Ageing of Scientific Literature: A Citation Analysis. *Journal of Documentation*, 35, 1979, pp. 179-196.

107. Brown, P. The Half-life of Chemical Literature. Journal of the American Society for Information Science, 31, 1979, pp. 179-196.

108. Balog, C. Multiple Authorship and Author Collaboration in Agricultural Research Publications. *Journal of Research Communication Studies*, 2, 1980, pp. 159-168.

109. Gordon, M.D. A Critical Reassessment of Inferred Relations between Multiple Authorship, Scientific Collaboration, the Production of Papers and their Acceptance for Publication. *Scientometrics*, 2, 1980, pp. 193-201.

110. Dewitt, T.W. and others. Science Citation Index and Chemistry. *Scientometrics*, 2, 1980, pp. 265-275.

111. White, H.D. and Griffith, B.C. Author Co-citation : A Literature Measure of Intellectual Structure. *Journal of the Amercian Society for Information Science*, 32, 1981, pp. 163-171.

112. Anand, A.K. Analysis of Communication in Journal of the Indian Chemical Society. *IASLIC Bulletin*, 26, 1979, pp. 17-21.

113. Ayers, Jerry B. Journals and Conference Proceedings of Chemical History, Education and Documentation. *Journal of Chemical Information and Computer Sciences*, 21, 1981, pp. 71-72.

114. Nagappa, B. and Maheswarappa, B.S. Most Frequently Cited Journals by Indian Phytopathologists. *Journal of Library and Information Science*, 6, 1981, pp. 1-17.

115. Maheswarappa, B.S. Bibliographical Phenomena of Phytomorphology Literature : A Citation Analysis. *Annals of Library Science and Documentation*, 30, 1983, pp. 22-30.

116. Gupta, Davendra K. Periodical Literature of Exploration Geophysics: Obsolescence Factors and Patterns. *Library Science with a Slant to Documentation*, 21, 1984, pp. 205-226.

117. Kapoor, S.K. Citation Analysis of Earth Science Literature. Annals of Library Science and Documentation, 31, 1984, pp. 56-62.

118. Bottle, R.T. and Gong, Y.T. A Bibliometric Study on the Ageing and Content Typology Relationship of the Biochemical Literature. *Journal of Information Science*, 13, 1987, pp. 59-63.

119. Stinson, E.R. and Lancaster, R.W. Synchronous Versus Diachronous Methods in the Measurement of Obsolescence by Citation Studies. *Journal of Information Science*, 13, 1987, pp. 65-74.

120. Gupta, Davendra K. Bibliometric Study of AIDS Literature. *Annals of Library Science and Documentation*, 36, 1988, pp. 34-42.

121. Ijari, S.R. and Kannappanavar, B.U. Periodical Literature of Geology: A Citation Analysis to Determine Obsolescence Factors and Patterns. *Indian Journal of Information, Library and Society*, 14(1), 1989, pp. 77-84.

122. Musib, S.K. Subject Dispersion Studies in International Economics. *Annals of Library Science And Documentation*, 36, 1989, pp. 36-40.

123. Sengupta, I.N. The Growth of Knowledge and Literature in Neuroscience. *Scientometrics*, 17, 1989, pp. 253-288.

124. Moed, H.F. and Vriens, M. Possible Inaccuracies Occurring in Citation Analysis. *Journal of Information Science*, 15, 1989, pp. 95-107.

125. Gupta, Usha. Obsolescence of Physics Literature: Exponential Decrease of the density of Citations to Physical Review Articles with Age. *Journal of the American Society for Information Science*, 41, 1990, pp. 282-287.

126. Usha, Mujoo-Munshi and others. Citation Behaviour of Chemical Scientists : A Case Study. *ILA Bulletin*, 27, 1991, pp. 47-53.

127. Deo, V.N. Citation Study of the Marathwada University Journal – A Case Study of the Use Patterns by Scholars. *Annals of Library Science and Documentation*, 38(4), 1991, pp. 131-147.

128. Hurd, Julie M. Interdisciplinary Research in the Sciences : Implications for Library Organization. *College and Research Libraries*, 53, 1992, pp. 283-297.

129. Mahapatra, G and Kaul, R. Self-citation by Indian Botanists. *ILA Bulletin*, 27, 1992, p. 161-167.

130. Diodata, Virgil and Smith, Fran. Obsolescence of Music Literature. *Journal of the American Society for Information Science*, 44(2), 1993, pp. 101-112

131. Parvathamma, N., Gunjal, S.R. and Nijagunappa. Growth Pattern of Literature and Scientific Productivity of Authors in Indian Earth Science (1978-88): A Bibliometric Study. *Library Science with a Slant to Documentation*, 30(2), 1993, pp. 54-64.

132. Norris, R.P. Authorship Pattern in CJNR : 1970-1991. *Scientometrics*, 28, 1993, pp. 151-158.

133. Kalyane, V.L. Informetrics on NEEM Research in India. *Library Science with a Slant to Documentation and Information Studies*, 30(4), 1993, pp. 139-145.

134. Milman, B. L. and Y. A. Gavrilova (1993). "Analysis of Citation and Cocitation in Chemical-Engineering." *Scientometrics* 27(1): 53-74.

135. Rana, Madan S. and Sunita Agarwal. Authorship Trends in Indian Wildlife and Fisheries Literature – A Bibliometric Study. *Annals of Library Science and Documentation*, 41(1), 1994, pp. 13-18.

136. Mahapatra, Gayatri and Kaul, Rama. Bibliometric Analysis of Citation Classics Classics in Life Sciences. *Library Science with a Slant to Documentation and Information Studies*, 31(3), 1994, pp. 129-134.

137. Braun, T. and Others. World Science in Eighties: National Performance in Publication Output and Citation Impact. 1985-1989 versus 1980-1984. Part II: Life Sciences, Engineering and Mathematics. *Scientometrics*, 31, 1994, pp. 3-30.

138. Arora, Jagadish and Kaur, Sharan Pal. Bibliometric Analysis of Core Journals of Immunology : A Study based on the Annual Review of Immunology. *Annals of Library Science and Documentation*, 41(3), 1994,p p. 81-94.

139. Mubeen, M.A. Bibliographic Coupling: An Empirical Study of Economics. *Annals of Library Science and Documentation*, 42(2), 1995, pp. 41-53.

140. Damodaram, T., Rajasekhar and Devarai, S. Growth of Research in Oilseeds and Collaboration Trends : A Case Study. *Library Science*, 32(4), 1995, pp. 172-175.

141. Dalai, B.K. and Ramesh, D.B. Publication Pattern in Scientific and Industria Research in India – A Bibliometric Study. *Annals of Library Science and Documentation*, 42(1), 1995, pp. 35-38.

142. Suchitra Das and Seth, M.K. Citation Analysis in Hydrometallurgy : A Bibliometric Study. *CLIS Observer*, 12(3-4), 1995, pp. 10-16.

143. Sarala, K.R. A Bibliometric Analysis of the Journal of Tropical Agriculture. *Library Science with a Slant to Documentation and Information Studies*, 32(4), 1995, pp. 165-171.

144. Senapati, S.K. Studies in Conservation : A Bibliometric Study. *Library Science with a Slant to Documentation and Information Studies*, 32(2), 1995, pp. 75-79.

145. Kalyane, V.L. and Sen, B.K. A Bibliometric Study of the Journal of Oil Seeds Research. *Annals of Library Science and Documentation*, 42(4), 1995, pp. 121-141.

146. Haiqi, Z. The Relationship of Authors to Multi-authored Pharmacology Research Papers. *International Forum on Information and Documentation*, 21, 1996, pp. 10-23.

147. Kulkarni, M.K. Scientific Research on Yoga : A Bibliometric Study. IASLIC Bulletin, 41(3), 1996, pp. 127-130.

148. Kajberg, L. A Citation Analysis of LIS Serial Literature Published in Denmark 1957-1986. *Journal of Documentation*, 52, 1996, pp. 69-85.

149. Joshi, Anupam N. and Maheswarappa, B.S. Multiple Authorship Trends and Collaborative Research among Indian Phytopathologists. *Indian Journal of Information, Library and Society*, 10, 1997, pp. 31-40.

150. Jose, Mercy and Korah, Accamma C. A Bibliometric Study of the 'Bibliography on Natural Rubber Research' of the RRII and the Rubber Board. *Library Science with a Slant to Documentation and Information Studies*, 34(4), 1997, pp. 191-195.

151. O'Neill, G.P. Authorship Pattern in Theory Based Versus Research Based Journals. *Scientometrics*, 41, 1998, pp. 291-298.

152. Sornam and Gopi. AIDS Literature : A Citation Study. *International Information Communication and Education*, 17(1), 1998, pp. 37-41.

153. Tiew, Wai Sin. Journal of Natural Rubber Research 1987-1996 : A Ten Year Bibliometric Study. *IASLIC Bulletin*, 43(2), 1998, pp. 49-57.

154. Meera. Plant Ecology Literature : A Bibliometric Study. *International Information Communication and Education*, 17, 1998, pp. 41-59.

155. Patil, Y.M. and Kumar, P.S.G. Pedological Literature Analysis. *Library Science with a Slant to Documentation and Information Studies*, 35(2), 1998, pp. 125-132.

156. Halkar, Senapati, S.K. and Salek Chand. Journal of Family Welfare : A Bibliometric Study. *IASLIC Bulletin*, 43(2), 1998, pp. 89-94.

157. Kambar, Mallinath and Akhtary, Syeda. Bibliometric Analysis of Ophthalmology Literature. *Library Science with a Slant to Documentation and Information Studies*, 35(3), 1998, pp. 201-207.

158. Fernandez, J. A. (1998). "The transition from an individual science to a collective one: The case of astronomy." *Scientometrics* 42(1): 61-74.

159. Rana, M.S. and Sunita Agarwal. A Bibliometric Study on Application of Telemetry in Wildlife Science. *Library Science with a Slant to Documentation and Information Studies*, 36(1), 1999, pp. 43-47.

160. Ming – Yueh Tsay. Library Journal Use and Citation Age in Material Science. *Journal of Documentation*, 55(5), 1999, 543-555.

161. Mahapatra, G. and Das, Bhagwan. Impact of Research Collaboration on Growth of Literature in Geology : A Bibliometric Study. *SRELS Journal of Information Management*, 37(2), 2000, pp. 95-105.

162. Bahr, Alice Harrison and Zemon, Mickey. Collaborative Authorship in the Journal Literature : Perspectives for Academic Librarians Who Wish to Publish. *College and Research Libraries*, 61, 2000, pp. 410-419.

163. Dutta, Bidyarthi and Sen, B.K. Indian Journal of Pure and Applied Physics – An Analysis of Citation Pattern. *ILA Bulletin*, 36(3), 2000, pp. 65-68.

164. Arundhaty Das. Bibliometric Analysis of Publications in Plasma Physics. *IASLIC Bulletin*, 45(4), 2000, pp. 145-160.

165. Dhiman, A.K. Ethno botany Journal: A Bibliometric Study. *IASLIC Bulletin*, 45(4), 2000, pp. 177-182.

166. Kannappanavar, B.U. and Vijaykumar, M. Authorship Trend and Solo V/S Team Research in International Monetary Fund Literature; A Bibliometric Study. *Annals of Library and Information Studies*, 48(3), 2001, pp. 117-120.

167. Kannappanavar, B.U. and Vijayakumar, M. Periodical Literature of Plant and Cell Physiology: A Citation Analysis Study to Determine Obsolescence Factors and Patterns. *SRELS Journal of Information Management*, 38(1), 2001, pp. 81-90.

168. Dutta, Bidyarthi and Sen, B.K. Indian Journal of Pure and Applied Mathematics: An Analysis of Citation Pattern. *IASLIC Bulletin*, 46(4), 2001, pp. 221-226.

169. Das, Anup Kumar. Collaboration Pattern in Computer Science Research in India: A Study. *ILA Bulletin*, 37(4), 2001, pp. 143-150.

170. Dhiman, A.K. and Sinha, S.C. Impact of Research Collaboration on Growth of Literature in Ethnobotany : A Bibliometric Study. *SRELS Journal of Information Management*, 38(1), 2001, pp. 53-62.

171. Das, Anup Kumar and Sen, B.K. Indian Journal of Medical Research – An Analysis of Citation Pattern. *ILA Bulletin*, 37(1), 2001, pp. 9-12.

172. Das, Anup Kumar and Sen, B.K. Journal of Biosciences – An analysis of Citation Pattern. *Annals of Library and Information Studies*, 48(2), 2001, pp. 59-63.

173. Sinha, S.C. and Dhiman, A.K. Bibliometric Study of Dr. R.C. Sinha, A Plant Patholist. *Annals of Library and Information Studies*, 48(2), 2001, pp. 73-84.

174. Biradar, B.S., Anita, S. and Ushalatha, D.K. Periodicals Use Pattern by Medical Practitioners of Shimoga City. *Annals of Library and Information Studies*, 48(2), 2001, pp. 65-71.

175. Sahoo, Jyotshna. Conservation of Cultural Property in India: A Bibliometric Appraisal. *IASLIC Bulletin*, 46(4), 2001, pp. 202-208.

176. Barooah, P.K. and Sharma, N.N. A Bibliometric Study of Research Papers to Evaluate the Collection Development Program of Library. *Annals of Library and Information Studies*, 48(4), 2001, pp. 157-165.

177. Gupta, B.M. and Suresh Kumar. Citation Analysis of Theoretical Population Genetics Literature. *Library Herald*, 39(4), 2001, pp. 208-226.

178. Dutta, Bidyarthi and Sen, B.K. Indian Journal of Chemistry Section A : An analysis of Citation Pattern. *Annals of Library and Information Studies*, 48(3), 2001, pp. 121-127.

179. Udofia, Udofia Iton. Bibliometric Studies on African Trypanosomiasis Research Literature: A Review of Authorship Pattern.

180. Dutta, Bidyarthi, Das, Anup Kumar and Sen, B.K. A New Indicator Based on Journal Self-citation. *CLIS Observer*, 19(1-2), 2002, pp. 110-119.

181. Glanzel, Wolfgang. Coauthorship Patterns and Trends in Sciences (1980-1998) : A Bibliometric Study with Implications for Database Indexing and Search Strategies. *Library Trends*, 50(3), 2002, pp. 461-473.

182. Hazarika, Tilak, Goswami, Kusuma and Das, Pritimoni. Bibliometric Analysis of Indian Forester: 1991-2000. *IASLIC Bulletin*, 48(4), 2003, pp. 213-223.

183. Hasan, Nabi and Singh, Mukhtiar. Himachal Journal of Agricultural Research 1990-1999: A Bibliometric Study. *CLIS Observer*, 20(1-2), 2003, pp. 31-33.

184. Johry, Nutan. International Social Science Journal : A Bibliometric Study. *Library Herald*, 41(2), 2003, p. 99-108.

185. Shokeen, Ashu and Kaushik, Sanjay. Indian Journal of Economics. *Library Herald*, 41(2), 2003, pp. 109-114.

186. Kaushik, Sanjay K. Citation Pattern of Sociologist. *ILA Bulletin*, 39(4), 2003, pp. 30-33.

187. Ganapathi, Batthini and Ashok, Madnani. The Journal of Entrepreneurship: A Bibliometric Study. *ILA Bulletin*, 39(4), 2003, pp. 34-39.

188. Senthilkumaran, P. and Vadivel, V. SPICE India: A Bibliometric Study. *SRELS Journal of Information Management*, 40(4), 2003, pp. 431-438.

189. Nalini, J.K. Occupational Health Related Publications in India: A Bibliometric Analysis of Journals. *SRELS Journal of Information Management*, 40(1), 2003, pp. 41-50.

190. Kannappanavar, B.U. Chidananda Swamy and Vijaykumar. *Publishing Trends of Indian Chemical Scientists: A Bibliometric Study*, 51(1), pp. 39-41.

191. Praseeda, K.R. and Vasudevan, T.M. The University News: A Bibliometric Analysis. *ILA Bulletin*, 40(1), 2004, pp. 46-47.

192. Narang, Asha. Indian Journal of Pure and Applied Mathematics: A Bibliometric Study. *Annals of Library and Information Studies*, 51(1), 2004, pp. 28-38.

193. Shokeen, Ashu and Kaushik, Sanjay K. Indian Journal of Plant Physiology: A Citation Analysis. *Annals of Library and Information Studies*, 51(3), 2004, pp. 104-107.

194. Mahapatra, P.K. and Panda, K.C. Health Research Literature on Orrissa: A Bibliometric Analysis. *SRELS Journal of Information Management*, 41(4), 2004, p. 383-392.

195. Mahapatra, R.K. and Rudranarayan. Tribal Studies on Orissa: A Bibliometric Analysis. *ILA Bulletin*, 40(2), 2004, pp. 11-15.

196. Senthilkumaran, P. and Vadivel, V. Journal of Spices and Aromatic Crops : A Bibliometric Appraisal. *SRELS Journal of Information Management*, 41(1), 2004, pp. 121-131.

197. Price, Derek J de Solla. *Little Science, Big Science*. New York: Columbia University Press, 1963

198. Hawkins, Donald T. Electrochemistry Journals. *Journal of Chemical Information and Computer Sciences*, 17, 1977, p. 41-45.

199. Maheswarappa, B.S. and Others. Collaborative Research in Science and Technology in India: A Bibliometric Study. *Journal of Library and Information Science*, 9, 1984, 154-159.

200. Guay, Y. Emergence of Basic Research on the Periphery: Organic Chemistry in India 1907-1926. *Scientometrics*, 10. 1986, pp. 77-94.

201. Maheswarappa, B.S. and Mathias, S.A. Authorial Collaboration in Various Disciplines of the Physcial Sciences in India: A Bibliometric Study. *Journal of Library and Information Science*, 12, 1987, pp. 136-155.

202. Klaic, B. Scientometric Analysis of the Research Activists of Chemists from the "Rugier Boskovic" Institute (Yugoslavia), 1976-1985. *Scientometrics*, 19, 1990, pp. 11-24.

203. Sanjaya Mishra and Mishra, Manoj K. Collaborative Research in Medicinal and Aromatic Plants. *Library Herald*, 30(1), 1991, pp. 30-34.

204. Sharada, B.A. Multiple Authorship Pattern in Linguistics. *Library Science with a Slant to Documentation and Information Studies*, 28(3), 1991, pp. 96-99.

205. Gupta, D.K. Scientometric Study of Exploration Geophysics – Author Productivity Trends. *Annals of Library Science and Documentation*, 39(4), 1992, pp. 145-152.

206. Vaishnav, A.A. and Deo, V.N. Literature of Computerised Library and Information Services: A Bibliometric Study. *Library Science*, 30(2), 1993, pp. 45-53.

207. Ramakrishna, N.V. and Panganayya, N.B. Growth of Biotechnology Literature: A Bibliometric Study. *Library Science with a Slant to Documentation*, 5(1), 1999, pp. 25-37.

208. Suresh Kumar. Lotka's Law and Author Productivity in the Field of Computer Science in India. *Library Herald*, 41(2), 2003, pp. 90-97

209. Gupta, B.M. and Jha, A.K. S&T Collaboration of India with Far East Asian Countries: A Quantitative Study Using Co-authored Papers. *ILA Bulletin*, 40(1), 2004, pp. 14-27.

210. Clarke, B.L. Multiple Authorship Trends in Scientific Papers. *Science*, 143, 1964, pp. 822-824.

211. Zuckerman, Harriet A. Nobel Laureates in Science: Patterns of Productivity, Collaboration and Authorship. *American Sociological Review*, 32, 1967, pp. 391-403.

212. Beaver, D de B. and Rosen, R. Studies in Scientific Collaboration. Part I. The Professional Orgins of Scientific Coauthorship. *Scientometrics*, 1, 1978, pp. 65-84.

213. Beaver, D de B. and Rosen, R. Studies in Scientific Collaboration. Part II. Scientific Coauthorship, Research Productivity and Visibility in the French Scientific Elite. *Scientometrics*, 1, 1979, pp. 133-149.

214. Beaver D de B. and Rosen, R. Studies in Scientific Collaboration. Part III Professionalization and Natural History of Modern Scientific Coauthorship. *Scientometrics*, 1, 1979, pp. 231-245.

215. Heffner, A.G. Funded Research, Multiple Authorship and Subauthorship Collaboration in Four Disciplines. *Scientometrics*, 3, 1981, pp. 5-12.

216. Lawani, S.M. On the Heterogenity and Classification of Author Self Citation. *Journal of the American Society for Information Science*, 33,,1982, pp. 281-284.

217. Subramanyam, K. and Stephens, Elsie M. Research Collaboration and Funding in Biochemistry and Chemical Engineering. *International Forum on Information and Documentation*, 7, 1982, pp. 26-29.

218. Subramanyam, K. Bibliometric Studies of Research Collaboration: A Review. *Journal of Information Science*, 6, 1983, pp. 33-38.

219. Sridhar, M.S. Citation Pattern of Indian Space Technologists. *International Library Review*, 17, 1985, 259-274.

220. Snyder, Herbert W. and Bonzi, Susan. An Enquiry into the Behaviour of Author Self-citation. In: Proceedings of the 52nd Annual Meeting of the American Society for Information Science. New Jersey: Learned Information Inc., pp. 147-151.

221. Bozni, Susan and Snyder, Herbert W. Patterns of Self-Citation across Fields of Enquiry. In. Proceedings of the 53rd Annual Meeting of the American Society for Information Science. New Jersey: Learned Institution Inc., pp. 204-207.

222. Kalyane, V.L. and Vidyasagar Rao, K. Collaboration Trends in Sugarcane Research: A Case Study. *Annals of Library Science and Documentation*, 39, 1992, pp. 9-11.

223. Sharada, B.A. Bibliometric Studies in Linguistics and Bibliometric Laws. *Library Science*, 30(2), 1993, pp. 71-75.

224. Joshi, Anupam N. and Maheswarappa, B.S. Multiple Authorship Trends in Different Subjects of Science and Technology: A Review of Literature. *ILA Bulletin*, 30, 1994, pp. 31-37.

225. Sudhier, K.G. Output of Scientific Research in Kerala: A Bibliometric Analysis. *Annals of Library Science and Documentation*, 44(4), 1997, pp. 113-126.

226. Gupta, B.M. Analysis of Distribution of the Age of Citations in Theoretical Population Genetics. *Scientometrics*, 40, 1997, pp. 139-162.

227. Kulkarni. Bibliometrical Portrait of a Scientist Working on Yoga: A Bibliometric Study. *IASLIC Bulletin*, 42(4), 1997, pp. 184-188.

228. Kalyane, V.L., Prakasan, E.R. and Vijaikumar. Scientometric Portrait of Ranjit Kumar Mitra. *ILA Bulletin*, 37(2), 2001, pp. 39-53.

229. Shukla, M.C., Saksena, S. and Riswadkar, M.R. Application of Bradford's and Lotka's Distribution to Bio-energy Literature: A Study based on Ten Abstracting Services. *Annals of Library and Information Studies*, 48(1), 2001, pp. 1-30.

3

Methodology

Bibliometrics is an emerging thrust area of research in the field of Library and Information Science. Bibliometrics can be traced back to early twentieth century and it is widely accepted term, but so too are terms such as Scientometrics, Informetrics and Librametrics. It can be defined as the study and measurement of the publication patterns of all forms of written communication and their authorship[1]. Today the importance of concept "Bibliometrics" has been widely recognized in the field of Library and information science and a number of studies have been conducted around the world in view of the practical applications.

The rising cost of periodicals, decreasing credit of Indian rupee abroad and shrinking fund position of the libraries have posed a serious threat before the librarian/ documentalist/ library administrator to acquire all the published materials in the field. Therefore, to streamline the acquisition policy of the library and to satisfy the majority of researchers to a maximum extent, an attempt is made to find a list of core journals in the field which is possible with the help of Bibliometric studies. Bibliometric techniques are also applied to identify the research trends and growth of knowledge in different disciplines, to identify authorship trends, to study obsolescence and dispersion of scientific literature, to predict productivity of publishers, to study the patter of scatter of literature on a subject in different periodicals, to develop and measure information and knowledge transfer.

Therefore Bibliometrics can be applied in many fields such as selection of books and periodicals, features of subject literature, evaluation of collection and bibliographies, historical and sociological studies.

71 Doctoral Dissertations submitted in the field of Library and information science during the period 1982-2004 to the four universities in Andhra Pradesh namely, Andhra University, Sri Venkateswara University, Osmania University and Sri Krishna Devaraya University has been the input for the present study. The citations appended to theses have been analysed to draw conclusions and inferences.

Table 3.1
Distribution of Theses in Library and Information Science and Its Subdisciplines

Sub-disciplines in Library and Information Science	*No. of Theses*	*No. of citations appended*	*Average no. of citations*
1	*2*	*3*	*4*
Agriculture Information, Libraries, Users and Services	3	538	179.33
Bibliometrics	5	1392	278.40
College Libraries, Users and Services	6	758	126.33
Libraries and I.T	4	780	195.00

(Contd...)

1	*2*	*3*	*4*
Marketing of Library Information Services and Products	2	448	224.00
Medical Information, Libraries, Users and Services	4	854	213.50
Other Aspects	11	2239	203.55
Other Libraries, Users and Services	4	756	189.00
Public Libraries and Community Information Services	8	1178	147.25
Scientific and Technical Libraries	7	1508	215.43

Out of 71 Theses submitted in the field of Library and information science and its sub-disciplines, University libraries, users and services with 17 theses stood in the first place followed by Other aspects which comprise of document delivery services, technical services, grey literature, reading habits, library thefts and mutilation, Library and Information Science education and library resources with 11 theses, Public libraries and community information services with 8 theses occupied third place followed by Scientific and technical libraries and College libraries, users and services with 7 and 6 theses respectively. For the purpose of present study, Legal Libraries, Government libraries, Museum libraries and Social sciences and Humanities libraries are categorised as Other Libraries.

Table 3.2
Period-wise Distribution of Theses

Period	*A.U*	*O.U*	*S.V*	*S.K*	*Total*
1982-86	3	0	0	0	3
R%	100.00	0.00	0.00	0.00	100.00
C%	7.89	0.00	0.00	0.00	4.43
1987-91	3	0	3	0	6
R%	50.00	0.00	50.00	0.00	100.00
C%	7.89	0.00	17.65	0.00	8.45
1992-96	15	3	3	0	21
R%	71.43	14.29	14.29	0.00	100.00
C%	39.47	27.27	17.65	0.00	29.58
997-2001	11	7	9	2	29
R%	37.93	24.14	31.03	6.90	100.00
C%	28.95	63.64	52.94	40.00	40.85
2002 Onwards	6	1	2	3	12
R%	50.00	8.33	16.67	25.00	100.00
C%	15.79	9.09	11.76	60.00	16.90
Total	38	11	17	5	71
R%	53.52	15.49	23.94	7.04	100.00
C%	100.00	100.00	100.00	10.00	100.00

Research in Library and Information Science was first initiated by Department of Library and Information Science, Andhra University and first theses was submitted in the year 1982. Later other universities have also followed the suit. Period-wise analysis of theses shows the most productive period of each university in terms of number of theses awarded in a particular period. Total period (1982-2004) has been divided into five classes. Table 3.2 shows period-wise distribution of theses in Library and information science awarded by different universities of Andhra Pradesh.

It may be observed from the above table that 41% of the theses were awarded during 1997-2001. From the year of introducing the Ph. D Programme in Library and information science by the university departments an increasing trend has been noticed.

University-wise distribution of theses also reveals clear domination of Andhra University by contributing to more than half of the total number of theses produced by all the four university departments in Library and information science. Andhra University also stood first in the list as the first university to award the first Ph. D degree during 1982-1986. Sri Venkateswara University stood in the second place with 24 percent of the total contributions of theses in the Library and information science field. Though the first thesis in department of Sri Venkateswara University has been awarded five years behind Andhra University, a steady growth in the number of theses awarded can be observed.

Objectives of the Study

a) To identify the different forms of literature used by LIS researchers or scientists.

b) Determine average number of references per dissertation.

c) The distribution of citations according to subject, language and country of origin has to be derived

d) Observe authorship pattern in the field of Library and information science

e) To study the self-citation behaviour of researchers in library and information science

f) Compile a ranked list of journals and books

g) Determine the half-life and obsolescence of the journal literature and productivity of journals

h) The researchers use pattern of journals in the field of LIS has to be examined by applying Bradford's law of scattering

i) Growth of knowledge and research trends in the field of LIS are to be studied

Need for The Study

In the recent times, the subject Library and information science has made rapid progress and has witnessed an enhanced research tempo and unprecedented growth of literature. The origin of new specializations due to the inter-disciplinary nature of subject has led to information explosion which posed serious threat to research in the field as well as to library professionals to cope up with the latest literature being produced in the discipline.

In order to withstand in these challenging situations, the librarians are required to adopt accurate acquisition policies within the limited budgetary provision and at the same time without affecting the requirements of the patrons. The characteristics of the literature have to be critically and carefully examined in order to meet the two objectives. Compiling core journals and books in any discipline through citation analysis is useful in building a organized collection to meet the requirements of the users, This policy will also assist in optimum use of collection in the library which confirms with the laws of library science propounded by Dr. S.R. Ranganathan, the father of library and information science in India.

A study of this nature in the field of Library and information science has not been undertaken in four universities i.e. Andhra University, Sri Venkateswara University, Osmania University and Sri Krishna Devaraya University to identify the core literature in any discipline and especially in the field of Library and information science. The University libraries have been spending crores of rupees on journals and in view of rising costs of periodicals it is necessary to take a intelligent decision on the part of the librarian / library administrator / documentalist to build a need-based acquisition of journals which satisfies both the budget limitations as well as the requirements of the users especially research scholars. The present study provides an insight into characteristics of literature used by the researchers in the field of Library and information science.

Methodology

The total population for the present study is citations appended to Doctoral dissertations in Library and information science and its sub-disciplines submitted to four universities in Andhra Pradesh i.e. Andhra University, Sri Venkateswara University, Osmania University and Sri Krishna Devaraya University till the end of 2004. This enables the researcher to derive the results and compare them, and also have better idea of the literature use pattern in different sub-disciplines of Library and information science.

Collection and Analysis of Data

The references appended to 71 theses submitted to four universities during the period 1982-2004 are collected for the purpose of citation analysis. All the references which are cited at the end of chapter and footnotes are taken into consideration for the study. A database covering all the theses and citations has been created with details of the citations using MS-Excel and later the data was converted to FOXPRO in order to draw tables, calculations

Part A: Citation Analysis

Part B: Validation of Hypothesis

Distribution of Citations

When we have closer look at the citations appeared in 71 theses which is the scope of study, we can identify different forms of literature used by researchers in the field of Library and information science.

The list of bibliographic forms are as follows:

a) Journals
b) Books
c) Editorial Works
d) Conference Proceedings
e) Reports
f) Reference Books
g) Theses
h) Newspapers
i) Dissertations
j) Unpublished
k) Acts
l) Bills
m) Standards

Analysis of citations appended to theses in LIS is done according to subject, country of origin and language. In order to identify the predominant medium of scientific communication, language wise distribution of citations has been presented in the study.

Multiple Authorship and Collaborative Research

Multiple authorship indicates development of a subject and a tendency of inter-institutional and inter disciplinary study. According to Arora and Pawan[2] increase in multiple authorship and collaboration between researchers is an indication of growing professionalism in different fields. For understanding the nature of authorship pattern journals and book citations have been grouped into five and ten year intervals. For each of the intervals (i.e. 5 years and 10 years) as well as for the total period the number of authors i.e. single or multiple are calculated.

The statistical techniques employed to study the trends in authorship pattern are:

Chi-Square Test

Line Diagrams

Curve Fitting.

Citations appeared in 71 theses submitted to four universities during the period 1983-2004 have been grouped into four groups with ten years interval excluding the first group which represents all the citations. For each of the intervals citations with single, two, three and more authors were calculated. Each interval is called reference period for the purpose of comparison and statistical analysis. On the basis of two dimensions i.e. reference period and number of authors the total citations are tabulated. Chi-Square test (1986) has been applied to find out significant relationship between number of authors and reference period.

On the X-axis, the values of percentage of citations and on Y-axis, reference period are plotted with single author, two authors, three and more authors for the purpose of drawing line diagrams.

The number of authors are added and divided by number of papers for each interval and whole period for calculating the author/article ratio or average number of authors per paper. A formula has been devised by Subramanyam(1983)[3] for deriving the degree of collaboration.

$$C = \frac{N_m}{N_m + N_s}$$

Where C = Degree of Collaboration in a discipline

N_m = Number of multi-authored papers

N_s = Number of single authored research papers

Self-Citations

There has developed a trend of citing own papers in a research article. Mostly, the persons who are from scientific fields cite their own papers more frequently whether they are relevant or not to the present study. Citing one's own earlier papers is known as Self-citation. Like other fields, there has started self-citation practice in the field of Library and information science.

In view of growing importance of self-citations, it is important to study the characteristics of self-citations. Two types of self-citations are computed in the present study. They are defined below:

- *Self-Citations of Type I*: The citation of a document which has been authored or co-authored by the researcher
- *Self-Citation of Type II*: The citation of a document which has been authored or co-authored by the research director

In order to identify the characteristics of self-citations two methods are employed. In the first method the ratio of self-citations to total number of citations which are appended to 71 theses is calculated in order to compute the percentage of self-citations. The ratio of number of theses containing at least one or more self-citations to the total number of theses in sample is calculated in order to find out the self-citation rate. In addition to these, the dispersion of self-citations among different bibliographic forms and the frequency citation of the age difference between the self-citations to journal articles and citing theses is also studied.

Ranking and Scattering of Cited Journals

Under this section we examine the ranked list of journals, productivity of cited journals, the relevance of Bradford's law of scattering, the distribution of cited journals among different countries and languages.

Ranked List of Cited Journals

The Compiled ranked list of journals can be utilised by librarians and research workers to select the journals of greater importance and productivity in the particular discipline and thereby overcome the budgetary constraints which is posing serious threat to librarians. The journals are arranged in terms of number of citations received by each individual journal and hence the highest rank will be occupied by journal with maximum number of citations to its credit followed by other journals.

The total number of journals observed in the present study are 773 and number of citations to journals comes to 7925.

Productivity of Journals

All the journal citations appended to sample has been bifurcated into four groups in such a manner that all the four groups contained approximately equal number of citations in order to measure the productivity of journals. The number of journals contributing the related citations in each group was computed. By dividing the number of citations in each group by the number of journals in that group, the average rate of productivity of journals is computed.

Application of Bradford's Law

Bradford law of scattering describes how the literature on a particular subject is scattered or distributed in the journals. The law is based on an investigation performed in 1933 by L. Jones in the Science Museum Library, London. It was first reported in 1934 in the Journal "Engineering" by Bradford and subsequently in a book entitled "Documentation" by the same author in 1948[4]. Bradford formulated his law as follows

"If scientific journals are arranged in order of decreasing productivity of articles on a given subject, they may be divided into a nucleus of periodicals more particularly devoted to the subject and several groups or zones containing the same articles as the nucleus, when the number of periodicals in the nucleus and succeeding zones will be as $1{:}n{:}n^2$

The application of Bradford's law to the present data is tested by plotting the logarithm of the cumulative number of journals on the X-axis and the cumulative number of articles on the Y-axis.

Bradford's Law applicability to the present citation data has been tested by using Leimkuhler's law (1990)[5]. After all the journals on a specific subject are arranged in decreasing order of productivity, if the journals are grouped into P groups such that each group contains the same number of citations (say Y_0), then ro, rok^2, rok^3, ... rok^{p-1} would be the number of citations in each group; (K>1). Denoting N; as the number of journals in the jth group (j=1 .... P)

Total number of journals $T = \sum_{j=1}^{P} Nj = ro\,(1+K+K^2.K^{p-1})$

$$ro = T(K-1)/.K^{p-1}$$

where k is degree of concentration;

ro = the number of journals in the first group where these

journals contain the maximum number of citations.

And total number of citations A = Yop (P is the number of groups)

According to Egghe and Rossueau (1990)[6] the degree of concentration K, can be calculated using the formula

$K = (C^y\,Ym)^{1/p}$ where Y=0.5772, Euler's number = $(1.781\ Ym)^{1/p}$ (2)

Where Ym is the number of citations contained in the 1st journal of the 1st group.

The value of K i.e. degree of concentration can be calculated by substituting the values of ym and p in the equation 2.

The number of journals in the first group can be identified by substituting values of K in equation (1)

Now the number of journals in the subsequent groups can be found using the values of k i.e.

rok = The number of journals in the second group

rok^2 = The number of journals in third group

rok^3 = The number of journals in fourth group and so on

The estimated number of citations in each group is derived on the basis of number of journals in each group. In order to identify the number of citations that should be present in each group, the ratio of total number of citations to total number of groups should be calculated. The total citations are divided into 3,4,5,6,7,8,9 and 10 groups respectively for applying the chi-square test of goodness of fit to the number of citations that should be present in each group and estimated number of citations in each group. With a view to calculate the number of journals in each group, the number of citations that should actually be present in each group, the estimated number of citations in each group, degree of concentration, chi-square values for different values of P (no. of groups) the researcher has developed Visual Basic program. However the decimal values in the computed value of the number of journals is not considered in the calculation of estimated citations.

Country-wise Distribution of Cited Journals

The journal citations are analysed according to country

of origin and countries that are contributing less than 0.5 percent of the total citations are grouped as "Others" category in order to lessen the lengthy list.

Language-wise Distribution of Cited Journals

In order to find out the predominant medium of scientific communication, the citations are analysed according to language of publication of cited journals.

Obsolescence of Literature

The term obsolescence frequently occurs in the literature of bibliometrics and citation analysis studies. Analysis of citations by the age of cited documents indicates the useful life of documents. Obsolescence is defined as the "decline over time in validity or utility of information (Line and Sandison, 1974)[7]. In the present study the source publications i.e. 71 theses of four universities in Andhra Pradesh does not share the common publication year we have to opt for multi-synchronous approach instead of synchronous where the source documents will have the same year of publication. The citation age is computed by comparing the date of publication of source document to the date of publication of the document cited by the author of the source publication. In the present study, the citation age is calculated by comparing the publication date of each cited document to the year of submission of citing theses.

To find out the half-life of the journal literature, the graph was plotted by taking period on the X-axis and the cumulative number of citations of the journals on the Y-axis. The maximum number of citations on Y-axis cuts at point 'P'. Half number of citations meet at point 'D' on Y-axis. A line drawn from point 'D' parallel to X-axis cuts the curved graph at 'B'. Again another line drawn from point 'B' parallel to Y-axis meets the X-axis at point 'C'. Distance from point 'D' to 'C' is the half-life of the total literature.

Availability of Cited Journal Literature and Books

The journal citation data in the present study has been compared with the database of the Andhra University, Sri Venkateswara University, Osmania University and Sri Krishna Devaraya University library in order to find out the percentage of availability of cited journals and books for Library and information Science and its sub-disciplines.

In-house Evaluation and Availability

Strohl's (1999)[8] definition of citation checking is also our point for the current study: "a sample of citations from text book, bibliographies, journal articles, student dissertations or other sources are checked against holdings to see what proportion is owned".

One type of in-house evaluation often used by librarian to assist insight on emerging and obsolescent research areas. Citation analysis is an excellent unobtrusive method to determine which resources doctoral students are using (Buttlar 1999)[9]. According to Buchanan and Herubel (1994)[10], "regular in-house collection evaluation enhances the management of collections in any research library's public service and collection development efforts for short and long term objectives". One of these researchers asserted that citation analysis was useful in determining current and future use of journals in their library.

Hypotheses

1. Hypothesis – 1

   Journals are important bibliographic form for the means of communication.

2. Hypothesis – 2

   The literature of library and information science is scattered over wide range of subjects

3. Hypothesis – 3

   Most of literature in Library and information science is published in English

4. Hypothesis – 4

   Developed countries are major producers of literature in the field of library and information science

5. Hypothesis – 5

   Collaborative research is more prevalent than Individual research in Library and information science

6. Hypothesis – 6

   Self-citation is a common phenomenon among the researchers in the field of library and information science

7. Hypothesis – 7

   In the discipline of library and information science, positive relation exists between period of the research and the number of total citations.

8. Hypothesis – 8

   The citations relating to journal literature in library and information science conforms to Bradford's law of scattering.

9. Hypothesis – 9

   The researchers in Library and information science generally utilize current information for their information requirements

10. Hypothesis – 10

    There is positive relation between the number of citations with multiple authors and period

11. Hypothesis – 11

    The citation behaviour of the scientists in the discipline of library and information science is generally influenced by place of publication

12. Hypothesis – 12

    The research activity in Library and information science is well augmented by University library.

Limitations of the Study

In the present study an effort has been made to identify the different aspects of literature use pattern by the researchers in the field of Library and Information Science. However due to time constraints and difficulties involved in personally interacting the research directors and researchers, the citation behaviour pattern of the researchers could not be included in the scope of the present study.

Bibliographic coupling could not be undertaken due to irregular and incomplete information especially in terms of author names in the cited data.

A comparative study between the ranked lists of journals ascertained from the study and cited journals in standard citation indexes could not be done due to non-availability of standard lists like science citation index to the researchers.

Due to lack of time the sample is limited only to theses awarded in Department of Library and Information Science of Andhra University, Sri Venkateswara University, Osmania University and Sri Krishna Devaraya University.

Bibliographic study of the researcher's publications such as journal articles, books, conference proceedings and patents would also be useful for understanding and measuring literature use and research output of the researcher but due to paucity of time, the study has not covered other sources like researchers publications.

Chapterization

Chapter I covers a brief introduction about the origin and development of bibliometrics, laws of bibliometrcs propounded by great library scientists and comparasion of the concept with related topics like Informetrics, Scientometrics, Cybermetrics and Webometrics. It also explains the practical applications of bibliometric studies in the field of library and information science.

Chapter II deals with various studies on bibliometrics and its related concepts conducted by Indian and foreign authors have been discussed

Chapter III envisages the scope, purpose and the methodology followed in order to achieve the objectives that were defined for the present study. A list of hypothesis is also formulated and its validity is tested with the findings of the study.

Chapter IV depicts the tabular presentation of the various aspects of the citation data.

Chapter V deals with the basis of analysis of the data, the summary and discussion of the findings is made. These discussions are made keeping in mind the results of the earlier studies, objectives and hypothesis formulated for various angles of research activity in Library and information science and their impact on collection development in Libraries and services to patrons. This chapter also covers the suggestions offered by the researcher.

This chapter covers the scope, purpose and methodology followed in order to accomplish the objectives defined for the present study. It also includes hypotheses formulated which are tested with the findings of the study, limitations of the study, and chapterisation.

REFERENCES

1. Levin, Richard I. *Statistics for Management*, New Delhi: Prentice-Hall of India, 1986.
2. Arora, Jagdish and Pawan, Usha. Collaborative research and authorship patterns in immunology: Correlation between multiple authorship and citedness. *IASLIC Bulletin*, 40(2), 73- 83, 1995.
3. Subramanyam, K. Bibliometric Studies of Research Collaboration: A Review, *Journal of Information Science*, 6, 1983, pp. 33-38.
4. Bradford, S.C. *Documentation*. London: Lockwood, 1948, p. 116.
5. Egghe, L. Application of the Theory of Bradford's Law to the Calculation of Leimkuhler's Law to the Compilation of Bibliographies. *Journal of the American Society for Information Science*, 41(7), 1990, pp. 469-492.
6. Egghe, L. and Rossueau. *Introduction to Informetrics*. Amsterdam: Elsevier, 1990.
7. Line, M.B. and Sandison, A. Obsolescence and Changes in the use of Literature with time. *Journal of Documentation*, 30, 1974, pp. 283-325.
8. Strohl, B. *Collection Evaluation Techniques: a short, selective, practical, current, annotated bibliography, 1990-1998*. Chicago: Reference and User Services Association, American Library Association, 1999.
9. Buttlar, L. Information Source in Library and Information Science Doctoral Research. *Library and Information Science Research*, 21(2), 1999, pp. 227-245.
10. Buchanan, A.L. and Herubel, J.P.V.M. Profiling Ph.D. Dissertation Bibliographies: Serials and Collection Development in Political Science, Behavioural and Social Sciences. *Librarian*, 13(1), 1994, pp. 1-10.

4

Citation Analysis

Citation analysis is one of the most commonly used forms of bibliometric studies. It makes use of bibliographic references which are essential part of the primary scientific communication. The technique of citation analysis involves the process of collection, counting, analysis and interpretation of citations given in various types of literature. Analysis of such references can reveal the relative use of different kinds of documents, age of used documents, most frequently used items, preferences of country and language, authorship pattern and scattering of literature. It is often used for journal ranking and also for evaluation of individuals and departments. Studies of this nature helps the librarian/ Documentalist/library administrator to solve problems regarding collection management which in view of rising cost of periodicals and shrinking fund position have been posing serious threat to present day library administrators. Similarly other crucial problems like space management, budget management can be solved with the help of these studies.

The input for the present study are citations appended to 71 theses submitted to four universities in Andhra Pradesh namely, Andhra University, Sri Venkateswara University,

Osmania University and Sri Krishna Devaraya University and data has been analysed keeping in view the objectives defined and hypothesis formulated by the researcher under the guidance of the research director. The results are critically examined in order to find out whether they confirm with the specified objectives and hypothesis formulated.

The citation details are presented in the form of tables for the purpose of analysis. Using different headings the data is analysed and presented.

Bibliometrics has established itself as a viable and distinctive research technique for studying science of science based on citation data. Citation analysis is one of the most important bibliometric techniques involving analysis of the references forming part of primary communication. Citations are the formal explicit linkages between publications that have particular points in common.

Distribution of Citations

The distribution of citations has been critically examined on their bibliographic form, subject, language and country of origin.

Bibliographic form-wise distribution of citations in LIS

The citations appended to 71 theses have been analysed to categorise the various sources of information used by researchers. The analysis revealed 12 bibliographic forms which are clearly explained in the tables to follow. The distribution of citations among different bibliographic forms in Library and Information Science is presented in the following table.

TABLE – 4.1
BIBLIOGRAPHIC FORM-WISE DISTRIBUTION OF CITATIONS IN LIBRARY AND INFORMATION SCIENCE

Sl. No.	*Form of Document*	*Number*	*Percentage*	*Cumulative Number*	*Cumulative Percentage*
1.	Journals	7925	57.59	7925	57.59
2.	Books	2863	20.81	10788	78.40
3.	Editorial Works	909	6.61	11697	85.00
4.	Conference Proceedings	629	4.57	12326	89.57
5.	Reports	597	4.34	12923	93.91
6.	Reference Books	446	3.24	13369	97.15
7.	Thesis	152	1.10	13521	98.26
8.	Others	240	1.74	13761	100.00

It is observed from the above table that Journals are most preferred bibliographic form for researchers with 7925 (57.59%) citations followed by Books with 2863 (20.81%) and Editorial Works with 909 (6.61%) citations.

While Journals account for (57.59%) of the total citations the other forms comes to (42.41%) which indicates the importance of Journals for research scholars. They report original research works and are considered as primary sources of information.

Citations to bibliographic forms accounting for less than one percent (1%) are grouped under others category. This category includes Newspapers, Ephemeral material, Dissertations, Unpublished, Acts, Bills and Standards. This category constitutes only 1.74 percent of the total citations cited by the researchers in the field of Library and information science.

TABLE – 4.2
BIBLIOGRAPHIC FORM-WISE DISTRIBUTION OF CITATIONS IN AGRICULTURE INFORMATION, LIBRARIES, USERS AND SERVICES

Sl. No.	*Form of Document*	*Number*	*Percentage*	*Cumulative Number*	*Cumulative Percentage*
1.	Journals	399	74.16	399	74.16
2.	Books	57	10.59	456	84.76
3.	Conference Proceedings	30	5.58	486	90.33
4.	Editorial Works	13	2.42	499	92.75
5.	Reports	13	2.42	512	95.17
6.	Reference Books	11	2.04	523	97.21
7.	Thesis	9	1.67	532	98.88
8.	Others	6	1.12	538	100.00

Bibliographic form wise distribution of citations in Agriculture Information, Libraries, Users and Services indicates that Journal is most cited form with 399 (74.16%) followed by Books (10.59%). However third preference is given to Conference Proceedings with (5.58%) citations.

Others category represents 1.12 percent of the total citations consisting of Newspapers, Unpublished, Dissertations and Ephemeral material.

TABLE – 4.3
BIBLIOGRAPHIC FORM-WISE DISTRIBUTION OF CITATIONS IN BIBLIOMETRICS

Sl. No.	*Form of Document*	*Number*	*Percentage*	*Cumulative Number*	*Cumulative Percentage*
1.	Journals	1131	81.25	1131	81.25
2.	Books	139	9.99	1270	91.24
3.	Reference Books	39	2.80	1309	94.04
4.	Conference Proceedings	31	2.23	1340	96.26
5.	Thesis	23	1.65	1363	97.92
6.	Editorial Works	15	1.08	1378	98.99
7.	Others	14	1.01	1392	100.00

Results of the above table gives a clear picture that majority of citations cited by researchers in Bibliometrics subject are Journals comprising (81.25%). Books with (9.99%) and Reference Books with (2.80%) occupy second and third places respectively.

Documents under others category include Reports, Unpublished materials, Dissertations and Ephemeral material.

TABLE – 4.4
BIBLIOGRAPHIC FORM-WISE DISTRIBUTION OF CITATIONS IN COLLEGE LIBRARIES, USERS AND SERVICES

Sl. No.	*Form of Document*	*Number*	*Percentage*	*Cumulative Number*	*Cumulative Percentage*
1.	Journals	447	58.97	447	58.97
2.	Books	141	18.60	588	77.57
3.	Reports	76	10.03	664	87.60
4.	Editorial Works	53	6.99	717	94.59
5.	Newspapers	15	1.98	732	96.57
6.	Reference Books	11	1.45	743	98.02
7.	Others	15	1.98	758	100.00

It is observed from the above table that Journals with 447 (58.97%) citations occupy the first place followed by Books with 141 (18.60%) citations and Reports with 76 (10.03%) citations.

The analysis of data on the preference for different bibliographic forms or category of documents exercised by the researchers in the area of College libraries, users and services also indicates the importance of report literature published by government and other agencies.

Others category include Conference proceedings, Thesis, Ephemeral material, Dissertations and Unpublished material constituting only 1.98 percent of the total citations.

TABLE – 4.5
BIBLIOGRAPHIC FORM-WISE DISTRIBUTION OF CITATIONS IN LIBRARIES AND I.T

Sl. No.	*Form of Document*	*Number*	*Percentage*	*Cumulative Number*	*Cumulative Percentage*
1.	Journals	358	45.90	358	45.90
2.	Books	219	28.08	577	73.97
3.	Editorial Works	71	9.10	648	83.08
4.	Reports	44	5.64	692	88.72
5.	Conference Proceedings	40	5.13	732	93.85
6.	Reference Books	21	2.69	753	96.54
7.	Ephemeral Material	11	1.41	764	97.95
8.	Thesis	10	1.28	774	99.23
9.	Others	6	0.77	780	100.00

The analysis of the table reveal that among the subject Libraries and I.T, Journals are most frequently cited form with 358 (45.90%) citations followed by Books 219 (28.08%) citations and Editorial Works with 71 (9.10%) citations.

Citations to Dissertations and Newspapers are included in others category.

TABLE – 4.6
BIBLIOGRAPHIC FORM-WISE DISTRIBUTION OF CITATIONS IN MARKETING OF LIBRARY INFORMATION SERVICES AND PRODUCTS

Sl. No.	*Form of Document*	*Number*	*Percentage*	*Cumulative Number*	*Cumulative Percentage*
1.	Journals	263	58.71	263	58.71
2.	Books	74	16.52	337	75.22
3.	Editorial Works	56	12.50	393	87.72
4.	Conference Proceedings	27	6.03	420	93.75
5.	Reference Books	27	6.03	447	99.78
6.	Reports	1	0.22	448	100.00

The bibliographic form wise distribution of citations in Marketing of Library and Information Services and Products represented the same trend as in the case of other sub-disciplines. The articles published in Journals accounted for 263 (58.71%).

TABLE – 4.7
BIBLIOGRAPHIC FORM-WISE DISTRIBUTION OF CITATIONS IN MEDICAL INFORMATION, LIBRARIES, USERS AND SERVICES

Sl. No.	*Form of Document*	*Number*	*Percentage*	*Cumulative Number*	*Cumulative Percentage*
1.	Journals	510	59.72	510	59.72
2.	Books	137	16.04	647	75.76
3.	Conference Proceedings	61	7.14	708	82.90
4.	Reference Books	51	5.97	759	88.88
5.	Reports	46	5.39	805	94.26
6.	Editorial Works	38	4.45	843	98.71
7.	Others	11	1.28	854	100.00

Table shows the distribution of citations among different documentary forms such as Journals, Books, Conference Proceedings, Reference Books etc in Medical Information, Libraries, Users and Services. It may be observed that 510 (59.72%) are citations to Journals; 137 (16.04%) are citations to Books; and 61 (7.14%) are citations to Conference Proceedings.

Others category (1.29%) covers Thesis, Ephemeral material and Newspapers.

Analysis of data in table gives a clear picture that majority of citations are Journals with 1278 (57.08%) citations followed by Books with 448 (20.01%) and Editorial Works with 155 (6.92%) citations.

Others category comprises of Theses, Dissertations, Newspapers, Unpublished and Ephemeral material accounting for 2.01 percent of the total citations.

TABLE – 4.8
BIBLIOGRAPHIC FORM-WISE DISTRIBUTION OF CITATIONS IN OTHER ASPECTS

Sl. No.	*Form of Document*	*Number*	*Percentage*	*Cumulative Number*	*Cumulative Percentage*
1.	Journals	1278	57.08	1278	57.08
2.	Books	448	20.01	1726	77.09
3.	Editorial Works	155	6.92	1881	84.01
4.	Conference Proceedings	148	6.61	2029	90.62
5.	Reports	87	3.89	2126	94.51
6.	Reference Books	78	3.48	2194	97.99
7.	Others	45	2.00	2239	100.00

TABLE – 4.9
BIBLIOGRAPHIC FORM-WISE DISTRIBUTION OF CITATIONS IN OTHER LIBRARIES, USERS AND SERVICES

Sl. No.	*Form of Document*	*Number*	*Percentage*	*Cumulative Number*	*Cumulative Percentage*
1.	Journals	420	55.56	420	55.56
2.	Books	122	16.14	542	71.69
3.	Editorial Works	77	10.19	619	81.88
4.	Conference Proceedings	72	9.52	691	91.40
5.	Reports	39	5.16	730	96.56
6.	Reference Books	20	2.65	750	99.21
7.	Others	6	0.79	756	100.00
	Total	756	100.00		

Since Legal libraries, Government libraries, Museum libraries and Social Sciences and Humanities libraries were represented as the subjects of few theses accounting for only 756 citations, they have been grouped under Other libraries category.

The study of this table shows that majority of citations cited by researchers in Other Libraries, Users and Services are Journals accounting for 55.56% of the total citations. Second preference has been given to Books with 16.14% followed by Editorial Works with 10.19% of the total citations.

Others category comprises only Newspapers with 6 citations out of the total citations.

TABLE – 4.10
BIBLIOGRAPHIC FORM-WISE DISTRIBUTION OF CITATIONS IN PUBLIC LIBRARIES AND COMMUNITY INFORMATION SERVICES

Sl. No.	*Form of Document*	*Number*	*Percentage*	*Cumulative Number*	*Cumulative Percentage*
1.	Journals	616	52.29	616	52.29
2.	Books	307	26.06	923	78.35
3.	Editorial Works	94	7.98	1017	86.33
4.	Reports	51	4.33	1068	90.66
5.	Conference Proceedings	47	3.99	1115	94.65
6.	Reference Books	33	2.80	1148	97.45
7.	Others	30	2.55	1178	100.00

The analysis of above table reveals that Journals with 616 (52.29%) citations stood in the first place followed by Books with 307 (26.06%) citations and Editorial Works with 94 (7.98%) citations respectively.

Newspapers, unpublished documents, Acts, Bills, theses and ephemeral material are included in others category as they constitute only 2.55 percent of the total citations.

TABLE – 4.11
BIBLIOGRAPHIC FORM-WISE DISTRIBUTION OF CITATIONS IN SCIENTIFIC AND TECHNICAL LIBRARIES

Sl. No.	*Form of Document*	*Number*	*Percentage*	*Cumulative Number*	*Cumulative Percentage*
1.	Journals	928	61.54	928	61.54
2.	Books	224	14.85	1152	76.39
3.	Editorial Works	99	6.56	1251	82.96
4.	Conference Proceedings	83	5.50	1334	88.46
5.	Reports	83	5.50	1417	93.97
6.	Reference Books	74	4.91	1491	98.87
7.	Others	17	1.13	1508	100.00

Results of this table indicate Journals as the most frequently cited form which confirms with other sub-disciplines. Books and Editorial Works are next to Journals in the number of citations.

Others category includes theses, ephemeral material, dissertations, newspapers, unpublished documents accounting for 1.13% only.

TABLE – 4.12
BIBLIOGRAPHIC FORM-WISE DISTRIBUTION OF CITATIONS IN UNIVERSITY LIBRARIES, USERS AND SERVICES

Sl. No.	*Form of Document*	*Number*	*Percentage*	*Cumulative Number*	*Cumulative Percentage*
1.	Journals	1575	47.58	1575	47.58
2.	Books	995	30.06	2570	77.64
3.	Editorial Works	238	7.19	2808	84.83
4.	Reports	152	4.59	2960	89.43
5.	Conference Proceedings	83	2.51	3043	91.93
6.	Reference Books	81	2.45	3124	94.38
7.	Thesis	67	2.02	3191	96.40
8.	Ephemeral Material	49	1.48	3240	97.89
9.	Others	70	2.12	3310	100.00

The results from the table shows Journals as the most bibliographic form for researchers with 1575 (47.58%) citations, followed by Books with 995 (30.06%) citations and Editorial Works 238 (7.19%) citations.

Others category represents 2.12 percent of the total citations comprising of newspapers, dissertations, unpublished documents and standards.

From the above analysis, we can conclude that there is slight variation in second and third place as reflected in Medical Information, Libraries, Users and Services, College Libraries, Users and Services; Bibliometrics and Agriculture Information, Libraries, Users and Services the bibliographic form wise distribution of citations reflected common pattern. Journals are found to occupying first place which clearly depicts that researchers are mostly dependent on Journals for their information needs as they are primary sources of information and also report the original research works. Books occupy the second place.

Subject-wise distribution of citations in Library and Information Science

The critical analysis of the citation data which is cited by researchers in the field of library and information science clearly indicates that these citations are scattered over a wide range of subjects which are the result of information explosion in the discipline. The first group includes the sub-disciplines of the library and information science where as the second group consists of further subdivision of these sub disciplines.

A close examination of subject-wise analysis depicts the distribution of citations among various subjects and also associated disciplines. This indicates the growth of specializations from the basic subject and also the interdisciplinary nature of the literature of the field.

The subject-wise distribution of citations in Library and Information Science is presented in Table-4.13.

TABLE – 4.13
SUBJECT-WISE DISTRIBUTION OF CITATIONS IN LIBRARY AND INFORMATION SCIENCE

Sl. No.	*Subject*	*No. of Citations*	*Per-centage*	*Cum Number*	*Cum Percentage*
1.	Special Libraries	1536	11.16	1536	11.16
2.	Bibliometrics	1413	10.27	2949	21.43
3.	LIS Research	1355	9.85	4304	31.28
4.	Humanities and Social Sciences	1347	9.79	5651	41.07
5.	Academic Libraries	1177	8.55	6828	49.26
6.	Library and Information Services	766	5.57	7594	55.18
7.	Libraries-General	756	5.49	8350	60.68
8.	Management	754	5.48	9104	66.16
9.	Information Systems and Networks	678	4.93	9782	71.08
10.	Library Automation	619	4.50	10401	75.58
11.	Library Management	580	4.21	10981	79.80
12.	Public Libraries	563	4.09	11544	83.89
13.	Information Sources	542	3.94	12086	87.83
14.	LIS Education and Training	371	2.70	12457	90.52
15.	Technical Services	245	1.78	12702	92.30
16.	Information Technology and Communication	213	1.55	12915	93.85
17.	Colleges and Universities	206	1.50	13121	95.35
18.	Others	640	4.65	13761	100.00

From the analysis of the above table it is evident that citations appended to theses have been scattered among 28 subjects. The highest number of publications fall under the broad field 'Special Libraries' with 1536 (11.16%) citations.

'Bibliometrics' and 'LIS Research' occupy the second and third place having 1413 and 1355 citations respectively. Humanities and Social Sciences and Academic Libraries stood in fourth and fifth place respectively. This finding indicates that the above mentioned areas represent the subjects in which maximum research work is done.

Subjects constituting less than 1 percent of the total citations are considered as others category. In the above table Others category comprise Library Associations, User Education and Training, Publishing and Printing, Education, Electronic and Digital Libraries, Social Science Libraries, Library Legislation, Research, Medical Education, Information and Knowledge, Sciences and Museums which constitute only 4.65 percent of the total citations of the study.

TABLE – 4.14
SUBJECT-WISE DISTRIBUTION OF CITATIONS IN AGRICULTURE INFORMATION, LIBRARIES, USERS AND SERVICES

Sl. No.	*Subject*	*No. of Citations*	*Per-centage*	*Cumulative Number*	*Cumulative Percentage*
1.	Special Libraries	276	51.30	276	51.30
2.	Information Systems and Networks	98	18.22	374	69.52
3.	LIS Research	48	8.92	422	78.44
4.	Information Technology & Communication	25	4.65	447	83.09
5.	Library and Information Services	22	4.09	469	87.17
6.	Bibliometrics	15	2.79	484	89.96
7.	Library Automation	13	2.42	497	92.38
8.	Libraries-General	7	1.30	504	93.68
9.	Others	34	6.32	538	100.00

It may be observed from the above table that Special Libraries occupied the first place in the list of subjects with

276 (51.30%) citations, followed by Information Systems and Networks with 98 (18.22%) citations and LIS Research with 48 (8.92%) citations.

Management, Information Sources, Academic Libraries, User Education and Training, Technical Services, Library Management, Public Libraries, Information and Knowledge, Colleges and Universities, Library Associations, Research, Sciences, Electronic and Digital Libraries, Humanities and Social Sciences and LIS Education and Training are included in Others category.

TABLE – 4.15
SUBJECT-WISE DISTRIBUTION OF CITATIONS IN BIBLIOMETRICS

Sl. No.	*Subject*	*No. of Citations*	*Per-centage*	*Cumulative Number*	*Cumulative Percentage*
1.	Bibliometrics	1301	93.46	1301	93.46
2.	Humanities and Social Sciences	27	1.94	1328	95.40
3.	LIS Research	17	1.22	1345	96.62
4.	Information Sources	15	1.08	1360	97.70
5.	Library and Information Services	14	1.01	1374	98.71
6.	Others	18	1.29	1392	100.00

The analysis of data in the above table clearly depicts that majority of citations are related to subject Bibliometrics with 1301 (93.46%) citations followed by Humanities and Social Sciences with 27 (1.94%) and LIS Research with 17 (1.22%) citations to their credit.

Others comprise Research, Library Management, Academic Libraries, Information Technology and Communication, Education, Management, Colleges and Universities and Special Libraries constituting only 1.29 percent of the total citations.

TABLE – 4.16
SUBJECT-WISE DISTRIBUTION OF CITATIONS IN COLLEGE LIBRARIES, USERS AND SERVICES

Sl. No.	*Subject*	*No. of Citations*	*Per-centage*	*Cumulative Number*	*Cumulative Percentage*
1.	Academic Libraries	338	44.59	338	44.59
2.	Humanities and Social Sciences	106	13.98	444	58.58
3.	Colleges and Universities	101	13.32	545	71.90
4.	Libraries-General	42	5.54	587	77.44
5.	Library Management	37	4.88	624	82.32
6.	Education	30	3.96	654	86.28
7.	LIS Research	27	3.56	681	89.84
8.	Information Sources	26	3.43	707	93.27
9.	User Education and Training	10	1.32	717	94.59
10.	Library Information Services	9	1.19	726	95.78
11.	Electronic and Digital Libraries	9	1.19	735	96.97
12.	Information Systems and Networks	8	1.06	743	98.02
13.	Others	15	1.98	758	100.00

The study of this table shows that maximum number of citations cited by researchers belongs to the subject Academic libraries accounting for 44.59% of the total citations. The next subject in the list is Humanities and Social Sciences with 13.98%, followed by Colleges and Universities with 13.32% of the total citations.

The subjects included in Others category are LIS Education and Training, Research, Library Automation, Management, Special Libraries, Technical Services and Special Libraries accounting for 1.98 percent of the total citations.

TABLE – 4.17
SUBJECT-WISE DISTRIBUTION OF CITATIONS IN LIBRARIES AND I.T

Sl. No.	*Subject*	*No. of Citations*	*Per-centage*	*Cumulative Number*	*Cumulative Percentage*
1.	Library Automation	370	47.44	370	47.44
2.	Academic Libraries	113	14.49	483	61.92
3.	Information Technology and Communication	63	8.08	546	70.00
4.	Humanities and Social Sciences	55	7.05	601	77.05
5.	Information Systems and Networks	35	4.49	636	81.54
6.	Libraries-General	34	4.36	687	85.90
7.	Library and Information Services	17	2.18	687	88.08
8.	Library Management	16	2.05	703	90.13
9.	Colleges and Universities	14	1.79	717	91.92
10	Special Libraries	13	1.67	730	93.59
11.	LIS Research	12	1.54	742	95.13
12.	Management	10	1.28	752	96.41
13.	Information Sources	8	1.03	760	97.44
14.	Others	20	2.56	780	100.00

The distribution of citations in Libraries and I.T indicates the scattering of citations among 18 subject areas. Library Automation with 370 (47.44%) citations and Academic Libraries with 113 (14.49%) stood in first and second places respectively. Next highest number of citations are related to the subject Information Technology and Communication (80.8%)

Subjects covered under Others category are Public Libraries, Electronic and Digital Libraries, LIS Education and Training, Education, Library Associations contributing only 20 (2.56%) citations of the total number.

TABLE – 4.18
SUBJECT-WISE DISTRIBUTION OF CITATIONS IN MARKETING OF LIBRARY INFORMATION SERVICES AND PRODUCTS

Sl. No.	*Subject*	*No. of Citations*	*Per-centage*	*Cumulative Number*	*Cumulative Percentage*
1.	Library and Information Services	345	77.01	345	77.01
2.	Special Libraries	24	5.36	369	82.37
3.	LIS Research	22	4.91	391	87.28
4.	Academic Libraries	18	4.02	409	91.29
5.	Library Management	11	2.46	420	93.75
6.	Information Sources	9	2.01	429	95.76
7.	Libraries-General	5	1.12	434	96.88
8.	Others	14	3.12	448	100.00

The Subject-Wise distribution of citations in the above sub-discipline are scattered among thirteen subjects. Among them, highest number of citations are from Library and Information Services (77.01%). The subject Special Libraries occupied second place with 24 (5.36%) citations followed by LIS Research with 22 (4.91%) citations.

Others category comprises Public Libraries, Management, Information Systems and Networks, Electronic and Digital Libraries, Research and Colleges and Universities.

TABLE – 4.19
SUBJECT-WISE DISTRIBUTION OF CITATIONS IN MEDICAL INFORMATION, LIBRARIES, USERS AND SERVICES

Sl. No.	*Subject*	*No. of Citations*	*Per-centage*	*Cumulative Number*	*Cumulative Percentage*
1.	Special Libraries	465	54.45	465	54.45
2.	LIS Research	149	17.45	614	71.90

(Contd...)

Sl. No.	*Subject*	*No. of Citations*	*Per-centage*	*Cumulative Number*	*Cumulative Percentage*
3.	Information Systems and Networks	61	7.14	675	79.04
4.	Information Technology and Communication	28	3.28	703	82.32
5.	Medical Education	22	2.58	725	84.89
6.	Library and Information Services	21	2.46	746	87.35
7.	Library Automation	13	1.52	759	88.88
8.	Libraries-General	11	1.29	770	90.16
9.	Bibliometrics	11	1.29	781	91.45
10.	Information Sources	11	1.29	792	92.74
11.	Academic Libraries	9	1.05	801	93.79
12.	Others	53	6.21	854	100.00

It may be observed from the above table that the citations in the field of Medical Information, Libraries, Users and Services are distributed among twenty two subjects. Maximum number of citations are cited from "Special Libraries" accounting for 465 (57.45%) citations, followed by LIS Research and Information Systems and Networks with 149 (17.45%) & 61 (7.14%) citations respectively.

The subject grouped under Others category are Library Management, Management, Information and Knowledge, Electronic and Digital Libraries, Public Libraries, Research, Colleges and Universities, Technical Services, Humanities and Social Sciences, Sciences and User Education and Training.

TABLE – 4.20
SUBJECT-WISE DISTRIBUTION OF CITATIONS IN OTHER ASPECTS

Sl. No.	*Subject*	*No. of Citations*	*Per-centage*	*Cumulative Number*	*Cumulative Percentage*
1.	LIS Education and Training	311	13.89	311	13.89
2.	Libraries-General	292	13.04	603	26.93
3.	Humanities and Social Sciences	211	9.42	814	36.36
4.	Information Sources	211	9.42	1025	45.78
5.	LIS Research	211	9.42	1236	55.20
6.	Special Libraries	184	8.22	1420	63.42
7	Academic Libraries	158	7.06	1578	70.48
8.	Library Management	131	5.85	1709	76.33
9.	Technical Services	123	5.49	1832	81.82
10.	Library Associations	119	5.31	1951	87.14
11.	Publishing and Printing	84	3.75	2035	90.89
12	User Education and Training	49	2.19	2084	93.08
13.	Information Systems and Networks	35	1.56	2119	94.64
14.	Library and Information Services	28	1.25	2147	95.89
15.	Bibliometrics	23	1.03	2170	96.92
16.	Others	69	3.08	2239	100.00

The examination of the above table reveals that the cited references in the field of Other Aspects are scattered among twenty six subjects. LIS Education and Training with 311 (13.89%) citations stood first. The second and third places are occupied by Libraries-General with 292 (13.04%) citations stood in second place. However third place is shared by three subjects namely, Humanities and Social Sciences, Information Sources and LIS Research with 211 (9.42%) citations respectively.

Others category comprises of subjects such as Information Technology and Communication, Library Automation, Education, Electronic and Digital Libraries, Public Libraries, Research, Colleges and Universities, Library Legislation, Information and Knowledge, Management and Sciences accounting for 3.08 percent of the total citations.

TABLE – 4.21
SUBJECT-WISE DISTRIBUTION OF CITATIONS IN OTHER LIBRARIES, USERS AND SERVICES

Sl. No.	*Subject*	*No. of Citations*	*Per-centage*	*Cumulative Number*	*Cumulative Percentage*
1.	Humanities and Social Sciences	153	20.24	153	20.24
2.	Special Libraries	135	17.86	288	38.10
3.	LIS Research	100	13.23	388	51.32
4.	Information Sources	84	11.11	472	62.43
5.	Library and Information Services	52	6.88	524	69.31
6.	Information Systems and Networks	48	6.35	572	75.66
7.	Library Automation	28	3.70	600	79.37
8.	Library Management	26	3.44	626	82.80
9.	Bibliometrics	24	3.17	650	85.98
10.	Information Technology and Communication	23	3.04	673	89.02
11.	Libraries-General	20	2.65	693	91.67
12.	Museums	15	1.98	708	93.65
13.	User Education and Training	10	1.32	718	94.97
14.	Academic Libraries	9	1.19	727	96.16
15.	Others	29	3.84	756	100.00

On careful examination of the above table it is clear that Humanities and Social Sciences with 153 (20.24%) citations dominated the list in the field of Other Libraries, Users and Services followed by Special Libraries with 135 (17.86%) citations and LIS Research with 100 (13.23%) citations respectively.

Subjects which are categorized as others include Management, Research, Public Libraries, Electronic and Digital Libraries, Technical Services, Education, Sciences and LIS Education and Training. The total number of citations of these subjects comes to 29 which is very minute number.

TABLE – 4.22
SUBJECT-WISE DISTRIBUTION OF CITATIONS IN PUBLIC LIBRARIES AND COMMUNITY INFORMATION SERVICES

Sl. No.	*Subject*	*No. of Citations*	*Per-centage*	*Cumulative Number*	*Cumulative Percentage*
1.	Public Libraries	504	42.78	504	42.78
2.	Libraries-General	163	13.84	667	56.62
3.	Humanities and Social Sciences	106	9.00	773	65.62
4.	Library and Information Services	98	8.32	871	73.94
5.	LIS Research	95	8.06	966	82.00
6.	Library Management	54	4.58	1020	86.59
7.	Library Legislation	47	3.99	1067	90.58
8.	Information Sources	30	2.55	1097	93.12
9.	Management	24	2.04	1121	95.16
10.	Information Systems and Networks	16	1.36	1137	96.52
11.	Others	41	3.48	1178	100.00

The examination of the table indicates that the distribution of citations in the field of Public Libraries and Community Information Services are scattered among twenty two subject areas. Public Libraries with 504 (42.78%) and Libraries-

General with 163 (13.84%) citations stood in first and second places respectively. Third place is occupied by Humanities and Social Sciences with 106 (9.00%) citations.

TABLE – 4.23
SUBJECT-WISE DISTRIBUTION OF CITATIONS IN SCIENTIFIC AND TECHNICAL LIBRARIES

Sl. No.	*Subject*	*No. of Citations*	*Per-centage*	*Cumulative Number*	*Cumulative Percentage*
1.	Special Libraries	364	24.14	364	24.14
2.	LIS Research	252	16.71	616	40.85
3.	Humanities and Social Sciences	161	10.68	777	51.53
4.	Library Automation	153	10.15	930	61.67
5.	Information Systems and Networks	116	7.69	1046	69.36
6.	Libraries-General	94	6.23	1140	75.60
7.	Library and Information Services	67	4.44	1207	80.04
8.	Library Management	64	4.24	1271	84.28
9.	Academic Libraries	60	3.98	1331	88.26
10.	Information Sources	35	2.32	1366	90.58
11.	Information Technology and Communication	29	1.92	1395	92.51
12.	Electronic and Digital Libraries	26	1.72	1421	94.23
13.	Bibliometrics	20	1.33	1441	95.56
14.	User Education and Training	19	1.26	1460	96.82
15.	Others	48	3.18	1508	100.00

Regarding the field of Scientific and Technical Libraries is concerned Special Libraries hold the first rank by receiving the maximum citations i.e. 364 (21.14%) citations, while LIS Research and Humanities and Social Sciences stood in second and third ranks with 254 (16.71%) and 161 (10.68%) citations to their credit.

LIS Education and Training, Public Libraries, Technical Services, Sciences, Medical Education, Information and Knowledge, Colleges and Universities, Library Associations, Research, Management and Publishing and Printing are treated as others as their contribution to the total citations is very minimal.

TABLE – 4.24
SUBJECT-WISE DISTRIBUTION OF CITATIONS IN UNIVERSITY LIBRARIES, USERS AND SERVICES

Sl. No.	*Subject*	*No. of Citations*	*Per-centage*	*Cumulative Number*	*Cumulative Percentage*
1.	Management	692	20.91	692	20.91
2.	Humanities and Social Sciences	523	15.80	1215	36.71
3.	Academic Libraries	461	13.93	1676	50.63
4.	LIS Research	422	12.75	2098	63.38
5.	Information Systems and Networks	259	7.82	2357	71.21
6.	Library Management	226	6.83	2583	78.04
7.	Information Sources	108	3.26	2691	81.30
8.	Technical Services	105	3.17	2796	84.47
9.	Library and Information Services	93	2.81	2889	87.28
10.	Libraries-General	88	2.66	2977	89.94
11.	Colleges and Universities	75	2.27	3052	92.21
12.	Special Libraries	69	2.08	3121	94.29
13.	Education	34	1.03	3155	95.32
14.	Others	155	4.68	3310	100.00

The above table represents that citations in the discipline University Libraries, Users and Services are scattered among 25 subjects. However the highest number of citations are related to the subject Management which has been cited maximum by the researchers with 692 (20.91%) citations, followed by Humanities and Social Sciences and Academic Libraries with 523 and 461 citations respectively. LIS Research with 422 (12.75%) and Information Systems and Networks with 259 (7.82%) citations stood in fourth and fifth place in the list.

The subjects covered under the Others category comprise Information Technology and Communication, Library Automation, LIS Education and Training, Public Libraries, Bibliometrics, Research, Sciences, Information and Knowledge, Electronic and Digital Libraries, User Education and Training, Library Legislation and Library Associations. The total contribution from these twelve subjects comes to 4.68 percent.

Language-wise Distribution of Citations

The literature in any discipline is published in many languages through out the world and at the same time the communication among the scientists and research scholars also follow the same pattern. The language in which the research scholars or scientists use to publish their research findings is generally main criteria to prefer a particular language. Besides these, there are various factors which influence the language selection like availability of literature, knowledge of research scholars to understand foreign languages and translation facilities. The language wise distribution of the cited literature in the field of Library and information science has been studied in order to identify the predominant language for scientific communication.

TABLE – 4.25

LANGUAGE WISE DISTRIBUTION OF CITATIONS

Sl. No.	*Language*	*No. of Citations*	*Per-centage*	*Cumulative Number*	*Cumulative Percentage*
1.	English	13719	99.69	13719	99.69
2.	Hindi	6	0.04	13725	99.74
3.	Telugu	36	0.26	13761	100.00
	Totals	13761	100.00		

The citations in the field of Library and Information Science are distributed among three languages. The above table reveals that English is the most dominant language with 99.69 percent of the total citations followed by Hindi and Telugu.

Country -wise Distribution of Citations

The Geographical distribution of literature in any discipline and for the present purpose in the field of Library and Information Science enables the researcher to identify the research output published by any country as the progress and development of any country depends upon its research productivity and research activities. Now Information is considered as a vital resource by all the nations.

The tables below represent the geographical distribution of citations cited by researchers in the field of Library and Information Science.

The country-wise distribution of citations in the field of Library and Information Science has been depicted in the Table 4.26.

TABLE – 4.26
COUNTRY-WISE DISTRIBUTION OF CITATIONS IN LIBRARY AND INFORMATION SCIENCE

Sl. No.	*Name of the Country*	*No. of Citations*	*Per-centage*	*Cumulative Number*	*Cumulative Percentage*
1.	India	5474	39.78	5474	39.78
2.	U.S.A.	4501	32.71	9975	72.49
3.	U.K.	2508	18.23	12483	90.72
4.	Netherlands	458	3.33	12941	94.05
5.	France	188	1.37	13129	95.42
6.	Others	632	4.58	13761	100.00

When we analyse the citations which are tabulated, we can get a clear idea about the countries which are major contributors in the field of Library and Information Science. India occupied the first position with 5474 (39.78%) citations followed by U.S.A with 4501 (32.71%) citations. U.K and Netherlands stood in third and fourth place with 2508 (18.23%) and 458 (3.33%) citations to their credit. However the fifth place goes to France accounting for 188 (1.37%) citations.

Countries with less than 1 percent contribution are grouped under others category. This category includes Australia, Canada, Germany, Denmark, Japan, China, Russia, Switzerland, South Africa, Ireland, Nigeria, New Zealand, Czech Republic, Pakistan, Singapore, Norway, Philippines, Sweden, Brazil, Finland, Hong Kong, Israel, Mexico, Slovenia, Romania, Austria, Bangladesh, Italy, Poland, Yugoslavia, Thailand, Indonesia, Jamaica, Jordan, Malawi, Malaysia, Nepal, Cuba, Fiji, Greece, Kenya, Papua New Guinea, Slovakia, Tanzania, Tunis, Uganda and Colombia accounting for 4.58 percent of the total citations.

TABLE - 4.27
COUNTRY-WISE DISTRIBUTION OF CITATIONS IN AGRICULTURE INFORMATION, LIBRARIES, USERS AND SERVICES

Sl. No.	*Name of the Country*	*No. of Citations*	*Per-centage*	*Cumulative Number*	*Cumulative Percentage*
1.	India	243	45.17	243	45.17
2.	U.S.A.	109	20.26	352	65.43
3.	Netherlands	100	18.59	452	84.01
4.	U.K.	58	10.78	510	94.80
5.	France	7	1.30	517	96.10
6.	Others	21	3.90	538	100.00

Country-wise distribution of citations in Agricultural Information, Libraries, Users and Services indicates that India with 243 (45.17%) citations clearly dominated the list followed by U.S.A with 109 (20.26%) and Netherlands with 100 (18.59%) citations. The fourth place is occupied by U.K and fifth place goes to France.

The countries which are included in Others category are Canada, Philippines, Australia, Denmark, Germany, Czech Republic, Mexico, Pakistan, South Africa contributing only 3.90 percent of the total citations.

TABLE – 4.28
COUNTRY-WISE DISTRIBUTION OF CITATIONS IN BIBLIOMETRICS

Sl. No.	*Name of the Country*	*No. of Citations*	*Per-centage*	*Cumulative Number*	*Cumulative Percentage*
1.	U.S.A.	471	33.84	471	33.84
2.	India	323	23.20	794	57.04
3.	U.K.	311	22.34	1105	79.38
4.	Netherlands	227	16.31	1332	95.69
5.	Denmark	20	1.44	1352	97.13
6.	Others	40	2.87	1392	100.00

Analysis of the table depicts U.S.A in the first place in terms of number of citations with 471 (33.84%). India took the second place with 323 (23.20%) citations and U.K stood in the third place with 311 (22.34%) citations. Netherlands and Denmark occupied fourth and fifth places respectively with 227 (16.31%) and 20 (1.44%) citations.

Others category comprises of countries namely France, Canada, Japan, Australia, Russia, Germany, Brazil, China, Finland, Hong Kong, Israel, Mexico, Nigeria, Pakistan, Czech Republic and Singapore contributing only 2.87 percent of the total citations reflecting the dependence of the researchers on few countries for their information requirements.

TABLE – 4.29
COUNTRY-WISE DISTRIBUTION OF CITATIONS IN COLLEGE LIBRARIES, USERS AND SERVICES

Sl. No.	*Name of the Country*	*No. of Citations*	*Per-centage*	*Cumulative Number*	*Cumulative Percentage*
1.	India	597	78.76	597	78.76
2.	U.S.A	123	16.23	720	94.99
3.	U.K	34	4.49	754	99.48
4.	Others	4	0.52	758	100.00

The above table represents the Country-Wise distribution of citations in the sub discipline College Libraries, Users and Services. The trend observed in the above table clearly indicates that India, U.S.A. and U.K. stood in the first three places contributing 99.48 percent of the total citations.

The countries that have been grouped under the category of others are China, Australia and Japan accounting for only 0.52 percent of the total citations.

TABLE – 4.30

COUNTRY-WISE DISTRIBUTION OF CITATIONS IN LIBRARIES AND I.T.

Sl. No.	*Name of the Country*	*No. of Citations*	*Per-centage*	*Cumulative Number*	*Cumulative Percentage*
1.	India	303	38.85	303	38.85
2.	U.S.A.	238	30.51	541	69.36
3.	U.K.	194	24.87	735	94.23
4.	Others	45	5.77	780	100.00

Geographical distribution of citations in Libraries and I.T reveal that India with 303 (38.85%) citations, U.S.A. with 238 (30.51%) citations and U.K. with 194 (24.87%) citations are ranked in the first, second and third place indicating the importance of the literature being published from these countries.

Others category represents 5.77 percent of the total citations consisting of Australia, Netherlands, France, Ireland, Canada, China, Germany, Pakistan, Russia, Austria, Denmark, Jamaica, Malaysia, New Zealand, Norway.

TABLE – 4.31
COUNTRY-WISE DISTRIBUTION OF CITATIONS IN MARKETING OF LIBRARY INFORMATION SERVICES AND PRODUCTS

Sl. No.	*Name of the Country*	*No. of Citations*	*Per-centage*	*Cumulative Number*	*Cumulative Percentage*
1.	U.S.A.	178	39.73	178	39.73
2.	India	136	30.36	314	70.09
3.	U.K.	79	17.63	393	87.72
4.	Netherlands	23	5.13	416	92.86
5.	Australia	9	2.01	425	94.87
6.	Denmark	6	1.34	431	96.21
7.	Canada	5	1.12	436	97.32
8.	Others	12	2.68	448	100.00

The number of citations appended to theses in the field of Marketing of Library and Information Services and Products accounts for 448 of the total citations analysed in Library and Information Science. Country-Wise distribution of citations in the Marketing of Library and Information Services and Products indicates that after U.S.A. (39.73%) and India (30.36%), U.K. occupies third place with 79 (17.63%) citations pushing Netherlands to fourth position with 23 (5.13%) citations. Australia with 9 (2.01%), Denmark with 6 (1.34%) and Canada with 5 (1.12%) citations stood in 5th, 6th and 7th places respectively in the ranked list.

The countries which were considered as others are Slovenia, China, France, Ireland, Japan and Russia contributing 2.68 percent of the total citations.

TABLE – 4.32
COUNTRY-WISE DISTRIBUTION OF CITATIONS IN MEDICAL INFORMATION, LIBRARIES, USERS AND SERVICES

Sl. No.	*Name of the Country*	*No. of Citations*	*Per-centage*	*Cumulative Number*	*Cumulative Percentage*
1.	U.S.A.	311	36.42	311	36.42
2.	India	239	27.99	550	64.41
3.	U.K.	230	26.93	780	91.33
4.	Switzerland	15	1.76	795	93.09
5.	Japan	14	1.64	809	94.73
6.	Australia	9	1.05	818	95.78
7.	Netherlands	9	1.05	827	96.84
8.	Others	27	3.16	854	100.00

The above table presents geographical distribution of citations to all bibliographic forms cited by researchers in the field of Library and Information Science. While U.S.A. takes the top position with its contribution covering 36.42 percent (311 citations), India occupied the second position by contributing 27.99 percent followed by U.K. with 230 (26.93%) citations to its credit. Switzerland occupied fourth place with 15 (1.76%) citations, while Japan stood in fifth place contributing 14 (1.64%) citations.

TABLE – 4.33
COUNTRY-WISE DISTRIBUTION OF CITATIONS IN OTHER ASPECTS

Sl. No.	*Name of the Country*	*No. of Citations*	*Per-centage*	*Cumulative Number*	*Cumulative Percentage*
1.	India	1074	47.97	1074	47.97
2.	U.S.A.	668	29.83	1742	77.80
3.	U.K.	321	14.34	2063	92.14
4.	Netherlands	39	1.74	2102	93.88
5.	Germany	25	1.12	2127	95.00
6.	Others	112	5.00	2239	100.00

Country-wise distribution of citations in Other Aspects shows that India occupies the first place with 1074 (47.97%) citations. U.S.A stands in second place with 29.83 percent contribution followed by U.K with 14.34 percent contributions and Netherlands with 1.74 percent contribution.

Others category comprises countries which have very less contribution to the total citations. The countries which have categorized under others category are France, Australia, Canada, Denmark, Japan, Czech Republic, Russia, Bangladesh, Poland, Yugoslavia, Brazil, Finland, Italy, Jordan, South Africa, Fiji, Hong Kong, Israel, Jamaica, Malaysia, Nigeria, Norway, Pakistan, Philippines, Slovakia, Sweden and Switzerland. The total contribution made by these countries comes to 5.00 percent of the total citations.

TABLE – 4.34
COUNTRY-WISE DISTRIBUTION OF CITATIONS IN OTHER LIBRARIES, USERS AND SERVICES

Sl. No.	*Name of the Country*	*No. of Citations*	*Per- centage*	*Cumulative Number*	*Cumulative Percentage*
1.	U.S.A.	356	47.09	356	47.09
2.	India	167	22.09	523	69.18
3.	U.K.	152	20.11	675	89.29
4.	Netherlands	26	3.44	701	92.72
5.	France	12	1.59	713	94.31
6.	Australia	9	1.19	722	95.51
7.	Others	34	4.49	756	100.00

Geographical distribution of citations in Other Libraries, Users and Services is represented in the above table. The contributions from United States are found to be high accounting for 47.09 percent of the total citations in Other Libraries, Users and Services. India stood in second place with 167 (22.09%) citations and U.K. in third place with 152 (20.11%) citations. However we can observe a significant gap in percentage of citations between the 3rd and 4th ranks respectively as it is clear that Netherlands stood in fourth place with only 26 (3.44%) citations.

Others category constitute 4.50 percent of the total citations comprise of Canada, Germany, Japan, Denmark, Austria, Czech Republic, Mexico, China, Colombia, Greece, Ireland, Nigeria, Russia and Singapore.

TABLE – 4.35
COUNTRY-WISE DISTRIBUTION OF CITATIONS IN PUBLIC LIBRARIES AND COMMUNITY INFORMATION SERVICES

Sl. No.	*Name of the Country*	*No. of Citations*	*Per- centage*	*Cumulative Number*	*Cumulative Percentage*
1.	India	486	41.26	486	41.26
2.	U.S.A.	369	31.32	855	72.58
3.	U.K.	183	15.53	1038	88.12
4.	France	63	5.35	1101	93.46
5.	Australia	32	2.72	1133	96.18
6.	Germany	12	1.02	1145	97.20
7.	Others	33	2.80	1178	100.00

The analysis of the data in the above table clearly reveals that India had received the maximum number of citations as far as the sub discipline Public Libraries and Community Information Services is concerned. U.S.A got 369 (31.32%) citations and stood in second place in the list followed by U.K with 183 (15.53%) citations. The fourth and fifth places have been occupied by France and Australia by contributing 5.35 and 2.72 percent of the total citations. Germany with 12 (1.02%) citations stood in the sixth place.

Countries under others category include Denmark, Canada, South Africa, Norway, China, Cuba, Hong Kong, Ireland, Papua New Guinea, Nigeria, Switzerland, Uganda.

TABLE – 4.36
COUNTRY-WISE DISTRIBUTION OF CITATIONS IN SCIENTIFIC AND TECHNICAL LIBRARIES

Sl. No.	*Name of the Country*	*No. of Citations*	*Per-centage*	*Cumulative Number*	*Cumulative Percentage*
1.	India	570	37.80	570	37.80
2.	U.S.A.	471	31.23	1041	69.03
3	U.K.	365	24.20	1406	93.24
4.	France	28	1.86	1434	95.09
5.	Others	74	4.91	1508	100.00

Geographical distribution of citations in Scientific and Technical Libraries is reflecting the general trend as in Library and Information Science discipline. Nearly 570 (37.80%) of the contributions are from India followed by 471 (31.23%) citations from United States of America. U.K. with 365 (24.20%) citations occupied the third place in the list and France stood in the fourth place with 28 (1.86%) citations.

Twenty one countries are included in others category namely, Australia, Russia, Canada, Netherlands, Japan, Germany, Denmark, China, Indonesia, Malawi, Nigeria, Singapore, South Africa, Czech Republic, Finland, Hong Kong, Israel, Sweden, Switzerland, Thailand and Tunis and their contribution is 4.91 percent of the total citations.

TABLE – 4.37
COUNTRY-WISE DISTRIBUTION OF CITATIONS IN UNIVERSITY LIBRARIES, USERS AND SERVICES

Sl. No.	*Name of the Country*	*No. of Citations*	*Per-centage*	*Cumulative Number*	*Cumulative Percentage*
1.	India	1336	40.36	1336	40.36
2.	U.S.A.	1207	36.47	2543	76.83
3.	U.K.	581	17.55	3124	94.38
4.	France	33	1.00	3157	95.38
5.	Others	153	4.62	3310	100.00

The Country-wise distribution of citations in the sub-discipline of University Libraries, Users and Services shows the same trend noticed in the basic subject i.e. Library and Information Science. India tops the list with 1336 (40.36%) citations and it is closely followed by United States of America with 1207 (36.47%) citations. United Kingdom with 581 (17.55%) citations stood in the third place, while France by contributing 33 (1.00%) citations occupied fourth place.

Others category (4.62%) covers Australia, Netherlands, Canada, Germany, Japan, New Zealand, China, Denmark, Nigeria, South Africa, Singapore, Pakistan, Romania, Ireland, Nepal, Russia, Switzerland, Brazil, Israel, Italy, Kenya, Sweden, Tanzania and Thailand.

Authorship Pattern of Citations in Library and Information Science

The authorship pattern of citations in the discipline Library and Information Science and its sub disciplines has been discussed in detail in this section.

To observe the change in authorship pattern over the years the chi-square test has been applied in order to verify any significant relationship between authorship and reference period. The distribution of citations in Library and Information Science and its sub-disciplines have been grouped into ten years interval according to number of authors and are represented in the following tables. For the purpose of applying chi-square test the pattern of authorship has been grouped under three categories only viz. Single, two authors and three and more authors (Tables 4.38 - 4.49).

TABLE – 4.38
AUTHORSHIP PATTERN IN LIBRARY AND INFORMATION SCIENCE
(10 YEARS INTERVAL)

Year	*Single author*	*Two authors*	*Three and above authors*	*Total*
Upto 1962	942	130	19	1091
	86.34	11.92	1.74	100.00
1963-72	1544	232	54	1830
	84.37	12.68	2.95	100.00
1973-82	2468	454	103	3025
	81.59	15.01	3.40	100.00
1983-92	2698	571	105	3374
	79.97	16.92	3.11	100.00
1993-02	1070	292	94	1456
	73.49	20.06	6.45	100.00
2003	11	1	0	12
	91.67	8.33	0.00	100.00
Total	8733	1680	375	10788
	80.95	15.57	3.48	100.00

CHI-SQUARE = 110.1226 DF = 10

TABLE – 4.39
AUTHORSHIP PATTERN IN AGRICULTURE INFORMATION, LIBRARIES, USERS AND SERVICES

Year	*Single author*	*Two authors*	*Three and above authors*	*Total*
Upto 1962	0	0	0	0
	0.00	0.00	0.00	0.00
1963-72	8	6	2	16
	50.00	37.50	12.50	100.00
1973-82	12	4	1	17
	70.59	23.53	5.88	100.00
1983-92	17	2	0	19
	89.47	10.53	0.00	100.00
1993-02	3	1	1	5
	60.00	20.00	20.00	100.00
2003	0	0	0	0
	0.00	0.00	0.00	0.00
Total	40	13	4	57
	70.17	22.81	7.02	100.00

CHI-SQUARE = 8.0534 DF = 6

TABLE – 4.40
AUTHORSHIP PATTERN IN BIBLIOMETRICS

Year	*Single author*	*Two authors*	*Three and above authors*	*Total*
Upto 1962	36	0	0	36
	100.00	0.00	0.00	100.00
1963-72	18	3	0	21
	85.71	14.29	0.00	100.00
1973-82	35	13	0	48
	72.92	27.08	0.00	100.00
1983-92	18	8	2	28
	64.29	28.57	7.14	100.00
1993-02	6	0	0	6
	100.00	0.00	0.00	100.00
2003	0	0	0	0
	0.00	0.00	0.00	0.00
Total	113	24	2	139
	81.29	17.27	1.44	100.00

CHI-SQUARE = 23.3093 DF = 8

TABLE – 4.41
AUTHORSHIP PATTERN IN COLLEGE LIBRARIES, USERS AND SERVICES

Year	*Single author*	*Two authors*	*Three and above authors*	*Total*
Up to 1962	10	1	0	11
	90.91	9.09	0.00	100.00
1963-72	24	4	1	29
	82.76	13.79	3.45	100.00
1973-82	18	8	1	27
	66.67	29.63	3.70	100.00
1983-92	43	4	1	48
	89.58	8.33	2.09	100.00
1993-02	24	2	0	26
	92.31	7.69	0.00	100.00
2003	0	0	0	0
	0.00	0.00	0.00	0.00
Total	119	19	3	141
	84.40	13.48	2.12	100.00

CHI-SQUARE = 9.7316 DF = 8

TABLE – 4.42
AUTHORSHIP PATTERN IN LIBRARIES AND I.T

Year	*Single author*	*Two authors*	*Three and above authors*	*Total*
Upto 1962	9	6	0	15
	60.00	40.00	0.00	100.00
1963-72	7	2	1	10
	70.00	20.00	10.00	100.00
1973-82	28	11	1	40
	70.00	27.50	2.50	100.00
1983-92	89	27	2	118
	75.42	22.88	1.70	100.00
1993-02	31	4	1	36
	86.11	11.11	2.78	100.00
2003	0	0	0	0
	0.00	0.00	0.00	0.00
Total	164	50	5	219
	74.89	22.83	2.28	100.00

CHI-SQUARE = 8.9096 DF = 8

TABLE – 4.43
AUTHORSHIP PATTERN IN MARKETING OF LIBRARY INFORMATION SERVICES AND PRODUCTS

Year	*Single author*	*Two authors*	*Three and above authors*	*Total*
Upto 1962	0	1	0	1
	0.00	100.00	0.00	100.00
1963-72	2	3	0	5
	40.00	60.00	0.00	100.00
1973-82	13	8	0	21
	61.90	38.10	0.00	100.00
1983-92	5	1	0	6
	83.33	16.67	0.00	100.00
1993-02	25	14	2	41
	60.98	34.15	4.87	100.00
2003	0	0	0	0
	0.00	0.00	0.00	0.00
Total	45	27	2	74
	60.81	36.49	2.70	100.00

CHI-SQUARE =5.6645 DF=8

TABLE – 4.44
AUTHORSHIP PATTERN IN MEDICAL INFORMATION, LIBRARIES, USERS AND SERVICES

Year	*Single author*	*Two authors*	*Three and above authors*	*Total*
Upto 1962	14	5	0	19
	73.68	26.32	0.00	100.00
1963-72	33	6	3	42
	78.57	14.29	7.14	100.00
1973-82	37	8	4	49
	75.51	16.33	8.16	100.00
1983-92	21	1	0	22
	95.45	4.55	0.00	100.00
1993-02	5	0	0	5
	100.00	0.00	0.00	100.00
2003	0	0	0	0
	0.00	0.00	0.00	0.00
Total	110	20	7	137
	80.29	14.60	5.11	100.00

CHI-SQUARE =8.8576 DF=8

TABLE – 4.45
AUTHORSHIP PATTERN IN OTHER ASPECTS

Year	*Single author*	*Two authors*	*Three and above authors*	*Total*
Upto 1962	38	5	0	43
	88.37	11.63	0.00	100.00
1963-72	87	1	3	91
	95.60	1.10	3.30	100.00
1973-82	145	11	2	158
	91.77	6.96	1.27	100.00
1983-92	112	10	5	127
	88.19	7.87	3.94	100.00
1993-02	28	0	1	29
	96.55	0.00	3.45	100.00
2003	0	0	0	0
	0.00	0.00	0.00	0.00
Total	410	27	11	448
	91.52	6.03	2.45	100.00

CHI-SQUARE =12.5296 DF=8

TABLE – 4.46
AUTHORSHIP PATTERN IN OTHER LIBRARIES, USERS AND SERVICES

Year	*Single author*	*Two authors*	*Three and above authors*	*Total*
Upto 1962	12	1	1	14
	85.72	7.14	7.14	100.00
1963-72	18	2	1	21
	85.72	9.52	4.76	100.00
1973-82	47	4	3	54
	87.04	7.41	5.55	100.00
1983-92	18	10	0	28
	64.29	35.71	0.00	100.00
1993-02	4	1	0	5
	80.00	20.00	0.00	100.00
2003	0	0	0	0
	0.00	0.00	0.00	0.00
Total	99	18	5	122
	81.15	14.75	4.10	100.00

CHI-SQUARE =14.6193 DF =8

TABLE – 4.47
AUTHORSHIP PATTERN IN PUBLIC LIBRARIES AND COMMUNITY INFORMATION SERVICES

Year	*Single author*	*Two authors*	*Three and above authors*	*Total*
Upto 1962	68	3	0	71
	95.77	4.23	0.00	100.00
1963-72	63	9	2	74
	85.14	12.16	2.70	100.00
1973-82	68	8	2	78
	87.18	10.26	2.56	100.00
1983-92	60	6	0	66
	90.91	9.09	0.00	100.00
1993-02	14	3	1	18
	77.78	16.67	5.55	100.00
2003	0	0	0	0
	0.00	0.00	0.00	0.00
Total	273	29	5	307
	85.93	9.45	1.62	100.00

CHI-SQUARE =9.3634 DF =8

TABLE – 4.48
AUTHORSHIP PATTERN IN SCIENTIFIC AND TECHNICAL LIBRARIES

Year	*Single author*	*Two authors*	*Three and above authors*	*Total*
Upto 1962	32	7	1	40
	80.00	17.50	2.50	100.00
1963-72	55	7	4	66
	83.33	10.61	6.06	100.00
1973-82	45	12	3	60
	75.00	20.00	5.00	100.00
1983-92	24	11	1	36
	66.67	30.56	2.77	100.00
1993-02	20	1	1	22
	90.92	4.54	4.54	100.00
2003	0	0	0	0
	0.00	0.00	0.00	0.00
Total	176	38	10	224
	78.57	16.96	4.47	100.00

CHI-SQUARE =10.1902 DF =8

TABLE – 4.49
AUTHORSHIP PATTERN IN UNIVERSITY LIBRARIES, USERS AND SERVICES

Year	*Single author*	*Two authors*	*Three and above authors*	*Total*
Upto 1962	143	39	9	191
	74.87	20.42	4.71	100.00
1963-1972	173	27	1	201
	86.07	13.43	0.50	100.00
1973-82	229	37	7	273
	83.88	13.55	2.57	100.00
1983-92	226	35	5	266
	84.96	13.16	1.88	100.00
1993-02	46	11	3	60
	76.67	18.33	5.00	100.00
2003	0	0	0	0
	0.00	0.00	0.00	0.00
Total	821	149	25	995
	82.51	14.97	2.52	100.00

CHI-SQUARE =16.4419 DF =8

Authorship Pattern: Single Vs Multiple Authorship

The examination of the authorship pattern reveals that majority of citations are by single author accounting for 80.95%. The remaining percent belongs to multiple authors i.e. 19.05%. Among the citations with multiple authorship majority belongs to two authors 1680 (15.57%) citations followed by citations by more than three authors with 2.37 percent of the total citations. Works done by three authors constitute only 1.10 percent. (Tables 4.38-4.49).

Period-wise Analysis

The period-wise distribution of citations reveals some important findings. Upto 1872-1882 there is no multiple authorship, out of total citations 2 (100.00) are written by single author which shows the absence of multiple authorship. We can observe a uniform trend regarding authorship pattern upto 1903-12 where the single authorship dominated the scene. During the period 1913-22 there is a swing in favour of multiple authorship. Except for that short period single authorship is in strong position than multiple authorship.

Among the citations by single author, majority of the citations belong to 1983-92. The least number of citations by single author were reported during the period 1883-92. The highest number of citations by two authors were reported during the period 1983-92. Among the citations by three authors, majority of the citations belong to 1993-2002.

The analysis of data in the table reveals that there is increasing trend of single authored citations. We can observe a irregular trend in case of single authorship upto 1913-22 and from there we can notice an increasing graph for single authored citations which shows the intention of authors to write individually in the field of Library and Information Science. Even though the single authorship dominated the proceedings there is changing scenario in multiple authorship as we can observe an increasing trend. Information explosion and inter-disciplinary nature of the subject have been compelling the authors to collaborate and hence the increasing trend towards multiple authorship can be observed in any discipline and for the present purpose in the field of Library and Information Science.

The reference period is plotted on X-axis the and values of percentage of citations are plotted on Y-axis for citations with single, two and three and above authors for the purpose of drawing line diagrams. The authorship trend has been clearly explained with the help of 3rd polynomial using MS-Excel software.

Degree of Collaboration among authors in the discipline of Library and Information Science

Subramanyam (1983) has worked out a formula to compute the degree of collaboration in a discipline by utilizing the data related to multi-authored research papers and single authored research papers. There was no collaboration for the periods 1872-1882 and 1883-1892. However the degree of collaboration started during the period 1893-1902. The table reveals that the degree of collaboration was highest during the period 1993-2002 in the discipline Library and Information Science and its sub-disciplines.

The Degree of Collaboration in the discipline Library and Information Science was found to be 0.2266. The collaboration started during the period 1893-1902. Among the sub-disciplines, the degree of collaboration has been highest in Bibliometrics (0.3045) followed by College Libraries, Users and Services (0.2880) and Agriculture Information, Libraries, Users and Services (0.2732). The degree of collaboration varied between 0.2060 and 0.3045 for all the sub-disciplines of Library and Information Science.

TABLE – 450
DEGREE OF COLLABORATION IN LIS AND ITS SUB DISCIPLINES

Subjects	*1872-1882*	*1883-1892*	*1893-1902*	*1903-1912*	*1913-1922*	*1923-1932*	*1933-1942*	*1943-1952*	*1953-1962*	*1963-1972*	*1973-1982*	*1983-1992*	*1993-2002*	*2003 & Above*	*Total*
	1	*2*	*3*	*4*	*5*	*6*	*7*	*8*	*9*	*10*	*11*	*12*	*13*	*14*	*15*
Agriculture	0.0000	0.0000	0.0000	0.0000	0.0000	0.0000	0.0000	0.0000	0.0000	0.0000	0.0000	0.0000	0.2732	0.0000	0.2732
Information, Libraries, Users and Services	0.0000	0.0000	0.0000	0.2732	0.0000	0.2732	0.0000	0.0000	0.0000	0.0000	0.0000	0.0000	0.3265	0.0000	0.3045
Bibliometrics	0.0000	0.0000	0.0000	0.3265	0.0000	0.3045	0.0000	0.0000	0.0000	0.0000	0.0000	0.1293	0.0714	0.1552	0.2880
College Libraries, Users and Services	0.0000	0.0000	0.1293	0.0714	0.1552	0.2880	0.0000	0.0000	0.0000	0.0000	0.0000	0.0000	0.2639	0.0000	0.2685
Libraries and IT	0.0000	0.0000	0.0000	0.2639	0.0000	0.2685	0.0000	0.0000	0.0000	0.0000	0.0000	0.0000	0.1931	0.0000	0.2639
Marketing of Library Information Services and Products	0.0000	0.0000	0.0000	0.1931	0.0000	0.2639	0.0000	0.0000	0.0000	0.0000	0.0000	0.2514	0.1953	0.0000	0.2572
Medical Information, Libraries, Users and Services	0.0000	0.0000	0.2514	0.1953	0.0000	0.2572	0.0000	0.0000	0.0000	0.0000	0.0000	0.0000	0.1619	0.0455	0.2386
Other Aspects															

(Contd...)

	1	2	3	4	5	6	7	8	9	10	11	12	13	14	15
Other Libraries, Users and Services	0.0000	0.0000	0.0000	0.1619	0.0455	0.2386	0.0000	0.0000	0.0000	0.0000	0.0000	0.1125	0.1722	0.0000	0.2241
Pblic Libraries and Community Information Services	0.0000	0.0000	0.1125	0.1722	0.0000	0.2241	0.0000	0.0000	0.0000	0.0000	0.0000	0.0913	0.1304	0.1346	0.2150
Scientific and Technical Libraries	0.0000	0.0000	0.0913	0.1304	0.1346	0.2150	0.0000	0.0000	0.0000	0.0000	0.0000	0.1896	0.1641	0.2892	0.2082
University Libraries, Users and Services	0.0000	0.0000	0.1896	0.1641	0.2892	0.2082	0.0000	0.0000	0.0000	0.0000	0.0000	0.2744	0.1690	0.1667	0.2060
Total	0.0000	0.0000	0.2744	0.1690	0.1667	0.2060	0.0000	0.0000	0.0000	0.0000	0.0000	0.2028	0.2073	0.2073	0.2266

Average Number of Authors per Citation in Library and Information Science

The type and nature of research conducted has a vast influence on the growth of collaborative papers and also number of authors in a discipline. The degree of collaboration in any discipline can be estimated by finding out the average number of authors per citation. The analysis of the main discipline Library and Information Science and its sub-disciplines shows a increase in average number of authors per citation from beginning to the current year. The average number of authors per citation in LIS and its sub-disciplines ranges from 1.17 to 1.49.

TABLE – 4.51
AVERAGE NUMBER OF AUTHORS PER CITATION IN LIBRARY AND INFORMATION SCIENCE

Year	*No. of Citations*	*No. of Authors*	*Average No. of Authors*
1872-82	2	2	1.00
1883-92	1	1	1.00
1893-02	4	4	1.00
1903-12	7	7	1.00
1913-22	12	18	1.50
1923-32	55	63	1.15
1933-42	90	103	1.14
1943-52	290	343	1.18
1953-62	678	792	1.17
1963-72	1924	2337	1.21
1973-82	3252	4065	1.25
1983-92	3704	4864	1.31
1993-02	1666	2414	1.45
2003 and Above	12	13	1.08
Total	11697	15026	1.28

The above table represents the average number of authors per citation in the field of Library and Information Science. The average number is steady in the initial years, fluctuated in later stage and showed a marked increase i.e. 1.21 (1963-1972) to 1.45 (1993-2002). The average number of authors per citation in this particular discipline is 1.28.

TABLE – 4.52
AVERAGE NUMBER OF AUTHORS PER CITATION IN AGRICULTURE INFORMATION, LIBRARIES, USERS AND SERVICES

Year	*No. of Citations*	*No. of Authors*	*Average No. of Authors*
1923-32	1	1	1.00
1933-42	1	1	1.00
1943-52	1	2	2.00
1953-62	2	2	1.00
1963-72	41	61	1.49
1973-82	111	146	1.32
1983-92	205	265	1.29
1993-02	107	153	1.43
2003 and Above	0	0	0.00
Total	469	631	1.35

The average number of authors per citation in sub-discipline "Agriculture Information, Libraries, Users and Services" is depicted in the above table. In the initial years i.e. 1872-1882 to 1913-19212 the average number is zero and after that there are fluctuations in the average number of authors. However the average number of authors for this field is 1.35.

TABLE – 4.53
AVERAGE NUMBER OF AUTHORS PER CITATION IN BIBLIOMETRICS

Year	*No. of Citations*	*No. of Authors*	*Average No. of Authors*
1893-02	2	2	1.00
1903-12	0	0	0.00
1913-22	6	12	2.00
1923-32	25	30	1.20
1933-42	12	12	1.00
1943-52	27	27	1.00
1953-62	45	55	1.22
1963-72	160	193	1.21
1973-82	402	564	1.40
1983-92	453	655	1.45
1993-02	153	246	1.61
2003 and Above	0	0	0.00
Total	1285	1796	1.40

The average number of authors per citation in "Bibliometrics" is presented in the above table. The average value increased from 1.00 to 2.00. The average number of authors per citation ratio is 1.40

TABLE – 4.54
AVERAGE NUMBER OF AUTHORS PER CITATION IN COLLEGE LIBRARIES, USERS AND SERVICES

Year	*No. of Citations*	*No. of Authors*	*Average No. of Authors*
1913-22	1	1	1.00
1923-32	0	0	0.00
1933-42	2	2	1.00
1943-52	12	12	1.00
1953-62	30	31	1.03
1963-72	140	153	1.09
1973-82	128	156	1.22
1983-92	180	224	1.24
1993-02	143	198	1.38
2003 and Above	5	5	1.00
Total	641	782	1.22

The average number of authors per citation in "College Libraries, Users and Services" is analysed in the above table. The results indicate that the ratio has increased from 1.00 (1943-52) to 1.38 (1993-2002). However the average number of author per citation ratio is 1.22.

TABLE – 4.55
AVERAGE NUMBER OF AUTHORS PER CITATION IN LIBRARIES AND I.T.

Year	*No. of Citations*	*No. of Authors*	*Average No. of Authors*
1903-12	2	2	1.00
1913-22	0	0	0.00
1923-32	0	0	0.00
1933-42	2	3	1.50
1943-52	6	8	1.33
1953-62	12	16	1.33
1963-72	43	60	1.40
1973-82	85	125	1.47
1983-92	309	399	1.29
1993-02	189	267	1.41
2003 and Above	0	0	0.00
Total	648	880	1.36

The average number of authors per citation in "Libraries and I.T" is shown in above table. The average number increased from 1.00 (1903-1912) to 1.50 (1933-1942) and average number of authors per citation is 1.36.

TABLE – 4.56
AVERAGE NUMBER OF AUTHORS PER CITATION IN MARKETING OF LIBRARY INFORMATION SERVICES AND PRODUCTS

Year	*No. of Citations*	*No. of Authors*	*Average No. of Authors*
1943-52	1	2	2.00
1953-62	6	6	1.00
1963-72	24	32	1.33
1973-82	105	123	1.17
1983-92	96	126	1.31
1993-02	161	297	1.84
2003 and Above	0	0	0.00
Total	393	586	1.49

The table presents the average number of authors per citation in "Marketing of Library Information Services and Products" even though it was zero from (1872-1882) to (1933-1942) the average number gradually presented a increasing trend. We can observe a steady increase in average number of authors from 1.17 (1973-1982) to 1.84 (1993-2002). The average number of authors per citation ratio is 1.49.

TABLE – 4.57
AVERAGE NUMBER OF AUTHORS PER CITATION IN MEDICAL INFORMATION, LIBRARIES, USERS AND SERVICES

Year	*No. of Citations*	*No. of Authors*	*Average No. of Authors*
1923-32	1	1	1.00
1933-42	2	3	1.50
1943-52	8	11	1.38
1953-62	28	37	1.32
1963-72	158	200	1.27
1973-82	185	244	1.32
1983-92	237	319	1.35
1993-02	66	77	1.17
2003 and Above	0	0	0.00
Total	685	892	1.30

The analysis of the table clearly depicts that average number of authors per citation in the field of "Medical Information, Libraries, Users and Services" has been highest (1.50) during the period 1933-1942 followed by (1.38) during the period 1943-52. The study of table shows that average number of authors per citation in this sub-discipline is 1.30.

TABLE – 4.58
AVERAGE NUMBER OF AUTHORS PER CITATION IN OTHER ASPECTS

Year	*No. of Citations*	*No. of Authors*	*Average No. of Authors*
1872-82	2	2	1.00
1883-92	1	1	1.00
1893-02	1	1	1.00
1903-12	1	1	1.00
1913-22	1	1	1.00
1923-32	3	3	1.00
1933-42	23	24	1.04
1943-52	56	64	1.14
1953-62	144	160	1.11
1963-72	331	369	1.11
1973-82	543	648	1.19
1983-92	555	774	1.39
1993-02	220	294	1.34
2003 and Above	0	0	0.00
Total	1881	2342	1.25

The findings of the above table indicates that average number of authors per citation is uniform with 1.00 from 1872-1882 to 1923-1932. However after this period there is some degree of fluctuation in the later years. The increase in average number of authors per citation in the sub-discipline of "Other Aspects" can be clearly observed if we examine the years 1872-1882 where the average number of authors per citation is 1.00 and 1983-1992 where the average number of authors per citation is 1.39. The average number of authors per citation for the entire period in this discipline is 1.25.

TABLE – 4.59
AVERAGE NUMBER OF AUTHORS PER CITATION IN OTHER LIBRARIES USERS AND SERVICES

Year	*No. of Citations*	*No. of Authors*	*Average No. of Authors*
1903-12	1	1	1.00
1913-22	0	0	0.00
1923-32	1	1	1.00
1933-42	2	2	1.00
1943-52	7	9	1.29
1953-62	22	25	1.14
1963-72	70	86	1.23
1973-82	225	275	1.22
1983-92	258	312	1.21
1993-02	33	44	1.33
2003 and Above	0	0	0.00
Total	619	755	1.22

The results of the table depicts average number of authors per citation in the field of "Other Libraries, Users and Services". The average number of authors per citation has presented a steady increase from 1.00 in (1903-1912) to 1.33 in (1993-2002). The average number of authors per citations for the period is 1.22.

TABLE – 4.60
AVERAGE NUMBER OF AUTHORS PER CITATION IN PUBLIC LIBRARIES AND COMMUNITY INFORMATION SERVICES

Year	*No. of Citations*	*No. of Authors*	*Average No. of Authors*
1	*2*	*3*	*4*
1903-12	1	1	1.00
1913-22	4	4	1.00
1923-32	7	7	1.00

(Contd...)

1	*2*	*3*	*4*
1933-42	12	12	1.00
1943-52	25	27	1.08
1953-62	71	76	1.07
1963-72	219	267	1.22
1973-82	354	404	1.14
1983-92	222	257	1.16
1993-02	99	129	1.30
2003 and Above	3	4	1.33
Total	1017	1188	1.17

The data in the table represents the average number of authors per citation in "Public Libraries and Community Information Services". The average value has marked a steady increase with passage of time. The average value increased from 1.00 (1903-1912) to 1.33 (2003 and above). The ratio of average number of authors per citation in the sub-field is 1.17.

TABLE – 4.61
AVERAGE NUMBER OF AUTHORS PER CITATION IN SCIENTIFIC AND TECHNICAL LIBRARIES

Year	*No. of Citations*	*No. of Authors*	*Average No. of Authors*
1903-12	1	1	1.00
1913-22	0	0	0.00
1923-32	3	3	1.00
1933-42	6	6	1.00
1943-52	52	57	1.10
1953-62	99	115	1.16
1963-72	212	263	1.24
1973-82	351	452	1.29
1983-92	269	360	1.34
1993-02	258	380	1.47
2003 and Above	0	0	0.00
Total	1251	1637	1.31

The average number of authors per citation in "Scientific and Technical Libraries" is depicted in the above table. The average value increased from 1.00 (1903-1912) to 1.47 (1993-2002). The ratio of average number of authors per citation for the entire period in the particular field is 1.31.

TABLE – 4.62
AVERAGE NUMBER OF AUTHORS PER CITATION IN UNIVERSITY LIBRARIES, USERS AND SERVICES

Year	*No. of Citations*	*No. of Authors*	*Average No. of Authors*
1872-82	0	0	0.00
1883-92	0	0	0.00
1893-02	1	1	1.00
1903-12	1	1	1.00
1913-22	0	0	0.00
1923-32	14	17	1.21
1933-42	28	38	1.36
1943-52	95	124	1.31
1953-62	219	269	1.23
1963-72	526	653	1.24
1973-82	763	928	1.22
1983-92	920	1173	1.28
1993-02	237	329	1.39
2003 and Above	4	4	1.00
Total	2808	3537	1.26

The data in the above table reveals the average number of authors per citation in the sub-discipline "University Libraries, Users and Services". In the initial years the average was zero. The average number of authors per citation ratio increased from 1.00 (1893-1902) to 1.39 (1993-2002). However we can observe a irregular trend regarding the average number over the entire period. The average number of authors per citation ratio is 1.26 in this specified sub-discipline.

Self Citations

Citation Analysis is one of the most important Bibliometric techniques involving analysis of the reference forming part of primary communication. There has developed a trend of citing own papers in a research article. The citing of own earlier published papers is known as Self-citation which has become a common phenomenon in all disciplines and for the present case in the field of Library and Information Science.

We shall discuss two types of self citations in this section. The reference to a document which has been authored or co-authored by the researcher himself is considered as Type I where as the reference to a document authored or co-authored by research director or guide is considered as Type II.

Distribution of Self Citations Subdiscipline-wise

TABLE – 4.63
DISTRIBUTION OF SELF CITATIONS SUB-DISCIPLINE-WISE

(TYPE – I)

Sl. No.	*Subject*	*Total No. of Citations*	*Total No. of Self Citations*	*Percentage of Self-Citation*
	1	*2*	*3*	*4*
1.	Agriculture Information, Libraries, Users and Services	538	1	0.19
2.	Bibliometrics	1392	0	0.00
3.	College Libraries, Users and Services	758	0	0.00
4.	Libraries and I.T	780	1	0.13

(Contd...)

1	*2*	*3*	*4*
5. Marketing of Library Information Services and Products	448	0	0.00
6. Medical Information, Libraries, Users and Services	854	0	0.00
7. Other Aspects	2239	4	0.18
8. Other Libraries, Users and Services	756	10	1.32
9. Public Libraries and Community Information Services	1178	3	0.25
10. Scientific and Technical Libraries	1508	7	0.46
11. University Libraries, Users and Services	3310	15	0.45
All Sub-disciplines	13761	41	0.30

The percentage of Self citations (Type I) in Library and Information Science and its sub-disciplines has been presented in the above table. It is noticeable form the table that Other Libraries, Users and Services stood in the first place with highest percentage of self citations i.e. 1.32, followed by Scientific and Technical Libraries with 0.46 percent and University Libraries, Users and Services with 0.45 percent. It is interesting to note that in certain sub-disciplines like Bibliometrics, College Libraries, Users and Services, Marketing of Library Information Services and Products and Medical Information, Libraries, Users and Services the self citation percentage is zero. The table reveals that self citation percentage in various sub disciplines of Library and Information Science varied from 0 to 1.32 percent.

TABLE – 4.64
DISTRIBUTION OF SELF CITATIONS
SUB DISCIPLINE-WISE

(TYPE – II)

Sl. No.	*Subject*	*Total No. of Citations*	*Total No. of Self Citations*	*Percentage of Self-Citation*
1.	Agriculture Information, Libraries, Users and Services	538	0	0.00
2.	Bibliometrics	1392	0	0.00
3.	College Libraries, Users and Services	758	0	0.00
4.	Libraries and I.T	780	0	0.00
5.	Marketing of Library Information Services and Products	448	0	0.00
6.	Medical Information, Libraries, Users and Services	854	0	0.00
7.	Other Aspects	2239	0	0.00
8.	Other Libraries, Users and Services	756	0	0.00
9.	Public Libraries and Community Information Services	1178	0	0.00
10.	Scientific and Technical Libraries	1508	0	0.00
11.	University Libraries, Users and Services	3310	0	0.00
	All Sub-disciplines	13761	0	0.00

Table 4.64 presents Percentage of Self citation of Type II in Library and Information Science and its sub-disciplines. However it is noticed that there is complete absence of self citation of this type.

Self Citation Rate

The following tables indicate the Self citation rate (Type I and Type II) in relation to citations appended to theses in the field of Library and Information Science and its sub-disciplines.

TABLE – 4.65
SELF CITATION RATE IN LIBRARY AND INFORMATION SCIENCE AND ITS SUB DISCIPLINES
(TYPE I)

Sub disciplines	*Total No. of Theses*	*No. of Theses with Self-Citations*	*No. of Theses without Self-Citations*	*Self citation rate*
1	*2*	*3*	*4*	*5*
Agriculture Information, Libraries, Users and Services	3	1	2	33.33
Bibliometrics	5	0	5	0.00
College Libraries, Users and Services	6	0	6	0.00
Libraries and I.T	4	1	3	25.00
Marketing of Library Information Services and Products	2	0	2	0.00
Medical Information,	4	0	4	0.00

(Contd...)

1	*2*	*3*	*4*	*5*
Libraries, Users and Services				
Other Aspects	11	2	9	18.18
Other Libraries, Users and Services	4	1	3	25.00
Public Libraries and Community Information Services	8	2	6	25.00
Scientific and Technical Libraries	7	1	6	14.29
University Libraries, Users and Services	17	2	15	11.76
All Sub-disciplines	71	10	61	14.08

Self citation rate (Type I) in Library and Information Science and its sub-disciplines are shown in the above table. The main observation from the data available in the data reveal that for sub-disciplines like Bibliometrics, College Libraries, Users and Services, Marketing of Library Information Services and Products and Medical Information, Libraries, Users and Services self citations are not present. The self citation rate in LIS and its sub-disciplines varies from 0 to 33.33 percent. The self citation behaviour (Type I) is high in sub-discipline Agriculture Information, Libraries, Users and Services with 33.33 percent followed by Libraries and I.T, Other Libraries, Users and Services and Public Libraries and Community Information Services with 25.00 percent each. The self citation rate in Other Aspects, Scientific and Technical Libraries and University Libraries, Users and Services is 18.18, 14.29, and 11.76 percent respectively. The self citation rate in Library and Information as a whole is 14.08 percent.

TABLE – 4.66
SELF CITATION RATE IN LIBRARY AND INFORMATION SCIENCE AND ITS SUB DISCIPLINES

(TYPE II)

Sub disciplines	*Total No. of Theses*	*No. of Theses with Self-Citations*	*No. of Theses without Self-Citations*	*Self citation rate*
Agriculture Information, Libraries, Users and Services	3	0	3	0.00
Bibliometrics	5	0	5	0.00
College Libraries, Users and Services	6	0	6	0.00
Libraries and I.T	4	0	4	0.00
Marketing of Library Information Services and Products	2	0	2	0.00
Medical Information, Libraries, Users and Services	4	0	4	0.00
Other Aspects	11	0	11	0.00
Other Libraries, Users and Services	4	0	4	0.00
Public Libraries and Community Information Services	8	0	8	0.00
Scientific and Technical Libraries	7	0	7	0.00
University Libraries, Users and Services	17	0	17	0.00
All Sub-disciplines	71	0	71	0.00

TABLE – 4.67
BIBLIOGRAPHIC FORM-WISE DISTRIBUTION OF SELF-CITATIONS IN LIS AND ITS SUB DISCIPLINES TYPE – I

Subjects	*Acts*	*Bills*	*Books*	*Conference proceedings*	*Disser-tations*	*Editorial works*	*Journals*	*News-papers*	*Others*	*Reference Books*	*Reports*	*Standards*	*Theses*	*Un-publi-shed*	*All Forms*
Agriculture Information, Libraries, Users and Services	0 0.00	0 0.00	0 0.00	1 100.00	0 0.00	0 0.00	0 0.00	0 0.00	0 0.00	0 0.00	0 0.00	0 0.00	0 0.00	0 0.00	1 100.00
Bibliometrics	0 0.00	0 0.00	0 0.00	0 0.00	0 0.00	0 0.00	0 0.00	0 0.00	0 0.00	0 0.00	0 0.00	0 0.00	0 0.00	0 0.00	0 0.00
College Libraries, Users and Services	0 0.00	0 0.00	0 0.00	0 0.00	0 0.00	0 0.00	0 0.00	0 0.00	0 0.00	0 0.00	0 0.00	0 0.00	0 0.00	0 0.00	0 0.00
Libraries and I.T	0 0.00	0 0.00	0 0.00	1 100.00	0 0.00	0 0.00	0 0.00	0 0.00	0 0.00	0 0.00	0 0.00	0 0.00	0 0.00	0 0.00	1 100
Marketing of Library Information Services and Products	0 0.00	0 0.00	0 0.00	0 0.00	0 0.00	0 0.00	0 0.00	0 0.00	0 0.00	0 0.00	0 0.00	0 0.00	0 0.00	0 0.00	0 0.00
Medical Information, Libraries, Users and Services	0 0.00	0 0.00	0 0.00	0 0.00	0 0.00	0 0.00	0 0.00	0 0.00	0 0.00	0 0.00	0 0.00	0 0.00	0 0.00	0 0.00	0 0.00
Other Aspects	0 0.00	0 0.00	0 0.00	1 25.00	0 0.00	0 0.00	2 50.00	0 0.00	0 0.00	0 0.00	0 0.00	0 0.00	0 0.00	1 25.00	4 100.00

(Contd...)

Subjects	*Acts*	*Bills*	*Books*	*Conference proceedings*	*Disser-tations*	*Editorial works*	*Journals*	*News-papers*	*Others*	*Reference Books*	*Reports*	*Standards*	*Theses*	*Un-publi-*	*All F*
Other Libraries, Users and Services	0	0	0	0	0	9	1	0	0	0	0	0	0	0	10
	0.00	0.00	0.00	0.00	0.00	90.00	10.00	0.00	0.00	0.00	0.00	0.00	0.00	0.00	100.00
Public Libraries and Community Information Services	0	0	0	0	0	0	3	0	0	0	0	0	0	0	3
	0.00	0.00	0.00	0.00	0.00	0.00	100.00	0.00	0.00	0.00	0.00	0.00	0.00	0.00	100.00
7Scientific and Technical Libraries	0	0	0	6	0	0	1	0	0	0	0	0	0	0	
	0.00	0.00	0.00	85.71	0.00	0.00	14.29	0.00	0.00	0.00	0.00	0.00	0.00	0.00	100.00
University Libraries, Users and Services	0	0	0	0	13	0	2	0	0	0	0	0	0	0	15
	0.00	0.00	0.00	0.00	86.67	0.00	13.33	0.00	0.00	0.00	0.00	0.00	0.00	0.00	100.00
All Subjects	0	0	0	9	13	9	9	0	0	0	0	0	0	1	41
	0.00	0.00	0.00	21.95	31.71	21.95	21.95	0.00	0.00	0.00	0.00	0.00	0.00	2.44	100.00

TABLE – 4.68
BIBLIOGRAPHIC FORM-WISE DISTRIBUTION OF SELF-CITATIONS IN LIS AND ITS SUB DISCIPLINES TYPE - II

Subjects	*Acts*	*Bills*	*Books*	*Conference proceedings*	*Disser-tations*	*Editorial works*	*Journals*	*News-papers*	*Others*	*Reference Books*	*Reports*	*Standards*	*Theses*	*Un-publi-shed*	*All Forms*
Agriculture Information, Libraries, Users and Services	0	0	0	0	0	0	0	0	0	0	0	0	0	0	0
	0.00	0.00	0.00	0.00	0.00	0.00	0.00	0.00	0.00	0.00	0.00	0.00	0.00	0.00	0.00
Bibliometrics	0	0	0	0	0	0	0	0	0	0	0	0	0	0	0
	0.00	0.00	0.00	0.00	0.00	0.00	0.00	0.00	0.00	0.00	0.00	0.00	0.00	0.00	0.00
College Libraries, Users and Services	0	0	0	0	0	0	0	0	0	0	0	0	0	0	0
	0.00	0.00	0.00	0.00	0.00	0.00	0.00	0.00	0.00	0.00	0.00	0.00	0.00	0.00	0.00
Libraries and I.T	0	0	0	0	0	0	0	0	0	0	0	0	0	0	0
	0.00	0.00	0.00	0.00	0.00	0.00	0.00	0.00	0.00	0.00	0.00	0.00	0.00	0.00	0.00
Marketing of Library Information Services and Products	0	0	0	0	0	0	0	0	0	0	0	0	0	0	0
	0.00	0.00	0.00	0.00	0.00	0.00	0.00	0.00	0.00	0.00	0.00	0.00	0.00	0.00	0.00
Medical Information, Libraries, Users and Services	0	0	0	0	0	0	0	0	0	0	0	0	0	0	0
	0.00	0.00	0.00	0.00	0.00	0.00	0.00	0.00	0.00	0.00	0.00	0.00	0.00	0.00	0.00

(Contd...)

Subjects	Acts	Bills	Books	Conference proceedings	Disser-tations	Editorial works	Journals	News-papers	Others	Reference Books	Reports	Standards	Theses	Un-publi-shed	All Forms
Other Aspects	0 0.00	0 0.00	0 0.00	0 0.00	0 0.00	0 0.00	0 0.00	0 0.00	0 0.00	0 0.00	0 0.00	0 0.00	0 0.00	0 0.00	0 0.00
Other Libraries, Users and Services	0 0.00	0 0.00	0 0.00	0 0.00	0 0.00	0 0.00	0 0.00	0 0.00	0 0.00	0 0.00	0 0.00	0 0.00	0 0.00	0 0.00	0 0.00
Public Libraries and Community Information Services	0 0.00	0 0.00	0 0.00	0 0.00	0 0.00	0 0.00	0 0.00	0 0.00	0 0.00	0 0.00	0 0.00	0 0.00	0 0.00	0 0.00	0 0.00
Scientific and Technical Libraries	0 0.00	0 0.00	0 0.00	0 0.00	0 0.00	0 0.00	0 0.00	0 0.00	0 0.00	0 0.00	0 0.00	0 0.00	0 0.00	0 0.00	0 0.00
University Libraries, Users and Services	0 0.00	0 0.00	0 0.00	0 0.00	0 0.00	0 0.00	0 0.00	0 0.00	0 0.00	0 0.00	0 0.00	0 0.00	0 0.00	0 0.00	0 0.00
All Subjects	0 0.00	0 0.00	0 0.00	0 0.00	0 0.00	0 0.00	0 0.00	0 0.00	0 0.00	0 0.00	0 0.00	0 0.00	0 0.00	0 0.00	0 0.00

The Self citation rate (Type II) in Library and Information Science and its sub-disciplines indicates that self citation rate (Type II) is zero for all sub-disciplines of Library and Information Science.

Bibliographic Form-wise Distribution of Self Citations in Library and Information Science and its Sub-disciplines

It is noticed from the present study that Self citations are disbursed among different bibliographic forms like Journals, Books, Conference Proceedings, Theses, Dissertations, Editorial Works, Reports, Acts, Bills, Standards, Newspapers, Reference Books and Others. The percentage of self citations to dissertations has been highest with 31.71 percent, in different sub-disciplines of Library and Information Science.

The Bibliographic form-wise distribution of citations (Type II) is absent for all sub-disciplines of Library and Information Science.

Ranking and Scattering of Journals

Rising costs of the journals on one hand and financial crunch on the other hand are posing serious threat to the librarians and library administrators of the present day. To acquire all journals is a big problem and at the same time the satisfaction of the users should not be neglected. The most productive journals are to be identified because they carry the core information that suit the requirements of the researchers as well as the general users which solves the acquisition problems and helps to weed out the journals which are unproductive. For this purpose the ranking of journals has to be undertaken. The ranked list shows the relative contribution of the each journal in the list of cited journals cited by the researcher. The journals which are placed in the beginning are considered to be most productive and contribute most number of citations in the field. Tables 4.69 – 4.80 depict the ranked list of journals in Library and Information Science and its sub-disciplines.

It is clear from the ranked list of journals in the field of Library and Information Science that first eighteen journals have contributed 50 percent of the citations cited by the researchers. The first eight journals accounted for 30 percent of the total journal citations. On the basis of their rank they can be considered as most productive journals. The remaining 50 percent is contributed by 755 journals. 75 percent of the citations are covered in 50 journals.

It is observed from the table that first two journals are published from United States of America contributing nearly 10 percent of the total citations. The first two journals are Library Trends and College and Research Libraries. ASLIB Proceedings which stood in third place is published from United Kingdom. Annals of Library Science and Documentation, University News, Herald of Library Science, ILA Bulletin which occupied fourth, fifth, sixth and seventh places respectively are published from India. United States is found to be the most productive country contributing 36 percent of the core journals followed by India with 32 percent.

The ranked list of journals in sub-discipline Agriculture Information, Libraries, Users and Services depicts that first seven journals contributed more than 50 percent of the total journal citations. 30 percent of the citations are contributed by first two journals i.e. International Journal of Agricultural Librarians and Documentalists and Indian Journal of Agricultural Library and Information Science. The remaining 70 percent of the citation are contributed by 68 journals.

Out of the first seven journals which are considered as core journals in this field, four journals are published from India while one each is published from Netherlands, United Kingdom and United States of America.

The productivity of cited journals in the field of Bibliometrics reveal that the first five journals contribute 50 percent of the total citations and the rest of the journals i.e. 46 contribute the remaining 50 percent which clearly proves the relevance of the first five journals. Scientometrics from Netherlands with 213 citations occupy the first place followed by *Journal of Documentation, Annals of Library Science and Documentation, Journal of the American Society for Information Science* and *IASLIC Bulletin.* Two out of the five core journals are published by India. United States of America, United Kingdom, Netherlands are publishing one journal each of the five core journals.

The rank-wise distribution of journals cited in the sub discipline College Libraries, Users and Services depict that the first five journals in this subject are found to be contributing more than 60 percent of the total citations. *University News* published from India stood in the first place with 104 (23.2662) citations. Out of the core five journals three journals are published from India and other two journals published from United States of America which clearly shows the domination of Indian Journals in the respective field.

The ranked list of journals cited in the sub discipline "Libraries and I.T." shows that the first 14 journals are found to be contributing to 50 percent of the citations in this discipline. The five core journals i.e. *Program, Library Trends, DESIDOC Bulletin of Information Technology, Annals of Library Science and Documentation* and *Information Technology and Libraries* have contributed 27 percent of the total citations. Out of the 14 most productive journals six, five and three are published from U.S.A., India and U.K. respectively.

The productivity of cited journals in field of Marketing of Library Information Services and Products indicate that the first five journals are found to be contributing 50 percent of the citations in Marketing of Library and Information Services and Products. Nearly half of them are from the first two ranked journals viz. ASLIB Proceedings and Special Libraries which are published from U.K and U.S.A respectively. Out of the first five core journals four journals are published from U.S.A and one journal is published from United Kingdom.

Analysis of the table gives a clear picture that core journals got the maximum number of citations which shows the importance and relevance of these journals in the subject "*Medical Information, Libraries, Users and Services*". The first fourteen journals contributed 50 percent of the total citations and rest 29 journals contributed the remaining 50 percent. Bulletin of Medical Library Association with 59 (11.5686%) citations occupied the first place followed by ASLIB Proceedings, Annual Review of Information Science and Technology, Journal of the American Society for Information Science and College and Research Libraries. Out of the fourteen core journals six are published from India, five from United States of America and three from United Kingdom.

The ranked list of journals in "*Other Aspects*" indicates that first thirteen journals in the list are contributing half of the citations cited by the researchers. Herald of Library Science topped the ranked list in this subject. Six out of thirteen journals are published each by India and United States of America which clearly depicts the importance of information being published from these two countries.

In the sub discipline Other Libraries, Users and Services the analysis of data in the table depicts Law Library Journal in the first place with 24 citations followed by Annual Review of Information Science and Technology, Library Trends, Lucknow Librarian and College and Research Libraries. The first 19 journals in the ranked list are contributing 50 percent of the total citations. The first six journals are contributing more than 25 percent and this indicates the importance among the research scholars who always look for original research works which are published in primary sources of information like journals. Four out of six journals are published from United States of America and one each from United Kingdom and India.

Ranked list of journals in the subject "*Scientific and Technical Libraries*" shows that *ASLIB Proceedings* from United Kingdom with 107 (11.5302%) citations stood in the first place. Second preference is given to *Special Libraries* with 72 (7.3276%) citations and *College and Research Libraries* with 52 (5.6034%) citations stood in the third place. Out of the first 10 core journals five are published from India, three journals are published from United States of America and two journals from United Kingdom. This comes to show that researchers mainly depend upon the literature being published from these three countries.

Analysis of data reveals that first twenty journals contributed 50 percent of total journal citations in the field of "*University Libraries, Users and Services*". First eight journals constituted 30 percent of the citations. Out of the eight core journals four originated from India, three from Untied States of America and one from United Kingdom. *College and Research Libraries* published from United States of America occupied the first position among the rank list of journals with 89 (5.6508%) citations.

The Ranked List of Journals in Library & Information science & its Sub-disciplines are presented in Tables 4.69-4.80.

TABLE-4.69

RANKED LIST OF JOURNALS IN LIBRARY AND INFORMATION SCIENCE

Sl. No	*Rank*	*Title of Journal*	*Country Name*	*No of Citations*	*Percent*	*Cum Number*	*Cum Percent*
	1	*2*	*3*	*4*	*5*	*6*	*7*
01	1	Library Trends	U.S.A	430	5.4259	430	5.4259
02	2	College and Research Libraries	U.S.A	329	4.1514	759	9.5773
03	3	ASLIB Proceedings	U.K	312	3.9369	1071	13.5142
04	4	Annals of Library Science and Documentation	India	287	3.6215	1358	17.1356
05	5	University News	India	267	3.3691	1625	20.5047
06	6	Herald of Library Science	India	259	3.2681	1884	23.7729
07	7	ILA Bulletin	India	248	3.1293	2132	26.9022
08	8	Special Libraries	U.S.A	234	2.9527	2366	29.8549
09	9	Scientometrics	Neth	216	2.7256	2582	32.5804
10	10	Journal of Documentation	U.K	214	2.7003	2796	35.2808
11	11	IASLIC Bulletin	India	196	2.4732	2992	37.7539
12	12	Journal of the American Society for Information Science	U.S.A	190	2.3975	3182	40.1514
13	13	Library Quarterly	U.S.A	174	2.1956	3356	42.3470
14	14	Library Herald	India	165	2.0820	3521	44.4290

(Contd...)

	1	2	3	4	5	6	7
15	15	Library Journal	U.S.A	150	1.8927	3671	46.3218
16	16	Indian Librarian	India	106	1.3375	3777	47.6593
17	17	International Library Review	U.K	97	1.2240	3874	48.8833
18	18	International Association of Agricultural Librarians and Documentalists	Neth	92	1.1609	3966	50.0442
19	19	Journal of Library and Information Science	India	91	1.1483	4057	51.1924
20	20	Lucknow Librarian	India	89	1.1230	4146	52.3155
21	21	Journal of Librarianship	U.K	88	1.1104	4234	53.4259
22	22	Library Science with a Slant to Documentation	India	83	1.0473	4317	54.4732
23	23	Annual Review of Information Science and Technology	U.S.A	82	1.0347	4399	55.5079
24	23	Journal of Education for Library and Information Science	U.S.A	82	1.0347	4481	56.5426
25	24	Journal of Information Science	U.K	80	1.0095	4561	57.5521
26	25	Bulletin of Medical Library Association	U.K	76	0.9590	4637	58.5110
27	26	Australian Library Journal	Aus	61	0.7697	4698	59.2808
28	26	Journalism Quarterly	U.S.A	61	0.7697	4759	60.0505
29	27	Libri	Den	59	0.7445	4818	60.7950

	1	2	3	4	5	6	7
30	28	UNESCO Bulletin for Libraries	France	57	0.7192	4875	61.5142
31	29	Canadian Library Journal	Canada	51	0.6435	4926	62.1577
32	30	DESIDOC Bulletin of Information Technology	India	48	0.6057	4974	62.7634
33	31	Library Association Record	U.K	46	0.5804	5020	63.3438
34	32	Library Science with a Slant to Documentation and Information Studies	India	43	0.5426	5063	63.8864
35	32	Science	U.S.A	43	0.5426	5106	64.4290
36	33	Journal of Applied Psychology	U.S.A	41	0.5174	5147	64.9464
37	34	Library Resources and Technical Services	U.S.A	39	0.4921	5186	65.4385
38	35	IFLA Journal	Ger	37	0.4669	5223	65.9054
39	35	Information Processing and Management	U.K	37	0.4669	5260	66.3722
40	36	Indian Journal of Information, Library and Society	India	36	0.4543	5296	66.8265
41	36	Program	U.K	36	0.4543	5332	67.2808
42	37	CLIS Observer	India	34	0.4290	5366	67.7098
43	37	Indian Journal of Agricultural Library and Information Science	India	34	0.4290	5400	68.1388
44	37	Journal of Academic Librarianship	U.S.A	34	0.4290	5434	68.5678

(Contd...)

	1	2	3	4	5	6	7
45	38	International Library Movement	India	31	0.3912	5465	68.9590
46	39	American Documentation	U.S.A	30	0.3785	5495	69.3375
47	40	Indian Journal of Psychology	India	29	0.3659	5524	69.7035
48	40	Wilson Library Bulletin	U.S.A	29	0.3659	5553	70.0694
49	41	Assistant Librarian	U.K	28	0.3533	5581	70.4227
50	41	Law Library Journal	U.S.A	28	0.3533	5609	70.7760
51	42	Drexel Library Quarterly	U.S.A	27	0.3407	5636	70.1167
52	43	Library Science	India	26	0.3281	5662	71.4448
53	43	New Frontiers in Education	U.S.A	26	0.3281	5688	71.7729
54	44	Journal of Education for Librarianship	U.S.A	25	0.3155	5713	72.0883
55	44	The Indian Journal of Technical Education	India	25	0.3155	5738	72.4038
56	45	Library and Information Science Research	U.S.A	23	0.2902	5761	72.6940
57	46	Journal of Library Administration	U.S.A	22	0.2776	5783	72.9716
58	47	Reference Quarterly	U.S.A	21	0.2650	5804	73.2366
59	48	Collection Management	U.S.A	20	0.2524	5824	73.4890
60	48	Library Review	U.K	20	0.2524	5844	73.7413
61	48	Modern Librarian	India	20	0.2524	5864	73.9937
62	49	Teaching at a Distance	U.K	19	0.2397	5883	74.2334

(Contd...)

	1	2	3	4	5	6	7
63	50	UNESCO Journal of Information Science Librarianship and Archives Administration	France	18	0.2271	5901	74.4606
64	50	Vidura	India	18	0.2271	5919	74.6877
65	51	International Information Communication and Education	India	17	0.2145	5936	74.9022
66	51	Journal of Higher Education	U.S.A	17	0.2145	5953	75.1167
67	51	Journal of Librarianship and Information Science	U.K	17	0.2145	5970	75.3312
68	51	NISSAT Newsletter	India	17	0.2145	5987	75.5457
69	52	Current Contents	U.S.A	16	0.2019	6003	75.7476
70	52	Indian Journal of Medical Education	India	16	0.2019	6019	75.9495
71	52	Journal of Medical Education	U.S.A	16	0.2019	6035	76.1514
72	52	Personnel Journal	U.S.A	16	0.2019	6051	76.3533
73	52	Yojana	India	16	0.2019	6067	76.5552
74	53	American Sociological Review	U.S.A	15	0.1893	6082	76.7445
75	53	Computers and the Humanities	Neth	15	0.1893	6097	76.9338
76	53	International Information and Library Review	U.K	15	0.1893	6112	77.1230
77	53	MLAI Bulletin	India	15	0.1893	6127	77.3123
78	54	American Libraries	U.S.A	14	0.1767	6141	77.4890
79	54	Government Information Quarterly	U.S.A	14	0.1767	6155	77.6656

(Contd...)

	1	2	3	4	5	6	7
80	54	Government Publications Review	U.K	14	0.1767	6169	77.8423
81	54	Personnel Psychology	U.S.A	14	0.1767	6183	78.0190
82	54	Serials Librarian	U.S.A	14	0.1767	6197	78.1956
83	55	Australian Academic and Research Libraries	Aus	13	0.1640	6210	78.3596
84	55	Information Technology and Libraries	U.S.A	13	0.1640	6223	78.5237
85	55	International Social Science Journal	U.K	13	0.1640	6236	78.6877
86	55	Nature	U.K	13	0.1640	6249	78.8517
87	55	SLA Geography and Map Division Bulletin	U.S.A	13	0.1640	6262	79.0158
88	56	Information Development	U.K	12	0.1514	6274	79.1672
89	56	International Association of Agricultural Information Specialists	Neth	12	0.1514	6286	79.3186
90	56	Online	U.S.A	12	0.1514	6298	79.4700
91	56	Prasar	India	12	0.1514	6310	79.6215
92	57	Canadian Journal of Information and Library Science	Canada	11	0.1388	6321	79.7603
93	57	Cataloguing and Classification Quarterly	U.S.A	11	0.1388	6332	79.8991
94	57	Industrial Relations	U.K	11	0.1388	6343	80.0379
95	57	International Forum on Information and Documentation	Russia	11	0.1388	6354	80.1767

(Contd...)

	1	2	3	4	5	6	7
96	57	Journal of Indian Management Association	India	11	0.1388	6365	80.3155
97	57	Journal of the Washington Academy of Sciences	U.S.A	11	0.1388	6376	80.4543
98	58	Indian Journal of Social Work	India	10	0.1262	6386	80.5804
99	58	Journal of Personality and Social Psychology	U.S.A	10	0.1262	6396	80.7066
100	58	Marketing Library Services	Neth	10	0.1262	6406	80.8328
101	58	Nauchno-Tekhnicheskaya Informatsiya	Russia	10	0.1262	6416	80.9590
102	59	Biblithekar	Ger	9	0.1136	6425	81.0726
103	59	British Medical Journal	U.K	9	0.1136	6434	81.1861
104	59	Computers in Libraries	Ireland	9	0.1136	6443	81.2997
105	59	Electronic Library	U.S.A	9	0.1136	6452	81.4132
106	59	FID News Bulletin	Neth	9	0.1136	6461	81.5268
107	59	ICSSR Newsletter	India	9	0.1136	6470	81.6404
108	59	Information Storage and Retrieval	U.K	9	0.1136	6479	81.7539
109	59	INSPEL	Ger	9	0.1136	6488	81.8675
110	59	Journal of Engineering Education	U.S.A	9	0.1136	6497	81.9811
111	59	Journal of Indian Education	India	9	0.1136	6506	82.0946
112	59	School Librarian	U.K	9	0.1136	6515	82.2082
113	59	Social Studies of Science	U.K	9	0.1136	6524	82.3218

(Contd...)

	1	2	3	4	5	6	7
114	59	Tendril	U.S.A	9	0.1136	6533	82.4353
115	59	The Progress of Education	India	9	0.1136	6542	82.5489
116	60	ALA Bulletin	U.S.A	8	0.1009	6550	82.6498
117	60	ALIS Bulletin	U.S.A	8	0.1009	6558	82.7508
118	60	College and Research Libraries News	U.S.A	8	0.1009	6566	82.8517
119	60	Indian Journal of Extension Education	India	8	0.1009	6574	82.9527
120	60	Journal of Educational Media and Library Sciences	China	8	0.1009	6582	83.0536
121	60	Journal of Educational Planning and Administration	India	8	0.1009	6590	83.1546
122	60	Library Hi Tech	U.S.A	8	0.1009	6598	83.2555
123	60	Psychological Review	U.S.A	8	0.1009	6606	83.3565
124	60	Pub. Astr. Soc.Pacific	U.S.A	8	0.1009	6614	83.4574
125	60	Social Science Information	U.K	8	0.1009	6622	83.5584
126	61	British Journal of Educational Technology	U.K	7	0.0883	6629	83.6467
127	61	Current Science	U.S.A	7	0.0883	6636	83.7350
128	61	Educational Libraries Bulletin	U.K	7	0.0883	6643	83.8233
129	61	Education Quarterly	India	7	0.0883	6650	83.9117
130	61	Engineering	U.K	7	0.0883	6657	84.0000

(Contd...)

	1	2	3	4	5	6	7
131	61	Grandhalaya Sarvaswamu	India	7	0.0883	6664	84.0883
132	61	Health Libraries Review	U.K	7	0.0883	6671	84.1767
133	61	Indian Journal of Industrial Relations	India	7	0.0883	6678	84.2650
134	61	Industrial and Engineering Chemistry	U.S.A	7	0.0883	6685	84.3533
135	61	Information Reports and Bibliography	U.S.A	7	0.0883	6692	84.4416
136	61	Journal of Library Automation	U.S.A	7	0.0883	6699	84.5300
137	61	Library and Information Science	Japan	7	0.0883	6706	84.6183
138	61	New Library World	U.K	7	0.0883	6713	84.7066
139	61	Scientific American	U.S.A	7	0.0883	6720	84.7950
140	61	Serials Review	U.S.A	7	0.0883	6727	84.8833
141	61	The Electronic Library	Aus	7	0.0883	6734	84.9716
142	61	Timeless Fellowship	India	7	0.0883	6741	85.0599
143	61	World Health Form	Switz	7	0.0883	6748	85.1483
144	62	ASLIB Information	U.K	6	0.0757	6754	85.2240
145	62	British Journal of Academic Librarianship	U.K	6	0.0757	6760	85.2997
146	62	Education for Information	Neth	6	0.0757	6766	85.3754
147	62	Human Relations	U.S.A	6	0.0757	6772	85.4511
148	62	Human Resource Management	U.S.A	6	0.0757	6778	85.5268

(Contd...)

	1	2	3	4	5	6	7
149	62	Information Today and Tomorrow	India	6	0.0757	6784	85.6025
150	62	ISTE Newsletter	India	6	0.0757	6790	85.6782
151	62	Journal of Chemical Documentation	U.S.A	6	0.0757	6796	85.7539
152	62	Journal of Marketing	U.S.A	6	0.0757	6802	85.8297
153	62	Library Management	U.K	6	0.0757	6808	85.9054
154	62	Mainstream	India	6	0.0757	6814	85.9811
155	62	Microcomputers for Information Management	U.S.A	6	0.0757	6820	86.0568
156	62	New England Journal of Medicine	U.K	6	0.0757	6826	86.1325
157	62	Public Library Quarterly	U.S.A	6	0.0757	6832	86.2082
158	62	Social Welfare	India	6	0.0757	6838	86.2839
159	63	Advances in Librarianship	U.S.A	5	0.0631	6843	86.3470
160	63	Bibliotek	Den	5	0.0631	6848	86.4101
161	63	Bibliothek	U.K	5	0.0631	6853	86.4732
162	63	Buch Und Bibliothek	Ger	5	0.0631	6858	86.5363
163	63	Bulletin of the American Society for Information Science	U.S.A	5	0.0631	6863	86.5994
164	63	Cape Librarian	S.Afr	5	0.0631	6868	86.6625
165	63	Collection Building	U.S.A	5	0.0631	6873	86.7256
166	63	Higher Education	U.S.A	5	0.0631	6878	86.7886
167	63	Indian Journal of Applied Psychology	India	5	0.0631	6883	86.8517
168	63	Indian Libraries	India	5	0.0631	6888	86.9148

(Contd...)

	1	2	3	4	5	6	7
169	63	Interlending Review	U.K	5	0.0631	6893	86.9779
170	63	ISI Bulletin	India	5	0.0631	6898	87.0410
171	63	Journal of Abnormal and Social Psychology	U.S.A	5	0.0631	6903	87.1041
172	63	Journal of Library History	U.K	5	0.0631	6908	87.1672
173	63	Library and Librarian	India	5	0.0631	6913	87.2303
174	63	Library Progress	India	5	0.0631	6918	87.2934
175	63	National Medical Journal of India	India	5	0.0631	6923	87.3565
176	63	Pakistan Library Bulletin	Pakistan	5	0.0631	6928	87.4196
177	63	Research Quarterly	Aus	5	0.0631	6933	87.4826
178	63	Scandinavian Public Library Quarterly	Norway	5	0.0631	6938	87.5457
179	63	Science Progress	U.K	5	0.0631	6943	87.6088
180	63	Serials	U.K	5	0.0631	6948	87.6719
181	63	The Library Bulletin	India	5	0.0631	6953	87.7350
182	64	American Economic Review	U.S.A	4	0.0505	6957	87.7855
183	64	American Psychologist	U.S.A	4	0.0505	6961	87.8360
184	64	American Society for Information Science	U.S.A	4	0.0505	6965	87.8864
185	64	Annals of Internal Medicine	U.S.A	4	0.0505	6969	87.9369
186	64	ASIS Proceedings	U.S.A	4	0.0505	6973	87.9874
187	64	Australian Public Libraries and Information Services	Aus	4	0.0505	6977	88.0379

(Contd...)

	1	2	3	4	5	6	7
188	64	Bulletin of Information	France	4	0.0505	6981	88.0883
189	64	CD-ROM Professional	U.S.A	4	0.0505	6985	88.1388
190	64	Citatel	Czech	4	0.0505	6989	88.1893
191	64	Convergence	Canada	4	0.0505	6993	88.2397
192	64	Cultural Forum	India	4	0.0505	6997	88.2902
193	64	Database	U.S.A	4	0.0505	7001	88.3407
194	64	Economic and Political Weekly	India	4	0.0505	7005	88.3912
195	64	Harvard Business Review	U.S.A	4	0.0505	7009	88.4416
196	64	Indian Education	India	4	0.0505	7013	88.4921
197	64	Indian Journal of Commerce	India	4	0.0505	7017	88.5426
198	64	Indian Library Journal	India	4	0.0505	7021	88.5931
199	64	Indian Pediatrics	India	4	0.0505	7025	88.6435
200	64	Information and referral	U.S.A	4	0.0505	7029	88.6940
201	64	Information Today	U.S.A	4	0.0505	7033	88.7445
202	64	Journal of American Medical Association	U.S.A	4	0.0505	7037	88.7950
203	64	Journal of Extension	U.S.A	4	0.0505	7041	88.8454
204	64	Journal of Indian Library Association	India	4	0.0505	7045	88.8959
205	64	Kniznice A Informacie	Slovakia	4	0.0505	7049	88.9464
206	64	Libra	U.K	4	0.0505	7053	88.9968
207	64	Library Focus	Nigeria	4	0.0505	7057	89.0473

(Contd...)

	1	2	3	4	5	6	7
208	64	Library Scientist	Nigeria	4	0.0505	7061	89.0978
209	64	Library World	India	4	0.0505	7065	89.1483
210	64	Maharastra Journal of Extension Education	India	4	0.0505	7069	89.1987
211	64	Manpower Journal	India	4	0.0505	7073	89.2492
212	64	Open	Neth	4	0.0505	7077	89.2997
213	64	Pharmaceutical Library Bulletin	Japan	4	0.0505	7081	89.3502
214	64	Research Strategies	U.S.A	4	0.0505	7085	89.4006
215	64	Scholarly Publishing	U.S.A	4	0.0505	7089	89.4511
216	64	Social Forces	U.S.A	4	0.0505	7093	89.5016
217	64	Sociology of Education	U.S.A	4	0.0505	7097	89.5521
218	64	South African Journal of Library and Information Science	S.Afr	4	0.0505	7101	89.6025
219	64	Span	Aus	4	0.0505	7105	89.6530
220	64	Times Higher Education Supplement	U.K	4	0.0505	7109	89.7035
221	65	ABGILA	India	3	0.0379	7112	89.7413
222	65	Access	Aus	3	0.0379	7115	89.7792
223	65	Administrative Science Quarterly	U.S.A	3	0.0379	7118	89.8170
224	65	Advances in Computers	U.S.A	3	0.0379	7121	89.8549
225	65	American Sociologist	U.S.A	3	0.0379	7124	89.8927
226	65	Annual Review of Psychology	U.S.A	3	0.0379	7127	89.9306
227	65	Art Libraries Journal	U.K	3	0.0379	7130	89.9685

(Contd...)

	1	2	3	4	5	6	7
228	65	ASEE	U.S.A	3	0.0379	7133	90.0063
229	65	Audiovisual Librarian	U.K	3	0.0379	7136	90.0442
230	65	Australian College Libraries	Aus	3	0.0379	7139	90.0820
231	65	BLLD Review	U.K	3	0.0379	7142	90.1199
232	65	CD-ROM Librarian	U.S.A	3	0.0379	7145	90.1577
233	65	Chronicle of Higher Education	U.S.A	3	0.0379	7148	90.1956
234	65	College Times	India	3	0.0379	7151	90.2334
235	65	CRUS News	U.K	3	0.0379	7154	90.2713
236	65	Ctenar	Czech	3	0.0379	7157	90.3091
237	65	Data Management	U.S.A	3	0.0379	7160	90.3470
238	65	Datamation	U.S.A	3	0.0379	7163	90.3849
239	65	Distance Education	India	3	0.0379	7166	90.4227
240	65	Eastern Librarian	Bangla	3	0.0379	7169	90.4606
241	65	Higher Education in Europe	Roma	3	0.0379	7172	90.4984
242	65	Higher Education Review	U.K	3	0.0379	7175	90.5363
243	65	Indian Management	India	3	0.0379	7178	90.5741
244	65	Indian Psychological Review	India	3	0.0379	7181	90.6120
245	65	Infromatik	Yug	3	0.0379	7184	90.6498
246	65	Information and Library Manager	U.K	3	0.0379	7187	90.6877
247	65	Information Scientist	U.K	3	0.0379	7190	90.7256
248	65	Information Services and Use	Neth	3	0.0379	7193	90.7634
249	65	Interlending and Document Supply	U.K	3	0.0379	7196	90.8013

(Contd...)

	1	2	3	4	5	6	7
250	65	International Development Review	U.S.A	3	0.0379	7199	90.8391
251	65	Joho No Kagaku to Gijutsu	Japan	3	0.0379	7202	90.8770
252	65	Journal of American Dietetic Association	U.S.A	3	0.0379	7205	90.9148
253	65	Journal of Information Processing and Management	Japan	3	0.0379	7208	90.9527
254	65	Journal of National Institute of Personnel Management	India	3	0.0379	7211	90.9905
255	65	Journal of Organizational Behavior	U.K	3	0.0379	7214	91.0284
256	65	Journal of Rural Development	India	3	0.0379	7217	91.0662
257	65	Journal of Scientific and Industrial Research	India	3	0.0379	7220	91.1041
258	65	Journal of University Education	India	3	0.0379	7223	91.1420
259	65	Kakatiya Journal of Distance Education	India	3	0.0379	7226	91.1798
260	65	LASIE	U.S.A	3	0.0379	7229	91.2177
261	65	Law Librarian	U.K	3	0.0379	7232	91.2555
262	65	Learning Resources Journal	U.K	3	0.0379	7235	91.2934
263	65	Library Research	U.S.A	3	0.0379	7238	91.3312
264	65	Medical Library Association Bulletin	U.K	3	0.0379	7241	91.3691
265	65	Methods of Information in Medicine	Ger	3	0.0379	7244	91.4069
266	65	Minerva	India	3	0.0379	7247	91.4448

(Contd...)

	1	*2*	*3*	*4*	*5*	*6*	*7*
267	65	Netlink	U.S.A	3	0.0379	7250	91.4826
268	65	Network	U.S.A	3	0.0379	7253	91.5205
269	65	Newzealand Libraries	Newz	3	0.0379	7256	91.5584
270	65	Nigerian Libraries	Nigeria	3	0.0379	7259	91.5962
271	65	Ontario Library Review	U.S.A	3	0.0379	7262	91.6341
272	65	Operational Research Quarterly	U.K	3	0.0379	7265	91.6719
273	65	Organizational Behaviour and Human Performance	U.S.A	3	0.0379	7268	91.7098
274	65	Phi Delta Kappan	U.S.A	3	0.0379	7271	91.7476
275	65	Physics Today	U.S.A	3	0.0379	7274	91.7855
276	65	Quality Progress	U.S.A	3	0.0379	7277	91.8233
277	65	Quarterly Journal of Local Self Government	India	3	0.0379	7280	91.8612
278	65	Reference Librarian	U.S.A	3	0.0379	7283	91.8991
279	65	Reference Services Review	U.S.A	3	0.0379	7286	91.9369
280	65	Research Policy	Neth	3	0.0379	7289	91.9748
281	65	Rural Libraries	U.S.A	3	0.0379	7292	92.0126
282	65	SAM Advanced Management Journal	U.S.A	3	0.0379	7295	92.0505
283	65	Science and Technology Libraries	U.S.A	3	0.0379	7298	92.0883
284	65	SLA News	U.S.A	3	0.0379	7301	92.1262
285	65	Social Action	India	3	0.0379	7304	92.1640
286	65	Social Science and Medicine	U.S.A	3	0.0379	7307	92.2019

(Contd...)

	1	2	3	4	5	6	7
287	65	Studies in Higher Education	U.K	3	0.0379	7310	92.2397
288	65	Supervision	U.S.A	3	0.0379	7313	92.2776
289	65	Technical Services Quarterly	U.S.A	3	0.0379	7316	92.3155
290	65	Vikasini : The Journal of Women Empowerment	India	3	0.0379	7319	92.3533
291	65	Vine	U.K	3	0.0379	7322	92.3912
292	65	Wisconsin Library Bulletin	U.S.A	3	0.0379	7325	92.4290
293	66	ABI Technic	U.S.A	2	0.0252	7327	92.4543
294	66	Academic Librarianship	U.S.A	2	0.0252	7329	92.4795
295	66	Advertising and Marketing	India	2	0.0252	7331	92.5047
296	66	American Journal of Clinical Nutrition	U.S.A	2	0.0252	7333	92.5300
297	66	American Journal of Sociology	U.S.A	2	0.0252	7335	92.5552
298	66	Art Documentation	U.S.A	2	0.0252	7337	92.5804
299	66	Assignation	U.K	2	0.0252	7339	92.6057
300	66	Association of Agricultural Libraries and Documentalists	Neth	2	0.0252	7341	92.6309
301	66	Australian Health Review	Aus	2	0.0252	7343	92.6562
302	66	Australian Medical Record Journal	Aus	2	0.0252	7345	92.6814
303	66	Bell System Technical Journal	U.S.A	2	0.0252	7347	92.7066
304	66	Bibliotheek En Samenleving	Neth	2	0.0252	7349	92.7319
305	66	Bibliothekarz	Poland	2	0.0252	7351	92.7571

(Contd...)

	1	2	3	4	5	6	7
306	66	Bogens Verden	Denm	2	0.0252	7353	92.7823
307	66	Bulletin of Library Association of China	China	2	0.0252	7355	92.8076
308	66	Bulletin-Des-Bibliotheques-France	France	2	0.0252	7357	92.8328
309	66	Business Horizon	U.S.A	2	0.0252	7359	92.8580
310	66	California Management Review	U.S.A	2	0.0252	7361	92.8833
311	66	Cathelic Library World	U.S.A	2	0.0252	7363	92.9085
312	66	COMLA Newsletter	Jamaica	2	0.0252	7365	92.9338
313	66	Computers Today	India	2	0.0252	7367	92.9590
314	66	Current Contents: Life Sciences	U.S.A	2	0.0252	7369	92.9842
315	66	Daedalus	U.K	2	0.0252	7371	93.0095
316	66	Documentaliste	France	2	0.0252	7373	93.0347
317	66	Documentation and Bibliothique	Canada	2	0.0252	7375	93.0599
318	66	Education	U.S.A	2	0.0252	7377	93.0852
319	66	Education for Library Information Science	Aus	2	0.0252	7379	93.1104
320	66	Educational Psychological Measurement	U.S.A	2	0.0252	7381	93.1356
321	66	Expert Systems	U.S.A	2	0.0252	7383	93.1609
322	66	Health Service Journal	U.K	2	0.0252	7385	93.1861
323	66	ASLIC Newsletter	India	2	0.0252	7387	93.2114
324	66	IATUL Proceedings	U.K	2	0.0252	7389	93.2366

(Contd...)

	1	2	3	4	5	6	7
325	66	IEEE Transactions on Education	U.S.A	2	0.0252	7391	93.2618
326	66	Illinois Libraries	U.S.A	2	0.0252	7393	93.2871
327	66	Indian Educational Review	India	2	0.0252	7395	93.3123
328	66	Indian Journal of Library Science	India	2	0.0252	7397	93.3375
329	66	Indian Journal of Maternal and Child Health	India	2	0.0252	7399	93.3628
330	66	Indian Journal of Public Health	India	2	0.0252	7401	93.3880
331	66	Indian Library Movement	India	2	0.0252	7403	93.4132
332	66	Indian Museum Bulletin	India	2	0.0252	7405	93.4385
333	66	Indian Press	India	2	0.0252	7407	93.4637
334	66	Information and the Transformation of the Society	U.S.A	2	0.0252	7409	93.4890
335	66	Information Science	China	2	0.0252	7411	93.5142
336	66	Information Studies	India	2	0.0252	7413	93.5394
337	66	Information Technology	U.S.A	2	0.0252	7415	93.5647
338	66	International Journal of Information Management	U.K	2	0.0252	7417	93.5899
339	66	Journal of Adult Education	U.S.A	2	0.0252	7419	93.6151
340	66	Journal of Advertising Research	U.S.A	2	0.0252	7421	93.6404
341	66	Journal of Association for Computing Machinery	U.S.A	2	0.0252	7423	93.6656
342	66	Journal of Chemical Education	U.S.A	2	0.0252	7425	93.6909

(Contd...)

	1	2	3	4	5	6	7
343	66	Journal of Experimental Social Psychology	U.S.A	2	0.0252	7427	93.7161
344	66	Journal of Government Information	U.K	2	0.0252	7429	93.7413
345	66	Journal of Indian Medical Association	India	2	0.0252	7431	93.7666
346	66	Journal of Information, Communication and Library Science	China	2	0.0252	7433	93.7918
347	66	Journal of Library Science	India	2	0.0252	7435	93.8170
348	66	Journal of Nepal Library Association	Nepal	2	0.0252	7437	93.8423
349	66	Journal of Political Economy	U.S.A	2	0.0252	7439	93.8675
350	66	Journal of Reading	U.S.A	2	0.0252	7441	93.8927
351	66	Journal of Royal Astronomical Society of Canada	U.S.A	2	0.0252	7443	93.9180
352	66	Journal of Social Issues	U.S.A	2	0.0252	7445	93.9432
353	66	Journal of Technical Vocational Education	India	2	0.0252	7447	93.9685
354	66	Kirjastotiede Ja Informatiikka	Finland	2	0.0252	7449	93.9937
355	66	Lancet	U.K	2	0.0252	7451	94.0189
356	66	Legal Reference Services Quarterly	U.S.A	2	0.0252	7453	94.0442
357	66	Liber-Bulletin	France	2	0.0252	7455	94.0694
358	66	Librarian Career Development	U.K	2	0.0252	7457	94.0946
359	66	Library Resources	U.S.A	2	0.0252	7459	94.1199

(Contd...)

	1	2	3	4	5	6	7
360	66	Library Science Research	U.K	2	0.0252	7461	94.1451
361	66	Library Sciences	India	2	0.0252	7463	94.1703
362	66	Library Work	U.S.A	2	0.0252	7465	94.1956
363	66	MALA Bulletin	Malawi	2	0.0252	7467	94.2208
364	66	Management Science	U.S.A	2	0.0252	7469	94.2461
365	66	Managing Information	U.K	2	0.0252	7471	94.2713
366	66	Medical Reference Services Quarterly	U.S.A	2	0.0252	7473	94.2965
367	66	Museums and Monuments	France	2	0.0252	7475	94.3218
368	66	Musion	Austria	2	0.0252	7477	94.3470
369	66	Nachr. Noue. Notiz	Ger	2	0.0252	7479	94.3722
370	66	Nachrichten Fuer Dokumentation	Ger	2	0.0252	7481	94.3975
371	66	New Quest	India	2	0.0252	7483	94.4227
372	66	New Scientist	U.K	2	0.0252	7485	94.4479
373	66	Notes	U.K	2	0.0252	7487	94.4732
374	66	OCLC News Letter	U.S.A	2	0.0252	7489	94.4984
375	66	Online Review	U.S.A	2	0.0252	7491	94.5237
376	66	Organisation Dynamics	U.S.A	2	0.0252	7493	94.5489
377	66	Philosophy of Science	U.S.A	2	0.0252	7495	94.5741
378	66	PNLA Quarterly	U.S.A	2	0.0252	7497	94.5994
379	66	Progressive Educational Herald	India	2	0.0252	7499	94.6246
380	66	Prolegomena Library Research	India	2	0.0252	7501	94.6498
381	66	Prospects	France	2	0.0252	7503	94.6751

(Contd...)

	1	2	3	4	5	6	7
382	66	Psychological Studies	India	2	0.0252	7505	94.7003
383	66	Public Health	U.K	2	0.0252	7507	94.7256
384	66	Publishing Research Quarterly	U.S.A	2	0.0252	7509	94.7508
385	66	Reading	India	2	0.0252	7511	94.7760
386	66	Reading teacher	U.S.A	2	0.0252	7513	94.8013
387	66	Region Health and Health Care	U.S.A	2	0.0252	7515	94.8265
388	66	Resourcesharing and Library Networks	U.S.A	2	0.0252	7517	94.8517
389	66	Revista Espanola De Documentacion Cientifica	U.S.A	2	0.0252	7519	94.8770
390	66	Rhod Librn	U.S.A	2	0.0252	7521	94.9022
391	66	Rissalat Al-Maktaba	Jordan	2	0.0252	7523	94.9274
392	66	S.Sfr. Lib	U.S.A	2	0.0252	7525	94.9527
393	66	School Library Media Quarterly	U.S.A	2	0.0252	7527	94.9779
394	66	Science Today	India	2	0.0252	7529	95.0032
395	66	Scottish Libraries	U.K	2	0.0252	7531	95.0284
396	66	Service Point	U.K	2	0.0252	7533	95.0536
397	66	Signum	Finland	2	0.0252	7535	95.0789
398	66	Social Science Medicine	U.K	2	0.0252	7537	95.1041
399	66	Social Science Research	U.S.A	2	0.0252	7539	95.1293
400	66	Sovetskoe	Russia	2	0.0252	7541	95.1546
401	66	State Librarian	U.K	2	0.0252	7543	95.1798

(Contd...)

	1	2	3	4	5	6	7
402	66	The Irish Library Bulletin	Ireland	2	0.0252	7545	95.2050
403	66	The Journal of Business Perspective	India	2	0.0252	7547	95.2303
404	66	The Orissa Education Magazine	India	2	0.0252	7549	95.2555
405	66	Toshokon Zasshi	Japan	2	0.0252	7551	95.2808
406	66	Training and Development Journal	U.S.A	2	0.0252	7553	95.3060
407	66	UNISIST Newsletter	France	2	0.0252	7555	95.3312
408	66	Universities Quarterly	U.K	2	0.0252	7557	95.3565
409	66	Women's Link	India	2	0.0252	7559	95.3817
410	66	Yad La-Kore	Israel	2	0.0252	7561	95.4069
411	66	YLG News	U.K	2	0.0252	7563	95.4322
412	67	American Sociologist	U.S.A	1	0.0126	7564	95.4448
413	67	Abacus	U.K	1	0.0126	7565	95.4574
414	67	Academe	U.S.A	1	0.0126	7566	95.4700
415	67	Administrative Change	India	1	0.0126	7567	95.4826
416	67	Adult Education	U.S.A	1	0.0126	7568	95.4953
417	67	Advanced Management Journal	U.S.A	1	0.0126	7569	95.5079
418	67	Advances in Nursing Science	U.S.A	1	0.0126	7570	95.5205
419	67	AGLIS Journal	India	1	0.0126	7571	95.5331
420	67	Agricultural Extension Review	Sou. Afr	1	0.0126	7572	95.5457
421	67	Aktuell	U.K	1	0.0126	7573	95.5584
422	67	ALTECH Journal	U.S.A	1	0.0126	7574	95.5710
423	67	Am. J. Hosp. Pharm.	U.S.A	1	0.0126	7575	95.5836

(Contd...)

	1	2	3	4	5	6	7
424	67	American Anthropologist	U.S.A	1	0.0126	7576	95.5962
425	67	American Bar Association Journal	U.S.A	1	0.0126	7577	95.6088
426	67	American Behavioural Scientist	U.S.A	1	0.0126	7578	95.6215
427	67	American Education	U.S.A	1	0.0126	7579	95.6341
428	67	American Industrial Hygiene Association Journal	U.S.A	1	0.0126	7580	95.6467
429	67	American Journal of Agricultural Economics	U.S.A	1	0.0126	7581	95.6593
430	67	American Journal of Psychology	U.S.A	1	0.0126	7582	95.6719
431	67	American Journal of Public Health	U.S.A	1	0.0126	7583	95.6845
432	67	American Patent Law Association Journal	U.S.A	1	0.0126	7584	95.6972
433	67	American Psychological Review	U.S.A	1	0.0126	7585	95.7098
434	67	American Scholar	U.S.A	1	0.0126	7586	95.7224
435	67	American Scientist	U.S.A	1	0.0126	7587	95.7350
436	67	Anabra State Librarian Association Bulletin	U.S.A	1	0.0126	7588	95.7476
437	67	Annals of Japan Society of Library Science	Japan	1	0.0126	7589	95.7603
438	67	Annals of New York Academy of Science	U.S.A	1	0.0126	7590	95.7729
439	67	Annual Review of Sociology	U.S.A	1	0.0126	7591	95.7855

(Contd...)

	1	2	3	4	5	6	7
440	67	Anthropological Linguistics	U.S.A	1	0.0126	7592	95.7981
441	67	APLA News	India	1	0.0126	7593	95.8107
442	67	Arch. Psychol	U.K	1	0.0126	7594	95.8233
443	67	Archives of Diseases in Childhood	U.K	1	0.0126	7595	95.8360
444	67	Artha Vijnana	India	1	0.0126	7596	95.8486
445	67	ASIS Bulletin	U.S.A	1	0.0126	7597	95.8612
446	67	ASLIB Managing Information	U.K	1	0.0126	7598	95.8738
447	67	ASLIB Social Sciences Information Group Newsletter	U.K	1	0.0126	7599	95.8864
448	67	ASTM Standardization News	U.S.A	1	0.0126	7600	95.8991
449	67	Australian Journal of Reading	Aus	1	0.0126	7601	95.9117
450	67	Australian Library Quarterly	Aus	1	0.0126	7602	95.9243
451	67	Australian School Librarian	Aus	1	0.0126	7603	95.9369
452	67	Australian Special Libraries News	Aus	1	0.0126	7604	95.9495
453	67	Australiasian College Libraries	Aus	1	0.0126	7605	95.9621
454	67	Bayern	Ger	1	0.0126	7606	95.9748
455	67	Behavioral and Social Sciences Librarian	U.S.A	1	0.0126	7607	95.9874
456	67	Bengal Library Association Bulletin	India	1	0.0126	7608	96.0000
457	67	Bibliography	U.S.A	1	0.0126	7609	96.0126
458	67	Bibliotecario	Italy	1	0.0126	7610	96.0252
459	67	Biblioteche Oggi	Italy	1	0.0126	7611	96.0379

(Contd...)

	1	*2*	*3*	*4*	*5*	*6*	*7*
460	67	Bibliotekarz	Poland	1	0.0126	7612	96.0505
461	67	Bibliotheck	U.K	1	0.0126	7613	96.0631
462	67	Bibliotheks Forum	Ger	1	0.0126	7614	96.0757
463	67	Bibliotheques-De-France	France	1	0.0126	7615	96.0883
464	67	Biometrika	U.S.A	1	0.0126	7616	96.1009
465	67	Bioscience	U.S.A	1	0.0126	7617	96.1136
466	67	Bollettino D' Informazioni	Italy	1	0.0126	7618	96.1262
467	67	Born and Boger	Den	1	0.0126	7619	96.1388
468	67	British Booksellers News	U.K	1	0.0126	7620	96.1514
469	67	British Journal of Healthcare Computing	U.K	1	0.0126	7621	96.1640
470	67	British Journal of Psychology	U.K	1	0.0126	7622	96.1767
471	67	British Journal of Technology	U.K	1	0.0126	7623	96.1893
472	67	British Library	U.K	1	0.0126	7624	96.2019
473	67	Bulletin of Information of ASS of Bibliothque Francies	France	1	0.0126	7625	96.2145
474	67	Business and Economic Review	U.S.A	1	0.0126	7626	96.2271
475	67	Business Information Review	U.K	1	0.0126	7627	96.2397
476	67	Byte	U.S.A	1	0.0126	7628	96.2524
477	67	Canadian Psychological Review	Canada	1	0.0126	7629	96.2650
478	67	Casopis	U.S.A	1	0.0126	7630	96.2776
479	67	CBE Views	U.S.A	1	0.0126	7631	96.2902

(Contd...)

	1	2	3	4	5	6	7
480	67	Centre for Library and Information Studies	Aus	1	0.0126	7632	96.3028
481	67	Ceskoslovenska-Informatiska	Czech R	1	0.0126	7633	96.3155
482	67	Change	U.S.A	1	0.0126	7634	96.3281
483	67	Chemical Industry	Czech R	1	0.0126	7635	96.3407
484	67	Choice	U.S.A	1	0.0126	7636	96.3533
485	67	Clearing House	U.S.A	1	0.0126	7637	96.3659
486	67	COFHE Bulletin	U.K	1	0.0126	7638	96.3785
487	67	Collaboration Computing	U.K	1	0.0126	7639	96.3912
488	67	College and Undergraduate Libraries	U.S.A	1	0.0126	7640	96.4038
489	67	College Librarian	India	1	0.0126	7641	96.4164
490	67	Colleges and Universities	U.K	1	0.0126	7642	96.4290
491	67	Colorado Libraries	U.S.A	1	0.0126	7643	96.4416
492	67	Communicator	U.S.A	1	0.0126	7644	96.4543
493	67	Community Librarian	U.K	1	0.0126	7645	96.4669
494	67	Computers and Automation	U.S.A	1	0.0126	7646	96.4795
495	67	Conservation Administration News	U.S.A	1	0.0126	7647	96.4921
496	67	CSI Communication	India	1	0.0126	7648	96.5047
497	67	Curator	U.S.A	1	0.0126	7649	96.5174
498	67	Data Quest	U.S.A	1	0.0126	7650	96.5300
499	67	Denwer University Library Administration and Management	U.S.A	1	0.0126	7651	96.5426

(Contd...)

	1	2	3	4	5	6	7
500	67	Directions in Higher Education	India	1	0.0126	7652	96.5552
501	67	Documentation	France	1	0.0126	7653	96.5678
502	67	Documentation Journal	U.K	1	0.0126	7654	96.5804
503	67	Education and Urban Society	U.S.A	1	0.0126	7655	96.5931
504	67	Education in Asia	Thailand	1	0.0126	7656	96.6057
505	67	Education World	India	1	0.0126	7657	96.6183
506	67	Educational Forum	India	1	0.0126	7658	96.6309
507	67	Educational Quarterly	India	1	0.0126	7659	96.6435
508	67	Educational Research	U.K	1	0.0126	7660	96.6562
509	67	Electrical Communication	U.S.A	1	0.0126	7661	96.6668
510	67	Electronic Networking	U.S.A	1	0.0126	7662	96.6814
511	67	Electronics For You	India	1	0.0126	7663	96.6940
512	67	Emergency Librarian	Canada	1	0.0126	7664	96.7066
513	67	EPA Bulletin	India	1	0.0126	7665	96.7192
514	67	European Journal	U.S.A	1	0.0126	7666	96.7319
515	67	European Journal of Cancer	U.K	1	0.0126	7667	96.7445
516	67	European Journal of Distance Education	U.K	1	0.0126	7668	96.7571
517	67	European Journal of Marketing	U.K	1	0.0126	7669	96.7697
518	67	European Journal of Operational Research	Neth	1	0.0126	7670	96.7823
519	67	Exceptional Children	U.S.A	1	0.0126	7671	96.7950

(Contd...)

	1	2	3	4	5	6	7
520	67	Expert Systems for Information Management	U.K	1	0.0126	7672	96.8076
521	67	Extension Service Review	U.S.A	1	0.0126	7673	96.8202
522	67	Fiji Library Association Journal	Fiji	1	0.0126	7674	96.8328
523	67	Financial Analyst Journal	U.S.A	1	0.0126	7675	96.8454
524	67	Focus on International and Comparative Librarianship	U.K	1	0.0126	7676	96.8580
525	67	Food Laboratory Newsletter	U.S.A	1	0.0126	7677	96.8707
526	67	Gender and Education	U.K	1	0.0126	7678	96.8833
527	67	Government Publication Quarterly	U.K	1	0.0126	7679	96.8959
528	67	Grandalaya	India	1	0.0126	7680	96.9085
529	67	Granthana	India	1	0.0126	7681	96.9211
530	67	Health Care Computing	U.S.A	1	0.0126	7682	96.9338
531	67	Health Education and Behaviour	U.S.A	1	0.0126	7683	96.9464
532	67	Health for the Millions	India	1	0.0126	7684	96.9590
533	67	Health Issues	Aus	1	0.0126	7685	96.9716
534	67	Higher Education and Research in the Netherlands	Neth	1	0.0126	7686	96.9842
535	67	Historical Methods	U.S.A	1	0.0126	7687	96.9968
536	67	History of Science	U.K	1	0.0126	7688	97.0095
537	67	Human Communication Research	U.S.A	1	0.0126	7689	97.0221
538	67	Human Development	U.S.A	1	0.0126	7690	97.0347

(Contd...)

	1	*2*	*3*	*4*	*5*	*6*	*7*
539	67	IASSIST Quarterly	U.S.A	1	0.0126	7691	97.0473
540	67	IATUL Quarterly	U.K	1	0.0126	7692	97.0599
541	67	ICCE Newsletter	U.S.A	1	0.0126	7693	97.0726
542	67	ICDE Bulletin	India	1	0.0126	7694	97.0852
543	67	ICMR Bulletin	India	1	0.0126	7695	97.0978
544	67	IEEE Internet Computing	U.S.A	1	0.0126	7696	97.1104
545	67	IEEE Transactions on Information Theory	U.S.A	1	0.0126	7697	97.1230
546	67	Impact of Science on Society	U.K	1	0.0126	7698	97.1356
547	67	Indian Book Industry	India	1	0.0126	7699	97.1483
548	67	Indian Economic Journal	India	1	0.0126	7700	97.1609
549	67	Indian Journal History of Medicine	India	1	0.0126	7701	97.1735
550	67	Indian Journal of Adult Education	India	1	0.0126	7702	97.1861
551	67	Indian Journal of Child Health	India	1	0.0126	7703	97.1987
552	67	Indian Journal of Communication	India	1	0.0126	7704	97.2114
553	67	Indian Journal of Community Health	India	1	0.0126	7705	97.2240
554	67	Indian Journal of Community Medicine	India	1	0.0126	7706	97.2366
555	67	Indian Journal of Distance Education	India	1	0.0126	7707	97.2492
556	67	Indian Journal of Open Learning	India	1	0.0126	7708	97.2618
557	67	Indian Journal of Public Administration	India	1	0.0126	7709	97.2744

(Contd...)

	1	2	3	4	5	6	7
558	67	Indian Journal of Training and Development	India	1	0.0126	7710	97.2871
559	67	Indiana Media Journal	U.S.A	1	0.0126	7711	97.2997
560	67	Information Today and Tomorrow	India	1	0.0126	7712	97.3123
561	67	Information and Management	Neth	1	0.0126	7713	97.3249
562	67	Information for the Management of Healthcare Newsletter	U.K	1	0.0126	7714	97.3375
563	67	Information Library and Society	India	1	0.0126	7715	97.3502
564	67	Information Library Review	U.K	1	0.0126	7716	97.3628
565	67	Information Management Report	U.K	1	0.0126	7717	97.3754
566	67	Information World Review	U.K	1	0.0126	7718	97.3880
567	67	INFOTOL	India	1	0.0126	7719	97.4006
568	67	Interlending Document Supply	U.K	1	0.0126	7720	97.4132
569	67	International Classification	Ger	1	0.0126	7721	97.4259
570	67	International Journal of Gynaecology and Obstetrics	Ireland	1	0.0126	7722	97.4385
571	67	International Journal of Information and Library Research	U.K	1	0.0126	7723	97.4511
572	67	International Journal of Legal Information	U.S.A	1	0.0126	7724	97.4637
573	67	International Journal of Technology Management	Switz	1	0.0126	7725	97.4763

(Contd...)

	1	2	3	4	5	6	7
574	67	International Librarian	India	1	0.0126	7726	97.4890
575	67	International Review of Education	Neth	1	0.0126	7727	97.5016
576	67	Investigacion Bibliotecologia E Information	Mexico	1	0.0126	7728	97.5142
577	67	Iron and Steel Review	India	1	0.0126	7729	97.5268
578	67	IT News	U.S.A	1	0.0126	7730	97.5394
579	67	Journal Information and Computers	U.S.A	1	0.0126	7731	97.5521
580	67	Journal of Administrative Management	Japan	1	0.0126	7732	97.5647
581	67	Journal of Aesthetic Art and Criticism	U.S.A	1	0.0126	7733	97.5773
582	67	Journal of Agricultural and Food Information	U.S.A	1	0.0126	7734	97.5899
583	67	Journal of Automation	U.S.A	1	0.0126	7735	97.6025
584	67	Journal of Broadcasting	U.S.A	1	0.0126	7736	97.6151
585	67	Journal of Business	U.S.A	1	0.0126	7737	97.6278
586	67	Journal of Clinical Documentation	U.S.A	1	0.0126	7738	97.6404
587	67	Journal of Computing and Information Technology	U.S.A	1	0.0126	7739	97.6530
588	67	Journal of Consulting Psychology	U.S.A	1	0.0126	7740	97.6656
589	67	Journal of Creative Behaviour	U.S.A	1	0.0126	7741	97.6782
590	67	Journal of Education and Psychology	India	1	0.0126	7742	97.6909

(Contd...)

	1	2	3	4	5	6	7
591	67	Journal of Environmental Education	U.S.A	1	0.0126	7743	97.7035
592	67	Journal of General Education	U.S.A	1	0.0126	7744	97.7161
593	67	Journal of Gerontology	U.S.A	1	0.0126	7745	97.7287
594	67	Journal of Hongkong Library Association	Hong	1	0.0126	7746	97.7413
595	67	Journal of Human Resources	U.S.A	1	0.0126	7747	97.7539
596	67	Journal of Humanistic Psychology	U.S.A	1	0.0126	7748	97.7666
597	67	Journal of Industrial Economics	U.K	1	0.0126	7749	97.7792
598	67	Journal of Informatics	U.K	1	0.0126	7750	97.7918
599	67	Journal of Legal Education	U.K	1	0.0126	7751	97.8044
600	67	Journal of Legal Information	U.S.A	1	0.0126	7752	97.8170
601	67	Journal of Patent Office Society	U.S.A	1	0.0126	7753	97.8297
602	67	Journal of Rural Development and Administration	Pakistan	1	0.0126	7754	97.8423
603	67	Journal of Secondary Education	U.S.A	1	0.0126	7755	97.8549
604	67	Journal of Special Education	U.S.A	1	0.0126	7756	97.8675
605	67	Journal of Systems Management	U.S.A	1	0.0126	7757	97.8801
606	67	Journal of Ugandan Libraries	Uganda	1	0.0126	7758	97.8927
607	67	Journal of Women in Culture and Society	U.S.A	1	0.0126	7759	97.9054
608	67	Journal Tribal	India	1	0.0126	7760	97.9180
609	67	Journal of Indian Management Association	India	1	0.0126	7761	97.9306

(Contd...)

	1	2	3	4	5	6	7
610	67	Journal of Technical and Vocational Education	India	1	0.0126	7762	97.9432
611	67	Juris Doctor	U.S.A	1	0.0126	7763	97.9558
612	67	Kelpro Bulletin	India	1	0.0126	7764	97.9685
613	67	KEM Hospital Newsletter	India	1	0.0126	7765	97.9811
614	67	Kniznice-A-Vedecke-Informacie	Slovakia	1	0.0126	7766	97.9937
615	67	Kurukshetra	India	1	0.0126	7767	98.0063
616	67	Language Arts	U.S.A	1	0.0126	7768	98.0189
617	67	Laserdisk Professional	U.S.A	1	0.0126	7769	98.0315
618	67	Law and Society Review	U.S.A	1	0.0126	7770	98.0442
619	67	Liberal Education	U.S.A	1	0.0126	7771	98.0568
620	67	Librarian and Book World	U.S.A	1	0.0126	7772	98.0694
621	67	Library Association Record	U.K	1	0.0126	7773	98.0820
622	67	Library Administration and Management	U.S.A	1	0.0126	7774	98.0946
623	67	Library and Information Science Research News	U.K	1	0.0126	7775	98.1073
624	67	Library and Libraries	U.S.A	1	0.0126	7776	98.1199
625	67	Library Bulletin	Aus	1	0.0126	7777	98.1325
626	67	Library College Journal	U.S.A	1	0.0126	7778	98.1451
627	67	Library Development in India	India	1	0.0126	7779	98.1577
628	67	Library Mosaics	U.S.A	1	0.0126	7780	98.1703

(Contd...)

	1	2	3	4	5	6	7
629	67	Library News	U.S.A	1	0.0126	7781	98.1830
630	67	Library Technology Reports	U.S.A	1	0.0126	7782	98.1956
631	67	Library Today	India	1	0.0126	7783	98.2082
.632	67	Literary and Linguistic Computing	U.K	1	0.0126	7784	98.2208
633	67	Local Studies Librarian	U.K	1	0.0126	7785	98.2334
634	67	Long-Range Planning	U.K	1	0.0126	7786	98.2461
635	67	Madurai University Newsletter	India	1	0.0126	7787	98.2587
636	67	Malaysian Journal of Library and Information Science	Malays	1	0.0126	7788	98.2713
637	67	Management Advisor	U.S.A	1	0.0126	7789	98.2839
638	67	Management and Change	India	1	0.0126	7790	98.2965
639	67	Management Review	India	1	0.0126	7791	98.3091
640	67	MARC User Group Newsletter	U.S.A	1	0.0126	7792	98.3218
641	67	March of Karnataka	India	1	0.0126	7793	98.3344
642	67	MCN American Journal of Maternal Child Nursing	U.S.A	1	0.0126	7794	98.3470
643	67	Media Studies Journal	U.S.A	1	0.0126	7795	98.3596
644	67	Microform Review	Ger	1	0.0126	7796	98.3722
645	67	Mousaion	Sou. Afr	1	0.0126	7797	98.3849
646	67	MSU Business Topics	U.S.A	1	0.0126	7798	98.3975
647	67	National Law School of India University Journal	India	1	0.0126	7799	98.4101

(Contd...)

	1	2	3	4	5	6	7
648	67	Nauchnye I Teknicheskie Biblioteki Sssr	Russia	1	0.0126	7800	98.4227
649	67	Naya Shikshak	India	1	0.0126	7801	98.4353
650	67	Nebraska Library Association Quarterly	U.S.A	1	0.0126	7802	98.4479
651	67	New Directions for Higher Education	U.S.A	1	0.0126	7803	98.4606
652	67	New Society	U.K	1	0.0126	7804	98.4732
653	67	Newspaper Journal	U.S.A	1	0.0126	7805	98.4858
654	67	Next Step Computers in Libraries	U.S.A	1	0.0126	7806	98.4984
655	67	NFI Bulletin	India	1	0.0126	7807	98.5110
656	67	NIE Journal	India	1	0.0126	7808	98.5237
657	67	Nigerbiblios	Nigeria	1	0.0126	7809	98.5363
658	67	NISG Newsletter	U.K	1	0.0126	7810	98.5489
659	67	Nurse Journal of India	India	1	0.0126	7811	98.5615
660	67	Nursing Times	U.K	1	0.0126	7812	98.5741
661	67	NY State Journal of Medicine	U.S.A	1	0.0126	7813	98.5868
662	67	Occupational Psychology	U.K	1	0.0126	7814	98.5994
663	67	Osmania Journal of Social Sciences	India	1	0.0126	7815	98.6120
664	67	Overseas Universities	U.K	1	0.0126	7816	98.6246
665	67	PC Quest	U.S.A	1	0.0126	7817	98.6372
666	67	Pediatrics	U.S.A	1	0.0126	7818	98.6498
667	67	Personal Psychology Autumn	U.K	1	0.0126	7819	98.6625

(Contd...)

	1	2	3	4	5	6	7
668	67	Personnel Management	U.K	1	0.0126	7820	98.6751
669	67	Personnel Practice Bulletin	Aus	1	0.0126	7821	98.6877
670	67	Personnel Training and Education	U.K	1	0.0126	7822	98.7003
671	67	Perspectives in Education	India	1	0.0126	7823	98.7129
672	67	Philips Professional Journal	Ger	1	0.0126	7824	98.7256
673	67	Philosophy Today	U.S.A	1	0.0126	7825	98.7382
674	67	Physics News	U.S.A	1	0.0126	7826	98.7508
675	67	PIMA Magazine	U.S.A	1	0.0126	7827	98.7634
676	67	PLA Bulletin	Pakistan	1	0.0126	7828	98.7760
677	67	PPST Bulletin	India	1	0.0126	7829	98.7886
678	67	Probl. Inf. Doc.	U.S.A	1	0.0126	7830	98.8013
679	67	Proc. Israel Acad. Science and Humanities	Israel	1	0.0126	7831	98.8139
680	67	Proceedings of Royal Society of Medicine	U.K	1	0.0126	7832	98.8265
681	67	Progress of Education	India	1	0.0126	7833	98.8391
682	67	Psychological Bulletin	U.S.A	1	0.0126	7834	98.8517
683	67	Psychological Monograph	U.S.A	1	0.0126	7835	98.8644
684	67	Psychological Reports	U.S.A	1	0.0126	7836	98.8770
685	67	Psychological Research Bulletin	Sweden	1	0.0126	7837	98.8896
686	67	Public Libraries	U.S.A	1	0.0126	7838	98.9022
687	67	Public Library Journal	U.K	1	0.0126	7839	98.9148

(Contd...)

	1	2	3	4	5	6	7
688	67	Quarterly Journal of the Pakistan Library Association	Pakistan	1	0.0126	7840	98.9274
689	67	Quest in Education	India	1	0.0126	7841	98.9401
690	67	Radical Humanist	India	1	0.0126	7842	98.9527
691	67	Reading Improvement	U.S.A	1	0.0126	7843	98.9653
692	67	Refer	U.K	1	0.0126	7844	98.9779
693	67	Refvista	Brazil	1	0.0126	7845	98.9905
694	67	Res. Librarianship	Aus	1	0.0126	7846	99.0032
695	67	Research and Review	U.S.A	1	0.0126	7847	99.0158
696	67	Review	Canada	1	0.0126	7848	99.0284
697	67	Revista	Brazil	1	0.0126	7849	99.0410
698	67	Revista Interamericana De-Bibliotecologia	Colom	1	0.0126	7850	99.0536
699	67	RILISAR Bulletin on Information	India	1	0.0126	7851	99.0662
700	67	Rural Sociology	U.S.A	1	0.0126	7852	99.0789
701	67	SALG Newsletter	U.K	1	0.0126	7853	99.0915
702	67	School Libraries in Canada	U.S.A	1	0.0126	7854	99.1041
703	67	Science and Public Policy	U.K	1	0.0126	7855	99.1167
704	67	Science Reporter	India	1	0.0126	7856	99.1293
705	67	Science Studies	U.K	1	0.0126	7857	99.1420
706	67	Scientific World	U.K	1	0.0126	7858	99.1546
707	67	Sloan Management Review	U.S.A	1	0.0126	7859	99.1672

(Contd...)

	1	2	3	4	5	6	7
708	67	Small Computers in Libraries	U.S.A	1	0.0126	7860	99.1798
709	67	Social Indicators Research	Neth	1	0.0126	7861	99.1924
710	67	Social Science Information Studies	France	1	0.0126	7862	99.2050
711	67	Social Science Progress	U.S.A	1	0.0126	7863	99.2177
712	67	Social Sciences Information Studies	U.K	1	0.0126	7864	99.2303
713	67	Society for Promotion of Engineering Education	U.S.A	1	0.0126	7865	99.2429
714	67	Society for Studies of Science Newsletter	U.S.A	1	0.0126	7866	99.2555
715	67	Sociological Inquiry	U.S.A	1	0.0126	7867	99.2681
716	67	Sociology	U.K	1	0.0126	7868	99.2808
717	67	Sociometry	U.S.A	1	0.0126	7869	99.2934
718	67	Software Review	U.S.A	1	0.0126	7870	99.3060
719	67	South Africa Library	Sou. Afr	1	0.0126	7871	99.3186
720	67	South Asia Library Group Newsletter	U.K	1	0.0126	7872	99.3312
721	67	South-Eastern Librarian	U.S.A	1	0.0126	7873	99.3438
722	67	Southern Economic Journal	U.S.A	1	0.0126	7874	99.3565
723	67	SRELS Journal of Information Management	India	1	0.0126	7875	99.3691
724	67	Studies in Adult Education	Tanz	1	0.0126	7876	99.3817
725	67	Studies in Personnel Psychology	Canada	1	0.0126	7877	99.3943

(Contd...)

	1	*2*	*3*	*4*	*5*	*6*	*7*
726	67	T. Dokument	Ger	1	0.0126	7878	99.4069
727	67	Teachers College Record	U.S.A	1	0.0126	7879	99.4196
728	67	Teaching and Learning	U.K	1	0.0126	7880	99.4322
729	67	Technicalities	U.S.A	1	0.0126	7881	99.4448
730	67	Technological Forecast and Social Change	U.S.A	1	0.0126	7882	99.4574
731	67	Technology Review	U.K	1	0.0126	7883	99.4700
732	67	Telecommunications Policy	U.K	1	0.0126	7884	99.4826
733	67	Telektronikk	Norway	1	0.0126	7885	99.4953
734	67	TES	U.K	1	0.0126	7886	99.5079
735	67	The Administrator	India	1	0.0126	7887	99.5205
736	67	The Association of American Teacher Bulletin	U.S.A	1	0.0126	7888	99.5331
737	67	The Educational Review	India	1	0.0126	7889	99.5457
738	67	The Futurist	U.S.A	1	0.0126	7890	99.5584
739	67	The Journal	U.S.A	1	0.0126	7891	99.5710
740	67	The Midwestern Archivist	U.S.A	1	0.0126	7892	99.5836
741	67	The Press Council of India Review	India	1	0.0126	7893	99.5962
742	67	The Public Access Computer System Review	U.S.A	1	0.0126	7894	99.6088
743	67	The Scientist	U.S.A	1	0.0126	7895	99.6215
744	67	The Tamilnadu Journal of Cooperation	India	1	0.0126	7896	99.6341

(Contd...)

	1	2	3	4	5	6	7
745	67	The Viswa Bharati Quarterly	India	1	0.0126	7897	99.6467
746	67	The Western Journal of Medicine	U.S.A	1	0.0126	7898	99.6593
747	67	Third World Libraries	U.S.A	1	0.0126	7899	99.6719
748	67	Tidsk Foer Dokumentation	Sweden	1	0.0126	7900	99.6845
749	67	Times Literary Supplement	U.K	1	0.0126	7901	99.6972
750	67	Tok Tok Bilong Haus Buk	Papua	1	0.0126	7902	99.7098
751	67	Top of the News	U.S.A	1	0.0126	7903	99.7224
752	67	Training and Education	U.K	1	0.0126	7904	99.7350
753	67	Trends in Special Librarianship	U.S.A	1	0.0126	7905	99.7476
754	67	Tribe	India	1	0.0126	7906	99.7603
755	67	Tropical and Geographical Medicine	Neth	1	0.0126	7907	99.7729
756	67	U.K Open University Library Bulletin	U.K	1	0.0126	7908	99.7855
757	67	UC&R Newsletter	U.S.A	1	0.0126	7909	99.7981
758	67	UNESCO Bulletin for Library Science, Librarianship and Archives Administration	France	1	0.0126	7910	99.8107
759	67	Universitas	U.S.A	1	0.0126	7911	99.8233
760	67	University Administration	India	1	0.0126	7912	99.8360
761	67	University Affairs	Canada	1	0.0126	7913	99.8486
762	67	Verband Dir Bibliotheken Des Landes	Ger	1	0.0126	7914	99.8612

(Contd...)

	1	2	3	4	5	6	7
763	67	Vocational Guidance Quarterly	U.S.A	1	0.0126	7915	99.8738
764	67	Western European Specialist Section Newsletter	U.S.A	1	0.0126	7916	99.8864
765	67	Western Journal of Nursing Research	U.S.A	1	0.0126	7917	99.8991
766	67	Women and Health	U.S.A	1	0.0126	7918	99.9117
767	67	World Hospitals	U.K	1	0.0126	7919	99.9243
768	67	World Patent Information	U.K	1	0.0126	7920	99.9369
769	67	World Wide Activities of Research Publications Serials	U.S.A	1	0.0126	7921	99.9495
770	67	Young Children	U.S.A	1	0.0126	7922	99.9621
771	67	Youth Times	China	1	0.0126	7923	99.9748
772	67	Zentralblattfur Bibliothekswessen	Ger	1	0.0126	7924	99.9874
773	67	ZIID-Z	Ger	1	0.0126	7925	100.0000

TABLE-4.70
RANKED LIST OF JOURNALS IN AGRICULTURE INFORMATION, LIBRARIES, USERS AND SERVICES

Sl. No	*Rank*	*Title of Journal*	*Country Name*	*No of Citations*	*Percent*	*Cum Number*	*Cum Percent*
	1	*2*	*3*	*4*	*5*	*6*	*7*
01.	1	International Journal of Agricultural Librarians and Documentalists	Neth	85	21.3033	85	21.3033
02.	2	Indian Journal of Agricultural Library and Information Science	India	34	8.5213	119	29.8246
03.	3	ASLIB Proceedings	U.K	22	5.5138	141	35.3383
04.	4	Annals of Library Science and Documentation	India	20	5.0125	161	40.3509
05.	5	Library Trends	U.S.A	18	4.5113	179	44.8622
06.	6	ILA Bulletin	India	14	3.5088	193	48.3709
07.	7	Herald of Library Science	India	13	3.2581	206	51.6291
08.	8	International Association of Agricultural Information Specialists	Neth	12	3.0075	218	54.6366
09.	8	Special Libraries	U.S.A	12	3.0075	230	57.6441
10.	9	IASLIC Bulletin	India	11	2.7569	241	60.4010
11	10	Journal of Library and Information Science	India	10	2.5063	251	62.9073

(Contd...)

	1	*2*	*3*	*4*	*5*	*6*	*7*
12	11	2 Journals with 8 Citations		16	4.0100	267	66.9173
13	12	4 Journals with 6 Citations		24	6.0152	291	72.9323
14	13	2 Journals with 5 Citations		10	2.5062	301	75.4386
15	14	5 Journals with 4 Citations		20	5.0125	321	80.45
11							
16	15	4 Journals with 3 Citations		12	3.0076	333	83.4586
17	16	11 Journals with 2 Citations		22	5.5143	355	88.9724
18	17	44 Journals with 1 Citation		44	11.0264	399	100.0000

TABLE-4.71
RANKED LIST OF JOURNALS IN BIBLIOMETRICS

Sl. No	*Rank*	*Title of Journal*	*Country Name*	*No of Citations*	*Percent*	*Cum Number*	*Cum Percent*
	1	*2*	*3*	*4*	*5*	*6*	*7*
01	1	Scientometrics	Neth	213	18.8329	213	18.8329
02	2	Journal of Documentation	U.K	115	10.1680	328	29.0009
03	3	Annals of Library Science and Documentation	India	107	9.4607	435	38.4615
04	4	Journal of the American Society for Information Science	U.S.A	93	8.2228	528	46.6844
05	5	IASLIC Bulletin	India	37	3.2714	565	49.9558
06	6	Library Trends	U.S.A	34	3.0062	599	52.9620
07	7	Journal of Information Science	U.K	30	2.6525	629	55.6145
08	8	Journal of Library & Information Science	India	29	2.5641	658	58.1786
09	9	ILA Bulletin	India	26	2.2989	684	60.4775
10	9	Library Quarterly	U.S.A	26	2.2989	710	62.7763
11	9	Science	U.S.A	26	2.2989	736	65.0752
12	10	American Documentation	U.S.A	20	1.7683	756	66.8435
13	10	Information Processing and Management	U.K	20	1.7683	776	68.6118
14	10	Libri	Denmark	20	1.7683	796	70.3802

(Contd...)

	1	*2*	*3*	*4*	*5*	*6*	*7*
15	11	College and Research Libraries	U.S.A	19	1.6799	815	72.0601
16	12	2 Journals with 15 Citations		30	2.6526	845	74.7126
17	13	2 Journals with 14 Citations		28	2.4756	873	77.1883
18	14	3 Journals with 11 Citations		33	2.9178	906	80.1061
19	15	1 Journal with 10 Citation		10	0.8842	916	80.9903
20	16	2 Journals with 8 Citations		16	1.4146	932	82.4050
21	17	2 Journals with 7 Citations		14	1.2378	946	83.6428
22	18	2 Journals with 6 Citations		12	1.0610	958	84.7038
23	19	4 Journals with 5 Citations		20	1.7684	978	86.4721
24	20	6 Journals with 4 Citations		24	2.1222	1002	88.5942
25	21	10 Journals with 3 Citations		30	2.6530	1032	91.2467
26	22	22 Journals with 2 Citations		44	3.8896	1076	95.1370
27	23	55 Journals with 1 Citations		55	4.8620	1131	100.0000

TABLE – 4.72

RANKED LIST OF JOURNALS IN COLLEGE LIBRARIES, USERS AND SERVICES

Sl. No	*Rank*	*Title of Journal*	*Country* Name	*No of* Citations	*Percent*	*Cum* Number	*Cum* Percent
01	1	University News	India	104	23.2662	104	23.2662
02	2	College and Research Libraries	U.S.A	58	12.9754	162	36.2416
03	3	Library Herald	India	47	10.5145	209	46.7562
04	4	ILA Bulletin	India	40	8.9485	249	55.7047
05	5	Library Trends	U.S.A	36	8.0537	285	63.7584
06	6	Indian Librarian	India	26	5.8166	311	69.5749
07	7	New Frontiers in Education	U.S.A	21	4.6980	332	74.2729
08	8	Herald of Library Science	India	19	4.2506	351	78.5235
09	9	Annals of Library Science and Documentation	India	9	2.0134	360	80.5369
10	9	Lucknow Librarian	India	9	2.0134	369	82.5503
11	10	Journal of Library and Information Science	India	8	1.7897	377	84.3400
12	11	3 Journals with 4 Citations		12	2.6847	389	87.0246
13	12	7 Journals with 3 Citations		21	4.6977	410	91.7226
14	13	6 Journals with 2 citations		12	2.6844	422	94.4072
15	14	25 Journals with 1 citation		25	5.5925	447	100.0000

TABLE – 4.73
RANKED LIST OF JOURNALS IN LIBRARIES AND I.T

Sl. No	*Rank*	*Title of Journal*	*Country* Name	*No of* Citations	*Percent*	*Cum* Number	*Cum* Percent
01	1	Program	U.K	28	7.8212	28	7.8212
02	2	Library Trends	U.S.A	26	7.2626	54	15.0838
03	3	DESIDOC Bulletin of Information Technology	India	17	4.7486	71	19.8324
04	4	Annals of Library Science and Documentation	India	14	3.9106	85	23.7430
05	5	Information Technology and Libraries	U.S.A	12	3.3520	97	27.0950
06	6	Library Review	U.K	11	3.0726	108	30.1676
07	6	University News	India	11	3.0726	119	33.2402
08	7	Journal of Personality and Social Psychology	U.S.A	10	2.7933	129	36.0335
09	8	College and Research Libraries	U.S.A	9	2.5140	138	38.5475
10	8	IASLIC Bulletin	India	9	2.5140	147	41.0615
11	9	2 Journals with 8 Citations		16	4.4692	163	45.5307
12	10	5 Journals with 7 Citations		35	9.7765	198	55.3073
13	11	2 Journals with 6 Citations		12	3.3520	210	58.6592
14	12	5 Journals with 5 Citations		25	6.9830	235	65.6425
15	13	8 Journals with 4 Citations		32	8.9384	267	74.5810

(Contd...)

Sl. No	*Rank*	*Title of Journal*	*Country* Name	*No of* Citations	*Percent*	*Cum* Number	*Cum* Percent
16	14	8 Journals with 3 Citations		24	6.7040	291	81.2849
17	15	11 Journals with 2 citations		22	6.1457	313	87.4302
18	16	45 Journals with 1 citation		45	12.5685	358	100.0000

TABLE – 4.74

RANKED LIST OF JOURNALS IN MARKETING OF LIBRARY INFORMATION SERVICES AND PRODUCTS

Sl. No	*Rank*	*Title of Journal*	*Country* Name	*No of* Citations	*Percent*	*Cum* Number	*Cum* Percent
01	1	ASLIB Proceedings	U.K	33	12.5475	33	12.5475
02	2	Special Libraries	U.S.A	31	11.7871	64	24.3346
03	3	Library Trends	U.S.A	24	9.1255	88	33.4601
04	4	College and Research Libraries	U.S.A	17	6.4639	105	39.9240
05	4	Journal of the American Society for Information Science	U.S.A	17	6.4639	122	46.3878
06	5	Marketing Library Services	Neth	10	3.8023	132	50.1901
07	6	Library Journal	U.S.A	8	3.0418	140	53.2319
08	7	Annals of Library Science Documentation	India	7	2.6616	147	55.8935
09	7	Australian Library Journal	Australia	7	2.6616	154	58.5551
10	8	4 Journals with 6 Citations		24	9.1256	178	67.6806
11	9	4 Journals with 5 Citations		20	7.6044	198	75.2852
12	10	3 Journals with 4 Citations		12	4.5627	210	79.8479
13	11	2 Journals with 3 Citations		6	2.2814	216	82.1293
14	12	13 Journals with 2 Citations		26	9.8865	242	92.0158
15	13	21 Journals with 1 Citation		21	7.9842	263	100.0000

TABLE – 4.75
RANKED LIST OF JOURNALS IN MEDICAL INFORMATION, LIBRARIES, USERS AND SERVICES

Sl. No	*Rank*	*Title of Journal*	*Country* Name	*No of* Citations	*Percent*	*Cum* Number	*Cum* Percent
01	1	Bulletin of Medical Library Association	U.K	59	11.5686	59	11.5686
02	2	ASLIB Proceedings	U.K	21	4.1176	80	15.6863
03	3	Annual review of Information Science and Technology	U.S.A	20	3.9216	100	19.6078
04	3	Journal of the American Society for Information Science	U.S.A	20	3.9216	120	23.5294
05	4	College and research Libraries	U.S.A	16	3.1373	136	26.6667
06	4	ILA Bulletin	India	16	3.1373	152	29.8039
07	4	Indian Journal of Medical Education	India	16	3.1373	168	32.9412
08	4	International Library Review	U.K	16	3.1373	184	36.0784
09	4	Journal of Medical education	U.S.A	16	3.1373	200	39.2157
10	5	Library Trends	U.S.A	15	2.9412	215	42.1569
11	6	3 Journals with 12 Citations		36	7.0587	251	49.2157
12	7	3 Journals with 11 Citations		33	6.4707	284	55.6863
13	8	5 Journals with 6 Citations		30	5.8825	314	61.5686
14	9	4 Journals with 5 Citations		20	3.9216	334	65.4902
15	10	8 Journals with 4 Citations		32	6.2744	366	71.7647

TABLE – 4.176
RANKED LIST OF JOURNALS IN OTHER ASPECTS

Sl. No	*Rank*	*Title of Journal*	*Country* Name	*No of* Citations	*Percent*	*Cum* Number	*Cum* Percent
01	1	Herald of Library Science	India	84	6.5728	84	6.5728
02	2	Special Libraries	U.S.A	74	5.7903	158	12.3631
03	3	ILA Bulletin	India	61	4.7731	219	17.1362
04	4	Journalism Quarterly	U.S.A	60	4.6948	279	21.8310
05	5	Indian Librarian	India	50	3.9124	329	25.7433
06	5	Library Journal	U.S.A	50	3.9124	379	29.6557
07	6	Journal of Education for Library and Information Science	U.S.A	45	3.5211	424	33.1768
08	6	Library Herald	India	45	3.5211	469	36.6980
09	7	College and Research Libraries	U.S.A	43	3.3646	512	40.0626
10	8	Library Trends	U.S.A	42	3.2864	554	43.3490
11	9	University News	India	33	2.5822	587	45.9311
12	10	ASLIB Proceedings	U.K	32	2.5039	619	48.4351
13	11	IASLIC Bulletin	India	29	2.2692	648	50.7042
14	12	Library Quarterly	U.S.A	27	2.1127	675	52.8169
15	13	Annals of Library Science and Documentation	India	25	1.9562	700	54.7731
16	14	International Library Review	U.K	21	1.6432	721	56.4163
17	15	Vidura	India	18	1.4085	739	57.8247

(Contd...)

Sl. No	Rank	Title of Journal	Country Name	No of Citations	Percent	Cum Number	Cum Percent
18	16	Journal of Education for Librarianship	U.S.A	17	1.3302	756	59.1549
19	17	Modern Librarian	India	16	1.2520	772	60.4069
20	18	Journal of Librarianship	U.K	15	1.1737	787	61.5806
21	19	3 Journals with 13 Citations		39	3.0516	826	64.6322
22	20	2 Journals with 12 Citations		24	1.8780	850	66.5102
23	21	2 Journals with 11 Citations		22	1.7214	872	68.2316
24	22	3 Journals with 10 Citations		30	2.3475	902	70.5790
25	23	6 Journals with 8 Citations		48	3.7560	950	74.3349
26	24	4 Journals with 7 Citations		28	2.1908	978	76.5258
27	25	6 Journals with 6 Citations		36	2.8170	1014	79.3427
28	26	5 Journals with 5 Citations		25	1.9560	1039	81.2989
29	27	9 Journals with 4 Citations		36	2.8170	1075	84.1158
30	28	13 Journals with 3 Citations		39	3.0511	1114	87.1674
31	29	33 Journals with 2 Citations		66	5.1645	1180	92.3318
32	30	98 Journals with 1 Citation		98	7.6636	1278	100.0000

TABLE – 4.77
RANKED LIST OF JOURNALS IN OTHER LIBRARIES, USERS AND SERVICES

Sl. *No*	*Rank*	*Title of Journal*	*Country* Name	*No of* Citations	*Percent*	*Cum* Number	*Cum* Percent
01	1	Law Library Journal	U.S.A	24	5.7143	24	5.7143
02	2	Annual Review of Information Science and Technology	U.S.A	22	5.2381	46	10.9524
03	3	Library Trends	U.S.A	19	4.5238	65	15.4762
04	4	Lucknow Librarian	India	15	3.5714	80	19.0476
05	5	College and Research Libraries	U.S.A	14	3.3333	94	22.3810
06	6	Government Publications Review	U.K	13	3.0952	107	25.4762
07	6	Library Quarterly	U.S.A	13	3.0952	120	28.5714
08	7	Computers and Humanities	Neth	12	2.8571	132	31.4286
09	7	Government Information Quarterly	U.S.A	12	2.8571	144	34.2857
10	8	Herald of Library Science	India	9	2.1429	153	36.4286
11	9	2 Journals with 8 Citations		16	3.8096	169	40.2381
12	10	2 Journals with 7 Citations		14	3.3334	183	43.5714
13	11	4 Journals with 6 Citations		24	5.7144	207	49.2857
14	12	5 Journals with 5 Citations		25	5.9525	232	55.2381
15	13	7 Journals with 4 Citations		28	6.6668	260	61.9048
16	14	8 Journals with 3 Citations		24	5.7144	284	67.6190
17	15	31 Journals with 2 citations		62	14.7622	346	82.3810
18	16	74 Journals with 1 citation		74	17.6194	420	100.0000

TABLE – 4.78

RANKED LIST OF JOURNALS IN PUBLIC LIBRARIES AND COMMUNITY INFORMATION SERVICES

Sl. No	*Rank*	*Title of Journal*	*Country* Name	*No of* Citations	*Percent*	*Cum* Number	*Cum* Percent
01	1	Library Trends	U.S.A	105	17.0455	105	17.0455
02	2	Library Quarterly	U.S.A	58	9.4156	163	26.4610
03	3	Herald of Library Science	India	41	6.6558	204	33.1169
04	4	Australian Library Journal	Aus	32	5.1948	236	38.3117
05	4	ILA Bulletin	India	32	5.1948	268	43.5065
06	5	Journal of Librarianship	U.K	30	4.8701	298	48.3766
07	5	Library Journal	U.S.A	30	4.8701	328	53.2468
08	6	UNESCO Bulletin for Libraries	France	28	4.5455	356	57.7922
09	7	ASLIB Proceedings	U.K	18	2.9221	374	60.7143
10	8	Assistant Librarian	U.K	13	2.1104	387	62.8247
11	9	IFLA Journal	Ger	12	1.9481	399	64.7727
12	9	Library Herald	India	12	1.9481	411	66.7208
13	10	Libri	Den	11	1.7857	422	68.5065
14	11	Tendril	U.S.A	9	1.4610	431	69.9675
15	12	4 Journals with 8 Citations		32	5.1948	463	75.1623
16	13	2 Journals with 7 Citations		14	2.2728	477	77.4351
17	14	1 Journal with 6 Citations		6	0.9740	483	78.4091
18	15	4 Journals with 5 Citations		20	3.2468	503	81.6558
19	16	6 Journals with 4 Citations		24	3.8964	527	85.5519

(Contd...)

Sl. No	Rank	Title of Journal	Country Name	No of Citations	Percent	Cum Number	Cum Percent
20	17	10 Journals with 3 Citations		30	4.8700	557	90.4221
21	18	9 Journals with 2 citations		18	2.9223	575	93.3442
22	19	41 Journals with 1 citation		41	6.6543	616	100.0000

TABLE – 4.79
RANKED LIST OF JOURNALS IN SCIENTIFIC AND TECHNICAL LIBRARIES

Sl. No	*Rank*	*Title of Journal*	*Country* Name	*No of* Citations	*Percent*	*Cum* Number	*Cum* Percent
01	1	ASLIB Proceedings	U.K	107	11.5302	107	11.5302
02	2	Special Libraries	U.S.A	68	7.3276	175	18..8578
03	3	College and Research Libraries	U.S.A	52	5.6034	227	24.4612
04	4	IASLIC Bulletin	India	42	4.5259	269	28.9871
05	5	Annals of Library Science and Documentation	India	38	4.0948	307	33.0819
06	6	Journal of Documentation	U.K	32	3.4483	339	36.5302
07	7	Herald of Library Science	India	28	3.0172	367	39.5474
08	7	Library Trends	U.S.A	28	3.0172	395	42.5647
09	8	Library Science with a Slant to Documentation	India	25	2.6940	420	45.2586
10	8	The Indian Journal of Technical Education	India	25	2.6940	445	47.9526
11	9	University News	India	21	2.2629	466	50.2155
12	10	Library Association Record	U.K	16	1.7241	482	51.9397
13	10	Library Science with a Slant to Documentation and Information Studies	India	16	1.7241	498	53.6638
14	11	DESIDOC Bulletin of Information Technology	India	15	1.6164	513	55.2802

(Contd...)

Sl. No	*Rank*	*Title of Journal*	*Country* Name	*No of* Citations	*Percent*	*Cum* Number	*Cum* Percent
15	11	ILA Bulletin	India	15	1.6164	528	56.8966
16	11	Library Quarterly	U.S.A	15	1.6164	543	58.5129
17	12	Lucknow Librarian	India	12	1.2931	555	59.8060
18	13	International Library Review	U.K	11	1.1853	566	60.9914
19	14	Journal of the American Society for Information Science	U.S.A	10	1.0776	576	62.0690
20	15	5 Journals with 9 Citations		45	4.8490	621	66.9181
21	16	3 Journals with 8 Citations		24	2.5863	645	69.5043
22	17	5 Journals with 7 Citations		35	3.7715	680	73.2759
23	18	7 Journals with 6 Citations		42	4.5262	722	77.8017
24	19	4 Journals with 5 Citations		20	2.1552	742	79.9569
25	20	6 Journals with 4 Citations		24	2.5860	766	82.5431
26	21	10 Journals with 3 Citations		30	3.2330	796	85.7759
27	22	24 Journals with 2 citations		48	5.1720	844	90.9483
28	23	84 Journals with 1 citations		84	9.0552	928	100.0000

TABLE – 4.80
RANKED LIST OF JOURNALS IN UNIVERSITY LIBRARIES, USERS AND SERVICES

Sl. No	*Rank*	*Title of Journal*	*Country* Name	*No of* Citations	*Percent*	*Cum* Number	*Cum* Percent
01	1	College and Research Libraries	U.S.A	89	5.6508	89	5.6508
02	2	Library Trends	U.S.A	83	5.2698	172	10.9206
03	3	University News	India	79	5.0159	251	15.9365
04	4	ASLIB Proceedings	U.K	60	3.8095	311	19.7460
05	5	Annals of Library Science Documentation	India	50	3.1746	361	22.9206
06	6	IASLIC Bulletin	India	43	2.7302	404	25.6508
07	7	Journal of Applied Psychology	U.S.A	40	2.5397	444	28.1905
08	8	Herald of Library Science	India	37	2.3492	481	30.5397
09	9	ILA Bulletin	India	34	2.1587	515	32.6984
10	10	Library Quarterly	U.S.A	32	2.0317	547	34.7302
11	11	Indian Journal of Psychology	India	29	1.8413	576	36.5714
12	12	Journal of Librarianship	U.K	28	1.7778	604	38.3492
13	12	Library Journal	U.S.A	28	1.7778	632	40.1270
14	13	Journal of the American Society for Information Science	U.S.A	27	1.7143	659	41.8413
15	13	Lucknow Librarian	India	27	1.7143	686	43.5556
16	14	Annual Review of Information Science and Technology	U.S.A	26	1.6508	712	45.2063

(Contd...)

Sl. No	*Rank*	*Title of Journal*	*Country* Name	*No of* Citations	*Percent*	*Cum* Number	*Cum* Percent
17	15	Journal of Documentation	U.K	25	1.5873	737	46.7937
18	16	Library Herald	India	21	1.3333	758	48.1270
19	17	Teaching at a Distance	U.K	19	1.2063	777	49.3333
20	18	3 Journals with 16 Citations		48	3.0477	825	52.3810
21	19	4 Journals with 15 Citations		60	3.8096	885	56.1905
22	20	2 Journals with 14 Citations		28	1.7778	913	57.9683
23	21	1 Journal with 13 Citations		13	0.8254	926	58.7937
24	22	4 Journals with 12 Citations		48	3.0476	974	61.8413
25	23	2 Journals with 11 Citations		22	1.3968	996	63.2381
26	24	4 Journals with 10 Citations		40	2.5396	1036	65.7778
27	25	3 Journals with 9 Citations		27	1.7142	1063	67.4921
28	26	1 Journal with 8 Citations		8	0.5079	1071	68.0000
29	27	6 Journals with 7 Citations		42	2.6664	1113	70.6667
30	28	5 Journals with 6 Citations		30	1.9050	1143	72.5714
31	29	9 Journals with 5 Citations		45	2.8575	1188	75.4286
32	30	10 Journals with 4 Citations		40	2.5400	1228	77.9683
33	31	28 Journals with 3 Citations		84	5.3340	1312	83.3016
34	32	61 Journals with 2 citations		122	7.7470	1434	91.0476
35	33	141 Journals with 1 citations		141	8.9535	1575	100.0000

Productivity of Journals and Books in Library and Information Science

With a view to measure the productivity of journals the journal citations are divided into four groups so that each group consists of almost equal number of citations based on ranked list of journals. The productivity of journals in Library and Information Science and its sub-disciplines is presented in the following tables. On clear examination of the results in the table it is evident that 25 percent of the citations are contributed by 6 journals in the field of Library and Information Science. However we can observe a marked increase in the number of journals as we shift on second, third and fourth groups. The values in the last column representing average productivity in first, second, third and fourth groups are 314.00, 180.91, 42.96, 2.81 respectively. This indicates the declining productivity of individual journals. We can observe inverse relationship between rank and productivity of the journals. As the rank of the journal increased there is decline in average productivity. Average productivity of 708 journals is only 2.81 which confirms with inverse relationship that exists between rank and average productivity of journals.

A. Productivity of Cited Journals in Library and Information Science

TABLE – 4.81
PRODUCTIVITY OF CITED JOURNALS IN LIBRARY AND INFORMATION SCIENCE

Sl. No	*Percentage of Citations*	*No. of Citations*	*No. of Journals Covered*	*Percentage of Journals*	*Average Productivity*
1	0-25%	1884	6	0.78	314.00
2	26-50%	1990	11	1.42	180.91
3	51-75%	2062	48	6.21	42.96
4	76-100%	1989	708	91.59	2.81
	Total	7925	773	100.00	10.25

TABLE – 4.82
PRODUCTIVITY OF CITED JOURNALS IN AGRICULTURE INFORMATION, LIBRARIES, USERS AND SERVICES

Sl. No	*Percentage of Citations*	*No. of Citations*	*No. of Journals Covered*	*Per-centage of Journals*	*Average Pro-ductivity*
1	0-25%	85	1	1.20	85.00
2	26-50%	108	5	6.02	21.60
3	51-75%	103	12	14.46	8.58
4	76-100%	103	65	78.31	1.58
	Total	399	83	100.00	4.81

The productivity of cited journals in sub-discipline "*Agriculture Information, Libraries, Users and Services*" is shown in the above table. The findings of the data clearly depicts that average productivity of one journal in the first group is 85 and it has declined to 1.58 in the fourth group. The average productivity for the entire field is 4.81. The details of the journal in the first group with an average productivity of 85.00 is *International Association of Agricultural Librarians* and *Documentalists.*

TABLE – 4.83
PRODUCTIVITY OF CITED JOURNALS IN BIBLIOMETRICS

Sl. No	*Percentage of Citations*	*No. of Citations*	*No. of Journals Covered*	*Per-centage of Journals*	*Average Pro-ductivity*
1	0-25%	213	1	0.79	213.00
2	26-50%	352	4	3.17	88.00
3	51-75%	280	12	9.52	23.33
4	76-100%	286	109	86.51	2.62
	Total	1131	126	100.00	8.98

The table 4.83 shows the average productivity of cited journals in the field of "*Bibliometrics*". Analysis of table shows that single journal in the first group has contributed 213 citations with an average productivity of 213.00. However we can observe a declining trend in average productivity of journals as we pass on to next groups. The average productivity has decreased from 213.00 in the first group to 2.62 in the 4th group. The name the journal in the first group is *Scientometrics*.

TABLE – 4.84
PRODUCTIVITY OF CITED JOURNALS IN COLLEGE LIBRARIES, USERS AND SERVICES

Sl. No	*Percentage of Citations*	*No. of Citations*	*No. of Journals Covered*	*Per-centage of Journals*	*Average Pro-ductivity*
1	0-25%	104	1	1.92	104.00
2	26-50%	105	2	3.85	52.50
3	51-75%	123	4	7.69	30.75
4	76-100%	115	45	86.54	2.56
	Total	447	52	100.00	8.60

The table presents details about the average productivity of cited journals in the discipline of College Libraries, Users and Services. In the first group the average productivity of one journal is 104.00. In the fourth group it has declined to 2.56. The name the journal in the first group with an average productivity of 104.00 is *University News*.

TABLE – 4.85
PRODUCTIVITY OF CITED JOURNALS IN LIBRARIES AND I.T

Sl. No	*Percentage of Citations*	*No. of Citations*	*No. of Journals Covered*	*Percentage of Journals*	*Average Productivity*
1	0-25%	85	4	4.17	21.25
2	26-50%	92	10	10.42	9.20
3	51-75%	90	18	18.75	5.00
4	76-100%	91	64	66.67	1.42
	Total	358	96	100.00	3.73

The average productivity of cited journals in the sub-discipline of "*Libraries and I.T*" is presented in the above table. It is noticed that the first group of citations are contributed by only 4 journals in the ranked list, thus signifying their high rate of productivity of 21.25. However we can observe that 64 journals could contribute only 91 citations with an average productivity of 1.42.

TABLE – 4.86
PRODUCTIVITY OF CITED JOURNALS IN MARKETING OF LIBRARY INFORMATION SERVICES AND PRODUCTS

Sl. No	*Percentage of Citations*	*No. of Citations*	*No. of Journals Covered*	*Percentage of Journals*	*Average Productivity*
1	0-25%	64	2	3.57	32.00
2	26-50%	58	3	5.36	19.33
3	51-75%	71	11	19.64	6.45
4	76-100%	70	40	71.43	1.75
	Total	263	56	100.00	4.70

Table shows the average productivity of journals cited by researchers in the sub-discipline "*Marketing of Library Information Services and Products*". The average productivity of journals has shown decreasing trend as we observe the four groups. The average productivity of each journal in first group accounted for 32.00 and it has declined to 1.75 in fourth group.

TABLE – 4.87
PRODUCTIVITY OF CITED JOURNALS IN MEDICAL INFORMATION, LIBRARIES, USERS AND SERVICES

Sl. No	*Percentage of Citations*	*No. of Citations*	*No. of Journals Covered*	*Percentage of Journals*	*Average Productivity*
1	0-25%	120	4	2.90	30.00
2	26-50%	131	9	6.52	14.56
3	51-75%	130	25	18.12	5.20
4	76-100%	129	100	72.46	1.29
	Total	510	138	100.00	3.70

The productivity of cited journals in the sub-discipline of Medical Information, Libraries, Users and Services has been tabulated. As observed in other sub-disciplines the average productivity of individual journals is high (30.00) in the first group and it decreased to (1.29) in fourth group. Four journals in the first group are found to be contributing 25 percent of the total citations. The remaining 75 percent in the field has been contributed by 134 journals. The decline in average productivity of journals among four groups is noticed from 30.00 to 1.29.

TABLE – 4.88
PRODUCTIVITY OF CITED JOURNALS IN OTHER ASPECTS

Sl. No	*Percentage of Citations*	*No. of Citations*	*No. of Journals Covered*	*Percentage of Journals*	*Average Productivity*
1	0-25%	279	4	1.96	69.75
2	26-50%	340	8	3.92	42.50
3	51-75%	338	25	12.25	13.52
4	76-100%	321	167	81.86	1.92
	Total	1278	204	100.00	6.26

Table indicates that 25 percent of the total citations are contributed by four journals with an average productivity of 69.75. The average productivity is 42.50, 13.52, and 1.92 in the second, third and fourth groups disclosing a declining or decreasing trend in average productivity.

TABLE – 4.89
PRODUCTIVITY OF CITED JOURNALS IN OTHER LIBRARIES, USERS AND SERVICES

Sl. No	*Percentage of Citations*	*No. of Citations*	*No. of Journals Covered*	*Per-centage of Journals*	*Average Pro-ductivity*
1	0-25%	94	5	3.50	18.80
2	26-50%	113	13	9.09	8.69
3	51-75%	107	35	24.48	3.06
4	76-100%	106	90	62.94	1.18
	Total	420	143	100.00	2.94

The productivity of cited journals in the field of "*Other Libraries, Users and Services*" is presented in the above table. Five journals in the first group are said to be contributing 25 percent of the total citations with an average productivity of 18.80. The average productivity of journals however declined with every group. The average productivity of journals in the first group is 18.80 and it is 1.18 in the fourth group which clearly indicates a decreasing trend in average productivity of journals.

TABLE – 4.90
PRODUCTIVITY OF CITED JOURNALS IN PUBLIC LIBRARIES AND COMMUNITY INFORMATION SERVICES

Sl. No	*Percentage of Citations*	*No. of Citations*	*No. of Journals Covered*	*Per-centage of Journals*	*Average Pro-ductivity*
1	0-25%	105	1	1.10	105.00
2	26-50%	193	5	5.49	38.60
3	51-75%	157	11	12.09	14.27
4	76-100%	161	74	81.32	2.18
	Total	616	91	100.00	6.77

Table depicts the average productivity of cited journals in the sub-discipline of "*Public Libraries and Community Information Services*". Average productivity of one journal in first group is 105.00 indicating the journal as the most productive among all the journals in this field. We can observe a declining trend in the next three groups. In the fourth group 74 journals contributed 161 citations with an average productivity of 2.18. The name of the journal in the first group with an average productivity of 105.00 is *Library Trends.*

TABLE – 4.91
PRODUCTIVITY OF CITED JOURNALS IN SCIENTIFIC AND TECHNICAL LIBRARIES

Sl. No	*Percentage of Citations*	*No. of Citations*	*No. of Journals Covered*	*Percentage of Journals*	*Average Productivity*
1	0-25%	227	3	1.80	75.67
2	26-50%	218	7	4.19	31.14
3	51-75%	247	24	14.37	10.29
4	76-100%	236	133	79.64	1.77
	Total	928	167	100.00	5.56

The average productivity of cited journals in the field of "*Scientific and Technical Libraries*" is presented in the above table. Average productivity of three journals in the first group is 75.67 indicating the importance of three journals. These three journals have contributed 25 percent of the total citations. The remaining 75 percent has been contributed by 164 journals indicating a declining trend in average productivity of journals.

TABLE – 4.92
PRODUCTIVITY OF CITED JOURNALS IN UNIVERSITY LIBRARIES, USERS AND SERVICES

Sl. No	*Percentage of Citations*	*No. of Citations*	*No. of Journals Covered*	*Percentage of Journals*	*Average Productivity*
	1	*2*	*3*	*4*	*5*
1	0-25%	361	5	1.65	72.20
2	26-50%	416	14	4.62	29.71

(Contd...)

	1	*2*	*3*	*4*	*5*
3	51-75%	401	42	13.86	9.55
4	76-100%	397	242	79.87	1.64
	Total	1575	303	100.00	5.20

The productivity of cited journals in the sub-discipline of "University Libraries, Users and Services" is shown in the above table. 25 percent of total citations are contributed by five journals in the ranked list with an average productivity of 72.20. The average productivity in the fourth group is 1.64 which confirms with the law that with an increase in rank of the journal there is decline in average productivity.

B. Productivity of Cited Books in Library and Information Science

The productivity of cited books is measured by grouping all the book citations into four groups so that each group contained equal number of citations approximately. The number of citations in each group and average productivity are computed. The average productivity of books is calculated by dividing the number of citations in each group by the number of books covered in the group.

The average productivity of books cited in Library and Information Science and its sub-disciplines is discussed in the following tables.

TABLE – 4.93
PRODUCTIVITY OF CITED BOOKS IN LIBRARY AND INFORMATION SCIENCE

Sl. No	*Percentage of Citations*	*No. of Citations*	*No. of Book Covered*	*Per-centage of Books*	*Average Pro-ductivity*
1	0-25%	715	98	5.82	7.30
2	26-50%	715	271	16.09	2.64
3	51-75%	717	599	35.57	1.20
4	76-100%	716	716	42.52	1.00
	Total	2863	1684	100.00	1.70

The analysis of table shows that 98 books contributed 25 percent of total citations with an average productivity of 7.30. The declining trend in average productivity can be observed very clearly and the average productivity in fourth group is 1.00 which confirms our statement above. The average productivity value range is between 1.00 and 7.30.

TABLE – 4.94
PRODUCTIVITY OF CITED BOOKS IN AGRICULTURE INFORMATION, LIBRARIES, USERS AND SERVICES

Sl. No	*Percentage of Citations*	*No. of Citations*	*No. of Books Covered*	*Per-centage of Books*	*Average Pro-ductivity*
1	0-25%	14	13	23.21	1.08
2	26-50%	14	14	25.00	1.00
3	51-75%	14	14	25.00	1.00
4	76-100%	15	15	26.79	1.00
	Total	57	56	100.00	1.02

TABLE – 4.95
PRODUCTIVITY OF CITED BOOKS IN BIBLIOMETRICS

Sl. No	*Percentage of Citations*	*No. of Citations*	*No. of Books Covered*	*Per-centage of Books*	*Average Pro-ductivity*
1	0-25%	33	5	5.75	6.60
2	26-50%	35	14	16.09	2.50
3	51-75%	36	33	37.93	1.09
4	76-100%	35	35	40.23	1.00
	Total	139	87	100.00	1.60

TABLE – 4.96
PRODUCTIVITY OF CITED BOOKS IN COLLEGE LIBRARIES, USERS AND SERVICES

Sl. No	*Percentage of Citations*	*No. of Citations*	*No. of Books Covered*	*Per-centage of Books*	*Average Pro-ductivity*
1	0-25%	34	14	12.28	2.43
2	26-50%	36	29	25.44	1.24
3	51-75%	35	35	30.70	1.00
4	76-100%	36	36	31.58	1.00
	Total	141	114	100.00	1.24

TABLE – 4.97

PRODUCTIVITY OF CITED BOOKS IN LIBRARIES AND I.T

Sl. No	*Percentage of Citations*	*No. of Citations*	*No. of Books Covered*	*Percentage of Books*	*Average Productivity*
1	0-25%	54	14	8.97	3.86
2	26-50%	55	32	20.51	1.72
3	51-75%	55	55	35.26	1.00
4	76-100%	55	55	35.26	1.00
	Total	219	156	100.00	1.40

TABLE – 4.98

PRODUCTIVITY OF CITED BOOKS IN MARKETING OF LIBRARY INFORMATION SERVICES AND PRODUCTS

Sl. No	*Percentage of Citations*	*No. of Citations*	*No. of Books Covered*	*Percentage of Books*	*Average Productivity*
1	0-25%	18	2	6.45	9.00
2	26-50%	18	4	12.90	4.50
3	51-75%	18	8	25.81	2.25
4	76-100%	20	17	54.84	1.18
	Total	74	31	100.00	2.39

TABLE – 4.99

PRODUCTIVITY OF CITED BOOKS IN MEDICAL INFORMATION, LIBRARIES, USERS AND SERVICES

Sl. No	*Percentage of Citations*	*No. of Citations*	*No. of Books Covered*	*Percentage of Books*	*Average Productivity*
1	0-25%	33	15	13.64	2.20
2	26-50%	35	26	23.64	1.35
3	51-75%	34	34	30.91	1.00
4	76-100%	35	35	31.82	1.00
	Total	137	110	100.00	1.25

TABLE – 4.100
PRODUCTIVITY OF CITED BOOKS IN OTHER ASPECTS

Sl. No	*Percentage of Citations*	*No. of Citations*	*No. of Books Covered*	*Percentage of Books*	*Average Productivity*
1	0-25%	108	8	2.99	13.50
2	26-50%	116	45	16.79	2.58
3	51-75%	112	103	38.43	1.09
4	76-100%	112	112	41.79	1.00
	Total	448	268	100.00	1.67

TABLE – 4.101
PRODUCTIVITY OF CITED BOOKS IN OTHER LIBRARIES, USERS AND SERVICES

Sl. No	*Percentage of Citations*	*No. of Citations*	*No. of Books Covered*	*Percentage of Books*	*Average Productivity*
1	0-25%	30	14	13.21	2.14
2	26-50%	31	31	29.25	1.00
3	51-75%	30	30	28.30	1.00
4	76-100%	31	31	29.25	1.00
	Total	122	106	100.00	1.15

TABLE – 4.102
PRODUCTIVITY OF CITED BOOKS IN PUBLIC LIBRARIES AND COMMUNITY INFORMATION SERVICES

Sl. No	*Percentage of Citations*	*No. of Citations*	*No. of Books Covered*	*Percentage of Books*	*Average Productivity*
1	0-25%	74	18	8.78	4.11
2	26-50%	79	37	18.05	2.14
3	51-75%	77	73	35.61	1.05
4	76-100%	77	77	37.56	1.00
	Total	307	205	100.00	1.50

TABLE – 4.103
PRODUCTIVITY OF CITED BOOKS IN SCIENTIFIC AND TECHNICAL LIBRARIES

Sl. No	*Percentage of Citations*	*No. of Citations*	*No. of Books Covered*	*Percentage of Books*	*Average Productivity*
1	0-25%	56	23	12.04	2.43
2	26-50%	56	56	29.32	1.00
3	51-75%	56	56	29.32	1.00
4	76-100%	56	56	29.32	1.00
	Total	224	191	100.00	1.17

TABLE – 4.104
PRODUCTIVITY OF CITED BOOKS IN UNIVERSITY LIBRARIES, USERS AND SERVICES

Sl. No	*Percentage of Citations*	*No. of Citations*	*No. of Books Covered*	*Percentage of Books*	*Average Productivity*
1	0-25%	248	51	7.86	4.86
2	26-50%	249	112	17.26	2.22
3	51-75%	249	237	36.52	1.05
4	76-100%	249	249	38.37	1.00
	Total	995	649	100.00	1.53

Application of Bradford's Law of Scattering

Bradford law of scattering describes how the literature on a particular subject is scattered or distributed in the journals. The law is based on an investigation performed in 1933 by L. Jones in the Science Museum Library, London. It was first reported in 1934 in the journal "Engineering" by Bradford and, subsequently in a book entitled "Documentation" by the same author in 1948. Bradford formulated his law as follows: "If scientific journals are arranged in order of decreasing productivity of articles on a given subject, they may be divided into a nucleus of periodicals more particularly to the subject and several groups or zones containing the same articles as the nucleus, when the number of periodicals in the nucleus and succeeding zones will be 1:

n: n^2 .... for some constant n. Thus, for a linear increase in the number of articles, the number of journals requires a geometric increase. This is popularly known as verbal formulation of Bradford's Law of Scattering.

In Chapter – 3 (Methodology), the application of Bradford's Law of Scattering (Verbal Formulation) to citation data was tested. The information from ranked list of journals in Library and Information Science (Tables 4.69-4.80) and its sub-disciplines has been used for this purpose.

Tables 4.105 to 4.112 presents Bradford groups for Library and Information Science representing 3,4,5,6,7,8,9, and 10 groups respectively. The computer Chi-square values are also presented.

The applicability of Bradford's Law of Scattering (graphical formulation) to citation data (Tables 4.69-4.80) in Library and Information Science and its sub disciplines was tested by plotting Bradford's bibliographs. Graphs were plotted on semi logarithmic papers, with the Y-axis representing the cumulative number of citations and the X-axis being the logarithm of the cumulative number of journals producing these citations.

TABLE – 4.105
BRADFORD GROUPS FOR LIBRARY AND INFORMATION SCIENCE

(3 GROUPS)

Groups	*No. of Journals (Computed)*	*No. of Journals (Considered)*	*Degree of Concentration*	*Citations that should be Present*	*Estimated Citations*
1	8.2361	9	9.1491	2641.6667	2582
2	75.3530	75	9.1491	2641.6667	3641
3	689.4109	689	9.1491	2641.6667	1702

Chi-square = 713.6406 Degree of Freedom = 2

Chi-square computed value (713.6406 and DF=2) computed to test the goodness of fit has proved that there is difference between number of citations that should have been present in each group and the estimated number of citations in each group, for the discipline Library and Information as a whole. However it tends to show that usage pattern of journals does not confirm with verbal representation of Bradford's law of scattering.

TABLE – 4.106
BRADFORD GROUPS FOR LIBRARY AND INFORMATION SCIENCE
(4 Groups)

Groups	*No. of Journals (Computed)*	*No. of Journals (Considered)*	*Degree of Concentration*	*Citations that should be Present*	*Estimated Citations*
1	4.3061	5	5.2606	1981.2500	1625
2	22.6525	23	5.2606	1981.2500	3134
3	119.1650	119	5.2606	1981.2500	2013
4	626.8764	627	5.2606	1981.2500	1153

Chi-square = 1081.5156 Degree of Freedom = 3

The scattering of citations among four groups of journals is show in the above table. The examination of the table indicates that the difference between the expected and estimated values using chi-square test has revealed that the scattering pattern has not been in line with pattern suggested by Bradford.

TABLE – 4.107
BRADFORD GROUPS FOR LIBRARY AND INFORMATION SCIENCE
(5 Groups)

Groups	*No. of Journals (Computed)*	*No. of Journals (Considered)*	*Degree of Concentration*	*Citations that should be Present*	*Estimated Citations*
1	2.8038	3	3.7742	1585.0000	1071
2	10.5823	11	3.7742	1585.0000	2450
3	39.9399	40	3.7742	1585.0000	2192
4	150.7419	151	3.7742	1585.0000	1336
5	568.9320	569	3.7742	1585.0000	876

Chi-square = 1227.4776 Degree of Freedom=4

The study of distribution of citations among five groups in the field of Library and Information Science is depicted in the above table. Significant difference has been observed between the expected and estimated values using chi-square test. The findings indicates the non-conformity of Bradford law of scattering even in five groups of journal distribution.

TABLE – 4.108
BRADFORD GROUPS FOR LIBRARY AND INFORMATION SCIENCE
(6 Groups)

Groups	*No. of Journals (Computed)*	*No. of Journals (Considered)*	*Degree of Concentration*	*Citations that should be Present*	*Estimated Citations*
1	2.0464	3	3.0247	1320.8333	1071
2	6.1898	6	3.0247	1320.8333	1511
3	18.7224	19	3.0247	1320.8333	2177
4	56.6306	57	3.0247	1320.8333	1477
5	171.2931	171	3.0247	1320.8333	981
6	518.1178	518	3.0247	1320.8333	708

Chi-square = 1019.8417 Degree of Freedom = 5

Table shows six group wise distribution of journals and corresponding number of citations (both expected and estimated). The Chi-Square value indicates high goodness of fit (DF=5) between the groups showing variation from Bradford law of scattering for journal literature for Library and Information Science discipline as a whole.

TABLE – 4.109
BRADFORD GROUPS FOR LIBRARY AND INFORMATION SCIENCE
(7 Groups)

Groups	*No. of Journals (Computed)*	*No. of Journals (Considered)*	*Degree of Concentration*	*Citations that should be Present*	*Estimated Citations*
1	1.5993	2	2.5824	1132.1429	759
2	4.1299	4	2.5824	1132.1429	1125
3	10.6650	11	2.5824	1132.1429	1990
4	27.5410	28	2.5824	1132.1429	1591
5	71.1212	71	2.5824	1132.1429	1085
6	183.6614	184	2.5824	1132.1429	791
7	474.2822	474	2.5824	1132.1429	584

Chi-square = 1329.1757 Degree of Freedom = 6

The above table shows the scattering pattern of citations among seven groups of journals. It is noticed that there is wide difference between expected and estimated values using Chi-Square test. The findings Chi-Square 1329.1757 and DF=6 is proving that journal usage pattern in Library and Information Science does not confirm with verbal representation of Bradford law of scattering.

TABLE – 4.110
BRADFORD GROUPS FOR LIBRARY AND INFORMATION SCIENCE
(8 Groups)

Groups	*No. of Journals (Computed)*	*No. of Journals (Considered)*	*Degree of Concentration*	*Citations that should be Present*	*Estimated Citations*
1	1.3074	2	2.2936	990.6250	759
2	2.9987	3	2.2936	990.6250	856
3	6.8777	7	2.2936	990.6250	1557
4	15.7747	16	2.2936	990.6250	1577
5	36.1808	36	2.2936	990.6250	1160
6	82.9842	83	2.2936	990.6250	853
7	190.3320	190	2.2936	990.6250	643
8	436.5444	437	2.2936	990.6250	510

Chi-square = 1143.9940 Degree of Freedom = 7

The Chi-Square value 1143.9940 and DF=7 calculated to test the fitness has clearly revealed the significant difference between the number of citations that should have been present in each group and estimated number of citations that should have been present in each group. It is concluded that the usage pattern of journals does not satisfy the verbal representation of Bradford law of scattering.

TABLE – 4.111
BRADFORD GROUPS FOR LIBRARY AND INFORMATION SCIENCE
(9 Groups)

Groups	*No. of Journals (Computed)*	*No. of Journals (Considered)*	*Degree of Concentration*	*Citations that should be Present*	*Estimated Citations*
	1	*2*	*3*	*4*	*5*
1	1.1032	2	2.0915	880.5556	759
2	2.3073	2	2.0915	880.5556	599

(Contd...)

	1	2	3	4	5
3	4.8257	5	2.0915	880.5556	1224
4	10.0930	10	2.0915	880.5556	1475
5	21.1095	21	2.0915	880.5556	1239
6	44.1506	44	2.0915	880.5556	927
7	92.3412	92	2.0915	880.5556	705
8	193.1323	193	2.0915	880.5556	551
9	403.9373	404	2.0915	880.5556	446

Chi-square = 1163.2113 Degree of Freedom = 8

The Chi-Square (1163.2113 DF=8) presented in the above table points out variation between the expected and estimated values using Chi-Square test. The results that are tabulated proves that application of Bradford law of scattering even in 9 group distribution futile.

TABLE – 4.112
BRADFORD GROUPS FOR LIBRARY AND INFORMATION SCIENCE
(10 Groups)

Groups	*No. of Journals (Computed)*	*No. of Journals (Considered)*	*Degree of Concen-tration*	*Citations that should be Present*	*Estimated Citations*
1	0.9528	1	1.9427	792.5000	430
2	1.8510	2	1.9427	792.5000	641
3	3.5961	4	1.9427	792.5000	1061
4	6.9862	7	1.9427	792.5000	1389
5	13.5724	14	1.9427	792.5000	1238
6	26.3675	26	1.9427	792.5000	954
7	51.2251	51	1.9427	792.5000	739
8	99.5168	100	1.9427	792.5000	597
9	193.3345	193	1.9427	792.5000	488
10	375.5975	376	1.9427	792.5000	388

Chi-square = 1393.3609 Degree of Freedom = 9

The Chi-Square test has been conducted to identify the distribution of citations among 10 groups of journals and degree of concentration. The computed value 1393.3609 DF=9 indicates that usage pattern of journals in the discipline Library and Information Science does not comply the verbal representation as suggested in Bradford law of scattering.

The chisquare values computed for sub-disuplines in LIS reveal the difference between the number of citations that should have been present in each group, and the estimated citations in each group. This difference comes to show the non-applicability of Bradford Law of Scattering.

Scattering of Journals and Books among Countries

The Country-wise distribution of journals and books reveals the productivity of countries in terms of their contributions in any discipline and in the present case in the field of Library and Information Science.

TABLE – 4.113
COUNTRY-WISE DISTRIBUTION OF JOURNALS IN LIBRARY AND INFORMATION SCIENCE

Sl. No	*Name of the Country*	*Number*	*Per-centage*	*Cum-ulative*	*Cumulative Percentage*
	1	*2*	*3*	*4*	*5*
1.	U.S.A.	2891	36.48	2891	36.48
2.	India	2602	32.83	5493	69.31
3.	U.K.	1437	18.13	6930	87.44
4.	Netherlands	380	4.79	7310	92.24
5.	Australia	116	1.46	7426	93.70
6.	France	96	1.21	7522	94.91
7.	Germany	76	0.96	7598	95.87
8.	Canada	74	0.93	7672	96.81
9.	Denmark	67	0.85	7739	97.65
10.	Russia	24	0.30	7763	97.96
11.	Japan	21	0.26	7784	98.22
12.	China	19	0.24	7803	98.46
13.	South Africa	14	0.18	7817	98.64
14.	Ireland	12	0.15	7829	98.79
15.	Nigeria	12	0.15	7841	98.94
16.	Czech. Republic	9	0.11	7850	99.05
17.	Pakistan	8	0.10	7858	99.15
18.	Switzerland	8	0.10	7866	99.26

(Contd...)

	1	*2*	*3*	*4*	*5*
19.	Norway	6	0.08	7872	99.33
20.	Finland	4	0.05	7876	99.38
21.	Slovenia	4	0.05	7880	99.43
22	7 Countries with 3 Citations	21	0.28	7901	99.70
23	7 Countries with 2 Citations	14	0.21	7915	99.87
24	10 Countries with 1 Citation	10	0.10	7925	100.00

Table above shows the geographical distribution of journals cited by researchers in the field of Library and Information Science. It reveals the research contribution of various countries in the discipline of Library and Information Science. U.S.A occupied the top position with 2891 (36.48%) citations to its credit, followed by India with 2602 (32.83%). U.K and Netherlands stood in third and fourth places respectively with 1437 (18.13%) and 380 (4.79%) citations. Next place is occupied by Australia and France with 116 and 96 citations.

The analysis of the table clearly indicates that research scholars depend upon U.S.A, India and U.K for their information requirements as the three countries stood in the first three place in the ranked list.

TABLE – 4.114
COUNTRY-WISE DISTRIBUTION OF JOURNALS IN AGRICULTURE INFORMATION, LIBRARIES, USERS AND SERVICES

Sl. No	*Name of the Country*	*Number*	*Percentage*	*Cumulative*	*Cumulative Percentage*
1.	India	169	42.36	169	42.36
2.	Netherlands	98	24.56	267	66.92
3.	U.S.A.	76	19.05	343	85.96
4.	U.K.	39	9.77	382	95.74
5.	Canada	4	1.00	386	96.74
6.	2 Countries with 3 Citations	6	1.50	392	98.25
7.	2 Countries with 2 Citations	4	1.00	396	99.25
8.	3 Countries with 1 Citation	3	0.75	399	100.00

TABLE – 4.115

COUNTRY-WISE DISTRIBUTION OF JOURNALS IN BIBLIOMETRICS

Sl. No	*Name of the Country*	*Number*	*Per-centage*	*Cum-ulative*	*Cumulative Percentage*
1.	U.S.A	351	31.03	351	31.03
2.	India	262	23.17	613	54.20
3.	U.K	245	21.66	858	75.86
4.	Netherlands	219	19.36	1077	95.23
5.	Denmark	20	1.77	1097	96.99
6.	Canada	7	0.62	1104	97.61
7.	2 Countries with 5 Citations	10	0.88	1114	98.50
8.	2 Countries with 4 citations	8	0.70	1122	99.20
9.	One Country with 2 Citations	2	0.18	1124	99.38
10.	7 Countries with 1 Citation	7	0.63	1131	100.00

TABLE – 4.116

COUNTRY-WISE DISTRIBUTION OF JOURNALS IN COLLEGE LIBRARIES, USERS AND SERVICES

Sl. No	*Name of the Country*	*Number*	*Per-centage*	*Cum-ulative*	*Cumulative Percentage*
1.	India	326	72.93	326	72.93
2.	U.S.A	103	23.04	429	95.97
3.	U.K	14	3.14	443	99.11
4.	China	2	0.45	445	99.55
5.	2 Countries with 1 Citation	2	0.44	447	100.00

TABLE – 4.117

COUNTRY-WISE DISTRIBUTION OF JOURNALS IN LIBRARIES AND I.T

Sl. No	*Name of the Country*	*Number*	*Per-centage*	*Cum-ulative*	*Cumulative Percentage*
1.	U.S.A	141	39.39	141	39.39
2.	India	96	26.82	237	66.20
3.	U.K	90	25.14	327	91.34
4.	Australia	6	1.68	333	93.02
5.	Ireland	5	1.40	338	94.41
6.	Canada	4	1.12	342	95.53
7.	Germany	4	1.12	346	96.65
8.	China	3	0.84	349	97.49
9.	2 Countries with 2 Citations	4	1.12	353	98.60
10.	5 Countries with 1 Citation	5	1.40	358	100.00

TABLE – 4.118

COUNTRY-WISE DISTRIBUTION OF JOURNALS IN MARKETING OF LIBRARY INFORMATION SERVICES AND PRODUCTS

Sl. No	*Name of the Country*	*Number*	*Per-centage*	*Cum-ulative*	*Cumulative Percentage*
1.	U.S.A	132	50.19	132	50.19
2.	U.K	46	17.49	178	67.68
3.	India	36	13.69	214	81.37
4.	Netherlands	19	7.22	243	88.59
5.	Australia	9	3.42	252	92.02
6.	Denmark	6	2.28	258	94.30
7.	Canada	5	1.90	263	96.20
8.	Slovenia	4	1.53	267	97.72
9.	China	3	1.14	270	98.86
10.	3 Countries with 1 Citation	3	1.14	273	100.00

TABLE – 4.119
COUNTRY-WISE DISTRIBUTION OF JOURNALS IN MEDICAL INFORMATION, LIBRARIES, USERS AND SERVICES

Sl. No	*Name of the Country*	*Number*	*Per-centage*	*Cum-ulative*	*Cumulative Percentage*
1.	U.S.A	186	36.47	186	36.47
2.	U.K	159	31.18	345	67.65
3.	India	122	23.92	467	91.57
4.	Australia	9	1.76	476	93.33
5.	Switzerland	7	1.37	483	94.71
6.	France	6	1.18	489	
	95.88				
7.	Canada	5	0.98	494	96.86
8.	Germany	5	0.98	499	97.84
9.	Japan	3	0.59	502	98.43
10.	2 Countries with 2 Citations	4	0.78	506	99.22
11.	4 Countries with 1 Citation	4	0.80	510	100.00

TABLE – 4.120
COUNTRY-WISE DISTRIBUTION OF JOURNALS IN OTHER ASPECTS

Sl. No	*Name of the Country*	*Number*	*Per-centage*	*Cum-ulative*	*Cumulative Percentage*
1.	U.S.A	487	38.11	487	38.11
2.	India	486	38.03	973	76.13
3.	U.K	173	13.54	1146	89.67
4.	Germany	25	1.96	1171	91.63
5.	Australia	15	1.17	1186	92.80
6.	Canada	15	1.17	1201	93.97
7.	France	14	1.10	1215	95.07
8.	Netherlands	13	1.02	1228	96.09
9.	Denmark	11	0.86	1239	96.95
10.	3 Countries with 4 Citations	12	0.93	1251	97.89
11.	3 Countries with 3 Citations	9	0.69	1260	98.59
12.	5 Countries with 2 Citations	10	0.80	1270	99.37
13.	8 Countries with 1 Citation	8	0.64	1278	100.00

TABLE – 4.121
COUNTRY-WISE DISTRIBUTION OF JOURNALS IN OTHER LIBRARIES, USERS AND SERVICES

Sl. No	*Name of the Country*	*Number*	*Per-centage*	*Cum-ulative*	*Cumulative Percentage*
1.	U.S.A	224	53.33	224	53.33
2.	India	75	17.86	299	71.19
3.	U.K	65	15.48	364	86.67
4.	Netherlands	19	4.52	383	91.19
5.	Australia	8	1.90	391	93.10
6.	France	7	1.67	398	94.76
7.	Germany	6	1.43	404	96.19
8.	Canada	5	1.19	409	97.38
9.	Denmark	3	0.71	412	98.10
10.	2 Countries with 2 Citations	4	0.96	416	99.05
11.	4 Countries with 1 Citation	4	0.96	420	100.00

TABLE – 4.122
COUNTRY-WISE DISTRIBUTION OF JOURNALS IN PUBLIC LIBRARIES AND COMMUNITY INFORMATION SERVICES

Sl. No	*Name of the Country*	*Number*	*Per-centage*	*Cum-ulative*	*Cumulative Percentage*
1.	U.S.A	250	40.58	250	40.58
2.	India	160	25.97	410	66.56
3.	U.K	94	15.26	504	81.82
4.	France	38	6.17	542	87.99
5.	Australia	32	5.19	574	93.18
6.	Germany	12	1.95	586	95.13
7.	Denmark	11	1.79	597	96.92
8.	Canada	7	1.14	604	98.05
9.	South Africa	4	0.65	608	98.70
10.	Norway	3	0.49	611	99.19
11.	5 Countries with 1 Citation	5	0.80	616	100.00

TABLE – 4.123
COUNTRY-WISE DISTRIBUTION OF JOURNALS IN SCIENTIFIC AND TECHNICAL LIBRARIES

Sl. No	*Name of the Country*	*Number*	*Per-centage*	*Cum-ulative*	*Cumulative Percentage*
1.	India	320	34.48	320	38.48
2.	U.S.A	300	32.33	620	66.81
3.	U.K	234	25.22	854	92.03
4.	France	18	1.94	872	93.97
5.	Australia	12	1.29	884	95.26
6.	Russia	10	1.08	894	96.34
7.	Canada	7	0.75	901	97.09
8.	Germany	5	0.54	906	97.63
9.	Denmark	4	0.43	910	98.06
10.	Japan	3	0.32	913	98.38
11.	5 Countries with 2 Citations	10	1.10	923	99.46
12.	5 Countries with 1 Citation	5	0.55	928	100.00

TABLE – 4.124
COUNTRY-WISE DISTRIBUTION OF JOURNALS IN UNIVERSITY LIBRARIES, USERS AND SERVICES

Sl. No	*Name of the Country*	*Number*	*Per-centage*	*Cum-ulative*	*Cumulative Percentage*
1.	U.S.A	641	40.70	641	40.70
2.	India	550	34.92	1191	75.62
3.	U.K	278	17.65	1469	93.27
4.	Australia	18	1.14	1487	94.41
5.	Canada	15	0.95	1502	95.37
6.	Germany	14	0.89	1516	96.25
7.	Netherlands	8	0.51	1524	96.76
8.	Denmark	7	0.44	1531	97.21
9.	China	6	0.38	1537	97.59
10.	Nigeria	6	0.38	1543	97.97
11.	France	5	0.32	1548	98.29
12.	Japan	4	0.25	1552	98.54
13.	South Africa	4	0.25	1556	98.79
14.	3 Countries with 3 Citations	9	0.57	1565	99.37
15.	3 Countries with 2 Citations	6	0.39	1571	99.75
16.	4 Countries with 1 Citation	4	0.24	1575	100.00

TABLE – 4.125
COUNTRY-WISE DISTRIBUTION OF BOOKS IN LIBRARY AND INFORMATION SCIENCE

Sl. No	*Name of the Country*	*Number*	*Per-centage*	*Cum-ulative*	*Cumulative Percentage*
1.	India	1131	39.50	1131	39.50
2.	U.S.A	915	33.50	2090	73.00
3.	U.K	678	23.68	2768	96.68
4.	France	34	1.19	2802	97.87
5.	Japan	20	0.70	2822	98.57
6.	Netherlands	19	0.66	2841	99.23
7.	New Zeeland	5	0.17	2846	99.41
8.	2 Countries with 3 Citations	6	0.20	2852	99.62
9.	4 Countries with 2 Citations	8	0.28	2860	99.90
10.	3 Countries with 1 Citation	3	0.09	2863	100.00

Analysis of the data tabulated reveals that COUNTRY-WISE distribution of books in the discipline of Library and Information Science proves that majority of books cited by researchers in the present study are published from India with 1131 (39.50%) citations. U.S.A and U.K occupied second and third place with 915 (33.50%) and 678 (23.68%) citations to their credit.

The study also revealed the domination of India, U.S.A and U.K and thereby the dependence of research scholars on the literature being published from these three countries.

TABLE – 4.126
COUNTRY-WISE DISTRIBUTION OF BOOKS IN AGRICULTURE INFORMATION, LIBRARIES, USERS AND SERVICES

Sl. No	*Name of the Country*	*Number*	*Per-centage*	*Cum-ulative*	*Cumulative Percentage*
1.	U.S.A	23	40.35	23	40.35
2.	India	22	38.60	45	78.95
3.	U.K	12	21.95	57	100.00

TABLE – 4.127
COUNTRY-WISE DISTRIBUTION OF BOOKS IN BIBLIOMETRICS

Sl. No	*Name of the Country*	*Number*	*Per-centage*	*Cum-ulative*	*Cumulative Percentage*
1.	U.S.A	58	41.73	58	41.73
2.	U.K	48	34.53	106	76.26
3.	India	26	18.71	132	94.96
4.	Netherlands	5	3.60	137	98.56
5.	2 Countries with 1 Citation	2	1.44	139	100.00

TABLE – 4.128
COUNTRY-WISE DISTRIBUTION OF BOOKS IN COLLEGE LIBRARIES, USERS AND SERVICES

Sl. No	*Name of the Country*	*Number*	*Per-centage*	*Cum-ulative*	*Cumulative Percentage*
1.	India	113	80.14	113	80.14
2.	U.K	17	12.06	130	92.20
3.	U.S.A	11	7.80	141	100.00

TABLE – 4.129
COUNTRY-WISE DISTRIBUTION OF BOOKS IN LIBRARIES AND I.T

Sl. No	*Name of the Country*	*Number*	*Per-centage*	*Cum-ulative*	*Cumulative Percentage*
1.	India	91	41.55	91	41.55
2.	U.K	70	31.96	161	73.52
3.	U.S.A	56	25.57	217	99.09
4.	2 Countries with 1 Citation	2	0.92	219	100.00

TABLE – 4.130
COUNTRY-WISE DISTRIBUTION OF BOOKS IN MARKETING OF LIBRARY INFORMATION SERVICES AND PRODUCTS

Sl. No	*Name of the Country*	*Number*	*Per-centage*	*Cum-ulative*	*Cumulative Percentage*
1.	U.S.A	29	39.19	29	39.19
2.	India	25	33.78	54	72.97
3.	U.K	16	21.62	70	94.59
4.	2 Countries with 2 Citations	4	5.40	74	100.00

TABLE – 4.131
COUNTRY-WISE DISTRIBUTION OF BOOKS IN MEDICAL INFORMATION, LIBRARIES, USERS AND SERVICES

Sl. No	*Name of the Country*	*Number*	*Per-centage*	*Cum-ulative*	*Cumulative Percentage*
1.	U.S.A	65	47.45	65	47.45
2.	U.K	43	31.39	108	78.83
3.	India	19	13.87	127	92.70
4.	Japan	5	3.65	132	96.35
5.	2 Countries with 2 Citations	4	2.92	136	99.27
7.	1 Country with 1 Citation	1	0.73	137	100.00

TABLE – 4.132
COUNTRY-WISE DISTRIBUTION OF BOOKS IN OTHER ASPECTS

Sl. No	*Name of the Country*	*Number*	*Per-centage*	*Cum-ulative*	*Cumulative Percentage*
1.	India	227	50.67	227	50.67
2.	U.S.A	107	23.88	334	74.55
3.	U.K	104	23.21	438	97.77
4.	2 Countries with 3 Citations	6	1.34	444	99.11
5.	1 Country with 2 Citations	2	0.45	446	99.55
6.	2 Countries with 1 Citation	2	0.44	448	100.00

TABLE – 4.133
COUNTRY-WISE DISTRIBUTION OF BOOKS IN OTHER LIBRARIES, USERS AND SERVICES

Sl. No	*Name of the Country*	*Number*	*Per-centage*	*Cum-ulative*	*Cumulative Percentage*
1.	U.S.A	49	40.16	49	40.16
2.	U.K	33	27.05	82	67.21
3.	India	33	27.05	115	94.26
4.	Japan	5	4.10	120	98.36
5.	2 Countries with 1 Citation	2	1.64	122	100.00

TABLE – 4.134
COUNTRY-WISE DISTRIBUTION OF BOOKS IN PUBLIC LIBRARIES AND COMMUNITY INFORMATION SERVICES

Sl. No	*Name of the Country*	*Number*	*Per-centage*	*Cum-ulative*	*Cumulative Percentage*
1.	India	156	50.81	156	50.81
2.	U.S.A	74	24.10	230	74.92
3.	U.K	62	20.20	292	95.11
4.	France	13	4.23	305	99.35
5.	2 Countries with 1 Citation	2	0.66	307	100.00

TABLE – 4.135
COUNTRY-WISE DISTRIBUTION OF BOOKS IN SCIENTIFIC AND TECHNICAL LIBRARIES

Sl. No	*Name of the Country*	*Number*	*Per-centage*	*Cum-ulative*	*Cumulative Percentage*
1.	U.S.A	78	34.82	78	34.82
2.	India	75	33.48	153	68.30
3.	U.K	64	28.57	217	96.88
4.	2 Countries with 3 Citations	6	2.68	223	99.55
5.	1 Country with 1 Citation	1	0.45	224	100.00

TABLE – 4.136
COUNTRY-WISE DISTRIBUTION OF BOOKS IN UNIVERSITY LIBRARIES, USERS AND SERVICES

Sl. No	*Name of the Country*	*Number*	*Per-centage*	*Cum-ulative*	*Cumulative Percentage*
1.	U.S.A	409	41.11	409	41.11
2.	India	344	34.57	753	75.68
3.	U.K	209	21.01	962	96.68
4.	France	12	1.21	974	97.89
5.	Japan	7	0.70	981	98.59
6.	New Zeeland	4	0.40	985	98.99
7.	Netherlands	3	0.30	988	99.30
8.	2 Countries with 2 Citations	4	0.40	992	99.70
9.	3 Countries with 1 Citation	3	0.30	995	100.00

Obsolescence of Literature and Half Life of Journal and Book Citations

Growth in collections of documents as well as files representing them affects all aspects of library management. Every addition of a document beyond a size calls for extra space, adds to maintenance problems and hampers easy and effective access to all documents. To overcome these problems or at least to minimize their adverse affects, there is need to exercise control over the size of collections. Discarding documents or relegating them to less frequented areas constitutes one such control. A discarding and/or relegating policy has to based on sound principles. Statistical methods aid in developing such principles. The relative importance or utility of a document is a key element of all such policies. This leads to the concept of Obsolescence.

In Bibliometrics and Citation analysis studies, obsolescence has become a common phenomenon. Obsolescence is defined as the "decline over time in validity or utility of information". The same applies to documents. Half-life of literature is the time by which one-half of the currently published literature becomes obsolescent.

The major factors which influence Obsolescence are information explosion, inter-disciplinary nature of the subject, growth in number of producers and users of literature and various social and political factors. The citation data in the present study has been analyzed to study both –

1. Age-wise distribution of citation to journals and books
2. Half-life of citations to journals and books.

A. Age-wise Distribution of Citations to Books and Journals

The Age-wise distribution of citations to journals and books in the discipline of Library and Information Science and its sub-disciplines have been discussed in the following tables.

A1. Age-wise Distribution of Citations to Journals

Table 4.137presents the Age-wise distribution of citations to journals in the field of Library and Information Science. The results of the table indicate wide range for the age of journal literature. The oldest citation cited was published 120 years ago. The article which has the age of 120 years was published in "Library Journal" in the year 1879 and it is very interesting to note that such an old article still catches the attention of the present day research scholars which shows the quality of the research article. This article is covered in the sub-discipline "Other Aspects".

25 percent of the journal citations are 7 year old, 50 percent of journal citations are 13 year old and about 75 percent of the journal citations are 22 year old.

The results of the Table- 4.138 show the Age-wise distribution of cited journals in Agriculture Information, Libraries, Users and Services. It is observed that 25 percent of the journal citations are 7 year old. 50 percent of the citations in Agriculture Information, Libraries, Users and Services are 12 year old. It may be seen from the table that the oldest journal cited was published 69 years ago. The title of the journal is BELL System Technical Journal published in the year 1928.

Table – 4.139 depicts Age-wise distribution of citations to journals in the field of Bibliometrics. 25 percent are of 8 years old and 51 percent are 15 years old. The oldest cited journal Science Progress in this sub-discipline is 82 years old and published in the year 1917.

Age-wise distribution of citations in College Libraries, Users and Services is revealed in Table – 4.140. It is clear from the results that nearly 26 percent of the citations are 9 years old, 50 percent of the citations are 16 years old, 75 percent of the journal citations are 28 years old. The citation with 57 years age is the oldest citation cited in the sub-discipline College Libraries, Users and Services. It is observed that Modern Librarian is the oldest journal cited in this sub-field published in the year 1941.

Table - 4.141 depicts the age of journal citations in the sub-discipline of Libraries and I.T. Nearly 25 percent of the journal citations are 5 years old, whereas 50 percent of the citations are 8 years old. Among all the citations, the age of the oldest citation is 89 years in this specified discipline. The title of the oldest journal cited is "Psychological Review" published in the year 1906.

The Age-wise distribution of journal citations in the sub-discipline Marketing of Library Information Services and Products reveal that 25 percent of the citations are 5 years old. About 50 percent of the journal citations are published 12 years ago. Nearly 75 percent of the citations are 19 years old. The oldest cited journal is 41 years old and the details are as follows: Library Trends published in the year 1958.

The Age-wise distribution of journal citations in the sub-discipline Medical Information, Libraries, Users and Services is presented in Table – 4.143. The maximum age of citation is 61 years. 29 percent of the journal citations are 6 years old. Nearly 52 percent of the citations are 10 years old and 75 percent of the journal citations are 19 years old. The title of oldest cited journals is BELL System Technical Journal published in the year 1928.

Table 4.144 shows the Age of the journal citations in the sub-field Other Aspects. 26 percent of the journal citations are published 9 years ago, whereas 50 percent of the citations are 17 years old. Among all the citations, the age of the oldest citation is 120 years. The name of the oldest journal cited is "Library Journal" published in the year 1879.

The table indicates age-wise distribution of journals cited in the sub-discipline Other Libraries, Users and Services. 27

percent of the journal citations are 6 years old. 50 percent of the citations are 11 years old and 75 percent of the citations are 17 years old. The maximum age of the journal citation among all the citations is 43 years. The title of the oldest cited journal is *Library Quarterly* published in the year 1949.

The age-wise distribution of citations in the field of Public Libraries and Community Information Services has been depicted in Table – 4.146. The conclusions derived indicate that 27 percent of the journal citations are 6 years old, nearly 50 percent of the citations are 13 years old while 75 percent of the journal citations are 19 years old. The oldest cited journal in this sub-discipline is 54 years old and it is Library Quarterly published in the year 1950.

Table – 4.147 presents Age wise distribution of citations to journals in sub-discipline Scientific and Technical Libraries, Users and Services. The analysis of the table depicts that 26 percent of citations are published 6 years ago, 50 percent of the citations are 12 years old, whereas 75 percent of the journal citations are 22 years old. One journal was found to be oldest one with 92 years of age. The title of the oldest journal is Society for Promotion of Engineering Education published in the year 1905.

The age-wise distribution of citations to journals in University Libraries, Users and Services is presented in Table – 4.148. It is observed from the table that nearly 25 percent of the citations are 7 years old, 50 percent of the citations are 14 years old and 75 percent of the citations are published 23 years ago. The citation with 95 years of age is oldest citation in the sub-discipline of University Libraries, Users and Services. The title of oldest journal is “American Economic Review” published in the year 1901.

Age-wise Distribution of Citations of Books in LIS

The age wise distribution of citations to books in Library

and Information Science and its sub-discipline are presented in the following tables in order to the identify the age wise preference given by researchers to the books cited.

Table – 4.149 indicates the age wise distribution of citations to books in the field of Library and Information Science. It is clearly observed from the data in the table that 26 percent of the cited books are 10 years old. About 50 percent of the book citations are 18 years old. Out of the all the books cited 75 percent are 27 years old. The title of the book with maximum age is History and Prospects of British Education in India by F.W. Thomas and it is published in the year 1891.

Agriculture Information Libraries, Users and Services

Table – 4.150 gives a clear picture about the age wise distribution of books in the sub-discipline Agriculture Information, Libraries, Users and Services. About 25 percent of the citations to books are published 9 years ago, 50 percent of the citations are 17 years old and 78 percent of the book citations are 25 years old. The oldest book cited in the sub-discipline Agriculture Information, Libraries, Users and Services is 38 years old. The details of the book are "Principles and Practice of Agricultural Research" by Salman, S.C. and published in the year 1964.

Bibliometrics

In the sub-discipline Bibliometrics, the age wise distribution of books cited by the researchers is shown in Table – 4.151. The results indicate that maximum age of cited books is 101 years. The title of the oldest book cited is Theory of National and International Bibliography by F. Campbell and published in the year 1896. 25 percent of the citations are 16 years old and 51 percent of the citations are 23 years old. 77 percent of the citations to books are published 35 years ago.

College Libraries, Users and Services

Table – 4.152 depicts the age wise distribution of book

citations which are cited by researchers in the sub-discipline College Libraries, Users and Services. 30 percent of the citations are 10 years old. 51 percent of the book citations are published 16 years ago. 80 percent of the citations are 27 years old. There is one citation with maximum age of 83 years and the details of this book are : University Education in India written by Ananth Nath Babu and published in the year 1921.

Libraries and I.T.

The age-wise distribution of citations to books in the sub-discipline Libraries and I.T is discussed in the Table – 4.153. The critical examination of the table clearly indicates that 25 percent of the citations to books in this specified field are only 6 years old. 53 percent of the citations are 11 years old. More than 75 percent of the citations are 17 years old. The maximum age in this sub-discipline is 67 years with details of the book as follows – *Attitudes: A Handbook of Social Psychology* authored by G.W. Allport.

Marketing of Library Information Services and Proudcts

Table – 4.154 presents the age wise distribution of citations to books in the sub-discipline Marketing of Library Information Services and Products. The study reveals that book citations with 4 years old contributed to 25 percent of the total book citations whereas book citations with 7 years age have contributed to 55 percent. Nearly 78 percent of the citations are 18 years old. The maximum age in the sub-discipline Marketing of Library Information Services and Products is 50 years and it received only one citation. The details of this book are: Public Relations in Management by J.H. Wright published in the year 1949.

Medical Information, Libraries, Users and Services

Table – 4.155 depicts data regarding age-wise distribution

of book citations in the sub-discipline Medical Information, Libraries, Users and Services. Nearly 25 percent of the citations are 8 years old, 50 percent of the citations are 16 years old. 80 percent of the citations are published 23 years ago. There is only one citation with maximum age i.e. 50 years. The information regarding this book are : Special Library Methods Chapter III : Medical and Scientific Libraries by J.L. Thornton.

Other Aspects

The age-wise distribution of books cited by researchers in the sub-discipline Other Aspects have been dealt with in Table 4.156. 25 percent of the citations are 12 years old. 51 percent of the citations to books are 19 years old. 75 percent of the citations are 26 years old. The oldest citation of all the citations in the sub-discipline is 121 years old which indicates the importance of the book for the present research activities. The book cited is Education in British India written by A.P. Howell and published in the year 1872.

Other Libraries, Users and Services

In the sub-discipline Other Libraries, Users and Services the maximum age of the cited books is 85 years. The title and author of the book are Where to Find Your Law by Earnest Arthur Jelf published in the year 1907. The books which are published 11 years ago could contribute 27 percent of the total book citations in the specified field. Nearly 50 percent of the citations are of 16 years old, and nearly 75 percent of the citations to books are 23 years old.

Public Libraries and Community Information Services

Table – 4.158 depicts age wise distribution of books cited in the sub-discipline Public Libraries and Community Information Services. The maximum age of the cited books is 70 years. The details of the oldest book cited are: Andhrula Charitam by Chilukuri Veerabhadra Rao published in the year 1912. About 25 percent of the books cited are 10 years old. 51 percent of the citations are 17 years old. 75 percent of the citations are 29 years old.

Scientific and Technical Libraries, Users and Services

The age-wise distribution of books cited by researchers in the sub-discipline Scientific and Technical Libraries, Users and Services is presented in Table – 4.159. Books with 13 years of age has contributed to 28 percent of the total book citations in the specified field. 50 percent of the citations are 21 years old. 75 percent of the citations to books are 31 years old. The maximum age is 67 years. The title of the book is History of Engineering Index by J.E. Hannum and published in the year 1930.

University Libraries, Users and Services

The age wise distribution of books cited in the sub-discipline University Libraries, Users and Services are presented in the following tables. The age wise distribution of books cited in this field indicate that 26 percent of the citations are 11 years old, while 51 percent of the citations are 20 years old. Books with 30 years of age contributed 75 percent of the book citations. The title of oldest book cited in the sub-discipline University Libraries, Users and Services is Philosophy of Management by Oliver Sheldon published in the year 1923.

The age wise distribution of citations to journals and books presented in the tables have revealed some important findings. It is interesting to note that in Library and Information Science discipline the older literature has caught the attention of the present day research scholars which indicates the quality of the research articles which were published way back.

The comparison of sub-disciplines in age wise distribution regarding journals has proved that more number of citations are published 5 years before in the case of Marketing of Library Information Services and Products, Other Libraries, Users and Services and Libraries and I.T. Citations within 10 years are more in Libraries and I.T, Medical Information, Libraries, Users and Services, Other Libraries, Users and Services. About 75 percent of the journal citations are less than 20 years in the case of Agriculture Information, Libraries, Users and Services, Libraries and I.T., Marketing of Library Information Services and Products, Medical Information, Libraries, Users and Services and Other Libraries, Users and Services.

It may be observed from the tables that maximum age of citations to journals is more in Agriculture Information, Libraries, Users and Services, Libraries and I.T., Medical Information, Libraries, Users and Services, Scientific and Technical Libraries and University Libraries, Users and Services whereas the maximum age of citations to books is more in Bibliometrics, College Libraries, Users and Services, Marketing of Library Information Services and Products, Other Aspects, Other Libraries, Users and Services and Public Libraries and Community Information Services.

Among the sub-disciplines the oldest citation to journal is 120 years cited in the sub-discipline Other Aspects followed by 95 years old cited in the sub-discipline University Libraries, Users and Services. The next oldest citation cited is 92 years old in the field of Scientific and Technical Libraries, Users and Services.

The age-wise distribution of citations to books has revealed that oldest citation to books is 121 years in the field of Other Aspects. The next oldest citation cited is 101 years old in the sub-discipline Bibliometrics.

Half-Life (Median Citation Age) of Citations

The data which is presented in the Tables – 4.290 to 4.318

are represented graphically by plotting the values of citation ages on X-axis and the cumulative number of citations on Y-axis in order to find out the half-life (median citation age) for journals and books in Library and Information Science and its sub-disciplines. The frequency polygons are also shown in the same figures.

To compute the half-life (median citation age) for journals and books in the discipline of Library and Information Science the data which is presented in Tables – 4.299 to 4.322 are represented graphically. The values of citation ages are plotted on X-axis and the cumulative number of citations are plotted on Y-axis for this purpose.

The figures indicate the half-life of period (median citation age) for journal citations in Library and Information Science and its sub-disciplines. The half-life value for LIS is 17.5. The half-life value for Agriculture Information, Libraries, Users and Services, Bibliometrics, College Libraries, Users and Services, Libraries and I.T, Marketing of Library Information Services and Products, Medical Information, Libraries, Users and Services, Other Aspects, Other Libraries, Users and Services, Public Libraries and Community Information Services, Scientific and Technical Libraries, University Libraries, Users and Services are 14, 18.5, 22.5, 11, 18, 15, 22, 14, 16, 16.5 and 19.

The half-life period (median citation age) for book citations for LIS is found to be 22. The half-life value for Agriculture Information, Libraries, Users and Services, Bibliometrics, College Libraries, Users and Services, Libraries and I.T, Marketing of Library Information Services and Products, Medical Information, Libraries, Users and Services, Other Aspects, Other Libraries, Users and Services, Public Libraries and Community Information Services, Scientific and Technical Libraries, University Libraries, Users and Services are 20, 27, 19.5, 14, 13.5, 19, 23, 19, 22, 27 and 24.

TABLE – 4.137
AGE-WISE DISTRIBUTION OF CITATIONS IN LIBRARY AND INFORMATION SCIENCE – JOURNALS

Age	*Number*	*Percentage*	*Cumulative*	*Cumulative Percentage*
1	*2*	*3*	*4*	*5*
0	20	0.2524	20	0.2524
1	139	1.7539	159	2.0063
2	189	2.3849	348	4.3912
3	320	4.0379	668	8.4290
4	336	4.2397	1004	12.6688
5	339	4.2776	1343	16.9464
6	379	4.7823	1722	21.7287
7	362	4.5678	2084	26.2965
8	324	4.0883	2408	30.3849
9	346	4.3659	2754	34.7508
10	318	4.0126	3072	38.7634
11	335	4.2271	3407	42.9905
12	273	3.4448	3680	46.4353
13	290	3.6593	3970	50.0946
14	217	2.7382	4187	52.8328
15	283	3.5710	4470	56.4038
16	259	3.2681	4729	59.6719
17	231	2.9148	4960	62.5868
18	238	3.0032	5198	65.5899
19	200	2.5237	5398	68.1136
20	238	3.0032	5636	71.1167
21	185	2.3344	5821	73.4511
22	166	2.0946	5987	75.5457
23	154	1.9432	6141	77.4890
24	145	1.8297	6286	79.3186
25	126	1.5899	6412	80.9085
26	132	1.6656	6544	82.5741
27	142	1.7918	6686	84.3659
28	110	1.3880	6796	85.7539
29	109	1.3754	6905	87.1293
30	108	1.3628	7013	88.4921
31	113	1.4259	7126	89.9180
32	100	1.2618	7226	91.1798
33	55	0.6940	7281	91.8738
34	55	0.6940	7336	92.5678

(Contd...)

1	*2*	*3*	*4*	*5*
35	64	0.8076	7400	93.3754
36	63	0.7950	7463	94.1703
37	38	0.4795	7501	94.6498
38	37	0.4669	7538	95.1167
39	54	0.6814	7592	95.7981
40	23	0.2902	7615	96.0883
41	26	0.3281	7641	96.4164
42	20	0.2524	7661	96.6688
43	35	0.4416	7696	97.1104
44	15	0.1893	7711	97.2997
45	30	0.3785	7741	97.6782
46	10	0.1262	7751	97.8044
47	14	0.1767	7765	97.9811
48	21	0.2650	7786	98.2461
49	14	0.1767	7800	98.4227
50	11	0.1388	7811	98.5615
51	9	0.1136	7820	98.6751
52	10	0.1262	7830	98.8013
53	11	0.1388	7841	98.9401
54	3	0.0379	7844	98.9799
55	3	0.0379	7847	99.0158
56	2	0.0252	7849	99.0410
57	9	0.1136	7858	99.1546
58	3	0.0379	7861	99.1924
59	6	0.0757	7867	99.2681
60	0	0.0000	7867	99.2681
61	11	0.1388	7878	99.4069
62	2	0.0252	7880	99.4322
63	3	0.0379	7883	99.4700
64	0	0.0000	7883	99.4700
65	4	0.0505	7887	99.5205
66	0	0.0000	7887	99.5205
67	0	0.0000	7887	99.5205
68	1	0.0126	7888	99.5331
69	3	0.0379	7891	99.5710
70	4	0.0505	7895	99.6215
71	9	0.1136	7904	99.7350
72	4	0.0505	7908	99.7855
73	4	0.0505	7912	99.8360
74	0	0.0000	7912	99.8360
75	0	0.0000	7912	99.8360

(Contd...)

1	*2*	*3*	*4*	*5*
76	0	0.0000	7912	99.8360
77	0	0.0000	7912	99.8360
78	0	0.0000	7912	99.8360
79	0	0.0000	7912	99.8360
80	3	0.0379	7915	99.8738
81	0	0.0000	7915	99.8738
82	3	0.0379	7918	99.9117
83	0	0.0000	7918	99.9117
84	0	0.0000	7918	99.9117
85	0	0.0000	7918	99.9117
86	0	0.0000	7918	99.9117
87	1	0.0126	7919	99.9243
88	0	0.0000	7919	99.9243
89	2	0.0252	7921	99.9495
90	0	0.0000	7921	99.9495
91	0	0.0000	7921	99.9495
92	1	0.0126	7922	99.9621
93	0	0.0000	7922	99.9621
94	0	0.0000	7922	99.9621
95	1	0.0126	7923	99.9748
96-104	0	0.0000	7923	99.9748
105	1	0.0126	7924	99.9874
106-119	0	0.0000	7924	99.9874
120	1	0.0126	7925	100.0000

TABLE – 4.138
AGE-WISE DISTRIBUTION OF CITATIONS IN AGRICULTURE INFORAMTION, LIBRARIES, USERS AND SERVICES - JOURNALS

Age	*Number*	*Percentage*	*Cumulative*	*Cumulative Percentage*
1	*2*	*3*	*4*	*5*
0	2	0.5013	2	0.5013
1	9	2.2556	11	2.7569
2	4	1.0025	15	3.7594
3	4	1.0025	19	4.7619
4	18	4.5113	37	9.2732
5	7	1.7544	44	11.0276
6	26	6.5163	70	17.5439
7	26	6.5163	96	24.0602

(Contd...)

1	*2*	*3*	*4*	*5*
8	16	4.0100	112	28.0702
9	24	6.0150	136	34.0852
10	22	5.5138	158	39.5990
11	33	8.2707	191	47.8697
12	25	6.2657	216	54.1353
13	23	5.7644	239	59.8997
14	16	4.0100	255	63.9098
15	10	2.5063	265	66.4160
16	8	2.0050	273	68.4211
17	14	3.5088	287	71.9298
18	8	2.0050	295	73.9348
19	18	4.5113	313	78.4461
20	11	2.7569	324	81.2030
21	6	1.5038	330	82.7068
22	6	1.5038	336	84.2105
23	16	4.0100	352	88.2206
24	11	2.7569	363	90.9774
25	5	1.2531	368	92.2306
26	5	1.2531	373	93.4837
27	2	0.5013	375	93.9850
28	3	0.7519	378	94.7368
29	2	0.5013	380	95.2381
30	6	1.5038	386	96.7419
31	3	0.7519	389	97.4937
32	0	0.0000	389	97.4937
33	1	0.2506	390	97.7444
34	1	0.2506	391	97.9950
35	1	0.2506	392	98.2546
36	0	0.0000	392	98.2546
37	0	0.0000	392	98.2456
38	2	0.5013	394	98.7469
39	1	0.2506	395	98.9975
40	0	0.0000	395	98.9975
41	0	0.0000	395	98.9975
42	1	0.2506	396	99.2481
43-53	0	0.0000	396	99.2481
54	1	0.2506	397	99.4987
55-61	0	0.0000	397	99.4987
62	1	0.2506	398	99.7494
63-68	0	0.0000	398	99.7494
69	1	0.2506	399	100.0000

TABLE – 4.139
AGE-WISE DISTRIBUTION OF CITATIONS IN BIBLIOMETRICS – JOURNALS

Age	*Number*	*Percentage*	*Cumulative*	*Cumulative Percentage*
1	*2*	*3*	*4*	*5*
0	0	0.0000	0	0.0000
1	20	1.7683	20	1.7683
2	27	2.3873	47	4.1556
3	37	3.2714	84	7.4271
4	24	2.1220	108	9.5491
5	37	3.2714	145	12.8205
6	43	3.8019	188	16.6225
7	58	5.1282	246	21.7507
8	42	3.7135	288	25.4642
9	56	4.9514	344	30.4156
10	49	4.3324	393	34.7480
11	45	3.9788	438	38.7268
12	33	2.9178	471	41.6446
13	34	3.0062	505	44.6508
14	29	2.5641	534	47.2149
15	43	3.8019	577	51.0168
16	48	4.2440	625	55.2608
17	35	3.0946	660	58.3554
18	51	4.5093	711	62.8647
19	32	2.8294	743	65.6941
20	34	3.0062	777	68.7003
21	31	2.7409	808	71.4412
22	24	2.1220	832	73.5632
23	27	2.3873	859	75.9505
24	26	2.2989	885	78.2493
25	36	3.1830	921	81.4324
26	11	0.9726	932	82.4050
27	31	2.7409	963	85.1459
28	18	1.5915	981	86.7374
29	11	0.9726	992	87.7100
30	19	1.6799	1011	89.3899
31	7	0.6189	1018	90.0088

(Contd...)

1	*2*	*3*	*4*	*5*
32	13	1.1494	1031	91.1583
33	6	0.5305	1037	91.6888
34	8	0.7073	1045	92.3961
35	9	0.7958	1054	93.1919
36	3	0.2653	1057	93.4571
37	8	0.7073	1065	94.1645
38	0	0.0000	1065	94.1645
39	8	0.7073	1073	94.8718
40	1	0.0884	1074	94.9602
41	1	0.0884	1075	95.0486
42	1	0.0884	1076	95.1370
43	0	0.0000	1076	95.1370
44	1	0.0884	1077	95.2255
45	2	0.1768	1079	95.4023
46	2	0.1768	1081	95.5791
47	0	0.0000	1081	95.5791
48	4	0.3537	1085	95.9328
49	3	0.2653	1088	96.1981
50	2	0.1768	1090	96.3749
51	3	0.2653	1093	96.6401
52	1	0.0884	1094	96.7286
53	2	0.1768	1096	96.9054
54-58	0	0.0000	1096	96.9054
59	1	0.0884	1097	96.9938
60-62	0	0.0000	1097	96.9938
63	3	0.2653	1100	97.2591
64	0	0.0000	1100	97.2591
65	4	0.3537	1104	97.6127
66-68	0	0.0000	1104	97.6127
69	2	0.1768	1106	97.7896
70	4	0.3537	1110	98.1432
71	9	0.7958	1119	98.9390
72	3	0.2653	1122	99.2042
73	3	0.2653	1125	99.4695
74-79	0	0.0000	1125	99.4695
80	3	0.2653	1128	99.7347
81	0	0.0000	1128	99.7347
82	3	0.2653	1131	100.0000

TABLE – 4.140
AGE-WISE DISTRIBUTION OF CITATIONS IN COLLEGE LIBRARIES, USERS AND SERVICES – JOURNALS

Age	*Number*	*Percentage*	*Cumulative*	*Cumulative Percentage*
1	*2*	*3*	*4*	*5*
0	1	0.2237	1	0.2237
1	11	2.4609	12	2.6846
2	17	3.8031	29	6.4877
3	21	4.6980	50	11.1857
4	10	2.2371	60	13.4228
5	3	0.6711	63	14.0940
6	4	0.8949	67	14.9888
7	12	2.6846	79	17.6734
8	16	3.5794	95	21.2528
9	22	4.9217	117	26.1745
10	21	4.6980	138	30.8725
11	24	5.3691	162	36.2416
12	21	4.6980	183	40.9396
13	9	2.0134	192	42.9530
14	13	2.9083	205	45.8613
15	18	4.0268	223	49.8881
16	8	1.7897	231	51.6779
17	7	1.5660	238	53.2438
18	8	1.7897	246	55.0336
19	7	1.5560	253	56.5996
20	11	2.4609	264	59.0604
21	9	2.0134	273	61.0738
22	15	3.3557	288	64.4295
23	6	1.3423	294	65.7718
24	13	2.9083	307	68.6801
25	5	1.1186	312	69.7987
26	6	1.3423	318	71.1409
27	16	3.5794	334	74.7204
28	3	0.6711	337	75.3915
29	14	3.1320	351	78.5235
30	14	3.1320	365	81.6555
31	9	2.0134	374	83.6689
32	15	3.3557	389	87.0246
33	5	1.1186	394	88.1432

(Contd...)

1	*2*	*3*	*4*	*5*
34	6	1.3423	400	89.4855
35	14	3.1320	414	92.6174
36	6	1.3423	420	93.9597
37	3	0.6711	423	94.6309
38	2	0.4474	425	95.0783
39	2	0.4474	427	95.5257
40	4	0.8949	431	96.4206
41	0	0.0000	431	96.4206
42	4	0.8949	435	97.3154
43	1	0.2237	436	97.5391
44	0	0.0000	436	97.5391
45	1	0.2237	437	97.7629
46	0	0.0000	437	97.7629
47	1	0.2237	438	97.9886
48-49	0	0.0000	438	97.9886
50	1	0.2237	439	98.2103
51	4	0.8949	443	99.1051
52	0	0.0000	443	99.1051
53	1	0.2237	444	99.3289
54	1	0.2237	445	99.5526
55	1	0.2237	446	99.7763
56	0	0.0000	446	99.7763
57	1	0.2237	447	100.0000

TABLE – 4.141
AGE-WISE DISTRIBUTION OF CITATIONS IN LIBRARIES AND I.T – JOURNALS

Age	*Number*	*Percentage*	*Cumulative*	*Cumulative Percentage*
1	*2*	*3*	*4*	*5*
0	1	0.2793	1	0.2793
1	8	2.2346	9	2.5140
2	15	4.1899	24	6.7039
3	17	4.7486	41	11.4525
4	20	5.5866	61	17.0391
5	27	7.5419	88	24.5810
6	38	10.6145	126	35.1955
7	29	8.1006	155	43.2961

(Contd...)

1	*2*	*3*	*4*	*5*
8	21	5.8659	176	49.1620
9	23	6.4246	199	55.5866
10	22	6.1453	221	61.7318
11	20	5.5866	241	67.3184
12	12	3.3520	253	70.6704
13	14	3.9106	267	74.5810
14	8	2.2346	275	76.8156
15	19	5.3073	294	82.1229
16	8	2.2346	302	84.3575
17	3	0.8390	305	85.1955
18	7	1.9533	312	87.1508
19	5	1.3966	317	88.5475
20	4	1.1173	321	89.6648
21	1	0.2793	322	89.9441
22	7	1.9553	329	91.8994
23	4	1.1173	333	93.0168
24	2	0.5587	335	93.5754
25	0	0.0000	335	93.5754
26	4	1.1173	339	94.6927
27	0	0.0000	339	94.6927
28	1	0.2793	340	94.9721
29	3	0.8380	343	95.8101
30	4	1.1173	347	96.9274
31	0	0.0000	347	96.9274
32	3	0.8380	350	97.7654
33	2	0.5587	352	98.3240
34-35	0	0.0000	352	98.3240
36	1	0.2793	353	98.6034
37	0	0.0000	353	98.6034
38	1	0.2793	354	98.8827
39-47	0	0.0000	354	98.8827
48	1	0.2793	355	99.1620
49-54	0	0.0000	355	99.1620
55	1	0.2793	356	99.4413
56-88	0	0.0000	356	99.4413
89	2	0.5857	358	100.0000

(Contd...)

TABLE – 4.142
AGE-WISE DISTRIBUTION OF CITATIONS IN MARKETING OF LIBRARY INFORMATION SERVICES AND PRODUCTS – JOURNALS

Age	*Number*	*Percentage*	*Cumulative*	*Cumulative Percentage*
0	2	0.7605	2	0.7605
1	9	3.4221	11	4.1825
2	8	3.0418	19	7.2243
3	9	3.4221	28	10.6464
4	22	8.3650	50	19.0114
5	18	6.8441	68	25.8555
6	8	3.0418	76	28.8973
7	10	3.8023	86	32.6996
8	19	7.2243	105	39.9240
9	4	1.5209	109	41.4449
10	6	2.2814	115	43.7262
11	5	1.9011	120	45.6274
12	9	3.4221	129	49.0494
13	8	3.0418	137	52.0913
14	3	1.1407	140	53.2319
15	4	1.5209	144	54.7529
16	15	5.7034	159	60.4563
17	9	3.4221	168	63.8783
18	15	5.7034	183	69.5817
19	13	4.9430	196	74.5247
20	8	3.0418	204	77.5665
21	13	4.9430	217	82.5095
22	10	3.8023	227	86.3118
23	5	1.9011	232	88.2129
24	2	0.7605	234	88.9734
25	2	0.7605	236	89.7338
26	1	0.3802	237	90.1141
27	3	1.1407	240	91.2548
28	3	1.1407	243	92.3954
29	1	0.3802	244	92.7757
30	7	2.6616	251	95.4373
31	3	1.1407	254	96.5779
32-34	0	0.0000	254	96.5779
35	3	1.1407	257	97.7186
36-40	0	0.0000	257	97.7186
41	6	2.2814	263	100.0000

TABLE – 4.143
AGE-WISE DISTRIBUTION OF CITATIONS IN MEDICAL INFORMATION, LIBRARIES, USERS AND SERVICES – JOURNALS

Age	*Number*	*Percentage*	*Cumulative*	*Cumulative Percentage*
1	*2*	*3*	*4*	*5*
0	1	0.1961	1	0.1961
1	10	1.9608	11	2.1569
2	19	3.7255	30	5.8824
3	29	5.6863	59	11.5686
4	26	5.0980	85	16.6667
5	23	4.5098	108	21.1765
6	42	8.2353	150	29.4118
7	34	6.6667	184	36.0784
8	35	6.8627	219	42.9412
9	28	5.4902	247	48.4314
10	19	3.7255	266	52.1569
11	16	3.1373	282	55.2941
12	14	2.7451	296	58.0392
13	16	3.1373	312	61.1765
14	13	2.5490	325	63.7255
15	11	2.1569	336	65.8824
16	19	3.7255	355	69.6078
17	13	2.5490	368	72.1569
18	10	1.9608	378	74.1176
19	9	1.7647	387	75.8824
20	16	3.1373	403	79.0196
21	21	4.1176	424	83.1373
22	8	1.5686	432	84.7059
23	13	2.5490	445	87.2549
24	7	1.3725	452	88.6275
25	5	0.9804	457	89.6078
26	13	2.5490	470	92.1569
27	7	1.3725	477	93.5294
28	3	0.5882	480	94.1176
29	4	0.7843	484	94.9020
30	2	0.3922	486	95.2941
31	11	2.1569	497	97.4510
32-33	0	0.0000	497	97.4510
34	2	0.3922	499	97.8431
35	0	0.0000	499	97.8431

(Contd...)

1	2	3	4	5
36	2	0.3922	501	98.2353
37	0	0.0000	501	98.2353
38	3	0.5882	504	98.8235
39	1	0.1961	505	99.0196
40-42	0	0.0000	505	99.0196
43	2	0.3922	507	99.4118
44	1	0.1961	508	99.6078
45-55	0	0.0000	508	99.6078
56	1	0.1961	509	99.8039
57-60	0	0.0000	509	99.8039
61	1	101961	510	100.0000

TABLE – 4.144
AGE-WISE DISTRIBUTION OF CITATIONS IN OTHER ASPECTS – JOURNALS

Age	*Number*	*Percentage*	*Cumulative*	*Cumulative Percentage*
1	2	3	4	5
0	3	0.2347	3	0.2347
1	6	0.4695	9	0.7042
2	15	1.1737	24	1.8779
3	40	3.1299	64	5.0078
4	54	4.2254	118	9.2332
5	44	3.4429	162	12.6761
6	31	2.4257	193	15.1017
7	38	2.9734	231	18.0751
8	61	4.7731	292	22.8482
9	47	3.6776	339	26.5258
10	28	2.1909	367	28.7167
11	45	3.5211	412	32.2379
12	34	2.6604	446	34.8983
13	60	4.6948	506	39.5931
14	23	1.7997	529	41.3928
15	41	3.2081	570	44.6009
16	37	2.8951	607	47.4961
17	37	2.8951	644	50.3912
18	38	2.9734	682	53.3646
19	30	2.3474	712	55.7121
20	44	3.4429	756	59.1549
21	26	2.0344	782	61.1894
22	30	2.3474	812	63.5368
23	18	1.4085	830	64.9452

(Contd...)

1	*2*	*3*	*4*	*5*
24	32	2.5039	862	67.4491
25	12	0.9390	874	68.3881
26	35	2.7387	909	71.1268
27	33	2.5822	942	73.7089
28	29	2.2692	971	75.9781
29	25	1.9562	996	77.9343
30	16	1.2520	1012	79.1862
31	33	2.5822	1045	81.7684
32	27	2.1127	1072	83.8811
33	20	1.5649	1092	85.4460
34	10	0.7825	1102	86.2285
35	19	1.4867	1121	87.7152
36	17	1.3302	1138	89.0454
37	13	1.0172	1151	90.0626
38	11	0.8607	1162	90.9233
39	23	1.7997	1185	92.7230
40	7	0.5477	1192	93.2707
41	9	0.7042	1201	93.9750
42	4	0.3130	1205	94.2879
43	16	1.2520	1221	95.5399
44	4	0.3130	1225	95.8529
45	9	0.7042	1234	96.5571
46	1	0.0782	1235	96.6354
47	2	0.1565	1237	96.7919
48	1	0.0782	1238	96.8701
49	3	0.2347	1241	97.1049
50	4	0.3130	1245	97.4178
51	2	0.1565	1247	97.5743
52	7	0.5477	1254	98.1221
53-55	0	0.0000	1254	98.1221
56	1	0.0782	1255	98.2003
57	5	0.3912	1260	98.5915
58	3	0.2347	1263	98.8263
59	3	0.2347	1266	99.0610
60	0	0.0000	1266	99.0610
61	7	0.5477	1273	99.6088
62	1	0.0782	1274	99.6870
63-71	0	0.0000	1274	99.6870
72	1	0.0782	1275	99.7653
73	1	0.0782	1276	99.8435
74-104	0	0.0000	1276	99.8435
105	1	0.0782	1277	99.9218
106-119	0	0.0000	1277	99.9218
120	1	0.0782	1278	100.0000

TABLE – 4.145
AGE-WISE DISTRIBUTION OF CITATIONS IN OTHER LIBRARIES, USERS AND SERVICES – JOURNALS

Age	*Number*	*Percentage*	*Cumulative*	*Cumulative Percentage*
1	*2*	*3*	*4*	*5*
0	4	0.9524	4	0.9524
1	15	3.5714	19	4.5238
2	14	3.3333	33	7.8571
3	24	5.7143	57	13.5714
4	21	5.0000	78	18.5714
5	14	3.3333	92	21.9048
6	24	5.7143	116	27.6190
7	29	6.9048	145	34.5238
8	11	2.6190	156	37.1429
9	19	4.5238	175	41.6667
10	24	5.7143	199	47.3810
11	13	3.0952	212	50.4762
12	27	6.4286	239	56.9048
13	15	3.5714	254	60.4762
14	18	4.2857	272	64.7619
15	19	4.5238	291	69.2857
16	9	2.1429	300	71.4286
17	16	3.8095	316	75.2381
18	11	2.6190	327	77.8571
19	19	4.5238	346	82.3810
20	8	1.9048	354	84.2857
21	16	3.8095	370	88.0952
22	5	1.1905	375	89.2857
23	5	1.1905	380	90.4762
24	4	0.9524	384	91.4286
25	5	1.1905	389	92.6190
26	1	0.2381	390	92.8571
27	2	0.4762	392	93.3333
28	1	0.2381	393	93.5714
29	8	1.9048	401	95.4762
30	5	1.1905	406	96.6667
31	3	0.7143	409	97.3810
32	1	0.2381	410	97.6190
33	2	0.4762	412	98.0952

(Contd...)

1	*2*	*3*	*4*	*5*
34	3	0.7143	415	98.8095
35	2	0.4762	417	99.2857
36-37	0	0.0000	417	99.2857
38	2	0.4762	419	99.7619
39-42	0	0.0000	419	99.7619
43	1	0.2381	420	100.0000

TABLE – 4.146
AGE-WISE DISTRIBUTION OF CITATIONS IN PUBLIC LIBRARIES AND COMMUNITY INFORMATION SERVICES – JOURNALS

Age	*Number*	*Percentage*	*Cumulative*	*Cumulative Percentage*
1	*2*	*3*	*4*	*5*
0	3	0.4870	3	0.4870
1	9	1.4610	12	1.9481
2	13	2.1104	25	4.0584
3	40	6.4935	65	10.5519
4	31	5.0325	96	15.5844
5	51	8.2792	147	23.8636
6	24	3.8961	171	27.7597
7	29	4.7078	200	32.4675
8	5	0.8117	205	33.2792
9	17	2.7597	222	36.0390
10	14	2.2727	236	38.3117
11	19	3.0844	255	41.3961
12	25	4.0584	280	45.4545
13	20	3.2468	300	48.7013
14	27	4.3831	327	53.0844
15	45	7.3052	372	60.3896
16	33	5.3571	405	65.7468
17	31	5.0325	436	70.7792
18	18	2.9221	454	73.7013
19	9	1.4610	463	75.1623
20	26	4.2208	489	79.3831
21	10	1.6234	499	81.0065
22	11	1.7857	510	82.7922
23	14	2.2727	524	85.0649
24	7	1.1364	531	86.2013

(Contd...)

1	2	3	4	5
25	23	3.7338	554	89.9351
26	5	0.8117	559	90.7468
27	8	1.2987	567	92.0455
28	9	1.4610	576	93.5065
29	4	0.6494	580	94.1558
30	5	0.8117	585	94.9675
31	4	0.6494	589	95.6169
32	3	0.4870	592	96.1039
33	6	0.9740	598	97.0779
34	1	0.1623	599	97.2403
35	1	0.1623	600	97.4026
36	2	0.3247	602	97.7273
37-38	0	0.0000	602	97.7273
39	2	0.3247	604	98.0519
40	2	0.3247	606	98.3766
41-42	0	0.0000	606	98.3766
43	1	0.1623	607	98.5390
44	1	0.1623	608	98.7013
45	1	0.1623	609	98.8636
46	0	0.0000	609	98.8636
47	1	0.1623	610	99.0260
48	2	0.3247	612	99.3506
49	2	0.3247	614	99.6753
50-52	0	0.0000	614	99.6753
53	1	0.1623	615	99.8377
54	1	0.1623	616	100.0000

TABLE - 4.147

AGE-WISE DISTRIBUTION OF CITATIONS IN SCIENTIFIC AND TECHNICAL LIBRARIES – JOURNALS

Age	*Number*	*Percentage*	*Cumulative*	*Cumulative Percentage*
1	*2*	*3*	*4*	*5*
0	1	0.1078	1	0.1078
1	11	1.1853	12	1.2931
2	34	3.6638	46	4.9569
3	32	3.4483	78	8.4052
4	55	5.9267	133	14.3319
5	53	5.7112	186	20.0431
6	56	6.0345	242	26.0776

(Contd...)

1	*2*	*3*	*4*	*5*
7	30	3.2328	272	29.3103
8	38	4.0948	310	33.4052
9	36	3.8793	346	37.2845
10	38	4.0948	384	41.3793
11	44	4.7414	428	46.1207
12	30	3.2328	458	49.3534
13	40	4.3103	498	53.6638
14	33	3.5560	531	57.2198
15	31	3.3405	562	60.5603
16	30	3.2328	592	63.7931
17	22	2.3707	614	66.1638
18	25	2.6940	639	68.8578
19	31	3.3405	670	72.1983
20	4	0.4310	674	72.6293
21	10	1.0776	684	73.7069
22	12	1.2931	696	75.0000
23	17	1.8319	713	76.8319
24	12	1.2931	725	78.1250
25	7	0.7543	732	78.8793
26	13	1.4009	745	80.2802
27	11	1.1853	756	81.4655
28	15	1.6164	771	83.0819
29	10	1.0776	781	84.1595
30	12	1.2931	793	85.4526
31	12	1.2931	805	86.7457
32	18	1.9397	823	88.6853
33	9	0.9698	832	89.6552
34	13	1.4009	845	91.0560
35	3	0.3233	848	91.3793
36	3	0.3233	851	91.7026
37	0	0.0000	851	91.7026
38	7	0.7543	858	92.4569
39	13	1.4009	871	93.8578
40	3	0.3233	874	94.1810
41	6	0.6466	880	94.8276
42	2	0.2155	882	95.0431
43	7	0.7543	889	95.7974
44	3	0.3233	892	96.1207
45	12	1.2931	904	97.4138
46	3	0.3233	907	97.7371
47	3	0.3233	910	98.0603
48	8	0.8621	918	98.9224

(Contd...)

1	*2*	*3*	*4*	*5*
49	1	0.1078	919	99.0302
50	1	0.1078	920	99.1379
51	0	0.0000	920	99.1379
52	1	0.1078	921	99.2457
53	3	0.3233	924	99.5690
54-56	0	0.0000	924	99.5690
57	2	0.2155	926	99.7845
58-67	0	0.0000	926	99.7845
68	1	0.1078	927	99.8922
69-91	0	0.0000	927	99.8922
92	1	0.1078	928	100.0000

TABLE – 4.148
AGE-WISE DISTRIBUTION OF CITATIONS IN UNIVERSITY LIBRARIES, USERS AND SERVICES – JOURNALS

Age	*Number*	*Percentage*	*Cumulative*	*Cumulative Percentage*
1	*2*	*3*	*4*	*5*
0	2	0.1270	2	0.1270
1	31	1.9683	33	2.0952
2	23	1.4603	56	3.5556
3	67	4.2540	123	7.8095
4	55	3.4921	178	11.3016
5	62	3.9365	240	15.2381
6	83	5.2698	323	20.5079
7	67	4.2540	390	24.7619
8	60	3.8095	450	28.5714
9	70	4.4444	520	33.0159
10	75	4.7619	595	37.7778
11	71	4.5079	666	42.2857
12	43	2.7302	709	45.0159
13	51	3.2381	760	48.2540
14	34	2.1587	794	50.4127
15	42	2.6667	836	53.0794
16	44	2.7937	880	55.8730
17	44	2.7937	924	58.6667
18	47	2.9841	971	61.6508
19	27	1.7143	998	63.3651
20	72	4.5714	1070	67.9365
21	42	2.6667	1112	70.6032

(Contd...)

1	*2*	*3*	*4*	*5*
22	38	2.4127	1150	73.0159
23	29	1.8413	1179	74.8571
24	29	1.8413	1208	76.6984
25	26	1.6508	1234	78.3492
26	38	2.4127	1272	80.7619
27	29	1.8413	1301	82.6032
28	25	1.5873	1326	84.1905
29	27	1.7143	1353	85.9048
30	18	1.1429	1371	87.0476
31	28	1.7778	1399	88.8254
32	20	1.2698	1419	90.0952
33	4	0.2540	1423	90.3492
34	11	0.6984	1434	91.0476
35	12	0.7619	1446	91.8095
36	29	1.8413	1475	93.6508
37	14	0.8889	1489	94.5397
38	9	0.5714	1498	95.1111
39	4	0.2540	1502	95.3651
40	6	0.3810	1508	95.7460
41	4	0.2540	1512	96.0000
42	8	0.5079	1520	96.5079
43	7	0.4444	1527	96.9524
44	5	0.3175	1532	97.2698
45	5	0.3175	1537	97.5873
46	4	0.2540	1541	97.8413
47	7	0.4444	1548	98.2857
48	5	0.3175	1553	98.6032
49	5	0.3175	1558	98.9206
50	3	0.1905	1561	99.1111
51	0	0.0000	1561	99.1111
52	1	0.0635	1562	99.1746
53	4	0.2540	1566	99.4286
54	0	0.0000	1566	99.4286
55	1	0.0635	1567	99.4921
56	0	0.0000	1567	99.4921
57	1	0.0635	1568	99.5556
58	0	0.0000	1568	99.5556
59	2	0.1270	1570	99.6825
60	0	0.0000	1570	99.6825
61	3	0.1905	1573	99.8730
62-86	0	0.0000	1573	99.8730
87	1	0.0635	1574	99.9365
88-94	0	0.0000	1574	99.9365
95	1	0.0635	1575	100.0000

TABLE – 4.149
AGE-WISE DISTRIBUTION OF CITATIONS IN LIBRARY AND INFORMATION SCIENCE – BOOKS

Age	*Number*	*Percentage*	*Cumulative*	*Cumulative Percentage*
1	*2*	*3*	*4*	*5*
0	4	0.1397	4	0.1397
1	29	1.0129	33	1.1526
2	39	1.3622	72	2.5148
3	75	2.6196	147	5.1345
4	86	3.0038	233	8.1383
5	117	4.0866	350	12.2249
6	91	3.1785	441	15.4034
7	81	2.8292	522	18.2326
8	74	2.5847	596	20.8173
9	89	3.1086	685	23.9260
10	72	2.5148	757	26.4408
11	82	2.8641	839	29.3049
12	84	2.9340	923	32.2389
13	77	2.6895	1000	34.9284
14	85	2.9689	1085	37.8973
15	108	3.7723	1193	41.6696
16	83	2.8991	1276	44.5686
17	96	3.3531	1372	47.9218
18	82	2.8641	1454	50.7859
19	127	4.4359	1581	55.2218
20	74	2.5847	1655	57.8065
21	88	3.0737	1743	60.8802
22	92	3.2134	1835	64.0936
23	59	2.0608	1894	66.1544
24	56	1.9560	1950	68.1104
25	52	1.8163	2002	69.9267
26	80	2.7943	2082	72.7209
27	55	1.9211	2137	74.6420
28	64	2.2354	2201	76.8774
29	57	1.9909	2258	78.8683
30	38	1.3273	2296	80.1956
31	38	1.3273	2334	81.5229
32	46	1.6067	2380	83.1296
33	50	1.7464	2430	84.8760
34	38	1.3273	2468	86.2033

(Contd...)

1	*2*	*3*	*4*	*5*
35	33	1.1526	2501	87.3559
36	33	1.1526	2534	88.5086
37	24	0.8383	2558	89.3468
38	25	0.8732	2583	90.2200
39	23	0.8034	2606	91.0234
40	15	0.5239	2621	91.5473
41	16	0.5589	2637	92.1062
42	22	0.7684	2659	92.8746
43	26	0.9081	2685	93.7827
44	16	0.5589	2701	94.3416
45	11	0.3842	2712	94.7258
46	9	0.3144	2721	95.0402
47	9	0.3144	2730	95.3545
48	13	0.4541	2743	95.8086
49	12	0.4191	2755	96.2277
50	14	0.4890	2769	96.7167
51	9	0.3144	2778	97.0311
52	3	0.1048	2781	97.1359
53	3	0.1048	2784	97.2407
54	8	0.2794	2792	97.5201
55	5	0.1746	2797	97.6947
56	7	0.2445	2804	97.9392
57	4	0.1397	2808	98.0789
58	5	0.1746	2813	98.2536
59	1	0.0349	2814	98.2885
60	7	0.2445	2821	98.5330
61	2	0.0699	2823	98.6029
62	5	0.1746	2828	98.7775
63	2	0.0699	2830	98.8474
64	0	0.0000	2830	98.8474
65	1	0.0349	2831	98.8823
66	6	0.2096	2837	99.0919
67	5	0.1746	2842	99.2665
68	2	0.0699	2844	99.3364
69	5	0.1746	2849	99.5110
70	1	0.0349	2850	99.5459
71-72	0	0.0000	2850	99.5459
73	1	0.0349	2851	99.5809
74	2	0.0699	2853	99.6507
75	0	0.0000	2853	99.6507
76	2	0.0699	2855	99.7206
77-81	0	0.0000	2855	99.7206
82	1	0.0349	2856	99.7555

(Contd...)

1	2	3	4	5
83	1	0.0349	2857	99.7904
84	0	0.0000	2857	99.7904
85	1	0.0349	2858	99.8254
86	1	0.0349	2859	99.8603
87-96	0	0.0000	2859	99.8603
97	1	0.0349	2860	99.8952
98-100	0	0.0000	2860	99.8952
101	1	0.0349	2861	99.9301
102	1	0.0349	2862	99.9651
103-120	0	0.0000	2862	99.9651
121	1	0.0349	2863	100.0000

TABLE – 4.150

AGE-WISE DISTRIBUTION OF CITATIONS IN AGRICULTURE INFORMATION, LIBRARIES, USERS AND SERVICES – BOOKS

Age	*Number*	*Percentage*	*Cumulative*	*Cumulative Percentage*
1	*2*	*3*	*4*	*5*
0	1	1.7544	1	1.7544
1	2	3.5088	3	5.2632
2	0	0.0000	3	5.2632
3	1	1.7544	4	7.0175
4	0	0.0000	4	7.0175
5	3	5.2632	7	12.2807
6	4	7.0175	11	19.2982
7	2	3.5088	13	22.8070
8	0	0.0000	13	22.8070
9	2	3.5088	15	26.3158
10	0	0.0000	15	26.3158
11	2	3.5088	17	29.8246
12	2	3.5088	19	33.3333
13	1	1.7544	20	35.0877
14	3	5.2632	23	40.3509
15	2	3.5088	25	43.8596
16	1	1.7544	26	45.6140
17	3	5.2632	29	50.8772
18	3	5.2632	32	56.1404
19	4	7.0175	36	63.1579
20	1	1.7544	37	64.9123

(Contd...)

1	*2*	*3*	*4*	*5*
21	1	1.7544	38	66.6667
22	0	0.0000	38	66.6667
23	3	5.2632	41	71.9298
24	0	0.0000	41	71.9298
25	4	7.0175	45	78.9474
26	2	3.5088	47	82.4561
27	4	7.0175	51	89.4737
28	1	1.7544	52	91.2281
29	1	1.7544	53	92.9825
30	0	0.0000	53	92.9825
31	1	1.7544	54	94.7368
32	2	3.5088	56	98.2456
33-37	0	0.0000	56	98.2456
38	1	1.7544	57	100.0000

TABLE – 4.151
AGE-WISE DISTRIBUTION OF CITATIONS IN BIBLIOMETRICS – BOOKS

Age	*Number*	*Percentage*	*Cumulative*	*Cumulative Percentage*
1	*2*	*3*	*4*	*5*
0	0	0.0000	0	0.0000
1	0	0.0000	0	0.0000
2	1	0.7194	1	0.7194
3	3	2.1583	4	2.8777
4	1	0.7194	5	3.5971
5	2	1.4388	7	5.0360
6	1	0.7194	8	5.7554
7	4	2.8777	12	8.6331
8	1	0.7194	13	9.3525
9	3	2.1583	16	11.5108
10	0	0.0000	16	11.5108
11	5	3.5971	21	15.1079
12	1	0.7194	22	15.8273
13	2	1.4388	24	17.2662
14	4	2.8777	28	20.1439
15	3	2.1583	31	22.3022
16	4	2.8777	35	25.1799
17	2	1.4388	37	26.6187
18	4	2.8777	41	29.4964
19	9	6.4748	50	35.9712
20	5	3.5971	55	39.5683

(Contd...)

1	*2*	*3*	*4*	*5*
21	9	6.4748	64	46.0432
22	4	2.8777	68	48.9209
23	4	2.8777	72	51.7986
24	8	5.7554	80	57.5540
25	2	1.4388	82	58.9928
26	2	1.4388	84	60.4317
27	2	1.4388	86	61.8705
28	1	0.7194	87	62.5899
29	2	1.4388	89	64.0288
30	1	0.7194	90	64.7482
31	2	1.4388	92	66.1871
32	2	1.4388	94	67.6259
33	3	2.1583	97	69.7842
34	4	2.8777	101	72.6619
35	7	5.0360	108	77.6978
36	3	2.1583	111	79.8561
37-39	0	0.0000	111	79.8561
40	2	1.4388	113	81.2950
41	0	0.0000	113	81.2950
42	1	0.7194	114	82.0144
43	0	0.0000	114	82.0144
44	3	2.1583	117	84.1727
45	0	0.0000	117	84.1727
46	1	0.7194	118	84.8921
47	1	0.7194	119	85.6115
48	3	2.1583	122	87.7698
49	2	1.4388	124	89.2086
50	3	2.1583	127	91.3669
51	2	1.4388	129	92.8058
52-56	0	0.0000	129	92.8058
57	1	0.7194	130	93.5252
58-59	0	0.0000	130	93.5252
60	1	0.7194	131	94.2446
61	0	0.0000	131	94.2446
62	1	0.7194	132	94.9640
63-65	0	0.0000	132	94.9640
66	1	0.7194	133	95.6835
67-73	0	0.0000	133	95.6835
74	2	1.4388	135	97.1223
75	0	0.0000	135	97.1223
76	2	1.4388	137	98.5612
77-96	0	0.0000	137	98.5612
97	1	0.7194	138	99.2806
98-100	0	0.0000	138	99.2806
101	1	0.7194	139	100.0000

TABLE – 4.152
AGE-WISE DISTRIBUTION OF CITATIONS IN COLLEGE LIBRARIES, USERS AND SERVICES – BOOKS

Age	*Number*	*Percentage*	*Cumulative*	*Cumulative Percentage*
1	*2*	*3*	*4*	*5*
0	1	0.7092	1	0.7092
1	1	0.7092	2	1.4184
2	2	1.4184	3	2.8369
3	5	3.5461	9	6.3830
4	8	5.6738	17	12.0567
5	7	4.9645	24	17.0213
6	1	0.7092	25	17.7305
7	3	2.1277	28	19.8582
8	4	2.8369	32	22.6950
9	5	3.5461	37	26.2411
10	6	4.2553	43	30.4965
11	4	2.8369	47	33.3333
12	5	3.5461	52	36.8794
13	4	2.8369	56	39.7163
14	6	4.2553	62	43.9716
15	5	3.5461	67	47.5177
16	6	4.2553	73	51.7730
17	1	0.7092	74	52.4823
18	7	4.9645	81	57.4468
19	9	6.3830	90	63.8298
20	4	2.8369	94	66.6667
21	4	2.8369	98	69.5035
22	1	0.7092	99	70.2128
23	2	1.4184	101	71.6312
24	0	0.0000	101	71.6312
25	2	1.4184	103	73.0496
26	7	4.9645	110	78.0142
27	3	2.1277	113	80.1418
28	3	2.1277	116	82.2695
29	1	0.7092	117	82.9787
30	3	2.1277	120	85.1064
31	1	0.7092	121	85.8156
32	1	0.7092	122	86.5248
33	5	3.5461	127	90.0709
34	3	2.1277	130	92.1986
35	0	0.0000	130	92.1986
36	1	0.7092	131	92.9078

(Contd...)

1	2	3	4	5
37	0	0.0000	131	92.9078
38	1	0.7092	132	93.6170
39	2	1.4184	134	95.0355
40	0	0.0000	134	95.0355
41	1	0.7092	135	95.7447
42	1	0.7092	136	96.4539
43-44	0	0.0000	136	96.4539
45	1	0.7092	137	97.1631
46-47	0	0.0000	137	97.1631
48	1	0.7092	138	97.8723
49-55	0	0.0000	138	97.8723
56	2	1.4184	140	99.2908
57-82	0	0.0000	140	99.2908
83	1	0.7092	141	100.0000

TABLE – 4.153
AGE-WISE DISTRIBUTION OF CITATIONS IN LIBRARIES AND I.T – BOOKS

Age	*Number*	*Percentage*	*Cumulative*	*Cumulative Percentage*
1	*2*	*3*	*4*	*5*
0	0	0.0000	0	0.0000
1	2	0.9132	2	0.9132
2	3	1.3699	5	2.2831
3	14	6.3927	19	8.6758
4	13	5.9361	32	14.6119
5	11	5.0228	43	19.6347
6	13	5.9361	56	25.5708
7	14	6.3927	70	31.9635
8	12	5.4795	82	37.4429
9	12	5.4795	94	42.9224
10	12	5.4795	106	48.4018
11	12	5.4795	118	53.8813
12	12	5.4795	130	59.3607
13	12	5.4795	142	64.8402
14	6	2.7397	148	67.5799
15	6	2.7397	154	70.3196
16	7	3.1963	161	73.5160
17	6	2.7397	167	76.2557
18	7	3.1963	174	79.4521
19	3	1.3699	177	80.8219
20	4	1.8265	181	82.6484

(Contd...)

1	*2*	*3*	*4*	*5*
21	3	1.3699	184	84.0183
22	4	1.8265	188	85.8447
23	1	0.4566	189	86.3014
24	4	1.8265	193	88.1279
25-26	0	0.0000	193	88.1279
27	1	0.4566	194	88.5845
28	4	1.8265	198	90.4110
29	1	0.4566	199	90.8676
30	2	0.9132	201	91.7808
31	0	0.0000	201	91.7808
32	1	0.4566	202	92.2374
33	0	0.0000	202	92.2374
34	1	0.4566	203	92.6941
35	1	0.4566	204	93.1507
36	1	0.4566	205	93.6073
37	1	0.4566	206	94.0639
38	2	0.9132	208	94.9772
39	1	0.4566	209	95.4338
40	0	0.0000	209	95.4338
41	2	0.9132	211	96.3470
42-43	0	0.0000	211	96.3470
44	3	1.3699	214	97.7169
45	1	0.4566	215	98.1735
46-48	0	0.0000	215	98.1735
49	1	0.4566	216	98.6301
50-57	0	0.0000	216	98.6301
58	1	0.4566	217	99.0868
59-65	0	0.0000	217	99.0868
66	1	0.4566	218	99.5434
67	1	0.4566	219	100.0000

TABLE – 4.154
AGE-WISE DISTRIBUTION OF CITATIONS IN MARKETING OF LIBRARY INFORMATION SERVICES AND PRODUCTS – BOOKS

Age	*Number*	*Percentage*	*Cumulative*	*Cumulative Percentage*
1	*2*	*3*	*4*	*5*
0	0	0.0000	0	0.0000
1	1	1.3514	1	1.3514
2	5	6.7568	6	8.1081

(Contd...)

1	*2*	*3*	*4*	*5*
3	5	6.7568	11	14.8649
4	8	10.8108	19	25.6757
5	4	5.4054	23	31.0811
6	12	16.2162	35	47.2973
7	6	8.1081	41	55.4054
8-9	0	0.0000	41	55.4054
10	2	2.7027	43	58.1081
11	0	0.0000	43	58.1081
12	1	1.3514	44	59.4595
13-14	0	0.0000	44	59.4595
15	3	4.0541	47	63.5135
16	0	0.0000	47	63.5135
17	7	9.4595	54	72.9730
18	4	5.4054	58	78.3784
19	3	4.0541	61	82.4324
20	0	0.0000	61	82.4324
21	2	2.7027	63	85.1351
22	2	2.7027	65	87.8378
23-25	0	0.0000	65	87.8378
26	2	2.7027	67	90.5405
27	1	1.3514	68	91.8919
28	0	0.0000	68	91.8919
29	2	2.7027	70	94.5946
30	0	0.0000	70	94.5946
31	3	4.0541	73	98.6486
32-49	0	0.0000	73	98.6486
50	1	1.3514	74	100.0000

TABLE – 4.155

AGE-WISE DISTRIBUTION OF CITATIONS IN MEDICAL INFORMATION, LIBRARIES, USERS AND SERVICES – BOOKS

Age	*Number*	*Percentage*	*Cumulative*	*Cumulative Percentage*
1	*2*	*3*	*4*	*5*
0	0	0.0000	0	0.0000
1	2	1.4599	2	1.4599
2	0	0.0000	2	1.4599
3	3	2.1898	5	3.6496

(Contd...)

1	*2*	*3*	*4*	*5*
4	5	3.6496	10	7.2993
5	4	2.9197	14	10.2190
6	4	2.9197	18	13.1387
7	6	4.3796	24	17.5182
8	10	7.2993	34	24.8175
9	7	5.1095	41	29.9270
10	2	1.4599	43	31.3869
11	9	6.5693	52	37.9562
12	3	2.1898	55	40.1460
13	4	2.9197	59	43.0657
14	1	0.7299	60	43.7956
15	7	5.1095	67	48.9051
16	2	1.4599	69	50.3650
17	9	6.5693	78	56.9343
18	6	4.3796	84	61.3139
19	13	9.4891	97	70.8029
20	3	2.1898	100	72.9927
21	1	0.7299	101	73.7226
22	0	0.0000	101	73.7226
23	8	5.8394	109	79.5620
24	3	2.1898	112	81.7518
25	1	0.7299	113	82.4818
26	2	1.4599	115	83.9416
27	1	0.7299	116	84.6715
28-31	0	0.0000	116	84.6715
32	1	0.7299	117	85.4015
33	7	5.1095	124	90.5109
34	3	2.1898	127	92.7007
35	1	0.7299	128	93.4307
36	1	0.7299	129	94.1606
37	0	0.0000	129	94.1606
38	1	0.7299	130	94.8905
39	1	0.7299	131	95.6204
40	1	0.7299	132	96.3504
41	1	0.7299	133	97.0803
42	0	0.0000	133	97.0803
43	1	0.7299	134	97.8102
44-47	0	0.0000	134	97.8102
48	2	1.4599	136	99.2701
49	0	0.0000	136	99.2701
50	1	0.7299	137	100.0000

TABLE – 4.156
AGE-WISE DISTRIBUTION OF CITATIONS IN OTHER ASPECTS – BOOKS

Age	*Number*	*Percentage*	*Cumulative*	*Cumulative Percentage*
1	*2*	*3*	*4*	*5*
0	0	0.0000	0	0.0000
1	7	1.5625	7	1.5625
2	7	1.5625	14	3.1250
3	8	1.7857	22	4.9107
4	13	2.9018	35	7.8125
5	23	5.1339	58	12.9464
6	10	2.2321	68	15.1786
7	11	2.4554	79	17.6339
8	8	1.7857	87	19.4196
9	7	1.5625	94	20.9821
10	3	0.6696	97	21.6518
11	3	0.6696	100	22.3214
12	11	2.4554	111	24.7768
13	21	4.6875	132	29.4643
14	8	1.7857	140	31.2500
15	22	4.9107	162	36.1607
16	15	3.3482	177	39.5089
17	11	2.4554	188	41.9643
18	10	2.2321	198	44.1964
19	33	7.3661	231	51.5625
20	11	2.4554	242	54.0179
21	14	3.1250	256	57.1429
22	33	7.3661	289	64.5089
23	9	2.0089	298	66.5179
24	6	1.3393	304	67.8571
25	15	3.3482	319	71.2054
26	19	4.2411	338	75.4464
27	11	2.4554	349	77.9018
28	26	5.8036	375	83.7054
29	9	2.0089	384	85.7143
30	5	1.1161	389	86.8304
31	2	0.4464	391	87.2768
32	4	0.8929	395	88.1696
33	8	1.7857	403	89.9554
34	1	0.2232	404	90.1786
35	1	0.2232	405	90.4018

(Contd...)

1	*2*	*3*	*4*	*5*
36	4	0.8929	409	91.2946
37	5	1.1161	414	92.4107
38	3	0.6696	417	93.0804
39	1	0.2232	418	93.3036
40	1	0.2232	419	93.5268
41	1	0.2232	420	93.7500
42	4	0.8929	424	94.6429
43	3	0.6696	427	95.3125
44-45	0	0.0000	427	95.3125
46	1	0.2232	428	95.5357
47	0	0.0000	428	95.5357
48	2	0.4464	430	95.9821
49	5	1.1161	435	97.0982
50	0	0.0000	435	97.0982
51	2	0.4464	437	97.5446
52-53	0	0.0000	437	97.5446
54	1	0.2232	438	97.7679
55-56	0	0.0000	438	97.7679
57	1	0.2232	439	97.9911
58	2	0.4464	441	98.4375
59	0	0.0000	441	98.4375
60	1	0.2232	442	98.6607
61-67	0	0.0000	442	98.6607
68	2	0.4464	444	99.1071
69-81	0	0.0000	444	99.1071
82	1	0.2232	445	99.3304
83-85	0	0.0000	445	99.3304
86	1	0.2232	446	99.5536
87-101	0	0.0000	446	99.5536
102	1	0.2232	447	99.7768
103-120	0	0.0000	447	99.7768
121	1	0.2232	448	100.0000

TABLE – 4.157
AGE-WISE DISTRIBUTION OF CITATIONS IN OTHER LIBRARIES, USERS AND SERVICES – BOOKS

Age	*Number*	*Percentage*	*Cumulative*	*Cumulative Percentage*
1	*2*	*3*	*4*	*5*
0	1	0.8197	1	0.8197
1	2	1.6393	3	2.4590
2	1	0.8197	4	3.2787

(Contd...)

1	*2*	*3*	*4*	*5*
3	2	1.6393	6	4.9180
4	3	2.4590	9	7.3770
5	3	2.4590	12	9.8361
6	4	3.2787	16	13.1148
7	3	2.4590	19	15.5738
8	4	3.2787	23	18.8525
9	4	3.2787	27	22.1311
10	1	0.8197	28	22.9508
11	6	4.9180	34	27.8689
12	7	5.7377	41	33.6066
13	1	0.8197	42	34.4262
14	3	2.4590	45	36.8852
15	7	5.7377	52	42.6230
16	7	5.7377	59	48.3607
17	11	9.0164	70	57.3770
18	6	4.9180	76	62.2951
19	4	3.2787	80	65.5738
20	4	3.2787	84	68.8525
21	3	2.4590	87	71.3115
22	1	0.8197	88	72.1311
23	3	2.4590	91	74.5902
24	4	3.2787	95	77.8689
25	2	1.6393	97	79.5082
26	2	1.6393	99	81.1475
27	0	0.0000	99	81.1475
28	2	1.6393	101	82.7869
29	2	1.6393	103	84.4262
30-31	0	0.0000	103	84.4262
32	5	4.0984	108	88.5246
33	1	0.8197	109	89.3443
34	0	0.0000	109	89.3443
35	1	0.8197	110	90.1639
36	5	4.0984	115	94.2623
37	1	0.8197	116	95.0820
38	1	0.8197	117	95.9016
39	1	0.8197	118	96.7213
40-41	0	0.0000	118	96.7213
42	1	0.8197	119	97.5410
43-53	0	0.0000	119	97.5410
54	1	0.8197	120	98.3607
55—65	0	0.0000	120	98.3607
66	1	0.8197	121	99.1803
67-84	0	0.0000	121	99.1803
85	1	0.8197	122	100.0000

TABLE – 4.158
AGE-WISE DISTRIBUTION OF CITATIONS IN PUBLIC LIBRARIES AND COMMUNITY INFORMATION SERVICES – BOOKS

Age	*Number*	*Percentage*	*Cumulative*	*Cumulative Percentage*
1	*2*	*3*	*4*	*5*
0	1	0.3257	1	0.3257
1	1	0.3257	2	0.6515
2	1	0.3257	3	0.9772
3	10	3.2573	13	4.2345
4	5	1.6287	18	5.8632
5	12	3.9088	30	9.7720
6	6	1.9544	36	11.7264
7	11	3.5831	47	15.3094
8	7	2.2801	54	17.5896
9	11	3.5831	65	21.1726
10	15	4.8860	80	26.0586
11	17	5.5375	97	31.5961
12	9	2.9316	106	34.5277
13	5	1.6287	111	36.1564
14	17	5.5375	128	41.6938
15	11	3.5831	139	45.2769
16	9	2.9316	148	48.2085
17	9	2.9316	157	51.1401
18	8	2.6059	165	53.7459
19	9	2.9316	174	56.6775
20	9	2.9316	183	59.6091
21	11	3.5831	194	63.1922
22	7	2.2801	201	65.4723
23	3	0.9772	204	66.4495
24	4	1.3029	208	67.7524
25	2	0.6515	210	68.4039
26	8	2.6059	218	71.0098
27	3	0.9772	221	71.9870
28	3	0.9772	224	72.9642
29	6	1.9544	230	74.9186
30	5	1.6287	235	76.5472
31	6	1.9544	241	78.5016
32	3	0.9772	244	79.4788
33	8	2.6059	252	82.0847
34	4	1.3029	256	83.3876
35	4	1.3029	260	84.6906

(Contd...)

1	*2*	*3*	*4*	*5*
36	4	1.3029	264	85.9935
37	2	0.6515	266	86.6450
38	2	0.6515	268	87.2964
39	3	0.9772	271	88.2736
40	1	0.3257	272	88.5993
41	2	0.6515	274	89.2508
42	4	1.3029	278	90.5537
43	3	0.9772	281	91.5309
44	2	0.6515	283	92.1824
45	0	0.0000	283	92.1824
46	1	0.3257	284	92.5081
47	3	0.9772	287	93.4853
48	1	0.3257	288	93.8111
49	1	0.3257	289	94.1368
50	2	0.6515	291	94.7883
51	1	0.3257	292	95.1140
52	0	0.0000	292	95.1140
53	1	0.3257	293	95.4397
54	2	0.6515	295	96.0912
55	2	0.6515	297	96.7427
56	1	0.3257	298	97.0684
57-62	0	0.0000	298	97.0684
63	1	0.3257	299	97.3941
64	0	0.0000	299	97.3941
65	1	0.3257	300	97.7199
66	1	0.3257	301	98.0456
67-68	0	0.0000	301	98.0456
69	5	1.6287	306	99.6743
70	1	0.3257	307	100.0000

TABLE – 4.159
AGE-WISE DISTRIBUTION OF CITATIONS IN SCIENTIFIC AND TECHNICAL LIBRARIES – BOOKS

Age	*Number*	*Percentage*	*Cumulative*	*Cumulative Percentage*
1	*2*	*3*	*4*	*5*
0	0	0.0000	0	0.0000
1	0	0.0000	0	0.0000
2	5	2.2321	5	2.2321
3	4	1.7857	9	4.0179
4	5	2.2321	14	6.2500
5	6	2.6786	20	8.9286
6	5	2.2321	25	11.1607

(Contd...)

1	*2*	*3*	*4*	*5*
7	1	0.4464	26	11.6071
8	5	2.2321	31	13.8393
9	6	2.6786	37	16.5179
10	5	2.2321	42	18.7500
11	3	1.3393	45	20.0893
12	7	3.1250	52	23.2143
13	11	4.9107	63	28.1250
14	3	1.3393	66	29.4643
15	6	2.6786	72	32.1429
16	5	2.2321	77	34.3750
17	9	4.0179	86	38.3929
18	2	0.8929	88	39.2857
19	11	4.9107	99	44.1964
20	9	4.0179	108	48.2143
21	5	2.2321	113	50.4464
22	7	3.1250	120	53.5714
23	4	1.7857	124	55.3571
24	4	1.7857	128	57.1429
25	4	1.7857	132	58.9286
26	8	3.5714	140	62.5000
27	3	1.3393	143	63.8393
28	15	6.6964	158	70.5357
29	3	1.3393	161	71.8750
30	4	1.7857	165	73.6607
31	5	2.2321	170	75.8929
32	12	5.3571	182	81.2500
33	3	1.3393	185	82.5893
34	4	1.7857	189	84.3750
35	4	1.7857	193	86.1607
36	2	0.8929	195	87.0536
37	7	3.1250	202	90.1786
38	1	0.4464	203	90.6250
39	3	1.3393	206	91.9643
40	4	1.7857	210	93.7500
41	2	0.8929	212	94.6429
42-43	0	0.0000	212	94.6429
44	2	0.8929	214	95.5357
45-46	0	0.0000	214	95.5357
47	1	0.4464	215	95.9821
48	1	0.4464	216	96.4286
49	1	0.4464	217	96.8750
50	1	0.4464	218	97.3214

(Contd...)

1	*2*	*3*	*4*	*5*
51	0	0.0000	218	97.3214
52	1	0.4464	219	97.7679
53-54	0	0.0000	219	97.7679
55	1	0.4464	220	98.2143
56	0	0.0000	220	98.2143
57	1	0.4464	221	98.6607
58-60	0	0.0000	221	98.6607
61	1	0.4464	222	99.1071
62	0	0.0000	222	99.1071
63	1	0.4464	223	99.5536
64-66	0	0.0000	223	99.5536
67	1	0.4464	224	100.0000

TABLE – 4.160

AGE-WISE DISTRIBUTION OF CITATIONS IN UNIVERSITY LIBRARIES, USERS AND SERVICES – BOOKS

Age	*Number*	*Percentage*	*Cumulative*	*Cumulative Percentage*
1	*2*	*3*	*4*	*5*
0	0	0.0000	0	0.0000
1	11	1.1055	11	1.1055
2	14	1.4070	25	2.5126
3	20	2.0101	45	4.5226
4	25	2.5126	70	7.0352
5	42	4.2211	112	11.2563
6	31	3.1156	143	14.3719
7	20	2.0101	163	16.3819
8	23	2.3116	186	18.6935
9	32	3.2161	218	21.9095
10	26	2.6131	244	24.5226
11	21	2.1106	265	26.6332
12	26	2.6131	291	29.2462
13	16	1.6080	307	30.8543
14	34	3.4171	341	34.2714
15	36	3.6181	377	37.8894
16	27	2.7136	404	40.6030
17	28	2.8141	432	43.4171
18	25	2.5126	457	45.9296
19	29	2.9146	486	48.8442
20	24	2.4121	510	51.2563
21	35	3.5176	545	54.7739
22	33	3.3166	578	58.0905

(Contd...)

1	*2*	*3*	*4*	*5*
23	22	2.2111	600	60.3015
24	23	2.3116	623	62.6131
25	20	2.0101	643	64.6231
26	28	2.8141	671	67.4372
27	26	2.6131	697	70.503
28	9	0.9045	706	70.9548
29	30	3.0151	736	73.9698
30	18	1.8090	754	75.7789
31	18	1.8090	772	77.5879
32	15	1.5075	787	79.0955
33	15	1.5075	802	80.6030
34	18	1.8090	820	82.4121
35	14	1.4070	834	83.8191
36	12	1.2060	846	85.0251
37	8	0.8040	854	85.8291
38	13	1.3065	867	87.1357
39	11	1.1055	878	88.2412
40	6	0.6030	884	88.8442
41	7	0.7035	891	89.5477
42	11	1.1055	902	90.6533
43	19	1.9095	921	92.5628
44	6	0.6030	927	93.1658
45	9	0.9045	936	94.0704
46	6	0.6030	942	94.6734
47	4	0.4020	946	95.0754
48	3	0.3015	949	95.3769
49	2	0.2010	951	95.5779
50	6	0.6030	957	96.1809
51	4	0.4020	961	96.5829
52	2	0.2010	963	96.7839
53	2	0.2010	965	96.9849
54	4	0.4020	969	97.3869
55	2	0.2010	971	97.5879
56	4	0.4020	975	97.9899
57	1	0.1005	976	98.0905
58	2	0.2010	978	98.2915
59	1	0.1005	979	98.3920
60	5	0.5025	984	98.8945
61	1	0.1005	985	98.9950
62	4	0.4020	989	99.3970
63-65	0	0.0000	989	99.3970
66	2	0.2010	991	99.5980
67	3	0.3015	994	99.8995
68-72	0	0.0000	994	99.8995
73	1	0.1005	995	100.0000

Availability of Journals and Books Cited by Researchers in Library and Information Science

Journal literature is the most important source of information for researchers in Library and Information Science. It is observed from the table that 773 journals contributed the highest number of citations (7925) accounting for 57.59% of the total citations. This section discusses the availability of the journals and books cited by the researchers in Library and Information Science in all the four university libraries studied. The number of cited journals available in the libraries and the number of citations available from these journals, the break up of these journals into Indian and foreign journals and their contributions are presented in Table 4.161 – 4. 164.

Out of 773 journals, the library of Andhra University is subscribing to 15 journals (1.94%) of which 10 are Indian and 5 are foreign. The distribution of these journals among various sub-disciplines has been presented in the Table 4.318.

Sub-discipline wise analysis of availability of journals indicates that highest number of journals in the library covered the sub-discipline Scientific and Technical Libraries. However, in the fields of Agricultural Libraries, Users and Services; Public Libraries and Community Information Services; Libraries and I.T; Marketing of Library Information Services and Products and Other Libraries, Users and Services the university library holds less than five percent of cited journals.

Sri Venkateswara University library acquires 11 journals of which all are Indian. The sub-discipline University Libraries, Users and Services stood in the first place regarding the percent of cited journals followed by Bibliometrics. Less than five percent of the cited journals are available in the sub-disciplines Medical Information, Libraries, Users and Services; Marketing of Library Information Services and Products; and Other Aspects.

TABLE – 4.161

AVAILABILITY OF CITED INDIAN AND FOREIGN JOURNALS IN ANDHRA UNIVERSITY LIBRARY

Subject	*Total No. of Journals*	*Total No. of Citations*	*No. of Indian Journals*	*No. of Citations to Indian Journals*	*No. of Foreign Journals*	*No. of Citations to Foreign Journals*
1	*2*	*3*	*4*	*5*	*6*	*7*
Agriculture Information, Libraries, Users and Services	9	64 4.22	7	47 5.52	2	17 2.56
Bibliometrics	11	183 12.06	7	107 12.56	4	76 11.43
College Libraries, Users and Services	12	181 11.93	8	118 13.85	4	63 9.47
Libraries and I.T	12	54 3.56	7	35 4.11	5	19 2.86
Marketing of Library Information Services and Products	9	43 2.83	5	7 0.82	4	36 5.41

(Contd...)

1	2	3	4	5	6	7
Medical Information, Libraries, Users and Services	10	78 5.14	7	49 5.75	3	29 4.36
Other Aspects	12	310 20.44	9	203 23.83	3	107 16.09
Other Libraries, Users and Services	5	23 1.52	1	1 0.12	4	22 3.31
Public Libraries and Community Information Services	7	52 3.43	4	37 4.34	3	15 2.26
Scientific and Technical Libraries	15	378 24.92	10	173 20.31	5	205 30.83
University Libraries, Users and Services	12	151 9.95	8	75 8.80	4	76 11.43
All Subjects	15	1517 100.00	10	852 100.00	5	665 100.00

TABLE – 4.162
AVAILABILITY OF CITED INDIAN AND FOREIGN JOURNALS IN SRI VENKATESWARA UNIVERSITY LIBRARY

Subject	*Total No. of Journals*	*Total No. of Citations*	*No. of Indian Journals*	*No. of Citations to Indian Journals*	*No. of Foreign Journals*	*No. of Citations to Foreign Journals*
1	*2*	*3*	*4*	*5*	*6*	*7*
Agriculture Information, Libraries, Users and Services	8	26 6.81	8	26 6.81	0	0 0.00
Bibliometrics	8	103 26.96	8	103 26.96	0	0 0.00
College Libraries, Users and Services	0	0 0.00	0	0 0.00	0	0 0.00
Libraries and I.T	0	0 0.00	0	0 0.00	0	0 0.00
Marketing of Library Information Services and Products	4	12 3.14	4	12 3.14	0	0 0.00

(Contd...)

1	*2*	*3*	*4*	*5*	*6*	*7*
Medical Information, Libraries, Users and Services	6	14 3.66	6	14 3.66	0	0 0.00
Other Aspects	3	6 1.57	3	6 1.57	0	0 0.00
Other Libraries, Users and Services	10	40 10.47	10	40 10.47	0	0 0.00
Public Libraries and Community Information Services	6	26 6.81	6	26 6.81	0	0 0.00
Scientific and Technical Libraries	0	0 0.00	0	0 0.00	0	0 0.00
University Libraries, Users and Services	10	155 40.58	10	155 40.58	0	0 0.00
All Subjects	11	382 100.00	11	382 100.00	0	0 0.00

TABLE – 4.163

AVAILABILITY OF CITED INDIAN AND FOREIGN JOURNALS IN OSMANIA UNIVERSITY LIBRARY

Subject	*Total No. of Journals*	*Total No. of Citations*	*No. of Indian Journals*	*No. of Citations to Indian Journals*	*No. of Foreign Journals*	*No. of Citations to Foreign Journals*
1	*2*	*3*	*4*	*5*	*6*	*7*
Agriculture Information, Libraries, Users and Services	2	2 2.11	1	1 2.22	1	1 2.00
Bibliometrics	3	6 6.32	2	4 8.89	1	2 4.00
College Libraries, Users and Services	3	5 5.26	3	5 11.11	0	0 0.00
Libraries and I.T	5	37 38.95	3	6 13.33	2	31 62.00
Marketing of Library Information Services and Products	0	0 0.00	0	0 0.00	0	0 0.00

(Contd...)

1	2	3	4	5	6	7
Medical Information, Libraries, Users and Services	0	0 0.00	0	0 0.00	0	0 0.00
Other Aspects	5	33 34.74	4	22 48.89	1	11 22.00
Other Libraries, Users and Services	0	0 0.00	0	0 0.00	0	0 0.00
Public Libraries and Community Information Services	4	8 8.42	3	4 8.89	1	4 8.00
Scientific and Technical Libraries	3	4 4.21	2	3 6.67	1	1 2.00
University Libraries, Users and Services	0	00.00	0	00.00	0	00.00
All Subjects	7	95 100.00	5	45 100.00	2	50 100.00

TABLE – 4.164
AVAILABILITY OF CITED INDIAN AND FOREIGN JOURNALS IN SRI KRISHNA DEVARAYA UNIVERSITY LIBRARY

Subject	*Total No. of Journals*	*Total No. of Citations*	*No. of Indian Journals*	*No. of Citations to Indian Journals*	*No. of Foreign Journals*	*No. of Citations to Foreign Journals*
1	*2*	*3*	*4*	*5*	*6*	*7*
Agriculture Information, Libraries, Users and Services	0	0 0.00	0	0 0.00	0	0 0.00
Bibliometrics	0	0 0.00	0	0 0.00	0	0 0.00
College Libraries, Users and Services	0	0 0.00	0	0 0.00	0	0 0.00
Libraries and I.T	0	0 0.00	0	0 0.00	0	0 0.00
Marketing of Library Information Services and Products	0	0 0.00	0	0 0.00	0	0 0.00

(Contd...)

1	2	3	4	5	6	7
Medical Information, Libraries, Users and Services	0	0 0.00	0	0 0.00	0	0 0.00
Other Aspects	0	0 0.00	0	0 0.00	0	0 0.00
Other Libraries, Users and Services	0	0 0.00	0	0 0.00	0	0 0.00
Public Libraries and Community Information Services	2	3 21.43	2	3 21.43	0	0 0.00
Scientific and Technical Libraries	0	0 0.00	0	0 0.00	0	0 0.00
University Libraries, Users and Services	2	11 78.57	2	11 78.57	0	0 0.00
All Subjects	3	14 100.00	3	14 100.00	0	0 0.00

Osmania University library houses 7 journals in the discipline of Library and Information Science. 5 journals are of Indian origin and 2 journals are foreign origin.

Majority of them are covering the subject Libraries and I.T and Other Aspects. The library holds less than fiver percent of cited titles in Scientific and Technical Libraries and Agricultural Information, Libraries, Users and Services.

Sri Krishna Devaraya University library is subscribing only 3 journals in the field of Library and Information Science. All the 3 journals are published in India. It is clear that the University library does not subscribe to journals published in foreign countries. The available journals mainly cover the sub-disciplines University Libraries, Users and Services and Public Libraries and Community Information Services.

The availability of cited books in the Andhra University library reveal that out of the total 1684 cited books, 681 books are available in the Andhra University library of which 324 are Indian books and 357 are foreign books.

The sub-discipline University Libraries, Users and Services stood in the first place with regarding percent of available books cited by researchers; followed by Scientific and Technical Libraries. However in the sub-disciplines Medical Information, Libraries, Users and Services; Other Libraries, Users and Services; Marketing of Library Information Services and Products; and Agriculture Information, Libraries, Users and Services the library holds less than three percent of cited books.

As far as Sri Venkateswara University is concerned, out of the total books cited in the present study 623 books are found to be available in this library of which 308 are Indian publications and 315 are foreign publications.

The sub-discipline University Libraries, Users and Services stood in the first place followed by Other Libraries,

Users and Services regarding the percent of availability of books cited by researchers .However in the sub-disciplines Medical Information, Libraries, Users and Services; Public Libraries and Community Information Services; Agriculture Information, Libraries, Users and Services; Other Aspects; Marketing of Library Information Services and Products and Bibliometrics the library holds less than ten percent of cited books.

Out of total books cited in the present study 518 books are available in Osmania University library. 270 books are Indian publications while 248 books are foreign publications.

The sub-discipline Libraries and I.T. occupied the first place in percent of availability of cited books, followed by Public Libraries and Community Information Services; Other Aspects; Bibliometrics; College Libraries, Users and Services; Scientific and Technical Libraries and Agriculture Information, Libraries, Users and Services.

The analysis of availability of cited books in Sri Krishna Devaraya University library indicates that out of total books cited in present study 388 are found to be available in this particular library of which 210 are Indian books and 178 are foreign books.

The percent of book citations reveal that University Libraries, Users and Services stood in the first place followed by Public Libraries and Community Information Services and Other Aspects.

Analysis of data on the availability of cited journals and books reveals some interesting findings. It is observed that out of 773 journals cited in Library and Information Science 15 journals are available in Andhra University Library (1.94%), 1.42% in Sri Venkateswara University Library, 0.90% in Osmania University Library and 0.39% in Sri Krishna Devaraya University Library. Out of the 167 Indian journals 5.99% are available in Andhra University Library, 6.58% in Sri Venkateswara University Library, 2.99% in Osmania University Library, 1.79% in Sri Krishna Devaraya University Library. Out of the 606 foreign journals 0.82% in Andhra University Library, 0.33%.

The library of Andhra University is found to be subscribing to highest number of journals in library and information science compared to other libraries. Out of the first fifteen journals in the ranked list 9 journals are available in this library. Further the information gathered about the history of periodical subscriptions of this library reveals that prior to 1992 this library was subscribing to 35 journals in Library and Information Science. Due to budget cut on journal subscriptions, subscriptions to many foreign journals have been stopped. However the library holds rich collection of back volumes of library science journals attracting number of researchers even from other states in India.

It is also observed that the library of Sri Venkateswara University is subscribing only to Indian journals. However the researchers have cited number of foreign journals which they might have obtained from other libraries other than the University library. Same trend is noticed in the case of Sri Krishna Devaraya University.

In terms of journal literature researchers in Library and Information Science in these universities are found to be depending mostly on other libraries in the country.

From the above discussion, it may be concluded that all the university libraries surveyed are able to cater to only 0.39% to 1.94% of the journal literature required by the researchers in Library and Information Science.

It is observed from the findings on the availability of cited books in the libraries of four universities that these libraries are in better position in terms of providing literature in the form of books compared to journal literature. Out of 1684 books cited 40.44% are available in Andhra University library, 36.99% in Sri Venkateswara University library, 30.76% in Osmania University library, and 23.04% in Sri Krishna Devaraya University library.

Majority of cited books available in these libraries are on University Libraries, College Libraries, Public Libraries in order of their priority. Compared to other sub disciplines in the field of Agriculture Information and Marketing of Library Information Services and Products limited number of books are available in these libraries.

This chapter presents all the findings based on analysis of data. The findings are arranged according to order of the objectives and hypotheses formulated. The next chapter deals with conclusions of the study and provides suggestions.

5

Summary and Conclusions

The budget constraints and ever changing demands of the clientele have compelled the librarians of today to make judgement regarding the procurement of journals which are primary sources of information. One of the vital areas of Bibliometrics is citation analysis which helps the librarians to recognize the core journals and for identifying the characteristic features of them in the discipline of Library and Information Science and its sub disciplines.

Summary

The purpose of the present study is to identify the characteristics of literature used by research scholars in the field of Library and Information Science as a whole and its sub disciplines Agriculture Information, Libraries, Users and Services; Bibliometrics; College Libraries, Users and Services; Libraries and I.T; Marketing of Library and Information Services and Products; Medical Information, Libraries, Users and Services; Other Aspects; Other Libraries, Users and Services; Public Libraries and Community Information Services; Scientific and Technical Libraries; University Libraries, Users and Services. The references appended to theses submitted to four universities in Andhra Pradesh i.e.

Andhra University, Sri Venkateswara University, Osmania University, Sri Krishna Devaraya University were analysed using citation analysis. Seventy One theses were awarded in the field of Library and Information Science during 1982-2004 by all the Universities in Andhra Pradesh put together. The citations cited in all these 71 theses of four universities form the basis for the present study. Journals, Books, Editorial Works, Conference Proceedings, Reference Books, Thesis, Dissertations, Acts, Bills, Newspapers, Reports, Standards, Unpublished and others are different forms cited by the researchers. The total number of theses were classified and grouped based on their subject into eleven sub disciplines of the major discipline Library and Information Science. The total number of citations in Agriculture Information, Libraries, Users and Services are 538 appended to 3 theses; in Bibliometrics 1392 citations are appended to 5 theses; in College Libraries, Users and Services 758 citations are appended to 6 theses; in Libraries and I.T 780 citations are appended to 4 theses; in Marketing of Library and Information Services and Products 448 citations are appended to 2 theses; in Medical Information, Libraries, Users and Services 854 citations are appended to 4 theses; in Other Aspects 2239 citations are appended to 11 theses; in Other Libraries, Users and Services 756 citations are appended to 4 theses; in Public Libraries and Community Information Services 1178 citations are appended to 8 theses; in Scientific and Technical Libraries 1508 citations are appended to 7 theses; in University Libraries, Users and Services 3310 citations are appended to 17 theses.

The Citation analysis has also been done in all the eleven sub disciplines of Library and Information Science and presented in tables and graphs.

The objectives of the study are:

1. To identify the different forms of literature used by Library and Information Science researchers or scientists.

2. Determine the average number of reference per dissertation.
3. The distribution of citations according to subject, language and country of origin has to be derived.
4. To study the self-citation behaviour of researchers in the discipline of Library and Information Science.
5. Compile a ranked list of journals and books.
6. Determine the half-life and obsolescence of journals and productivity of journals.
7. The researchers use pattern of journals in the field of Library and Information Science has to be examined by applying Bradford's Law of Scattering.
8. Growth of knowledge and research trends in the field of Library and Information Science are to be studied.

For the purpose of testing the following hypotheses is formulated

1. Journals are important bibliographic form for the means of communication
2. Hypothesis 2

   The literature of Library and Information Science is scattered over wide range of subjects
3. Hypothesis 3

   Most of the literature in Library and Information Science is published in English language.
4. Hypothesis 4

   Developed countries are major producers of literature in the field of Library and Information Science

5. Hypothesis 5

   Collaborative research is more prevalent than individual research in Library and Information Science.

6. Hypothesis 6

   Self-citation is a common phenomenon among the researchers in the field of Library and Information Science.

7. Hypothesis 7

   In the discipline of Library and Information Science, positive relation exists between period of the research and the number of total citations.

8. Hypothesis 8

   The citations relating to journal citations in Library and Information Science conforms to Bradford's Law of Scattering.

9. Hypothesis 9

   The researchers in Library and Information Science generally utilize current information for their day to day requirements.

10. Hypothesis 10

    There is positive relation between the number of citations with multiple authors and period.

11. Hypothesis 11

    The citation behaviour of scientists in the discipline of Library andInformation Science is generally influenced by place of publication.

12. Hypothesis 12

The research activity in Library and Information Science is well augmented by University library.

Conclusions

The conclusions incurred from the study under investigation are depicted in various headings in the following paragraphs.

Average Number of Citations

The average number of citations appended per thesis in the discipline Library and Information Science is 193.82. Bibliometrics stood in the first place with 278.40 citations per thesis followed by Marketing of Library Information Services and Products with 224.00 citations per thesis. The third and fourth places were occupied by Scientific and Technical Libraries and Medical Information, Libraries, Users and Services with 215.43 and 213.50 citations respectively. Doctoral dissertations in Other Aspects and Libraries and I.T stood in fifth and sixth places respectively. The sub discipline College Libraries, Users and Services have received the least number of citations per thesis i.e. 126.33. Compared to earlier studies (Vijaykumar and others), the average number per thesis is very high as per the findings of the present study. The findings of earlier studies indicated the average number as 39 per thesis.

Distribution of Citations

The citations appended to the theses under the present study have been categorized among different forms, subjects, countries, languages and are discussed in the following paragraphs.

The bibliographic form-wise distribution of citations in Library and Information Science and its sub disciplines followed a more or less a similar pattern. Journals and books occupy the first and second places in Library and Information Science and its sub disciplines indicating the importance of journals and books as primary sources of information for researchers in this field.

The findings of the study supports the fact that journals are main sources for research scholars as they report original research literature and are considered to be primary channels of scientific communication.

Subject-wise Analysis

The examination of subject wise analysis of citations in the discipline Library and Information Science has indicated wide scatter of literature. The analysis reveals that literature in LIS is distributed among 28 subjects. Special Libraries and Bibliometrics received maximum number of citations and stood in the first and second places respectively. LIS research with 1355 citations to its credit stood in the third place.

Earlier studies of LISA (2002-2003) and doctoral dissertations in LIS (Vijay Kumar and Others) revealed different findings. Thrust areas identified through studies on LISA in the order of priority are Library technical services, Information storage, Librarianship, Information science, Publishing and book selling and On-line information retrieval. On the other hand, Vijay Kumar and others have identified 'College libraries' as the most focused subject area in LIS research.

Results of another study by Chatterjee and others (1995) also found 'Academic Libraries' as the most popular subject of research covered by LIS research in India. It is observed from another study (Rajeev Vij, 2001) on LISA database (1969-2000) that Internet and World Wide Web are evolving subjects, where as CD-ROMs, Information storage, medical informatics and telecommunications are showing trends of decay.

Earlier study by Vaishnav (1993) has shown that among different areas of literature on computerized LIS, much attention was given to computerized cataloguing, databases, information retrieval, computerized information services and computerized information storage and retrieval. The study has also noted some of the evolving subjects like computer skills, computerized accounting, computerized administration, computerized authority files, computerized book trade, computerized classification, computerized current awareness service, computerized reference sources and computerized user training programmes. Under the category of decaying subjects, this study identified subjects like computer output microforms, computerized printed catalogues, computerized data processing.

Language-wise Distribution

As far as the language wise distribution is concerned, English is identified as dominant language accounting for 99.69 percent of the total citations. Telugu with 0.26 percent and Hindi with 0.04 percent of the citations stood in second and third places respectively. These findings have reiterated the findings of earlier studies showing English as a predominant language.

The clear domination of English as a medium for scientific communication can be attributed to the fact that it is a universal language which can bring scientists, research scholars, and educationists from different countries, backgrounds, cultures, languages on to a common platform to share their experiences.

All the research findings are being published in English. To stay in tune with the latest developments in a discipline, English language plays a vital role. The library and information science professionals have also followed the same pattern and accessed the literature published in English. The use of literature in English has helped the LIS professionals in India to take up the challenges and to update their knowledge on par with international standards.

Information is considered as a vital resource by all the nations. The distribution of citations country wise in the discipline Library and Information Science enables the researcher to measure the research output published by a country, as the progress and development of any country depends on its research activities. Though the literature cited by researchers is scattered among various countries, it is clear that the research activity is high only in some countries. In the present study India stood in the first place as the most productive country with 39.78 percent of the total citations, followed by United States of America with 32.71 percent and United Kingdom with 18.23 percent of the total citations. These findings confirm the findings of earlier studies (Mahapatra, 1994) on Indian Library and Information Science Literature.

Bibliometrics, Marketing of Library Information Services and Products; Medical Information, Libraries, Users and Services and Other Libraries are the four sub-disciplines where United States of America stood in the first place followed by India. Except for these four sub-disciplines, India is found to be the most productive country.

The results reveal that research scholars have mostly relied on the information published from India, U.S.A, U.K and Netherlands. It is very interesting to note that these four countries have contributed 94.05 percent of the total citations in Library and Information Science and its sub-disciplines.

Authorship Pattern and Collaborative Research

The distribution of citations authorship wise indicates same pattern in Library and Information Science and its sub-disciplines. Single author papers were the maximum in number. However when we observe the findings in the field of Library and Information Science as a whole we can identify that collaborative papers started from the period 1913-1922. The increasing trend in the multi-authored papers indicates growing inter-disciplinary nature of the discipline Library and Information Science. Among multiple authors, papers written by two authors are more compared to three and four and above authors which is similar in Library and Information Science and its sub-disciplines. These findings reiterate the findings of the earlier studies on authorship pattern in LIS literature (Rajeev Vij 2001, Parameswaran and Smitha, 2001).

The relationship between authorship and reference period (10 years intervals) in Library and Information Science and its sub-disciplines have been presented with the application of chi-square test.

The authorship wise distribution of books cited in the present study indicates a similar pattern in Library and Information Science and its sub-disciplines. Books authored by single author are the maximum. However we can observe an increasing trend in multi authored books.

The average number of authors per citation in the field of Library and Information Science was found to be 1.28. The number of authors per citation in the sub-disciplines varies between 1.17 and 1.49.

Marketing of Library Information Services and Products occupies the first place regarding average number of authors.

The average number of authors per citation in journals in Library and Information Science stood at 1.26. The average number of authors per citation in the sub-disciplines varies from 1.12 to 1.42.

Bibliometrics stood in the first place regarding average number of authors per citation in journals whereas Public Libraries and Community Information Services occupied the last place.

As far as books is concerned the average number of authors per book in Library and Information Science is 1.22.

The average number of authors per book in the sub-disciplines varies from 1.13 to 1.45.

The sub-discipline Marketing of Library Information Services and Products occupied the first position with 1.45 average number of authors per each cited book.

The Degree of Collaboration in the discipline Library and Information Science was found to be 0.2266. The collaboration started during the period 1893-1902. Among the sub-disciplines, the degree of collaboration has been highest in Bibliometrics (0.3045) followed by College Libraries, Users and Services (0.2880) and Agriculture Information, Libraries, Users and Services (0.2732). The degree of collaboration varied between 0.2060 and 0.3045 for all the sub-disciplines of Library and Information Science. According to a study by Humayoon Kabir (1994), the degree of collaboration among authors in Library and Information Science ranged between 0.20 to 0.35 and the overall average is 0.31

Self-Citations

The results of the study clearly indicate that the practice of self-citations (Type-I) in the field of Library and Information Science and its sub-disciplines is not significant. The percentage of self-citations (Type-I) in Library and Information Science as a whole is 0.30. Other Libraries, Users and Services occupied the first place, followed by Scientific and Technical Libraries with 1.32 percent and 0.46 percent. Earlier studies on Self citations practices among the authors of journal articles revealed different findings. A study on international library and information science journals by Raptis (1992) found a self-citation rate of 27.6 percent whereas it was 6 percent according to a study by Dimitroff and Arlitsch (1995) and 14 percent by a study conducted by Kundu (1981). The findings of the present study on self citations appended to theses differed from the self citation practices noticed in library science journals. Self citation to theses and conference proceedings were found to be more than to journal literature.

However, the practice of self-citations (Type-II) depicts a contrasting picture from Type-I. We can observe from the findings that there is complete absence of self-citations (Type-II).

The findings of the present study reveals that the self-citation rate (Type-II) is absent completely among the researchers in Library and Information Science.

The bibliographic form wise distribution of self-citations in Library and Information Science and its sub-disciplines is disbursed among different categories of documents like – Journals, Books, Conference Proceedings, Theses, Dissertations, Editorial Works, Reports, Acts, Bills, Standards, Newspapers, Reference Books, Ephemeral material and others. The percentage of self-citations to dissertations has been the highest with 31.71 percent. Journals, Conference Proceedings, Editorial works jointly stood in the second place respectively. It may be concluded from the findings that the practice of making self citations is not as common with writers and researchers in the field of Library and Information Science as in other disciplines. The above findings comply with the findings of the earlier studies (Dhiman 2002).

Ranked List of Journals and Books

Journals

The ranked list of journals in the field of Library and Information Science and its sub-disciplines is distributed among 773 journals. The first seven journals in the ranked list contributed to more than 25 percent of the total citations. The first eighteen journals contributed to 50 percent of the total journal literature. The first sixty six journals contributed to 75 percent of the total journal citations.

Out of first seven journals which contributed more than 25 percent, 4 journals are of Indian origin, 2 are of United States of America origin and 1 journal published from U.K.

This indicates that scholars in the discipline mainly depend upon literature published from India, U.S.A and U.K. for their information requirements.

In the sub-discipline Agriculture Information, Libraries, Users and Services the citations are scattered over 83 journals. It is observed from the findings that first two journals have contributed nearly 30 percent of the total journal citations. It is interesting to observe that the first two journals are related to subject of the sub-discipline Agriculture Information, Libraries, Users and Services.

The journal citations in the sub-discipline Bibliometrics are scattered over 126 journals. The findings depict that first two journals in the ranked list have contributed 30 percent of the total journal citations. The first six journals are found to be contributing more than 50 percent of the total journal citations. Eighteen journals contributed 75 percent of the total citations. The rest were covered by 108 journals.

Ranking of journals in tne sub-discipline College Libraries, Users and Services shows that nearly 25 percent of the citations are contributed by one journal i.e. University News. The first four journals have contributed 55 percent of the total citations. 75 percent of the citations are contributed by first seven journals. The remaining citations in College Libraries, Users and Services are covered by 45 journals. The result shows that the journal "University News" attaches more importance to the subject college libraries.

Distribution of citations in the sub-discipline Libraries and I.T shows that the journal citations are scattered over 96 journals. The first five journals contributed 27 percent of the total journal citations. First 15 journals in the ranked list contributed 50 percent of the total citations. 75 percent of the citations are covered by 33 journals. The remaining 25 percent were covered by 63 journals.

The journal citations in the sub-discipline Marketing of Library Information Services and Products are scattered over 56 journals. The first two journals in the ranked list are found to be contributing 25 percent of the journal citations. First six journals contributed 50 percent of the total citations. 75 percent of the citations are contributed by first seventeen journals in the ranked list. Thirty-Nine journals in the list covered the rest of the citations in Marketing of Library Information Services and Products.

The ranked list of journals in Medical Information, Libraries, Users and Services shows that more than 25 percent of the journal citations are contributed by first five journals. More than 50 percent was contributed by 14 journals. 39 journals in the list covered 75 percent of the citations. The rest of the citations were covered by 99 journals.

In the sub field Other Aspects, journal articles cited by researchers are scattered over 204 journals. The first five journals in the ranked list are found to be contributing 25 percent of the total journal citations. 50 percent of the citations are covered by the first thirteen journals. 75 percent of citations are contributed by 38 journals. The remaining percent is covered by 166 journals.

The journal citations in the sub-discipline Other Libraries, Users and Services are scattered over 143 journals which are published from different countries. The first six journals in the ranked list are found to be contributing 25 percent of the total citations. 50 percent of the citations are covered by 19 journals. 54 journals are said to have contributed 75 percent of the total journal citations. 89 journals in the ranked list covered the rest of the citations.

In the sub-discipline Public Libraries and Community Information Services, the citations are dispersed over 91 journals. It is interesting to note that the first two journals could contributed more than 25 percent of the total journal citations. The first seven journals contributed 53 percent of the total citations. 75 percent of the citations are contributed by 18 journals in the ranked list. The remaining 25 percent of citations are scattered over 73 journals.

The journal citations in the sub-discipline Scientific and Technical Libraries are scattered over 167 journals. The first three journals in the ranked list are said to have contributed more than 25 percent of the total citations. 50 percent of the citations are said to be covered by 11 journals in the ranked list. Thirty five journals covered 75 percent of the total citations. One hundred and thirty two journals in the list covered the remaining citations in the sub field Scientific and Technical Libraries.

Distribution of citations in sub discipline University Libraries, Users and Services is observed among 303 journals. The first six journals in the ranked list are contributing 25 percent of the total journal citations. Twenty journals in the ranked list are found to be contributing 50 percent of the total journal citations. 62 journals covered 75 percent of the citations. Two hundred and forty one journals covered the remaining citations in the sub-discipline University Libraries, Users and Services.

The ranked list of journals in the discipline Library and Information Science indicates that "Library Trends" published from U.S.A. and "College and Research Libraries" which is also published from U.S.A. stood in the first and second position. This indicates that journals published from United States of America are mostly referred by scholars for their information requirements.

Sub-discipline-wise ranking shows that in Agriculture Information, Libraries, Users and Services "International Association of Agricultural Librarians and Documentalists" stood in the first place, in Bibliometrics "Scientometrics" published from Netherlands stood in the first place, in College

Libraries, Users and Services "University News" published from India occupied the first position, in Libraries and I.T. "Program" from United Kingdom topped the list, in Marketing of Library Information Services and Products "ASLIB Proceedings", in Medical Information, Libraries, Users and Services "Bulletin of Medical Library Association" published from U.K. stood in the first rank, in Other Aspects "Herald of Library Science" topped the list, in Other Libraries, Users and Services "Law Library Journal" from U.S.A. stood in first place, in Public Libraries and Community Information Services "Library Trends" from U.S.A. occupied the top position, in Scientific and Technical Libraries "ASLIB Proceedings" and in University Libraries, Users and Services "College and Research Libraries" published from U.S.A. occupied the top rank.

The country-wise distribution of journals which are cited in the discipline of Library and Information Science and its sub-disciplines also shows the ratio of Indian and foreign journals. Journals published other than in India are categorised as foreign publications for the purpose of the study.

Out of the total journals cited 21.60 percent are Indian journals and 78.40 percent are foreign journals. The ratio of Indian and foreign journals in Library and Information Science is 1:3.63.

The percentage of citations contributed by 167 Indian journals is 32.83 where as percentage of citations contributed by 606 foreign journals are 67.17.

The ranked list of ten Indian and foreign core journals shows that Annals of Library Science and Documentation and Library Trends are the top Indian and foreign journals respectively. The findings related to top most Indian journal confirms to the findings of the earlier study by Mahapatra (1994).

It is highly impossible for any individual library to satisfy the information requirements of all the users with limited financial resources. The ever rising cost of journals is becoming a major problem for the librarians and it calls for judicious selection. Analysis based on citations will help to overcome all these problems. The document being cited is a more valuable record than the use of document as shown in the transactions log of the circulation section. Hence citation analysis has become a vital aspect of Bibliometrics.

Books

Citations to books in the discipline Library and Information Science and its sub-disciplines are distributed over 1684 books. The ranked list of books reveal that "*The Foundations of Education for Librarianship*" by J.H. Shera, "*World Trends in Library Education*" by G. Bramley and "*The University Library: the organization and administration and functions of academic libraries*" by L.R. Wilson and M.F. Tauber occupied the first, second and third places respectively. Sub-discipline wise ranked list also indicates the most cited titles. They are "*Library Networks*" by Susan K. Martin in Agriculture Information, Libraries, Users and Services; "*Little Science and Big Science*" by Derek J. De Solla Price in Bibliometrics; "*Libraries in Higher Education*" by M. Bavakutty in College Libraries, Users and Services; "*Library Automation*" *by Robert M. Hayes* in Libraries and I.T; "*Strategic Marketing for Non-Profit Organization*" by Philip Kotler in Marketing of Library Information Services and Products; "*Medical Librarianship*" by D.A. Mathews in Medical Information, Libraries, Users and Services; "*World Trends in Library Education*" by G. Bramley in Other Aspects; "*Management*" *by Harold Koontz* in Other Libraries, Users and Services; "Engineering as a Career" *by Ralph J. Smith* in Scientific and Technical Libraries; "*The University Library: the organization, administration and functions of academic libraries" by L.R. Wilson and M.F. Tauber* in University Libraries, Users and Services.

The country wise distribution of books cited in Library and Information Science indicates the ratio of Indian books to foreign books. Out of the total number of books, 1037 are foreign publications accounting to 61.58 percent of the total books cited in the study. 647 books are of Indian origin accounting to 38.42 percent of the total books. The ratio of Indian books to foreign books is 1:1.6. All books published outside India are considered as foreign for the purpose of present study.

The book titles topped in the ranked list of Indian books are as follows: Library and Information Science – *Library Administration: theory and practice;* Agriculture Information, Libraries, Users and Services – *A Report on the Feasibility Study on Automation and Networking of Delhi Libraries*; Bibliometrics – *Quantitative Methods for Library and Information Science;* College Libraries, Users and Services – *Libraries in Higher Education;* Libraries and I.T – *Resource Sharing in Public and Academic Libraries*; Marketing of Library Information Services and Products – *Marketing Management: analysis, planning, implementation and control*; Medical Information, Libraries, Users and Services – *Documentation and Information : services, techniques systems;* Other Aspects – *Librarianship as Profession in India*; Other Libraries, Users and Services – *Fundamentals of Museology*; Public Libraries and Community Information Services – *Rural Library Services in India;* Scientific and Technical Libraries – *Attitude, Concept, Formation and Change;* University Libraries, Users and Services – *Resource Sharing in Public and Academic Libraries.*

Titles that topped the ranked list of foreign books are as follows : Library and Information Science – *The Foundations of Education for Librarianship*; Agriculture Information, Libraries, Users and Services – *Library Networks*; Bibliometrics – *Little Science and Big Science*; College Libraries, Users and Services – *Library Surveys : An Introduction to the Use, Planning, Procedure and Presentation of Surveys*; Libraries and I.T – *A Bibliography of Bibliometrics and Citation Indexing and Analysis*; Marketing of Library Information Services and Products – *Strategic Marketing for Non-Profit Organization;* Medical Information, Libraries, Users and Services – *Medical Librarianship*; Other Aspects – *World Trends in Library Education;* Other Libraries, Users and Services – *Management*; Public Libraries and Community Information Services – *Public Library Finance*; Scientific and Technical Libraries – *Engineering as a Career*; University Libraries, Users and Services – *A Bibliography of Bibliometrics and Citation Indexing and Analysis..*

Productivity of Journals and Books in Library and Information Science

The distribution of cited journals in the discipline of Library and Information Science and its sub-disciplines shows that a few number of journals are contributing maximum number of citations. The number of journals covering half of the citations range between 1 to 14 journals. In LIS as a whole journals are producing half of the literature required by researchers in this field. The ranked list of journals and books enables us to identify the most productive among them. "Library Trends" from United States of America and "The Foundations of Education for Librarianship" by J.H. Shera occupied the first place in journals and books respectively.

Applicability of Bradford's Law of Scattering

The method developed by Levin Kuhler has been utilized in the present study in order to test the application of Bradford's Law of Scattering (Verbal formulation) to the citation data. The scattering of articles over 773 journals cited by researchers is observed by grouping the total citations into three to ten groups. For each group of citations, the degree of concentration, the number of citations that should present, the estimated citations in each group are calculated. The Chi-Square values are computed using a Visaul Foxpro programme. The Chi-Square values which are computed indicates that there is significant difference between the number of citations in each group and the estimated number of citations that should have been present in each group for Library and Information Science and its sub-disciplines.

The application of graphical formulation of Bradford's Law of Scattering of journal citations in the discipline Library and Information Science and its sub-disciplines has been tested by plotting Bradford's bibliographs. A close look at graphs drawn show a initial rising curve followed by linearity and towards the end show the groos droop which is not in conformity with the Bradford's hyperbolic curve. From this we can conclude that use pattern of the journal literature by the researchers in Library and Information Science and its sub-dsicipilines does not support the verbal or graphic formulation of the Bradford's Law of Scattering.

Country-wise Distribution of Cited Journals

The geographical distribution of journals and books cited by research scholars have been taken up in the present study. The results reveal that journals cited in the study are published from 46 countries. It shows the relative research contribution of different countries in the discipline Library and Information Science. United States of America (U.S.A) with 2921 journal citations to its credit took the lead position. India with 2584 journal citations stood in the second position, United Kingdom with 1432 journal citations and Netherlands with 380 citations stood in third and fourth places respectively. The ratio of citations to Indian journals to American journals is 1:1.1. Where as the ratio of citation to Indian journals to British journals is 1.8:1.

On the whole the country wise distribution of journal citations in Library and Information Science and its sub-disciplines followed a similar pattern with slight variations.

United States of America, India and United Kingdom are found to be the most productive countries as researchers mostly relied on the information published from these three countries. These findings differ from the ranked list of contributing countries based on earlier studies. (Rajeev Vij, 2001) and (Paramaeswaran and Smitha, 2001).

It is interesting to note that Netherlands which occupied fourth place in Library and Information Science as a whole stood in second rank in the sub-discipline Agriculture Information, Libraries, Users and Services.

Obsolescence of Literature

The citations to journals and books have been analysed to study obsolescence of literature in the discipline Library and Information Science and its sub-disciplines. The age wise distribution of citations to journals and books reveal that nearly one fourth of the total citations are seven years old, more than half are 15 years old and nearly three fourth are 23 years old. There are some variations in case of sub-disciplines.

The age wise distribution of journal citations reflects similar pattern. More than 25 percent of the journal citations are 7 years old, 50 percent of the journal citations are 13 years old and 75 percent are 22 years old.

The age wise distribution of book citations in Library and Information Science is also presented in the study. More than 25 percent of book citations are 10 years old, 50 percent of citations are 18 years old and 75 percent are 27 years old.

The age wise distribution of journals and book citations combined and individually indicate that mostly researchers in LIS referred twenty five years old back literature to meet their information requirements.

The maximum age of journal in the present study is 120 years whereas in the case of books it is 121 years. The title of the oldest cited journals is "*Library Journal*" in the sub-discipline Other Aspects. The oldest cited book is "*History and Prospects of British Education in India by F.W. Thomas*" in the sub-discipline Other Aspects.

Compared to book citations the journal citations are more aged in Agriculture Information, Libraries, Users and Services; Libraries and I.T; Medical Information, Libraries, Users and Services; Scientific and Technical Libraries; University Libraries, Users and Services.

It is evident from the findings that an article published in "*Library Journal*" in the year 1879 still catches the attention of present day scholars which indicates the importance attached to that article.

Similarly it is also interesting to note that the book "*History and Prospects of British Education in India*" published in 1891 is still referred by LIS researchers of 21st century. This clearly shows the value of content for the researchers in the modern times.

The results in the present study indicate that the half-life of period (median citation age) for journal literature in Library and Information Science is 17.5 years. These findings differ from earlier studies by Mahendra and Deshmukh (1996). They found that for LIS journal literature the half life period is 8 years. The half-life value for Agriculture Information, Libraries, Users and Services is 14; for Bibliometrics 18.5; for College Libraries, Users and Services 22.5; for Libraries and I.T 11; for Marketing of Library

Information Services and Products 18; for Medical Information, Libraries, Users and Services 15; for Other Aspects 22; for Other Libraries, Users and Services 14; for Public Libraries and Community Information Services 16; Scientific and Technical Libraries 16.5 and University Libraries, Users and Services 19.

The half-life period (median citation age) for book citations in Library and Information Science is found to be 22 years. Earlier studies by Mahendra and Deshmukh (1996) found that half life of books in LIS as 12 years. The half-life values for the sub-disciplines Agriculture Information, Libraries, Users and Services; Bibliometrics; College Libraries, Users and Services; Libraries and I.T; Marketing of Library Information Services and Products; Medical Information, Libraries, Users and Services; Other Aspects; Other Libraries, Users and Services; Public Libraries and Community Information Services; Scientific and Technical Libraries; University Libraries, Users and Services are 20, 27, 19.5, 14, 13.5, 19, 23, 19, 22, 27, 24.

Availability of Cited Journals and Books in Andhra University, Sri Venkateswara University, Osmania University and Sri Krishna Devaraya University.

The results of this study University wise are depicted as follows. The Andhra University library procures 15 journals of which 10 are Indian and five are foreign.

Sub-discipline wise analysis of availability of journals indicates that highest number of journals in the library covered the sub-discipline Scientific and Technical Libraries. However, in the fields of Agricultural Libraries, Users and Services; Public Libraries and Community Information Services; Libraries and I.T; Marketing of Library Information Services and Products and Other Libraries, Users and Services the university library holds less than five percent of cited journals.

Sri Venkateswara University library acquires 11 journals of which all are Indian. The sub-discipline University Libraries, Users and Services stood in the first place regarding the percent of cited journals followed by Bibliometrics. Less than five percent of the cited journals are available in the sub-disciplines Medical Information, Libraries, Users and Services; Marketing of Library Information Services and Products; and Other Aspects.

Osmania University library houses 7 journals in the discipline of Library and Information Science. 5 journals are of Indian origin and 2 journals are foreign origin.

Majority of them are covering the subject Libraries and I.T and Other Aspects. The library holds less than five percent of cited titles in Scientific and Technical Libraries and Agricultural Information, Libraries, Users and Services.

Sri Krishna Devaraya University library is subscribing only 3 journals in the field of Library and Information Science. All the 3 journals are published in India. It is clear that the University library does not subscribe to journals published in foreign countries. The available journals mainly cover the sub-disciplines University Libraries, Users and Services and Public Libraries and Community Information Services.

The availability of cited books in the Andhra University library reveal that out of the total cited books, 681 (40.43%) books are available in the Andhra University library of which 324 are Indian books and 357 are foreign books. The research scholars of Andhra University have referred 401 books for their research requirements of which 196 are Indian origin and 205 are foreign origin.

The sub-discipline University Libraries, Users and Services stood in the first place with regarding percent of available books cited by researchers; followed by Scientific and Technical Libraries. However in the sub-disciplines

Medical Information, Libraries, Users and Services; Other Libraries, Users and Services; Marketing of Library Information Services and Products; and Agriculture Information, Libraries, Users and Services the library holds less than three percent of cited books.

As far as Sri Venkateswara University is concerned, out of the total books cited in the present study 623 (36.99%) books are found to be available in this library of which 308 are Indian publications and 315 are foreign publications.

The scholars in the discipline Library and Information Science have referred to 215 books of which 86 are of Indian origin and 129 are foreign origin. The sub-discipline University Libraries, Users and Services stood in the first place followed by Other Libraries, Users and Services regarding the percent of availability of books cited by researchers .However in the sub-disciplines Medical Information, Libraries, Users and Services; Public Libraries and Community Information Services; Agriculture Information, Libraries, Users and Services; Other Aspects; Marketing of Library Information Services and Products and Bibliometrics the library holds less than ten percent of cited books.

Out of total books cited in the present study 518 (30.76%) books are available in Osmania University library. 270 books are Indian publications while 248 books are foreign publications. Out of these 518 books, the research scholars affiliated to Osmania University referred 104 books.

The sub-discipline Libraries and I.T. occupied the first place in percent of availability of cited books, followed by Public Libraries and Community Information Services; Other Aspects; Bibliometrics; College Libraries, Users and Services; Scientific and Technical Libraries and Agriculture Information, Libraries, Users and Services.

The analysis of availability of cited books in Sri Krishna Devaraya University library indicates that out of total books cited in present study 388 (23.04%) are found to be available in this particular library of which 210 are Indian books and 178 are foreign books. The researchers of the Sri Krishna Devaraya University have referred 64 books. Out of these 64 books, 37 books are Indian publications and 27 books are foreign publications.

The percent of book citations reveal that University Libraries, Users and Services stood in the first place followed by Public Libraries and Community Information Services and Other Aspects.

Validation of Hypotheses

The researcher has arrived at the following conclusions by testing the validity of hypotheses formulated.

The first hypothesis states that journals are important bibliographic form for means of communication. This statement is found to be true as the present study suggest journals as the most preferred vehicles of scholarly communication. Most of the researchers depend upon journals to meet their day to day information requirements. The results in the study indicate that journal citations come to 7925 (57.59%).

The second hypothesis states that literature in Library and Information Science is scattered over wide range of subjects. The statement is also found to be valid as the literature in the discipline Library and Information Science is distributed among 28 subjects.

The third hypothesis states that most of the literature in Library and Information Science is published in English. The statement stands out to be valid as very high percentage of literature cited in Library and Information Science theses is published in English language which reflects the global nature of this language and hence it can be concluded that English is a universal language for scholarly communication.

The fourth hypothesis states that major producers of literature in Library and Information Science are developed countries. This statement is true as the findings in the study show that most of the literature cited in Library and Information Science is published from United States of America and United Kingdom. This shows the importance of literature published from the developed countries and their concern for research activity.

The fifth hypothesis states that collaborative research is more prevalent than individual research in Library and Information Science. This is not true as single authorship is more than collaborative authorship. But we can observe an increasing trend towards collaborative research and this is clear from the period 1913-1922.

The sixth hypothesis states that self-citation is a common phenomenon among the researchers in the field of Library and Information Science. This statement is not valid as the results in the study indicate low self-citation rate in the literature of Library and Information Science.

The seventh hypothesis states that positive relation exists between reference period and the number of citations in the discipline Library and Information Science. This point seems to be valid, since the findings of the present study depict an increasing trend in the number of citations with an increase in the age of citations.

According to eighth hypothesis citations relating to journal literature in Library and Information Science conforms to Bradoford's Law of Scattering. The findings of both verbal and graphical formulation however does not support this hypothesis. Hence the Bradford's Law of Scattering is found to be invalid in the discipline of Library and Information Science.

The ninth hypothesis formulated states that researchers in Library and Information Science generally utilizes current information for their information requirements. However this statement is not completely true as the results in the present study indicates that researchers in Library and Information Science discipline have used both current and aged literature to conduct their research activity.

The tenth hypothesis states that there exists a positive relation between the number of citations with multiple authors and period. However the hypothesis formulated is found to be valid from the findings as we can observe an increase in the number of multi-authored papers with a progress in reference period. This clearly indicates that there is an increasing trend towards collaborative research activities in the discipline Library and Information Science.

According to eleventh hypothesis, the citation behaviour of scientists in Library and Information Science is generally influenced by place of publication. The statement, indicates that a research scholar utilizes information produced in his or her own country compared to literature produced in other countries. This statement is found to be invalid as the researchers have equally relied upon the publications from foreign countries like U.S.A. and U.K.

The twelfth hypothesis indicates that the University library plays a vital role in augmenting the research activity in the discipline Library and Information Science. But the results indicate that the statement is partially true as the University libraries surveyed are found to be subscribing to only small percent of cited journals by the LIS researchers. Similar findings are noticed in terms of availability of books as limited numbers of cited books are available in university libraries to the researchers.

Various sections in this chapter discussed about the major findings of the study. The validity of the findings have also been assessed keeping in view the objectives and hypothesis of the study on one hand and the findings of earlier studies on the other hand. The following section covers general observations made and suggestions offered by the researcher pertaining to the future research as well as quality of research in Library and Information Science.

Suggestions

Bibliometrics is an emerging thrust area of research in the field of Library and Information Science. Bibliometric studies are used to identify the pattern of publication, authorship and citation analysis with the hope that such regularities can give an insight into the dynamics of the area under consideration. This consequently sheds more light on our knowledge of the structure of subject literature for better organization of information resources.

Further, Bibliometrics has established itself as a viable and distinctive research technique for studying science of science based on citation data. Citoanalytical study of doctoral dissertations or theses which are the products of research activity form an important source of information. Such studies may be useful for acquisition of materials, provision of better services to patrons. Answers to questions like what part of literature is cited most, for how long the literature remains useful to readers, and languages of most cited publications provides guidance to collection development policies, individual item selection, and retention and binding decision.

Such studies have been attempted in different subjects in natural and physical sciences but paucity of such works exists in humanities and social sciences. However, some significant studies have been conducted in some areas of social sciences such as history, anthropology, political sciences, sociology and agricultural economics (Kaiser and Sharda).

Moreover, researchers' citation patterns reflect dynamic research priorities, by offering guidance to academic libraries which support campus research and teaching activities. Library support for scientific research has become quite a challenge towards the end of the 20th century due to shrinking budgets, escalating cost of scientific journals, and the advent of the electronic journals. So local citation patterns can help the librarians make objective selection decisions and create a collection that will be more widely used.

Citation studies reveal much about scholarly communication and can be an effective tool to guide collection development in academic libraries. These studies typically take one of the two directions: "local" or "global". It is believed that studies of local faculty yield more relevant results than "global" research to assist librarians making serial selection decisions for their institutions. Aside from practical applications, citation studies offer objective insight into the fundamental research behaviour of researchers.

Research is the most remarkable phenomena of development in any subject. It is the most important tool for the advancement of knowledge, scientific discoveries, technological achievement and scholarly publications. It is carried out to develop new concepts and theories and to contribute towards new knowledge.

All subjects require continuous research support to develop as a discipline. Library and information science which has developed as an independent and vital discipline in the last century needs constant improvement and development through research.

Like any other discipline, the levels of research in LIS extend from book writing, paper writing to writing of learned treatise and monograph. The aim of research work in LIS like any other discipline has been towards the advancement of subject and contributing towards new knowledge. Though research in LIS started during the second decade of this century, substantial growth has been registered during the

1990's only. The research under university supervision started after independence, but individual research started in thirties with Dr. S.R. Ranganathan whose research contribution in various areas of librarianship is still considered to be relevant and valuable in promoting and motivating the scientific and pragmatic research in LIS both at national and international level.

Traditionally LIS research activities in India have been dominated by qualitative research methods. Therefore, in order to broaden the research perspectives in LIS, it is important to introduce current research programmes in quantitative research paradigm. In this context, Bibliometrics has prime relevance since it represents a unique set of techniques for monitoring and analysis of information resource and for the management of knowledge in social and organizational contexts. Keeping this purpose in view the present study has investigated the use of literature in the doctoral dissertations of Library and Information Science researchers accepted by different Universities of Andhra Pradesh through the analysis of citations.

The review of literature reveals that several studies have been made on the application of Bibliometric techniques to various disciplines. The sources chosen for study includes journal literature, theses, citation indexes, individual and organizational contributions in different disciplines. Number of review articles comparing the application, limitation and advantages of different techniques also have been published. The studies ranged from the bibliometric study of individual journal contributions to the analysis of the content of online databases .The area of bibliometrics attracted the attention of many researchers to conduct studies at MLISc, MPhil and PhD levels in Library and Information Science schools in India. Majority of them are found to be citation studies using citation analysis techniques aimed at researching the literature use pattern of researchers in a particular subject.

The present study is also one among them conducted at the doctoral level to make an in-depth analysis of literature used by the researchers in the discipline of Library and Information Science in their research pursuit.

It is also observed that collaborative efforts are being made at the international level to study the research trends in Library and Information Science. Number of countries has collaborated for making Bibliometric study of their research literature in order to examine the growth of research and its development over a period of time and identify any changes in the topics studied. These studies will reflect variations of emphasis and trends in research in the countries examined. Each country will have its own research profile, which may not follow very closely the international trends. Earlier studies have proved these observations. Based on such studies we can seek explanation for national differences of individual countries so that, one can suggest how the social institutionalization of LIS has an effect on research output. Findings from earlier studies pointed out that a developed social structure of the discipline has a positive impact on the quality and quantity of research output. The review of literature by the researcher also supports the above findings. LIS professionals in India should also start making such efforts to collaborate with other countries to take up such projects in LIS to help the profession develop and gain international recognition.

The overall distribution of theses submission indicates that there were 9 submissions only from 1982-1991, and 62 submissions from 1992-2004, on an average 3 theses were produced by the four universities in Andhra Pradesh. The LIS theses submissions across the state reflect that Andhra University received the highest number of awardees followed by Sri Venkateswara University, Osmania University and Sri Krishna Devaraya University.

It is observed that a large proportion of doctoral research in LIS is produced in LIS departments of well established old Universities. Another interesting observation is that men are more in number among those awarded with doctoral degree.

The study carried out revealed that the research topics undertaken by LIS scholars of Library and Information Science at doctoral level in the universities of Andhra Pradesh were done on varied subjects like Agriculture Information, Libraries, Users and Services; Bibliometrics; College Libraries, Users and Services; Libraries and IT; Marketing of Library Information Services and Products; Medical Information, Libraries, Users and Services; Other Aspects; Other Libraries, Users and Services; Public Libraries and Community Information Services; Scientific and Technical Libraries; and University Libraries, Users and Services. It is also observed that areas like academic libraries, in particular the University Libraries and College Libraries have gained noticeable attention by LIS researchers. Most of the research studies are found to be limited to local libraries and issues. This may be due to lack of financial aid to conduct research. However there is ample scope for further research in the above mentioned areas.

The findings of the study indicates that LIS research in the state of Andhra Pradesh is not progressing much towards the new and emerging areas of librarianship. But the library profession has widely accepted the challenges of information and communication technology. The shift from collection management to information and knowledge management, the change in its domain and structure calls for a change in the mind set of the library professionals. Areas like management of electronic library, virtual library, multimedia, web based services, Internet, commercial information system, use of new and advanced management techniques, online education and training for users need the attention of LIS researchers.

However, the findings reveal that LIS research in Andhra Pradesh is gathering momentum and generating confidence among the LIS professionals. Factors like recognition of official position, salary scale, UGC norms for career promotion etc have been the motivating factors. Since users are most important for the libraries, most of the researchers have been concentrating on user information needs and information seeking behaviour. Citation analysis and biographical studies have also been popular topics of research, as they provide useful feedback and helps in developing a relevant and user oriented collections. Most of the research done in these areas justifies the relevance of research. Certain areas like cost effectiveness, quality control, publishing pattern, etc. that have been neglected need to be explored more. Since IT has been challenging the LIS Profession, more IT-based research needs to be taken up by the LIS researchers. Such studies help to assess the impact of emerging technologies on library management and services on one hand and give direction in exploiting the advantage of these technologies in providing improved and qualitative services to the users on the other.

Journal Ranking

Under the crucial situation of the increasing size and complexity of the subject, mounting pressure of readers and the multiplying financial crunch of the library, the rank list of periodicals can serve as a tool in selection of core journals in the field.There is a great deal of advice in the library and documentation literature on how to decide which periodicals to buy. Techniques suggested often involve ranking the 'potential' journals in some way, e.g., by citation analysis, usage, time spent on reading, user preferences etc., with the implication that the ones coming out on top are the most likely best buys. Garfield (1976), therefore, confidently said that the result of this type of citation analysis appear to be of great potential value in the management of library journal collection.

The present study presents a ranked list of journals in library and information science based on citation analysis. This list, also serves as an authentic tool to the librarians and information scientists in selecting journals in LIS for subscription. This in turn helps them in the optimum utilization of their library budget for the benefit of their clientele, and in preparation of documentation lists for circulation.

Education & Training in the use of Bibliometric techniques

At present in India, syllabus of few LIS departments have an independent paper on Bibliometrics covering both theory and application of Bibliometric techniques. There is a need to introduce such courses at postgraduate level or at doctoral level programmes in more number of LIS departments. Such courses will also meet the demand of refreshing and stimulating the use of quantitative studies in the field of library and information science.

The proposed course on Bibliometrics may cover areas like: concept of Bibliometrics, review of historical development of Bibliometrics, Bibliometric laws and interpretations; information retrieval and search techniques; mapping of social and cognitive structure; Webometrics; text and data mining; developing and implementing bibliometric research design models; collecting, organising and visualizing bibliometric data; application of statistical tests to bibliometric data; demonstration of practical tools and application areas and discussion on research students design of topic of research at micro level.

Furthermore, Bibliometrics can be applied in a large number of contexts, for example scientific and social studies, research evaluation, knowledge management, environment scanning, tracing trends and development in a particular field, optimizing library and information resources.

Information input is crucial for conducting the research activity in any field of knowledge. Scientist's approach to information varies based on the various stages of research activity. Their current needs for information are usually coupled with retrospective information needs. A universal finding of many surveys of the literature use habits of researchers is that the frequently used sources of information are periodicals which account for over half of their reading. The same has been traced in the present study. In addition to journals, other sources occasionally referred by scientists include books, conference proceedings, reports, theses, standards and patents. Each of these documents has a specific role to play in the dissemination of research information.

Another important observation made by the researcher is that for collection of research data the researchers have depended mostly on the available information from the organisational and other local libraries and information centers. Availability and access to required information are the two factors that influence the quality of any research activity. The university library is bestowed with this responsibility to serve the information needs of researchers by making available the pertinent information to them. Maintaining the up to date and relevant collection of different forms and providing wider access to remotely available information sources are the effective means for meeting the objectives of the library. Dr V S K Library, Andhra University is one of the oldest university libraries in South India acting as a rich source of information to the researchers. Researchers from different parts of the country, working especially in Science and Technology areas visit the library for consulting the valuable collection in the library. Very often, the library also supplies the xerox copies of required material on demand to the external users through postal services. Since its inception the collection in the library is steadily growing in its size. The proportion of relevant collections in various subjects is satisfactory, since the selection of the titles is based on the suggestions from the concerned subject teachers. The study of the composition of the collection in Library and Information Science shows that most of the standard subject books available are older editions. Hence there is a need to update with latest editions. Further, the status of book collection in the university libraries warrants formulation of sound acquisition policies to improve the quality of the library collections.

Regarding the availability of journal literature in Library and Information Science, few of the journals in the ranked list are available in the holding of these libraries. This may be due to the cuts in periodical budgets in recent years and also due to the hike in periodical subscriptions thereby affecting the research activity in the campus. However, from 1st January 2004, University Grants Commission (UGC), India has initiated a consortia of universities in India to provide online access to electronic journals to facilitate and sustain the on going research programs at the university level. To launch this program, to offer value added services to the university's academic and research communities, powerful Internet connectivity through ERNET, India has been provided. The total cost of launching the UGC INFONET program was borne by the UGC. As per the MOU the universities have to bear only the yearly maintenance cost. INFLIBNET, Ahmedabad is a coordinating agency for this program, which on behalf of the individual universities, bargains with different publishers and vendors of electronic journals and suppliers of databases in number of subjects. Based on the feedback about the journal requirement of individual universities, INFIBNET decides the number and types of the journals and databases to be subscribed and accessed. UGC INFONET service is really a boon to the Indian academic and research community. The present study reveals that all the four University libraries covered in the study have the UGC INFONET facility from 2004 onwards. The facility was introduced in Andhra University, Sri Venkateswara University, Osmania University in different years. They started providing access to Electronic journals through the UGC INFONET programme from 2004, where as Sri Krishnadevaraya University started offering this service from 2005 onwards. Overcoming the barriers of distance and time, it is providing seamless and fast access to the global information. The current researchers in LIS in these four universities now can access freely a wide range of information sources covering both current and historical information available through UGC Internet services. They can update their knowledge with the latest advances in their field of interest accessing the current information related to latest techniques, methods and processes. The research community now can share and exchange their research findings with fellow researchers through powerful electronic messaging system.

In addition to this, database management and net working technologies are supporting the librarians and information scientists and the users of information in many ways. Besides helping in enhancing access to the internal information base of the local information center, they have the potential to assist in developing and distributing qualitative value added services to users. Effective reference and current awareness services may be offered by the libraries exploiting the resources available on-line using these networking technologies.

Another important technological revolution that is alarming the library professionals is digital revolution. An increasing proposition of information being produced is created, stored and can be retrieved in digital form. Just to keep pace with the flood of new information, the libraries of the future must be able to handle the digital and electronic resources available in different subject fields. Number of digital resources in Library and Information Science and its sub disciplines are available on Internet. They have to be exploited by the libraries to provide better services to the researchers. And also skills and tools need to be developed to use digital libraries and Internet resources effectively.

Latest technologies no doubt are opening new horizons for the libraries and information centers in developing countries and are enabling them to handle the challenges posed by changes in internal and external environment in a cost-effective manner. We have almost reached the fourth stage of Lancaster's prediction and must also realize that technology is going to play a significant role during the twenty first century in the field of scholarly communication. The role of library professionals is also changing. Their new roles as network navigator, consultant, instructor intermediary and searcher will accelerate since most of the end users are not equipped with required skills and experience to handle the latest technologies. The changing environment also necessitates the end-user training programmes for the efficient use of the technology adopted in libraries.

It is hoped that this study would provide some insights into literature use pattern of Indian researchers in Library and Information Science. With in the limitations and parameters of its scope and design it is hoped that the research work presented in the foregoing chapters has thrown up some interesting results and intervenes. Bibliometric studies have been made in various areas especially in science and pertaining to various aspects of citation analysis and citation behavioral patterns. The present study aims to draw the attention to the literature use pattern by the researchers in Library and Information Science and to provide insight into some of the trends that may affect the future research. There are many other applications of bibliometric laws and techniques that may be studied in depth in future by the researchers in this field.

Regarding the future research in the field, the following observations have been made. Despite the fact that the LIS research has made significant studies during the last few decades, we must concentrate on building a stronger conceptual/theoretical framework. The academics should seriously consider the scope and importance of their research topics before publishing. The profession must be on a continuous spiral upward and conduct more theory building research.

The LIS researchers should consider "branching out" by conducting and publishing research in non-traditional areas of Library and Information Science. The profession also must examine and cite more research conducted in other related disciplines and incorporate those findings, conclusions and recommendations to build a stronger framework and continue broadening the LIS academics focus and breadth of knowledge.

Studies on LIS research productivity should be replicated periodically, at least once in ten years to determine the changes that have taken place as a result of research and development in the profession. Such studies may help the profession to adequately respond to the challenges faced by the profession.

Another area which also warrants further study is into published research as most of the findings are not published. Research into these areas raise a number of interesting questions which could take the studies on published research output forward.

After independence, number of LIS schools offering research programmes in India at Masters, M.Phil and doctoral levels have been increased.

It is observed that publications in the form of books arising from the 71 analysed theses are minimal. This may be due to the fact that where there is no pressure to publish for career growth, graduates publish less or nothing. Arguably, research is complete only when it is published. However, some of the researchers have published their research findings in professional journals. The tradition that requires research supervision to produce joint publication with their students from the research project or encourage their students to publish should be promoted. This would attract good research work, where the authors are reluctant to publish because they are not under any pressure or obliged to do so as opposed to university academics that is compelled to publish.

The study also reveals that specialization and location of senior academics that determine the doctoral research levels, topics, output and other staff related variables favour previously advantaged universities. In this context, also there is a need to conduct future research on the post research publication activities of the researchers in the discipline of Library and Information Science.

Findings from the present study provide data on issues like, determining doctoral research capacity in LIS in Andhra Pradesh; knowledge and comparison of doctoral level research potential; selection of doctoral research institution; staff exchange programmes; research partnership. The rapidly growing research capacity in the state and the country offers promising opportunities for research and professional linkages as well as manpower training at graduate levels for the people of Andhra Pradesh and India. LIS institutions in the country have the potential to play a leading role with regard to LIS research in India.

In conclusion it may be said that, this study provided new and foundational data to characterize and measure the doctoral research activity of a group of library information scientists in the state of Andhra Pradesh. This data could contribute to a larger project where results could be compared with other disciplines, both closely and distantly related. Objective and substantive information gathered through present study will provide logical base for taking decisions on collection development.

Bibliography

Aflolabi, M. Productivity of Journals, which Published Nigeraian Library Literature 1910-198. *Annals of Library Science and Documentation*, 39, 1992, p. 139-144.

Aiyepeku, Wilson O. The Bradord Distribution Theory: The Compounding of Bradford Periodical Literature in Geography. *Journal of Documentation*, 33(3), 1977, p. 210-219.

Alabi, G. Bradford's Law and its Application. *International Library Review*, 11, 1979, p. 151-158.

Alvarez, P. and Pulgarin, A. The Research Model, Measuring the Impact of Scientific Journals: Analytical Chemsitry. *Journal of the American Society of Information Science*, 47, 1996, p. 458-467.

Anand, A.K. Analysis of Communication in Journal of the Indian Chemical Society. *IASLIC Bulletin*, 26, 1981, p. 17-21.

Anand, J.K. Journal of Documentation 1980-1989: Analytical Study. *Library Herald*, 30, 1991, p. 81-123.

Aravind, P. The Literature of Physical Anthropology: A Citation Analysis. Sri Padmavathi Mahila Viswa Vidyalayam, Ph.D. Thesis, 1996.

Aravinda, P. Bibliometric Study of Citations in Annual Review of Anthropology. Tirupati, Sri Venkateswara University. M.L.I.Sc, 1986 (Unpublished).

Arjunlal. Ranking of Periodicals in the field of Soil Science. *Annals of Library Science and Documentation*, 37, 1990, p. 67-73.

Atkins, P.W. Physical Chemistry. In: McGraw-Hill Encyclopaedia of Science and Technology. Parker, S.P. Ed. Vol. 10. New York: McGraw-Hill, p. 263-266

Ayers, Jerry B. Journals and Conference Proceedings of Chemical History, Education and Documentation. *Journal of Information and Computer Sciences*, 21, 1981, p. 71-72.

Balog, C. Multiple Authorship and Author Collaboration in Agricultural Research Publications. *Journal of Research Communication Studies*, 2, 1980, p. 159-168.

Bankapur, M.B and Kumbhar, M. Bibliometrics and Scienometric Tools for Measurement of Productivity in Agricultural Research. *Indian Journal at information Library and Society,* 6, 199, p. 169-178.

Baraua, D.K. and Indranarayana Sengupta: An Evaluation, *Indian Journal of Information, Library and Society*. 5, 1992, p. 1-23.

Baugham, J C. A Structural analysis of the Literature of Sociology. *Library Quarterly*. 44, 1 974, p. 293-307.

Beaver, D de B and Rosen, R. Studies in Scientific Collaboration. Part I. The Professional Origins of Scientific Coauthorship. *Scientometrics,* 1, 1978, p. 65-84.

Beaver, D de B and Rosen, R. Studies in Scientific Collaboration. Part II. The Professional Origins of

Scientific Coauthorship, Research Productivity and Visibility in the French Scientific Elite. *Scientometrics*, 1, 1979, p. 133-149.

Begum, K.J. and Rajendra N. Research Collaboration in Zoological Literature A citation analysis. *ILA Bulletin*. 25, 1989, p. 19-28.

Bonitz, M. "Evidence for the Invalidity of the Bradford's Law for the Single Scientist. *Scientometrics*. 2, 1980, p. 203-220.

Bonzi, Susan. And Snyder, Herbert W. Pattern of Self-citation across the Fields of Inquiry. In: Proceedings of the 53rd Annual Meeting of the American Society for Information Science. New Jersey: Learned Information Inc., 1990, p. 204-207.

Bookstein, A. The Bibliometric Distributions. *Library Quarterly*. 46, 1976, p. 416-425.

Borgman, C. Bibliometrics and Scholarly Communication: Editor's Introduction. *Communication Research*, 16, 1989, p. 583-599.

Bottle, R.T. and Gong, Y.T. A Bibliometric Study on the Ageing and Content Topology Relationship of the Biochemical Literature. *Journal of Information Science*, 13, 1987, p. 59-63.

Brace, W. Frequently Cited Authors And Periodicals in Library and Information Science dissertations 1941-71. *Journal of Library and Information Science*. 2, 1976, p. 16-34.

Bradford, S.C. Sources of Information on Specific Subjects. *Engineering*, 137, 1934, p. 85-86.

Bradford, S.C. Sources of Information on Specific Subjects. *Engineering*. 137, 1934, p.85-86.

Braun, T. and Others. The Scientometric Weight of 50 Nations in 27 Science Areas, 1989-1993. Part I. All fields Combined, Mathematics, Engineering, Chemistry and Physics. *Scientometrics*, 33, 1995, p. 263-293.

Braun, T. and Others. World Science in Eighties: National Performance in Publication Output and Citation Impact, 1985, 1989 versus 1980-1984.

Brayn, T. and Others. World Science in Eighties: National Performance in Publication Output and Citation Impact, 1985 ; 1989 versus 1980-1984. Part I. All Science Fields Combined, Physics and Chemistry. *Scientometrics*, 29, 1994, p. 299-334.

British Standard Glossary of Documentation of Terms. London: British Standard Institution, 1976.

Broadman, E. Choosing Psychology Journals. *Medical Library Association Bulletin*. 32, 1944, p. 479-483.

Brookes, B.C. The Derivation and Application of the Bradford-Zipf Distribution. *Journal of Documentation*, 24, 1968, p. 247-265.

Brookes, B.C. The Growth, Utility and Obsolescence of Scientific Periodical Literature. *Journal of Documentation*, 26, 1970, p. 283-294.

Brookes, B.C. The Growth, Utility and Obsolescence of Scientific Periodical Literature. *Journal of Documentation*. 26, 1970, p. 283-285.

Brookes, B.C. Theory of the Bradford's Law. *Journal of Documentation* .33, 1977, p. 285-290.

Brown, C.H. Scientific Serials. Association of College and Research Libraries Monograph No. 16. U.S.A.: Chicago Libraries,1956.

Brown, P. The Half-Life of the Chemical Literature. *Journal of the American Society for Information Science*, 31, 1980, p. 61-63.

Burton, R.E and Kesler R.W. Hatf-life of Some Scientific and Technical Literature. *American Documentation* 11, 1960, p.18~25.

Burton, R.E. and Kebler, R.W. Half-life of some Scientific and Technical Literature. *American Documentation*, 11, 1960, p. 18-22.

Campbell, F. Theory of the National and International Bibliography. London, 1896.

Chakraborty, R. Citation Analysis of Petrological Literature. *Lucknow Librarian*. 15, 1983, p. 98-105.

Chakraborty, R. Journal Citation in Masters Theses : one Measurement of Journal Collection. *Journal of American Society for Information Science*. 24, 1973, p. 347-355.

Chen, Ching-Chin. How do the Scientists meet their Information Needs? *Special Libraries*, 65, 1974, p. 272-280.

Chen, Ching-Chin. The Use Patten of Physics Literature in a Large Academic Research Library. *Journal of the American Society for Information Science*, 23, 1972, p. 254-270.

Clarke, B.L. Multiple Authorship Trends in Scientific Papers. *Science*, 143, 1964, p. 822-824.

Clenens et al. Careers in Print: Books, Journals and Scholarly Reputations. *The American Journal of Sociology*, 101(2), 1995, p. 433-494.

Cline G.S. Application of Bradford's Law to Citation Data. *College and Research Libraries*. 42, 1981 p. 53-67.

Coats, A.W. The role of Scholarly Journals in the History of Economics: An Essay, *Journal of Economic Literature*, 9(1), 1971, p. 29-44.

Cole, F.J. and Eales, N.B. The History of Comparative Anatomy. Part I. A Statistical Analysis of the Literature. *Science Progress*, 11, 1917, p. 578-596.

Coleman, S.R. Disciplinary Variables that Affect the Shape of the Bradford's Bibliograph. *Scientometrics*, 29, 1994, p. 59-81.

Coupe, T. Revealed Performances. Worldwide Rankings of Economists and Economic Departments. Unpublished Manuscripts, Free University of Brussels. http://homepages.ulb.ac.be\~tcoupe. 2000

Cronin, B. Comparative Citation Rankings of Authors in Mongographic Journal Literature: A Study of Sociology, 101(2), 1997, p. 433-494.

De Oliveira, Silas Marques. Citation Pattern in Veterinary Medicine Dissertations. *Annals of Library Science and Documentation*, 31, 1984, p. 147-155.

Deo, V.N. Citation Study of the Marathwada University Journal: A case Study of the use Patterns by Scholars. *Annals of Library Science and Documentation*, 38, 1991, p. 85-99.

Devarajan, G and Vijayalakshmi, V. Applied Economics Dissertations: A citation study. *IASUC Bulletin*. 27, 1982, p. 9-15.

Dewitt, T.W. Science Citation Index and Chemistry. *Scientometrics*, 2, 1980, p. 265-275.

Diamond, A.M. The Core Journals in Economics, *Current Contents*, 21, 1989, p. 4-11.

Dimitroff, A. and Arlitsch, K. Self-citations in Library and Information Science Literature. *Journal of Documentation*, 51, 1995, p. 44-56.

Diodato, V. Dictionary of Bibliometrics. New York: Haworth Press, 1994.

Egghe, L. and Rousseau, R. Introduction to Informetrics. Amsterdam: Elsevier, 1990.

Egghe, L. and Rousseau, R. Reflections on a Deflection: A note on different causes of the Gross Droop. *Scientometrics*, 14, 1988, p. 493-511.

Elish Raju and Kavitha. Frequently Cited Periodicals by Indian Organic Chemistry: A citation analysis. *Annals of Library Science and Documentation.* 33, 1986, p. 56-67.

Fairthorne, R.A. Empirical Hyperbolic Distributions (Bradford-Zipf-Mandelbrot) for Bibliometric Description and Prediction. *Journal of Documentation*, 25, 1969, p. 319-343.

Ferguson, R.D. Information Science: A Bibliometric Evaluation of the Information Analysis Concept Boston. Boston University, Ph.D. 1980 (Unpublished).

Flowers, B.H. Survey of Information Needs of Physicists and Chemists. *Journal of Documentation*, 21, 1965, p. 83-112.

Fussler, R.H. Characteristics of Research Literature Used by Chemists and Physicists in the United States. *Library Quarterly*, 19, 1949, p. 19-35.

Garfield, E. Citation Analysis as a Tool in Journal. Analysis. *Science*. 1978, 1972, p. 471-478.

Garfield, E. Citation Indexing its theory and application in Science, Technology and Humanities. New York: John Wiley, 1979.

Garfield, E. Essays of an Information Scientists. 3vols. Philadelphia: ISI Press, 1977, 1980.

Garfield, E. Significant Journals of Science. *Nature*, 264, 1976, p. 609-615.

Garfield, E. Social Science Citation Index Journal Citation Reports. Philadelphia: Institute for Scientific Information, 1987, 1992.

Garfield, E. Who will win the Noble Prize in Economics? Here is a Forecast based on Citation Indicators. *Current Contents*, 11, 1990, p. 3-7.

Garg, K.C. and Rag M.K.D. Bibliornetric Analysis of Scientific productivity: A case study of an Indian Physics Laboratory. *Scientometrics*. 13, 1988, p. 261-268.

Garg, Kailash Chandra. and Ashok Kumar. Information Gathering Habits of the R&D Scientists: A Survey. *Annals of Library Science and Documentation*, 31, 1984, p. 63-74.

Garrett, A.B. Chemistry In: McGraw-Hill of Encyclopaedia of Science and Technology. Parker, S.P. Ed. New York: McGraw-Hill, 1982, p. 84-87.

Garudadwajan, Murthy, H.S.S. Bradford Distribution: An Application to the Study of Core Collection of Periodicals in Aeronautics and Related Subjects. *Library Science*, 20(3), 1983, p. 159-190.

Goffman, W. and Morris, Thomas G. Bradford's Laws and Library Acquistions, *Nature*, 226, 1970, p. 922-923.

Goffman, W. and Warren, K.S. Dispersion of Papers among Journals based on a Mathematical Analysis of two diverse Medical Literature, *Nature*, 221, 1969, p. 1205-1207.

Gordon, M.D. A Critical Reassessment of Inferred Relations between Multiple Authorship, Scientific Collaboration, the Production of Papers and their Acceptance for Publication. *Scientometrics*, 2, 1980, p. 193-201.

Govinda Raju, N., *Bibliometric Applications: Study of Literature Use Patterns,* Akansha Publishing House, New Delhi, 2009.

Grefrath, Richard W. A Study of Citations to 308 Journal Articles in Chemistry Published in 1963. *Journal of Chemical Documentation*, 14, 1974, p. 95-98.

Griffith, B.C. and Others. The Ageing of Scientific Literature: A Citation Analysis. *Journal of Documentation*, 35, 1979, p. 179-196.

Griffith, B.C. Bibliometrics: some tools and results. In: Egghe, L; Rousseau, R. Ed. Informatics 85/88. Amsterdam: Elsevier, 1988, p. 85-95.

Gross, O.V. Bradford's Law and the Kenanatherton Data. *American Documentation*, 19(1), 1967, p. 46.

Gross, P.L.K. and Gross, E.M. College Libraries and Chemical Education. *Science*, 66, 1927, p. 385-389.

Guay, Y. Emergence of Basic Research on the Periphery: Organic Chemistry in India. 1907-1926. *Scientometrics*, 10, 1986, p. 77-94.

Gupta. B.M. Application of Bradford's Law to Citation Data of Ethiopian Medical Journal. *Annals of Library Science and Documentation*. 38, 1991, p. 85-98.

Gupta, B.M. Analysis of Distribution of the Age of the Citations in Theoretical Population Genetics. *Scientometrics*, 40, 1997, p. 139-162.

Gupta, B.M. and Nagpal, M.P.K. Citation Analysis and its Applications: A Review. *Herald of Library Science*, 18, 1979, p. 86-93.

Gupta, D.K. A Citography on Lepichon's Article on Sea-floor Spreading on Continental Drift: Application of Bradford's Law. *IASLIC Bulletin*, 28(2), 1960, p. 31-36.

Gupta, D.K. Application of Bradford's Law to Citation Data of Ethiopian Medical Journal. *Annals of Library Science and Documentation*, 38, 1991, p. 85-98.

Gupta, D.K. Collaborative Research Trends in Geophysics. *Scientometrics*, 28, 1993, p. 287-296.

Gupta, Davendra K. Bibliometric Study of AIDS Literature. *Annals of Library Science and Documentation*, 36, 1988, p. 34-42.

Gupta, Davendra K. Periodical Literature of Exploration of Geophysics: Obsolescence Factors and Patterns. *Library Science with a Slant to Documentation*, 21, 1984, p. 205-226.

Gupta, R.C. and Others. Maintenance of Periodicals Collection: A Statistical Case Study. *Annals of Library Science and Documentation*, 25, 1978. p. 101-105.

Gupta, Usha. Obsolescence of Physics Literature: Exponential Decrease of the Density of Citations to Physical Review Articles with Age. *Journal of the American Society*, 1990.

Hadley, E.H. Organic Chemistry. In: *Encyclopaedia of Chemistry*. Hampel, C.A. and Gessner, G.H. Eds. New York: Van Nostrand Reinhold, 1973. p. 763-765.

Haiqi, Z. The relationship of Authors to Multi-authored Pharmacology Research Papers. *International Forum on Information and Documentation*, 21, 1996, p. 10-23.

Hampel, C.A. and Hawley, G.G. Eds. Glossary of Chemical Terms. New York: Van Nostrand Reinhold, 1976.

Hart, R and Others. Funded and Non Funded Research: Characteristics of Authorship and Pattern of Collaboration in the 1986 Library and Information Science Literature. *Library and Information Science Research*, 12, 1990, p. 72-86.

Hawkins, Donald T. Electrochemistry Journals. *Journal of Chemical Information and Computer Sciences*, 17, 1977, p. 41-45.

Hawkins, Donald T. Unconventional Use of On-line Information Retrieval System: Online Bibliometric Studies. *Journal of American Society for Information Science*, 28, 1977, p. 13-18.

Heffner, A.G. Funded Research, Multiple Authorship and Subauthorship in four disciplines. *Scientometrics*, 3, 1981, p. 5-12.

Herner, S. Information Gathering Habits of Workers in Pure and Applied Sciences. *Industrial and Engineering Chemistry*, 46, 1954, p. 228-236.

Hertzel, D.H. History of the Development of Ideas in Bibliometrics. In: *Encyclopaedia of Library and Information Science*, Kent, A. and Lancour, H. Eds. Vol.42. New York: Marcel Dekker, 1987, p. 144-219.

Herubel, J.P. and VM and Buchannan, A.L. Citation Studies in the Humanities and Social Sciences: A Selective and Annotated Bibliography. *Collection Management*, 18, 1994, p. 89-137.

Hireppe, R. Supplement to a Bibliography of Bibliometrics and Citation Indexing, *Scientometrics*, 4, 1982, p. 241-270.

Hjerppe, R.A Bibliography of Bibliometrics and Citation Indexing and Analysis. Stockholm, Royal Institute of Technology Library, 1980.

Houghton, B. *Scientific Periodicals: Their Historical Development, Characteristics and Control*. London: Clive Bingley, 1975.

Hulme, E.W. *Statistical Bibliography in Relation to the Growth of Modern Civilization*. London: Grafton, 1923.

Hurd, Julie M. Interdisciplinary Research in the Sciences: Implications for the Library Organization. *College and Research Libraries*, 53, 1992, p. 283-297.

Joshi, Anupam N. and Maheswarappa, B.S. Multiple Authorship Trends in Different Subjects of Science and Technology: A Review of Literature. *ILA Bulletin*, 30, 1994, p. 31-37.

Joshi, Anupam N. and Maheswarappa, B.S. Multiple Authorship Trends and Collaborative Research among Indian Phytopathologists (1950-1989). *Indian Journal of Information, Library and Society*, 10, 1997, p. 31-40.

Kajberg, L. A Citation Analysis of Lis Serial Literature published in Denmark 1957-1986. *Journal of Documentation*. 52, 1996, 69-85.

Kalaitzidakis, Petal. - Ranking of Academic Journals and Institutions in Economics. 2001.

Kalyane V.L and Vidyasagar Rao, K. Collaboration trends in Sugarcane Research: A case study. *Annals of library science and documentation*. 39, 1992, P. 9-11.

Kannappanavar, B.U. and Nulvi C.N. Authorship Trend and Solo Research in Rural Transformation D.A Bibliometric Study: *ILA Bulletin*. 27, 1991, p. 38-39.

Kapoor, S.K. Citation Analysis of Earth Science Literature. *Annals of Library Science and Documentation*. 31, 1984, p. 56-62.

Kapoor, S.K. Citation Analysis of Earth Science literature. *Annals of Library Science and Documentation*. 31, 1984, p. 56-62.

Karisiddappa C.R. etc. Authorship Pattern and Collaborative Research Psychology. *IASUC Bulletin*. 35, 1990, p.73~78.

Katz, J.J. Inorganic chemistry. In: McGraw-Hill Encyclopaedia of Science and Technology. Parker SP, Ed. V 7. 1982. New York, McGraw-Hill, 1982, p. 167.

Kelland, J.l. and Young A.P. Citation as a form of library use Collection Management. 19, 1994, p.81-100.

Kendall, M.G. The Bibliography of Operations Research *Operations Research Quarterly*. 2, 1960, p.31-36.

Kessler, M.M. Bibliographic Coupling Between Scientific Papers. *American Documentation*. 14,1963, p.10 -11

King, J. A Review of Bibliometric and Other Science Indicators and their Role in Research Evaluation. *Journal of Information Science*. 13, 1987, p. 261-276.

Klaic, B. Scientometric Analysis of The Research Activities of Chemists from the "Rugjer Boskovic" Institute (Yugoslavia), 1976 -1985. *Scientometrics*. 19, 1990, p 11-24.

Krishan Kumar. Users Survey Concerning Teachers and Research Scholars in the Department of Chemistry, University of Delhi. *Annals of Library Science and Documentation*. 15, 1968, p.175-207.

Kronick D A. Authorship and Authority in the Scientific Periodicals of Seventeenth and Eighteenth Centuries. *The Library Quarterly*. 48, 1978, p. 255-275.

Kubota, Akiko. A Citation Analysis of Graduation Theses of the School of Library and Information Science, Keio University. *Library and Information Science*. 14, 1976, p. 193-209.

Kundu, A.K. Self-citations by Indian Library Scientists. *Annals of Library Science and Documentation*. 28, 1981, p.39-41.

Laband and Piette. The Relative Impact of Economics Journals. *Journal of Economic Literature*, 32, 1994, p. 640-666.

Laborie, Tim and Halperin, M. Citation Patterns In Library and Information Science Dissertations. *Journal of Education for Librarianship*. 16, 1976, p. 271 283.

Laitinen, H.A. Analytical Chemistry. In: McGraw-Hill Encyclopaedia of Science and Technology. Parker, S.P. Ed. V 1. New York: McGraw-Hill, 1982, p 494 497.

Lancaster, F.W. and Mehrotra, R. Where Indian Scientists Publish. *Current Science.* 53, 1984, p. 684-689.

Lancaster, F.W. Bibliometric Methods in Assessing Productivity and Impact Of Research. Sarada Ranganathan Endowment for Library Science : Bangalore, 1991.

Lancaster, F.W. The Measurement and Evaluation of Library Services. Washington D.C.: Information Resources Press, 1977.

Lawani, S.M. Bibliometrics: Its theoretical foundations, methods and applications. *Libri.* 31, 1981, p. 294-315.

Lawani, S.M. On The Heterogeneity and Classification of Author Self Citation. *Journal of the American Society for Information Science.* 33, 1982, p. 281-284.

Leimkuhler, F.F. The Bradford Distribution. *Journal of Documentation.* 13, 1967, p.197-207.

Levin, Richard 1. Statistics for Management. New Delhi: Prentice-Hall of India,1986.

LiBorie, T. and Halperin, M. Citation Pattern in Library and Information Science Dissertations. *Journal of Education for Librarianship*, 16, 1976, p. 271-283.

Liebowctz, S.J. and Palmer, J.P. Assessing the Relative Impact of Economics Literature, 21, 1984, p. 77-88.

Liebowitz S.J and Palmer J.P. Assessing the Relative Impacts of Economics Journals, *Journal of Economics Literature*, Vol. XXIII, 1984 p.77-88.

Line, M.B. and Sandison A. Obsolescence and Changes in the use of Literature with Time. *Journal of Documentation.* 30, 1974, p.283-325.

Line, M.B. The Half-Life of Periodical Literature: Apparent and Real Obsolescence. *Journal of Documentation.* 26, 1970, p. 46-52.

Line, M.B. The Influences of Types of Sources Used on the Results of Citation Analysis. *The Journal of Documentation*, 35, 4, 1979, p. 265-284.

Liner, G.H. Core Authors and Rankings in Economics, *Atlantic Economic Journal*, 29, 4, 2001, p.439-469.

Liu, M. The Complexities of Citation Practice: A Review of Citation Studies. *Journal of Documentation.* 49, 1993, p. 370-408.

Locketi, Mary, W. The Bradford's Distribution: A Review of the Literature, *Library and Information Science Research.* 11, 1989, 1934-1987, p. 21-36.

Longyear, R.M. Article Citations and Obsolescence in Musicological. Journals. *Notes.* 33, 1977, p. 563-571.

Lotka, A.J. Statistics - The Frequency Distribution of Scientific Productivity. *Journal of the Washington Academy of Sciences.* 16, 1926, p. 317-325

Mac Roberts, M.H. and Mac Roberts, B.R. Problems of Citation Analysis: A critical review. *Journal of the American Society for Information Science.* 40, 1989, p. 342-349.

Madkey, V.D and Rajyalakshmi, D. Citation Analysis of Ph.D. Theses in Environmental Science and Engineering Used By Neeri Scientists During 1977-1991. *Annals of Library Science and Documentation.* 41, 1994, p. 63-78.

Mahapatra, G. and Kaul R. Bibliometric Analysis of Citation Classics in Life Sciences. *Library Science with a Slant to Documentation and Information Studies.* 31, 1994, p. 129-134.

Mahapatra, G. and Kaul R. Self-Citation by Indian Botanists. *ILA bulletin.* 27, 1992, p. 161-167.

Mahapatra, M. Inclusion of Bibliometrics in Library and Information Curricula in India : A Proposal of a sample. IASUC Bulletin. 30, 1988, 173-179.

Mahendra, V. Mete and Deshmukh, P.P. Citation Analysis of Annals of Library Science and Documentation. *Annals of Library Science and Documentation.* 43, 1996, p. 11-25.

Maheswarappa, B.S. and Mathias, S.A. Authorial Collaboration in Various Disciplines of the Physical Sciences in India: 1987. A Bibliometric Study. *Journal of Library and Information Science.* 12, 1987, p. 136-155.

Maheswarappa, B.S. and Others. Collaborative Research in Science and Technology in India: A Bibliometric Study. *Journal of Library and Information Science.* 9, 1984, p. 154-159.

Maheswarappa, B.S. and Prakash, S.P. Literature use Pattern by the Researchers in the Field of Botany: A Citation Study of Doctoral Theses. *Journal of library and information science.* 7, 1982, p. 15-32.

Maheswarappa, B.S. Bibliographical Phenomena of Phytomorphology Literature: A Citation Analysis. *Annals of Library Science and Documentation.* 30, 1983, p. 22: 30.

Malin, M.Y. The Science Citation Index: A New Concept in Indexing. *Library Trends.* 16, 1968. p.374-387.

Martyn, J. Citation Analysis. *Journal of Documentation.* 31, 1975, p.290-297.

Meera. Plant Ecology Literature: A Bibliometric study. *International Information Communication and Education.* 17, 1998, p.41-59.

Miller, E. and Truesdell, E. Citation indexing: History and applications. *Drexel Library Quarterly*. 8, 1972, p. 159-172.

Mitra, A.C. Bibliographical Reference: A Review of Its Role. *Annals of Library Science and Documentation*. 17, 1970, p. 117-123.

Moed, H.F. and Vriens. M. Possible Inaccuracies Occurring in Citation Analysis. *Journal of Information Science*. 15, 1989, p.95-107.

Mohinder Singh. Studies of Chemical Literature and Changes in the Ranking of Periodicals by Citation Analysis of Data for 1967 -76. *Annals of Library Science and Documentation*. 25, 1978, p. 55-61.

Mubeen, M.A. Citation Analysis of Doctoral Dissertations in Chemistry. *Annals of Library Science and Documentation*. 43, 1996, p. 48-58.

Nagappa, B, and Maheswarappa, B.S. Journals Cited Most Frequently by Indian Plant Physiologists. *Library Herald*. 20, 1981, 130-139.

Nagappa, B. and Maheswarappa, B.S. Most Frequently cited Journals by Indian Phytopathologists. *Journal of Library and Information Science*. 6, 1981, p. 1-17.

Narayana N.S.S. Random Reflections on Some Aspects of Informetics. DRTC Workshop on Informetrics and Scientometrics. Paper BA. Documentation Research & Training Centre, Bangalore. 1988.

Narin, F. and Moll, J.K. Bibliometrics. In: *Annual Review of Information Science and Technology*. Williams ME, Ed. V 12. New York: Elsevier Science, 1977, p.35-38.

Nederholf, A.J. and Zwaan, R.A. Quality Judgment of Journals as Indicators of Research Performance in the Humanities and the Social and Behavioural Sciences.

Journal of the American Society for Information Science, 42, 5, 1991, p. 332-340.

Nicholas, D. and Ritchie, M. *Literature and Bibliometrics*, London, Clive Bingley, 1978.

Norris, R.P. Authorship pattern in CJNR: 1970-1991, *Scientometrics*. 28, 1993, p.151-158.

Nweke Ken, MC. The Language and Format of the Literature Used by Research Scholars in Zoology at the Ibadan University, Nigeria. *Annals of Library Science and Documentation*. 35, 1988, p. 128-133.

Olsgaard, J.N. and Olsgaard, J.K. Authorship Five Library Science Periodicals. *College and Research Libraries*. 41, 1980, 59-62.

Omoruyi, J. Social Science Dissertations: Characteristics of bibliographic citations. *UNESCO Bulletin for Libraries*. 32, 1978, p. 172-177.

Oneill, G.P. Authorship Pattern in Theory based versus Research Based Journals. *Scientometrics*. 41, 1998, p.291-298.

Osareh F. Bibliometrics, Citation Analysis and Co-Citation Analysis: A Review of Literature II. *Libri*. 46, 1996, p. 217-225.

Osareh, F. Bibliometrics, Citation Analysis and Co-Citation" Analysis: A Review of Literature I. *Libri*. 46, 1996, p.149-158.

Pestana, et al Scientometric evaluation of R&D activities in medium-size institutions. In the proceedings of the Fifth International Conference of the International Society for Scientometrics and Informetics Ed. By Michael Koenig and Abraham Book Stein. 1995 p.425-434.

Potter, W.G. Introduction to Bibliometrics. *Library Trends*. 30, 1981, p. 5-7.

Price Derek J De Solla. *Little Science, Big Science*. New York: Columbia University Press, 1963.

Pritchard, Alan. *Computers, Statistical Bibliography and Abstracting Services*. Unpublished. 1968.

Pritchard, Alan. Statistical Bibliography or Bibliometrics. *Journal of Documentation*. 25, 1969.p.348-349.

Pulla Reddy, M. and Sharma, C.B.S.R. Bibliometric Study of research publications In Indian Environmental Genetic Toxicology. *IASUC Bulletin*. 33, 1988, 7-15.

Qiu, L. and Tague. Complete or incomplete data sets; the Groos droop investigated. *Scientometrics*. 19, 1990, p.3-237.

Quandt, Richard E. Some Quantitative Aspects of the Economic Journal Literature, *Journal of Political Economy*, Vol. 84, 1976, p. No.4.

Raina Roshan. A Study towards Achieving Stability in the Ranks of Some Important Journals in Biochemistry. *Annals of Library Science and Documentation*. 31,1984, p.162-172.

Raisig, L.M. Mathematical Evaluation of the Scientific Serials. *Science*. 131, 1960.p. 1417-1419.

Rangana, Than S.R. Librametry and its scope. 7th Annual Seminar Paper D.A. 285-301, Documentation Research & Training Centre, Bangalore. 1969.

Ranganathan, S.R. Proceedings of the Aslib's Annual Conference. Great Britain, Leamington Spa, 1948.

Rangra, V.K and Others. Reporting of Indian chemical literature in Referativinyi Zhurnal - Khimiya. *Annals of Library Science and Documentation*. 19, 1972, p. 81-86.

Raptis, P. Authorship Characteristics in Five International Library Science Journals. *Libri*. 42, 1992, p. 35-52.

Ravichandra Rao, I.K. Growth of Periodicals and Obsolescence of Articles in Periodicals: A Case Study in Sociology. *Library Science with a Slant to Documentation.* 11, 1974, p. 92-96.

Ravichandra Rao. I.K. *Quantitative Methods for Library and Information Science.* New Delhi: Wiley Eastern, 1983.

Renuka, P., *Library & Information Services in Agricultural Education, Research and Extension,* Akansha Publishing House, New Delhi, 2009.

Sangam, S.L and Biradar, B.S. Patterns of information use by Indian surgical scientists. *Annals of Library Science and Documentation.* 37, 1990, p.133-142.

Sangam, S.L. A Citation analysis of Doctoral Dissertations in Social Science Accepted by the Karnataka University, Dharwad, during 1964 to 1982. Gulbarga University, Ph.D. (Unpublished). 1985.

Sangam, S.L. Obsolescence of Literature in Economics. *ILA Bulletin.* 29, 1989.p. 59-66.

Saraswathi, M. etc. Bibliometric Study of Tribal Linguistics in India. *International Library Movement.* 15, 1993, 17-27.

Satariano, W.A. Journal Use in Sociology Citation Analysis Verses Readership Patterns. *The Library Quarterly.* 48, 1978, 293-301.

Schrader, A.M. Teaching Bibliometrics. *Library Trends.* 30. 1981. p. 151-172.

Sen, B.K. and Narendra Kumar. Indian Contributions in Bibliometrics: 1958-1984: A review. *Annals of Library Science and Documentation.* 33, 1986, p. 85-103.

Sengupta I.N. Bibliometrics, Librametrics: An Overview. *Libri.* 42, 1992, p. 75-98.

Sengupta I.N. Bibliometrics: A Bird's Eye View. *IASLIC Bulletin.* 60; 167-174.

Sengupta I.N. The Growth of Biophysical Literature. *Scientometrics.* 8, 1985, p. 365-375.

Sengupta I.N. Three New Bibliometric Parameters and Their Applications to Rerank Periodicals in the Field of Pharmacology. *ILA Bulletin.* 24, 1988, 61-68.

Sengupta, I.N and Others. Evaluation of Periodicals in Respect of Their Significance to Present Day Research Activity in the Field of Neuroscience. *Herald of Library Science.* 19, 1980, p. 312-318.

Sengupta, I.N. A Weightage Formula to Rerank Biochemical periodicals. *International Library Review.* 16, 1984, p. 447-458.

Sengupta, I.N. A Weightage Formula to Rerank Periodicals in the Field of Microbiology. *Scientometrics.* 17, 1989. p. 289-300.

Sengupta, I.N. Bibliometrics: A Bird's Eye View *IASUC Bulletin.* 30, 1985, 165-175.

Sengupta, I.N. Choosing Microbiology Periodicals: Study of the Growth of the Literature in the Field. *Annals of Library Science and Documentation.* 21, 1974. p. 95-.

Sengupta, I.N. Choosing pharmacology periodicals: Study of the growth of literature in the field. *Annals of Library Science and Documentation.* 21, 1974 p.1-21.

Sengupta, I.N. Role of Bibliometry in Journal Selection and Library Management. *ASUC Bulletin.* 25, 1980, 87-93.

Sengupta, I.N. The growth of Knowledge and Literature in Neuroscience. *Scientometrics.* 17, 1989, p. 253-288.

Sengupta, I.N. Three New Parameters in Bibliometric Research and their Application to Rerank Periodicals in the Field of Biochemistry. *Scientometrics.* 10, 1986, p. 235-242.

Seymour, C.A. Weeding the Collection: A Review of Research on Identifying Obsolete Stock Part I: Monographs. *Libri.* 22, 1972, p 137-148.

Seymour, C.A. Weeding the Collection: A Review of Research on Identifying Obsolete Stock Part IT: Serials. *Libri.* 22, 1972, p. 183-189.

Sharma, R.C. Citation Indexing : An Appraisal. *ILA Bulletin.* 25, 1979, 117-125.

Shaukebdra, K etc. Bibliometrics: A Tool for Scientific Evaluation. *lLA Bulletin.* 24 : 1989 , 207.

Simon, H.R. Why Analyse Bibliographies. *Library Trends.* 22, 1973, p. 3-8

Singh, J.P. Citations of Optical Engineering. *JLA Bulletin.* 25, 1989, 26-29.

Singh, R.S. Ranking of periodicals in chemistry from the point of view of Indian Scientists. *Annals of Library Science and Documentation.* 21, 1974, p. 55-67.

Sinha, S.C. A Bibliometric Analysis of a Research field (Literature of Building and Science). *International Library Movement* 11, 1989, 22-380

Sinha, S.C. and Ullan, M.F. Information Profile of an Indian Bibliometrician': Bibliometric Study of Dr. LN. Sengupta's Publications. Indian Journal of Information. *Library and Society.* 7, 1994, 250-262.

Small, H.G. Co-Citation in the Scientific Literature: A New Measure of the Relationship Between Two Documents. *Journal of the American Society for Information Science.* 24, 1973 p. 265-269.

Smith Linda, C. Citation Analysis. *Library Trends.* 30, 1981 p. 83-106.

Snyder Herbert, W. and Bonzi Susan. An Enquiry into the Behaviour of Author Self-Citation. In: *Proceedings of the 52nd Annual Meeting of the American Society for Information Science.* New Jersey: Learned Information Inc., 1989. P. 147 -151.

Sridhar, M.S. Citing Pattern of Indian Space Technologists. *International Library Review.* 17, 1985, p. 259-274.

Stinson, E.R and Lancaster R.W. Synchronous Versus Diachronous Methods in the Measurement of Obsolescence by Citation Studies. *Journal of Information Science.* 13, 1987, p. 65-74.

Stranks, D.R. Radio chemistry. In: *McGraw-Hill Encyclopaedia of Science and Technology.* PARKER SP, Ed. V 11. McGraw-Hill, New York, 1982. p 338--340.

Studies in Scientific Collaboration. Part III. Professionalisation and Natural History of Modern Scientific Coauthorship. *Scientometrics,* 1, 1979, p. 231-245.

Subba Rao, C.R. Calculations, Errors and Methodology in Bibliometry: The Need for Statistician's Collaboration. *ILA Bulletin.* 25, 1989, 130-142.

Subramanyam K and Stephens Elsie M. (1982). Research Collaboration and Funding in Biochemistry and Chemical Engineering. *International Forum on Information and Documentation.* 7, 1983, p. 26-29.

Subramanyam, K. Bibliometric studies of Research Collaboration: A Review. *Journal of Information Science.* 6, 1983, p. 33-38.

Sylvia Margaret and Lesher Marcella. What Journals do Psychology Graduate Students Need? A Citation Analysis of Thesis References. *College & Research Libraries.* 56, 1995, 313-318.

Tagliacozzo, R. Self-citations in Scientific Literature. *Journal of Documentation*. 33, 1977, p. 251-265.

Tague, J. and others. The Law of Exponential Growth: Evidence, Implications and Forecasts. *Library Trends*. 30, 1981 p. 125-149.

Todorov, R. and Glanzel. W. Journal Citation Measures: A Concise Review. *Journal of Information Science*. 14, 1981 p. 47-56.

Upadhyay, J.L. Bibliometric analysis of Breast Cancer Literature. Indian *Journal of Information Library and Society*. 2, 1989.

Usha, M. etc. Research Collaborations in Agricultural Sciences. *ILA Bulletin* 28, 1993, 57-62.

Usha, Mujoo-Munshi and Others. Citation Behaviour of Chemical Scientists: A case study. *ILA Bulletin*. 27, 1991, p. 47-53.

Uzun, A. A Bibliometric analysis of Physics Publications from Middle Eastern countries. *Scientometrics*. 36, 1996, p. 259-269.

Verma B.C and Murthy A.T. Use of Literature by Research Scholars in Political Science and Economics. *Library Herald*. 12, 1970, p, 58-69.

Vickery, B.C. Bradford's Law of Scattering. *Journal of Documentation*. 4, 1948, p. 198-203.

Vimala, V. Bibliometric Study of Citations in Ph.D. Theses in Biological Sciences. Sri Venkateswara University, Ph.D. (Unpublished). 1997.

Webster Polish Sociology Citation Index as an Example of Usage of National Citation Indexes in Scientometric Analysis of Social Sciences. *Journal of Information Science*, 24, 1, 1998, p. 19-32.

Weinstock, M. Citation indexes. In: Kent A and Lancour H, Eds. *Encyclopaedia of Library and Information Science.* Vol. 5. New York : Marcel Dekker, 1971.p 16-40

White, H.D and Griffith, B.C. Author Co-Citation: A Literature Measure of intellectual Structure. *Journal of the American Society for Information Science.* 32, 1981, p.163-171.

White, H.D. and McCain KW. Bibliometrics. In: *Annual Review of Information Science and Technology*. Williams M.E. Ed. Vol. 24. Elsevier Science, New York. 1989, p119-186.

Wilkinson E.A. The Ambiguity of Bradford's law. *Journal of Documentation.* Vol. 31(1), 1972, p. 122-130.

Wood, D.N. and Bower, C.A. The use of social science. Periodical literature. *Journal of Documentation.* 25: 1969, 108-109.

Worthen, D.B. The Application of Bradford's Law to Monographs. *Journal of Documentation.* Vol.31 (1), 1975, p.19-25.

Yanovsky, V. Citation Analysis. Significance of Scientific Journals. *Scientometrics.* 3, 1981, 223-236.

Zipf, G.K. *Human Behaviour and Principle of Least Effort.* Cambridge. Addison-Wesley, 1949.

Zthian, J.M. *Public Knowledge: An Essay Concerning the Social Dimension of Science.* Cambridge: Cambridge University Press, 1968.

Zuckerman Harriet, A. Nobel Laureates in Science: Patterns of Productivity, Collaboration and Authorship. *American Sociological Review.* 32, 1967, p. 391-403.

APPENDIX – I

LIST OF THESES SUBMITTED TO ANDHRA UNIVERSITY

Theses No.	*Title of the Theses*	*Name of the Scholar*	*Year*	*Name of the Guide*	*Name of the Branch*
	1	*2*	*3*	*4*	*5*
1.	Effect of Library Legislation on Public Library Development in Andhra Pradesh	G.V.S.L. Narasimha Raju	1982	K. Ramakrishna Rao	Public Libraries and Community Information Services
2.	Rural Library Services and Community Analysis: A Study of an Andhra Village	K. Sarada	1983	K. Siva Reddy	Public Libraries and Community Information Services
3.	Role of the University Library in Supporting Research: A Case Study of Andhra University	P. Soma Raju	1983	A. Neelameghan	University Libraries, Users and Services

(Contd...)

	1	2	3	4	5
4.	Medical College Libraries of Andhra Pradesh: A Study	R.S.R. Varalakshmi	1990	K. Siva Reddy	Medical Information, Libraries, Users and Services
5.	Industrial Libraries of Andhra Pradesh: A Study	C. Sasikala	1991	K. Siva Reddy	Scientific and Technical Libraries
6.	Public Library and Tribal Community: A Study in Andhra Pradesh	V. Chandrasekhara Rao	1991	K. Sarada	Public Libraries and Community Information Services
7.	Information Generation and Library Use by University Teachers: A Case Study of S.V. University	A. Durvasa Babu	1992	G.V.S.L. Narasimha Raju	University Libraries Users and Services

(Contd...)

	1	2	3	4	5
8.	Pattern and Development of University Libraries in Andhra Pradesh	V. Venkata Ramana	1992	K. Siva Reddy	University Libraries, Users and Services
9.	Junior College Libraries in Andhra Pradesh: Emergence, Services, Trends and Problems	K. Somasekhara Rao	1992	K. Siva Reddy	College Libraries, Users and Services
10.	Evaluation of Catalogue Use: A Study of Dr. V.S. Krishna Library, Andhra University (India)	T.M.K. Gandhi	1992	K. Sarada	University Libraries, Users and Services
11.	The I.I.T. Libraries: A Study	P. Bhaskara Rao	1992	B. Vijaya Lakshmi	Scientific and Technical Libraries

(Contd...)

	1	2	3	4	5
	of their Resources, Services, and Users, with Proposal for Setting up a Library and Information Network				
12.	User Behavioural Pattern towards Theft and Mutilation in the University Libraries: A Case Study of Andhra University	K. Tata Rao	1993	P. Soma Raju	Other Aspects
13.	The Library System of Andhra Pradesh	A.P.S.V.V.S.N.L. Raju	1993	B. Vijaya Lakshmi	University Libraries, Users and Services

(Contd...)

	1	*2*	*3*	*4*	*5*
	Open Universities: Evaluation of Library Facilities, Resources and Services				
14.	Escalating Periodical Prices and its Impact on Library Subscriptions: An Economic Analysis	Y. Nagi Reddy	1993	P. Soma Raju	Other Aspects
15.	Information Services and Use Pattern in Humanities: Survey and	M. Kanakachari	1993	B. Vijaya Lakshmi	Other Libraries, Users and Services

(Contd...)

	1	2	3	4	5
	Proposal for Setting up a National Documentation Centre				
16.	Public Library Services and Community Analysis in an Urban Setting: A Study of the District Central Library of Visakhapatnam and its Community	M. Satyanarayana	1993	K. Sarada	Public Libraries and Community Information Services
17.	Indian Library Association: A Critical Evaluation of its Contribution	V. Vijaya Sudha	1994	G.V.S.L. Narasimha Raju	Other Aspects

(Contd...)

	1	2	3	4	5
	to the Library and Information Science Profession in India				
18.	Professional Attitudes Towards Library Computerization: A Study of University and Special Libraries in Andhra Pradesh	J. Vijaya Kumar	1995	G.V.S.L. Narasimha Raju	Libraries and I.T.
19.	A Study of the Libraries of Government Polytechnics in Andhra Pradesh	N. David Livingstone	1995	B. Vijaya Lakshmi	Scientific and Technical Libraries

(Contd...)

	1	2	3	4	5
20.	A Study of Resource Sharing and Networking of University Libraries in Andhra Pradesh	G. Sujatha	1996	K. Sarada	University Libraries, Users and Services
21.	Human Resources Development (HRD) in University Libraries of Andhra Pradesh – A Study of the Professionals in the University Libraries of Osmania, Andhra, Sri Venkateswara and The University of Hyderabad	G. Babu Rao	1996	G.V.S.L. Narasimha Raju	University Libraries, Users and Services

(Contd...)

	1	2	3	4	5
22.	Publishing Pattern of Scientists in India with Special Reference to Astronomers and Astrophysicists	G. Vageswari	1997	B. Vijaya Lakshmi	Bibliometrics
23.	Promotion of Reading Habits of School Children: A Survey of Schools in Visakhapatnam City	B. Bhaskara Kumar	1997	P. Soma Raju	Other Aspects
24.	Literature Use Pattern of Scholars in Telugu	G. Valasayya	1997	B. Vijaya Lakshmi	Bibliometrics

(Contd...)

	1	2	3	4	5
	Language and Literature: A Bibliometric Study of the Ph.D. Theses Submitted to Andhra University during 1946-1992				
25.	Information Use Pattern in Private Engineering College Libraries in Andhra Pradesh	K. Satyanarayana	1997	R.S.R. Varalakshmi	Scientific and Technical Libraries
26.	Higher Education Libraries in the State of Tripura: An Analytical Study	Hari Sankar Chakraborty	1998	P. Soma Raju	College Libraries, Users and Services

(Contd...)

	1	*2*	*3*	*4*	*5*
27.	Working of Libraries in Multi-faculty Colleges Affiliated to Andhra University – A Comparative Study	U. Sudhakara Rao	1998	P. Soma Raju	College Libraries, Users and Services
28.	Bibliometric Study of Citations in Ph.D. Theses in Chemistry Accepted by S.V. University, Tirupati	C. Arun Prasad Reddy	1999	B. Vijaya Lakshmi	Bibliometrics
29.	University Management Engineering College Libraries	M. Krishna Murthy	1999	P. Soma Raju	Scientific and Technical Libraries

(Contd...)

	1	*2*	*3*	*4*	*5*
	in Andhra Pradesh: An Evaluative Study				
30.	Off-Campus Library and Information Science Education Programmes in South India – An Evaluative Study	K. Sugathri Devi	1999	R.S.R. Varalakshmi	Other Aspects
31.	Communication Patterns and Information Seeking Behaviour of Health Science Researchers/ Scientists – A Study of ICMR Institutes	B. Solomon Raju	1997	R.S.R. Varalakshmi	Medical Inforamtion, Libraries, Users and Services
32.	Marketing of Library Information	K. Rama Patnaik	2000	C. Sasikala	Marketing of Library Information Services

(Contd...)

	1	*2*	*3*	*4*	*5*
	Services and Products in India: Present Trends and Future Perspectives				and Products
33.	The Organisation and Management of Map Collections in Indian Libraries: A Study	K. Satyavati Patnaik	2002	K. Somasekhara Rao	Other Aspects
34.	Evaluation of Agricultural Information Faculty in Andhra Pradesh for Agricultural Education, Research and Extension	P. Renuka	2002	C. Sasikala	Agriculture Information, Libraries, Users and Services

(Contd...)

	1	*2*	*3*	*4*	*5*
35.	Attitudes Towards Information Technology : A Study of Professionals in Research and Academic Libraries in Hyderabad and Secunderabad (A.P.)	V. Nireekshana Babu	2002	K. Somasekhara Rao	Libraries and I.T.
36.	Information Sources, Services and User Survey of B.Ed College Libraries in Andhra Pradesh	P. Swarna Kumari	2003	R.S.R. Varalakshmi	College Libraries, Users and Services
37.	Professional Attitudes of Librarians	C. Nageswara Rao	2003	K. Somasekhara Rao	Scientific and Technical Libraries

(Contd...)

	1	*2*	*3*	*4*	*5*
	towards Information Technology: A Survey of Polytechnic Libraries in Andhra Pradesh (India)				
38.	Autonomous College Libraries in Andhra Pradesh (India) : A Study on Emergence, Services, Standards and Professional Attitudes towards Automation	G.A. Prasad Rao	2003	K. Somasekhara Rao	College Libraries, Users and Services

LIST OF THESES SUBMITTED TO SRI VENKATESWARA UNIVERSITY

Theses No.	*Title of the Theses*	*Name of the Scholar*	*Year*	*Name of the Guide*	*Name of the Branch*
	1	*2*	*3*	*4*	*5*
1.	Finances of Public Libraries	N. Guruswamy Naidu	1988	L.K. Naidu	Public Libraries and Community Information Services
2.	A Critical Study of Information Seeking Behaviour of Medical Specialists in Madras City (India)	T. Raja Gopal	1989	G.V.S.L. Narasimha Raju	Medical Information, Libraries, Users and Services
3.	Job Satisfaction of Library Professional Staff	V. Pulla Reddy	1991	V. Pulla Reddy	University Libraries, Users and Services
4.	A Critical Study of the Information Needs of the Legal Profession	G. Saroja	1992	N. Guruswamy Naidu	Other Libraries, Users and Services

(Contd...)

	1	*2*	*3*	*4*	*5*
	and Legal Information Systems with Particular Reference to Andhra Pradesh (India)				
5.	Newspaper as a Source of Information: A Survey of Tirupati	K. Padmini	1994	N. Guruswamy Naidu	Other Aspects
6.	Planning Function in the Management of University Libraries in Andhra Pradesh	D. Chandran	1994	N. Guruswamy Naidu	University Libraries, Users and Services
7.	A Study on Agricultural Information Systems in	K. Veeranjaneyulu	1997	T. Rajagopal	Agriculture Information, Libraries, Users and Services

(Contd...)

	1	2	3	4	5
	Andhra Pradesh (India)				
8.	User Satisfaction in University Libraries	V. Sudhakara Rao	1997	V. Pulla Reddy	University Libraries, Users and Services
9.	Bibliometric Study of Citations in Ph.D. Theses in Biological Sciences	V. Vimala	1997	V. Pulla Reddy	Bibliometrics
10.	Public Access to Government Information: A Study with Special Reference to Rayalaseema Districts of Andhra Pradesh (India)	K. Durga Devi-	1997	T. Raja Gopal	Other Libraries, Users and Services

(Contd...)

	1	2	3	4	5
11.	Manpower Planning in University Libraries in Andhra Pradesh	C. Muralikrishna	1997	N. Guruswamy Naidu	University Libraries, Users and Services
12.	A Study and Assessment of Selected Museum Information Systems in India	B. Rajagopal	1998	T. Rajagopal	Other Libraries, Users and Services
13.	Organisation of University Libraries in Rayalaseema	N. Thulasi Rami Reddy	1999	N. Guruswamy Naidu	University Libraries, Users and Services
14.	Marketing of Information Services by Industries in Andhra Pradesh	I. Chandraiah	1999	N. Guruswamy Naidu	Marketing of Library Information Services and Products

(Contd...)

	1	2	3	4	5
15.	Health Care Information to Rural People in Andhra Pradesh with Special Reference to Chittoor District	K. Surendra Babu	2000	V. Pulla Reddy and C.K. Ramaiah	Medical Information, Libraries, Users and Services
16.	Contribution of Faculty Members to the Flow of Information: A Study at Selected Universities in Andhra Pradesh	M.R. Murali Prasad	2002	K. Padmini	University Libraries, Users and Services
17.	Non-Print Media as a Source of Information: A Study of Selected University Libraries of Andhra Pradesh	B. Vijaya Kumar	2002	K. Padmini	University Libraries, Users and Services

LIST OF THESES SUBMITTED TO OSMANIA UNIVERSITY

Theses No.	*Title of the Theses*	*Name of the Scholar*	*Year*	*Name of the Guide*	*Name of the Branch*
	1	*2*	*3*	*4*	*5*
1.	Planning and Implementation of Automated Circulation System for Osmania University Library System	N. Laxman Rao	1993	A.V. Satyanarayana	Libraries and I.T.
2.	Community Information and the Library in the Developing Society: A State-of-the-Art and Prognostic Study with Particular Reference to Rural Andhra Pradesh	V. Vishwa Mohan	1995	A.A.N. Raju	Public Libraries and Community Information Services

(Contd...)

	1	2	3	4	5
3.	Serial Literature in Sociology and its Document Delivery Capacity in India: A Bibliographical Study	S. Sudarshan Rao	1995	A.A.N. Raju	Other Aspects
4.	Information Needs and Sources of Information of Subject Matter Specialists in the Training and Visit System of Agricultural Extension	C. Sugunavathy	1997	D.B. Eswara Reddy	Agriculture Information, Libraries, Users and Services
5.	Personnel in Public Library System in Andhra Pradesh: A Study of Career Development	J. Yadagiri Reddy	1997	A.A.N. Raju	Public Libraries and Community Information Services

(Contd...)

	1	2	3	4	5
6.	A Study of State Policy and Administration of Collegiate Education in Andhra Pradesh	G. Narasimha Murthy	1998	D.B. Eswara Reddy	College Libraries, Users and Services
7.	Treatment of Indic Names in AACR 2 – A Study	Devendra Kumar Kaushik	1998	D.B. Eswara Reddy	Other Aspects
8.	Design and Development of a National Information System in Nutrition Science for India (NISNUTS): A Study	K. Sampatha Chary	1998	A.A.N. Raju	Scientific and Technical Libraries
9.	Bibliometric Analysis of Citation	P.T. Dheerendra	1999	A.A.N. Raju	Bibliometrics

(Contd...)

	1	2	3	4	5
	Patterns in Indian Periodical Literature on Economics				
10.	Use of Information Technology in Central University Libraries in India	P. Venkataramana	2001	V. Chandrasekhara Rao	Libraries and I.T.
11.	Use of Grey Literature by Social Scientists in India with Special Reference to Hyderabad	T. Rama Devi	2002	N. Laxman Rao	Other Aspects

LIST OF THESES SUBMITTED TO SRI KRISHNA DEVARAYA UNIVERSITY

Theses No.	*Title of the Theses*	*Name of the Scholar*	*Year*	*Name of the Guide*	*Name of the Branch*
	1	*2*	*3*	*4*	*5*
1.	A Study of the Use of Information Sources in Sciences and Social Sciences by the Faculty and Research Scholars in Women University Libraries in India	D. Rajeswari	1997	P. Kamaiah	University Libraries, Users and Services
2.	Quality of Worklife in the University Libraries of Andhra Pradesh: A Case Study	P. Rajaratnam Chetty	1998	P. Kamaiah	University Libraries, Users and Services
3.	Publication of Library Science Literature in	Paturi Sarada	2003	P. Kamaiah	Other Aspects

(Contd...)

	1	2	3	4	5
	Telugu: A Critical Evaluation				
4.	Delegation of Authority in the University Libraries with Special Reference to Andhra Pradesh: A Study	M. Ramchander	2004	P. Kamaiah	University Libraries, Users and Services
5.	Education and Information for Empowering Women through Public Libraries with a Special Reference to Andhra Pradesh	B.A. Ravi	2004	P. Kamaiah	Public Libraries and Community Information Services

Index